CW00796861

Norway's Foreign Relations
– A History

Olav Riste

Norway's Foreign Relations
– A History

Universitetsforlaget
Oslo

ISBN 82-15-00051-7

Published with a grant from the Research Council of Norway, and a Norwegian Ministry of Foreign Affairs.

www. universitetsforlaget.no

Universitetsforlaget AS
P.O Box 508 Sentrum
NO-0105 Oslo
Norway

Cover: Kristin Berg Johnsen
Maps: Sverre Mo
Printed: PDC Tangen 2001

Contents

Foreword

This book has a dual background. On the one hand it arises out of a major research project, financed by the Royal Norwegian Ministry for Foreign Affairs, which resulted in the multi-authored six-volume series *Norsk utenrikspolitikks historie*, published during the years 1995-7. Already in the plan for that project the need for a survey volume in English, aimed towards a foreign readership, was included. The present author, as the initiator and leader of the project, was then charged with that task. On the other hand the book evolves from an ambition by the author, after a lifetime devoted to study and research into the development of the Norwegian foreign policy tradition, to summarise and make accessible to a wider readership his views and conclusions.

This dual background is reflected in the book. It draws heavily, albeit in varying degrees, on the work done by the nine authors of the six-volume series. Each chapter has been submitted to the author of that particular part of the series, for critical comments. It is with pleasure that I record my gratitude to Narve Bjørgo, Øystein Rian, Alf Kaartvedt, Roald Berg, Odd-Bjørn Fure, Knut Einar Eriksen, Helge Øystein Pharo, and Rolf Tamnes, for their comments and encouragement (Jakob Sverdrup sadly having died shortly after completing volume 4). When I add that none of them is in any way responsible for mistakes, flaws and weaknesses in the present book, there is more than the usual author's "mea culpa" in this: Just as each of the authors has had – and expressed – his own particular views, so I have – and express – mine. This is therefore not a mere summary of the nine authors' views and conclusions, but my version of the course of Norway's foreign relations as they have developed over time, in the overall perspective of "Norway in the world" rather than "Norway and the world", and with an emphasis on long term trends.

In the Norwegian language the term "utenrikspolitikk" commonly covers both "foreign policy"- defined by the Oxford English Dictionary as "a course of action adopted and pursued by a government" – and "foreign relations" – defined as "the various modes in which one country, state, etc., is brought into contact with another by political or commercial interests"

(I would here add "cultural"). Hence the title of the six-volume work referred to above. The purpose of the project and the work which resulted from it, and my purpose in this book, was and is however to review the wider field of Norway's foreign relations.

The decision to write an historical survey of Norway's foreign relations in English begs a question: Why should an international readership be interested in the foreign relations of a very minor power on the international stage (unless of course they have a special interest in Norway and things Norwegian)? One answer may be that Norwegian foreign policy reflects particularly clearly a dilemma facing all small, democratic countries trying to find their way in international affairs. On the one side Norway's smallness both facilitates and requires a national consensus on foreign policy: compared to most other countries the distance in Norway between the governors and the governed is remarkably short. Hence Norwegian citizens, either directly or through their representatives or corporate organs, have unusually great influence on national decisions that are perceived as having an impact on their life or livelihood. For a small country such a consensus is a *conditio sine qua non* for an ability to play a role in foreign affairs. (The drawback is of course that when a consensus on important issues is unobtainable, indecision results.) At the same time the smallness of the country reduces its impact on international affairs: because Norway is so small, the country has relatively little influence over the international conditions that determine its integrity and welfare.

In different ways the three trends identified in this book as formative in the development of Norwegian foreign policy – neutralism/isolationism, moralism, and internationalism – reflect that dilemma. Neutralism/isolationism was – and is – in many ways a defensive response to Norway's perceived impotence in international politics. The strong streak of moralism can be seen as an attempt to bypass that lack of power, seeking instead a role as the champion of ideals. Norway's internationalism, on the other hand, reflects in part a realisation that it is only by being a player that she can have an impact in international affairs, and in part a growing self-confidence in her ability to play a part commensurate with – and sometimes greater than – her place in the ranking order of power.

This book, like the six-volume series that preceded it, is not primarily aimed at an academic readership. The principal aim has been to provide a readable survey for the general reader with an interest in the subject, research-based, but without the encumbrance of theoretical or methodological exegeses. The treatment is broadly chronological, but in view of the complexity of the last half-century it was felt necessary to deal with that period in thematic fashion. The number of endnotes has been kept to a minimum, also because the bulk of the literature and sources is in Norwegian and therefore inaccessible to foreign readers. Anyone wishing to explore the issues in greater detail should therefore consult the six-volume series. Furthermore, in order to produce a reasonably brief, continuous and coherent narrative I have had to refrain from frequent excursions into general Norwegian or international history. Instead I have inserted a number of "frames", often combined with illustrations, to provide necessary "bridges" to a wider historical context. I owe thanks to Knut Amund Surlien for his valuable assistance with the groundwork and drafting of those texts. Odd Engdahl has earned my gratitude for his help with the maps and illustrations. My English wife Ruth has once again helped me to avoid many of the pitfalls that arise when writing in a language which is not my own.

Finally, while recording with pleasure my gratitude to the Royal Norwegian Ministry of Foreign Affairs for its continuing support of the entire project, I wish to make it clear that no part of this book has been reviewed or submitted for clearance or approval by the Ministry. Officialdom has therefore had no influence on its contents, nor has anyone in an official position expressed any wish for such influence.

Billingstad, in May 2001

Olav Riste

1. The Middle Ages

Introduction

It has been said that Norway's history has three time dimensions. As a people and as a nation, that history covers more than a thousand years, beginning with the Age of the Vikings. As an autonomous state with a continuous tradition embodied in a Constitution and in political institutions, Norway's lifespan stretches from 1814 and the end of the Napoleonic wars. As a fully sovereign nation with her own foreign policy, however, Norway goes back less than a hundred years – to 1905 and the break-up of the union with Sweden. Strictly speaking the entire history of Norwegian foreign policy unfolds within the confines of our own century. Yet the history of Norway's foreign relations, which is our concern here, begins with the early middle ages.

The question of when a people may properly be called a nation has been the subject of many learned volumes. For our purpose it is sufficient to begin with the period from the end of the ninth century, when several of the regions constituting the geographical term *Norvegr* – the way to the North – were for the first time brought together under one King. The first written record containing reference to Norway and the Norwegians appears in the Anglo-Saxon King Alfred's world history, based on what he was told by the northern Norwegian chieftain Ottar who came to King Alfred's court around 890. The process of establishing and consolidating the Kingdom of Norway, beginning with the coastal regions of south-western Norway and gradually extending inland and eastward, lasted for about 150 years. Without pretending to enter into the mindset of the peoples populating the areas which at any time during that process were subject to the King of Norway, it seems reasonable to speak in general terms of their relations with the outside world as "Norway's foreign relations", while reserving the term "foreign policy" for the policy of the Kings.

The end of the first millennium was a period marked by a strong expansion of trade relations among the peoples of north-western Europe, in which the sea-faring Vikings and their longships played a prominent part.[1] Their maritime expertise and navigational skills opened up areas of activity and interests for successive generations of Norwegians, in three different

Ottar at the Court of King Alfred

Around the year 890 the merchant Ottar visited the court of the Wessex King Alfred the Great. Ottar's story was taken down, and has been preserved. Ottar's home was in the Malangen area of northern Norway, near present-day Tromsø. The description of his voyage suggests that he had been as far east as the Dvina river in the White Sea, roughly where Archangel is today, and had found there a people he called 'Bjarmi'. Ottar then described how he had followed the coast southward along what he called 'the land of the Norsemen' to a trading town near present-day Oslo, and from there to the old commercial centre of 'Hedeby' in southern Denmark, before crossing the North Sea to England. He made it clear that his voyage was for trade purposes, and in the Far North he had been looking for walrus tusks which were a treasured luxury item in Europe.

Ottar's voyage demonstrate the importance of the sea as a link between distant areas, and as a channel of communication for commercial purposes.

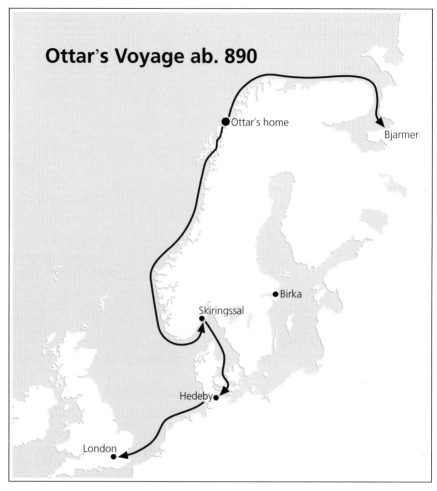

Ottar's Voyage ab. 890

directions: towards the south and south-east, in contact with and also increasingly in conflict with the Danes and the expansive ambitions of the Danish Kings; westward, where greener pastures invited trade, settlement, and imperialist expansion in the British Isles and even further afield; and northward in the search for fur, hides, and other products for export. Contemporary accounts dwell on the ferocious conduct of the Viking barbarians, but archaeological evidence also points to a civilisation with highly developed agricultural skills and a city life where handicraft and artistic activities flourished. From people-to-people relations of a commercial nature came organised trade between states, and from expansionist raids and settlements came inter-state conflicts – in other words foreign relations, and the foreign policy of Kings.

The "Norwegian Empire[2]"

The first western and south-western expansion of the Norwegians preceded the Viking age proper, as settlers from the western coast of Norway established themselves in Iceland, Greenland, the Faeroes and the northernmost parts of the British isles. When some of those settlements reached a critical mass, political organisation ensued, around three main centres. The one whose population was almost exclusively Norwegian was the earldom of the Orkneys. It was established around 900 but became extended a hundred years later to include Shetland, as well as Caithness and Sutherland on the Scottish mainland. A second one was on the islands known as Sodor – now the Hebrides – and Man, which constituted a separate Kingdom of sorts albeit marked by much internal strife. Here Celtic peoples were strongly present.[3] Finally there was the Norwegian-Irish Kingdom based on Dublin, which came into existence in the middle of the ninth century.

Whereas the Orcadian earldom was predominantly agricultural and initially peaceful, the western Kingdoms of Man and Dublin combined internal squabbles with expansive designs on the British mainland. The first Norwegian King, Harald 'Fairhair', looked askance at the ambitions of such upstarts which, if they became too powerful, might threaten his already tenuous hold on his burgeoning empire. This led him into a political alliance with England's King Athelstan, whose ambition was to extend his realm to include northern England and Scotland, and who was therefore equally perturbed at the prospect of northern England falling into Dublin's hands.

The Dublin-York axis seemed to have lost its strength before the middle of the tenth century, but by then the restless and ambitious eldest son of King Harald, Eirik 'Bloodaxe', had made the Orkneys his political base for incursions into the mainland as far south as York. While it is doubtful whether his brother Haakon 'the Good', who had succeeded his father as King of Norway, connived in Eirik's belligerent adventures, the growth of the Orkneys as a centre for Norwegian power projection was actively sup-

---

The Vikings

In Norwegian history the 9th and 10th centuries are referred to as the era of the Vikings, although recent research suggests that Vikings, or Norsemen, whether Norwegian or Danish, may have criss-crossed the North Sea as early as the 7th or 8th centuries. European historians, taking their cue from contemporary descriptions, long tended to portray the Vikings as particularly cruel and mindless brigands, assailing and looting peaceful monasteries and farming communities. In Scandinavian historiography, on the other hand, the period was for a long time regarded as a pride-inspiring period of great achievements. Recently, more balanced assessments have prevailed. The British historian Peter Sawyer has described the activities of the Vikings as well within the pattern of general political and military events at the time: a period of near anarchic conditions interspersed with essentially short-lived reigns by warlords, marked by political turmoil, roaming bands of warriors, and ever changing alliances. In such an environment the Vikings hardly stood apart from the general picture, except that they came from far away, and in ships.

A more interesting question is why the Vikings ventured so far from home? It seems to have had much to do with rapid population growth, outstripping the natural resources at home. Some then sought wealth by plunder, others loaded their ships with domestic products like hides and skins for sale or barter abroad, and others again emigrated to what seemed like greener pastures in other lands. And they could do all this because of superior skills in ship-building and ocean sailing.

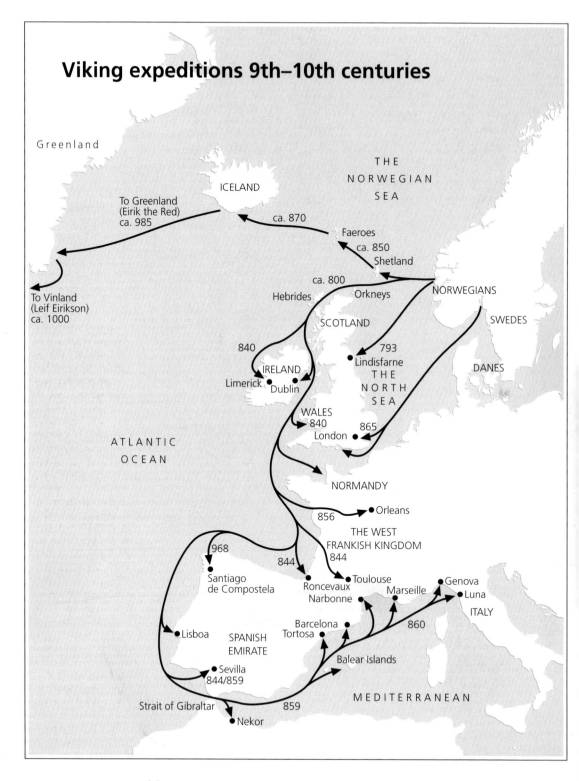

Viking expeditions 9th–10th centuries

ported by Haakon and his successors. The northern parts of Scotland, and Sodor and Man, were at least in part controlled by the Earls of the Orkneys and their Norwegian sovereigns, but attempts to include Ireland in the empire failed when King Magnus 'Barefoot' died in a battle near Dublin in 1103.

The death of King Magnus 'Barefoot' in fact marked the end of more than a half-century of extraordinary attempts to build a Norwegian North Sea empire on the ruins of the Danish King Knut's Anglo-Danish realm.

The previous King Magnus, son of St. Olav who had died in battle against a coalition of dissatisfied regional chieftains in 1030, had managed by a combination of luck and astute diplomacy to join the Danish throne to his own, thus creating a powerful economic and military basis for a possible attempt to restore King Knut's empire. Magnus did not live long enough to realise such ambitions – he died in 1046, but his uncle Harald in 1064 decided to surrender his increasingly tenuous control of Denmark, and turned to England. There the dying King Edward Confessor had no clear heirs, and Harald saw himself as a candidate by virtue of being the heir of King Knut.

With a large fleet King Harald 'Hard-ruler' and his invading army landed in northern England in September 1066, hoping to make York his base. But England's King Harold Godwinsson, in spite of having lined up the greater part of his army to meet an expected Norman invasion in the south, defeated the Norwegian army at the battle of

The Viking Longships
Round the turn of the last century excavations in both Norway and Denmark brought to light several well preserved ships from the second half of the first millennium. They showed that there must have been a revolution in shipbuilding during the seventh and eighth centuries. Based on the design of the common rowing-boats, but given a strong keel to provide strength, new and longer ships were built and equipped with a square sail in addition to oars. One of the best preserved Norwegian longships, the Gokstad ship now in the Viking Ship Museum in Oslo, has a keel hewn from a single 25 by 20 centimetres thick oak plank, 15 metres long. With ships of up to twice that size, eminently seaworthy, large areas of Western Europe came within reach: The distance from Bergen on Norway's west coast to Lerwick in the Shetlands, 187 nautical miles, took hardly more than two days. Such speed and mobility were also important for force projection and 'hit-and-run' raids in coastal areas. With their shallow draught they could also navigate on rivers.

17

Stamford Bridge where the Norwegian King Harald was killed. From an Anglo-Saxon viewpoint Harald Godwinsson's victory at Stamford Bridge was a pyrrhic one, since the effort there fatally weakened his resistance against the invading Normans three weeks later. But the military strength of Norman England also signalled the futility of any dreams of expanding the "Norwegian empire" on the British mainland. There remained only the need to consolidate Norway's hold over the western islands.

There is no clear consensus among historians as to the aims and purposes of the belligerent expansionism of the Norwegian Kings in this period[4]. Personal ambitions and prestige must have played a role, perhaps also bonds of blood relations or friendship between Kings and local chieftains. For the consolidation of empire, however, more was needed. First came the need for the King of Norway to provide extended security. The primary hallmark of empire has at all times been the establishment of common security against outsiders. As long as the King could provide solid military assistance to repel hostile incursions, his vassals in the islands and outlying provinces would continue to pay the taxes due to him. Another important motivation for the establishment as well as the maintenance of the "Norwegian empire" was the expansion of trade relations with the British isles, and with it the securing of the trade routes across the North Sea. To the extent that one can speak of a Norwegian Viking empire, therefore, it was not least a trading empire. The territorial expansion of the tenth and eleventh centuries was followed in the next century by a significant growth of trade relations, particularly between Norway and the east coast of Britain. The basic trade pattern was that of fish in exchange for grain and cloth. And the great number of special emissaries sent from Norway to the English King from about 1150 onwards attest to the growing importance of Anglo-Norwegian political relations. With trade there also developed close cultural relations, and church ties. A Norwegian church province was established in 1152/53, by which six bishoprics in the western isles were subsumed under the archbishop of Nidaros (Trondheim). This fact in turn strengthened the Norwegian Kings' ambition as well as their ability to maintain their suzerainty over the areas.

Another reason why the "Norwegian empire" assumed a more defensive stance from the middle of the twelfth century was that the Norwegian Kings became elsewhere engaged. Internal strife, periodically developing into civil wars, made it more difficult to muster the naval and military power necessary to intervene in their lieges' disputes with Scotland and England. At home they also had to contend with Danish and Swedish attempts to exploit, for their own ends, the turmoil created by pretenders who took up arms against the reigning Norwegian Kings. In Denmark the royal house had by 1150 consolidated its power over the state, and used its strength to reassert Denmark's position as the predominant Baltic power.

18

**Defence of the Realm
– the Leidang**
In addition to the King's
own Guards, the defence
of the Realm relied since
the tenth century on the
system of the Leidang.
The law required the
peasants to possess personal arms. The kingdom was
further divided into dis-
tricts called 'skipreide',
each of which had to
equip, maintain, and man
a longship. The ships
could then be mobilised
by the King, and assem-
bled in defence against an
invading force. Together
those ships represented a
formidable force, which
successive kings were also
tempted to use in foreign
adventures, although such
use was not strictly war-
ranted by the laws. An
example of the Leidang
fleet used as a force
demonstration or in
offensive operations is
King Haakon Haakonson's
naval expedition to
Scotland in 1263.

The Norwegian Kings had in the meantime profited from their hold on
northern Norway to expand the valuable fur trade, with tentacles eastward
to the White Sea, and from there southward to Novgorod. But from the
middle of the twelfth century Norway, weakened by internal power strug-
gles, was displaced in the east by Swedish, Danish, and German efforts to
extend their influence in the Baltic. In the north the Norwegian Kingdom
also had to contend with Russian and Finnish attempts to encroach on the
profitable fur trade with the Sami areas.

In those circumstances it was both desirable and necessary for the
Norwegian King to strengthen his links with the English King. Documents
from the period contain mention of a confederation established between
Norway's King Inge and King John I of England at the beginning of the
thirteenth century. This had the double purpose of strengthening peace and
friendship and thereby securing the maritime trade between the two countries, and it was renewed by King Haakon Haakonson through a formal
agreement with Henry III in 1223.

Diplomacy and Power Projection

The consolidation of the Norwegian Kingdom that began with Haakon
Haakonson meant renewed efforts to expand and secure Norway's hold
over the increasingly unruly western provinces. The period from 1240
onwards was to have its share of armed struggle, in which Norwegian sea
power played a prominent role. The ability of the Norwegian Kings to
muster large fleets of longships manned with foot soldiers was based on the
institution of the leidang. Established by force of law, that institution
required each district to build, man, maintain and provision a certain num-

ber of longships for the defence of the realm against foreign invaders. Against the promise of rich rewards, either with shares in the plundering or with landed property at home, the King could then on occasion use the fleet also for foreign adventures.

The dominant feature of the foreign policy of Haakon Haakonsson and his successors, however, was the sophisticated use of diplomacy, interspersed with threats of the use of force. For a period of nearly eighty years Norway, backed by her considerable naval strength, was able to play a significant role as a middle power in European international politics. Mediaeval diplomacy was from the beginning characterised by *ad hoc* missions by the Kings' special envoys. In the Norwegian context the sources record an increasing number of such missions from the beginning of the second millennium. 250 years later this had become institutionalised to the extent that to all intents and purposes it constituted an organised foreign service. This was sub-divided into a nucleus of more professional diplomats, charged with the most important affairs of state-to-state relations, and a more numerous group of more occasional envoys who often combined diplomatic missions of less consequence with private business abroad. One study of this Norwegian *corps diplomatique*, for the thirteenth century, has identified over a hundred such envoys and nearly ninety diplomatic missions.

Recruited into this diplomatic corps were a high number of ecclesiastic persons, but also an increasing proportion of nobles and courtiers. A fact which at first sight seems surprising is that quite a few of them were of foreign origin. But being in the service of the King of Norway, owing their loyalty and allegiance to him, their "nationality" of origin hardly mattered against the advantage brought by intimate knowledge of the way of thinking of their opposite numbers. One example is Sir Askatin, probably English by birth, who rose to become the first known bearer of the title of Chancellor in Norway, and who led the negotiations with England and Scotland in the 1260s. The lack of means of rapid communication with the King made the envoys plenipotentiaries in the fullest sense of the word. If successful they would be rewarded with prestige, honours, and wealth, but there were considerable risks involved: take the example of Baron Audun Hugleiksson, whose extravagant promises in 1295 to the French King Philip IV, of 300 ships and 50 000 men for his wars with England in return for his support for Norwegian claims to Scotland, seem to have been one of the reasons for his death at the gallows in Bergen in 1302.

Documents from that period are eloquent evidence of the pre-eminence of relations with England, quantitatively as well as qualitatively. But Haakon Haakonsson's initial successes were in relations with the Papacy. His coronation by a cardinal from Rome – in spite of being an illegitimate son – was accompanied by his promise to be "defender of the faith" against the Mongol threat in the north. A consequent peace treaty with Novgorod strengthened Norway's political and economic dominance north of the arctic circle, and the resulting increase in wealth and power gave Haakon considerable prestige on the European diplomatic stage. Henry III of England extended special commercial privileges to Norway, and Louis IX of France asked for his collaboration in crusading ventures. The pinnacle of Haakon's prestige was the marriage of his daughter Kristin to the son of the Spanish King Alfonso X in 1257, clearly connected with the latter's hope of Norwegian naval support against Morocco.

This western orientation of Norwegian foreign policy was in the second half of the thirteenth century gradually replaced by efforts to exploit the erosion of the power of the Danish Kings after the death of Valdemar the Victorious. Haakon Haakonson's expansive policy towards Denmark and the Baltic was spurred by the prospect of both economic and territorial gains. One tempting prize was the customs and excise income from control of the maritime trade passing through the narrow Sound between Denmark and Sweden on the way from the Baltic to the ports of western Europe. His method was partly political, by means of an alliance with Sweden, partly dynastic, through the marriage of his son Magnus to the Danish Princess Ingeborg, and partly naked force projection, mustering 3-400 longships to back his claims. This burst of activity came to an end when, in one of those shifts of alliance so typical of the period, Denmark and Sweden joined forces to oppose him.

The setback to Haakon's southward thrust against Denmark coincided with new threats against Norway's control of the north-western fringes of Scotland. The Scottish Kings had for some time been trying to establish suzerainty over the Hebrides by negotiating a treaty to that effect with Norway. Sharply rebuffed by Haakon, the Scots began a series of hit-and-run raids on the islands. Attempts by King Henry III of England to mediate were unsuccessful, and in 1262 he threw his weight behind Haakon, promising armed intervention if a war should become inevitable. Haakon now decided to mobilise the Norwegian fleet, and sailed towards the Scottish coast with 160 longships. His plan of action involved a feint towards the east coast, to draw the main Scottish army away from the west coast and the islands where the bulk of his armada would operate. But as the men on the detached squadron refused to go ashore in the absence of the King, who had stayed with the main fleet, the strategy had to be changed to one of patrolling the west coast in the hope of drawing the Scots out to sea. When this failed, as the Scots stayed in their forts on shore while the Norwegian fleet began to suffer serious supply problems, the Norwegian marines grew restless. In early October 1263 a clash occurred at Largs, as a storm drove some of the Norwegian ships on to the shore and a landing party was attacked by a Scottish cavalry force led by King Alexander III.

The continuing stalemate, and the onset of autumn and winter storms,

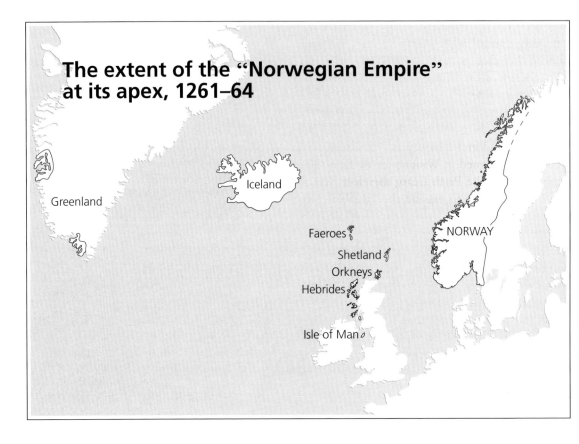

The extent of the "Norwegian Empire" at its apex, 1261–64

Greenland

Iceland

Faeroes

Shetland

Orkneys

Hebrides

Isle of Man

NORWAY

soon forced the Norwegian fleet to withdraw to the Orkneys. There King Haakon became ill and died before the end of the year, and with that the ill-fated venture to reassert Norwegian power in western Scotland came to an end. King Haakon's son Magnus now engaged in a long drawn-out process of negotiations with the Scottish King, during which King Henry III of England made it clear that a continuation of the treaty of friendship and trade relations between Norway and England required that Magnus made his peace with Scotland. A peace treaty was finally concluded at Perth in 1266. There King Magnus had to relinquish sovereignty over the Hebrides and Man to the Scottish King, against payment of a basic indemnity and an annual fee usually referred to later as "the Annuals". The Orkneys and Shetland were however to remain under the sovereignty of the Norwegian King, and the Sodor and Man bishopric would still be under the archbishop of Nidaros.

The Perth settlement, while superficially appearing as an imperial setback for the Norwegian Kingdom, in fact was a tribute to King Magnus' statesmanship. The economic and military resources required to maintain real control of the Hebrides and Man were clearly not available to the Norwegian crown. Shedding that burden, while retaining control of the Orkneys and Shetland, should therefore be seen as a wise consolidation of the King of Norway's sphere of influence on the western side of the North Sea. The Perth treaty also opened the way to a renewal of the beneficial relations of trade and friendship between England and Norway, as sanctioned by a peace treaty signed at Winchester in 1269. The main effect of the Perth treaty, therefore, was to leave Norway free to expand the valuable commerce with England, and also to consolidate her hold on the northern parts of the empire, from Greenland to the Orkneys. But it also created a long-term bone of contention in the shape of "the Annuals". This the Scottish Kings paid only intermittently to 1389, and thereafter not at all.

In the North Atlantic area Iceland had been populated by settlers from Norway in the ninth and tenth centuries. Although they as early as in the year 930 established an independent regime of law and order centred on the Allthing, considered to be the oldest parliamentary institution in the world, internal strife was rampant. Iceland's links with Norway, apart from its economic dependence, centred on the church's allegiance to the archbishop of Nidaros. Since the archbishop and the Norwegian King had common interests in pacifying the island's warring tribes, a fruitful cooperation between the temporal and spiritual power led to a settlement at the Allthing in 1262.

The Governance of Norway in the High Middle Ages

In Norway as in the other European countries the High Middle Ages were marked by the strengthening of royal power and influence. At the local level the king could build on the ancient institution of regional 'ting' or lawmaking assemblies, now chaired by a lawman as the king's representative. Tax collection, defence organisation, and the administration of justice, was in the hands of a regional governor appointed by the king. An attempt at a more centralised governance of the realm, in the form of a national assembly, proved too unwieldy for Norway's widely scattered population. Hence the end of the 13th century brought the establishment of a more permanent 'council of the realm' composed of a small number of aristocrats and senior officials, to which the king sought for advice and consent in the exercise of his personal reign.

In the conduct of foreign relations the king made extensive use of envoys on special missions to foreign princes. But for important or delicate negotiations with foreign heads of state he had a small group of senior grandees or statesmen, of whom at least one was also a member of the 'council of the realm'. With such a group of 'diplomats' at its centre we see the beginning of an institutionalised foreign service, which in the 13th century seems to have numbered over a hundred persons.

There the majority of the local chieftains swore eternal allegiance to the Norwegian crown, but retained an important measure of self-government in that all laws promulgated by the Norwegian King required formal sanction by the Allthing. In the meantime some Icelanders had ventured further west and established small settlements on the western coast of Greenland – a name which was hardly a fair description of that vast island, although the climate at that time was far more temperate than in modern times. Those outposts were of course totally dependent on trading links with Norway via Iceland, and would later die out as that connection lapsed. In the Faeroes, completing the southern tier of the realm, the pattern of establishing local chieftains with ties of loyalty to the Norwegian King was repeated.

1270 to 1319: Towards Sunset for the "Empire"

While King Magnus Haakonson continued until his death in 1280 to conduct a policy of pacification and consolidation, the guardians of his young
son and heir Eirik took a different line. A new challenge had appeared on
the scene in the shape of a trading empire known as the Hanse or the
Hanseatic League, from a mediaeval German word for "guild" or "association". Centred in the cities on the southern shores of the North Sea and
the Baltic, and occasionally supported by the Danish Kings, the German
merchants and their "guilds" had for some time been extending their grip
on trade and shipping in the area, forming permanent commercial enclaves
and claiming trading privileges in a number of foreign towns.[5] With a firm
foothold in the most important Norwegian port, Bergen, they were seen by
Eirik's guardians as presenting a threat against the position of the Norwegian merchants there. In the trade war that followed, Eirik's guardians were
supported by England, which also saw her trading empire being challenged.
After five years of war a treaty of arbitration reaffirmed the privileges of the
Hanseatic merchants, but Eirik's conflict with Denmark continued, based
on Eirik's claim to the Danish throne through his mother, the widowed
Danish princess Ingeborg. Four times in the course of six years the Norwegian leidang fleet attacked Danish territory, until in 1295 the eroded Danish
Kingdom had to submit to a peace treaty. By that treaty Eirik Magnusson's
claim to the Danish throne on behalf of Queen Ingeborg was recognised.

Dynastic considerations, coupled with an ambition to get money owed
to Norway through the terms of the Perth treaty, also lay behind Eirik's
attempt to resurrect claims on Scotland, this time in alliance with King
Edward I of England. By the fortuitous death within two years of both the
Scottish crown prince and his father King Alexander III, Eirik's infant
daughter had emerged as the heir to the throne. In 1289, at the tender age
of six, she was formally acknowledged as Queen of Scotland, and one year
later a marriage contract was arranged between her and the English prince
regent of Scotland. Sadly, the death of the young princess in 1290 put an
end to Eirik Magnusson's dream of a partly resurrected "Norwegian empire". The Scottish throne now passed to John Balliol, who promptly allied
himself with France with the aim of stemming England's expansionist policy both in France and on the British isles. It was to this alliance that King
Eirik Magnusson's adventurist "envoy extraordinary", Audun Hugleiksson,
grandly pledged the active participation of 300 Norwegian longships and
50 000 soldiers, against a hefty subsidy for which the envoy himself collect-
ed a substantial advance. What is perhaps historically significant about that
incident is not that the promised armed assistance was way beyond Norway's means, but what it may tell us about Norway's reputation as a naval
and military power.

Despite his alliance with France and the promise of Norwegian armed support – bought with the additional promise of payment of outstanding Norwegian claims – John Balliol proved powerless to prevent an English conquest of most of Scotland. Both common sense and "realpolitik" hence convinced Haakon Magnusson, who ascended to the Norwegian throne after his brother Eirik's death in 1299, that Norway's best interests lay in a renewal of friendship and trade relations with England. This made it possible for Haakon – styled Haakon V – to turn his attention to inter-Nordic politics. An initial alliance with Sweden, directed against Denmark, was in 1309 replaced by an alliance of the three Nordic Kings against Erik Magnusson, the ambitious brother of the King of Sweden and pretender to the Swedish throne. But in 1312 Erik married Haakon V's daughter Ingebjørg, and when Haakon died in 1319 without a male heir, their son Magnus Eriksson became heir to both Norway and the now vacant Swedish throne. 1319 thus came to mark the end of a separate Norwegian Kingdom with its own native royal house, and ushered in a period of personal unions among the Nordic Kingdoms in which Norway was to become a junior partner.

The year 1319 is well established as a turning-point in Norwegian history. But to historians, turning-points are never as

The Hanseatic League

Originally composed of the trading cities of northern Germany, the Hanseatic League grew in the 14th century into a tightly knit network that dominated industry and trade in the whole of Northern Europe. Its headquarters were in Lübeck, and by 1400 it had established strongholds in about seventy towns, including – since 1360 – Bergen on the west coast of Norway. There the German merchants obtained what was in fact extra-territorial rights, with their own jurisdiction, financial regime, and even military means. Through their control of the markets around the Baltic and the North Sea they provided secure outlets for Norwegian fish products, and could guarantee the import of cereals which the fishermen needed in return – granting credits if required when the fish catch failed. The goods were transported in the Hanse's own cargo ships, and Norwegian shipping went into a steep decline.

The native merchants of Bergen, as well as their traditional British trading partners, gradually lost out in the face of such a powerful organisation. As for the Kings of Denmark-Norway, they did occasionally try to limit the powers and privileges of the Hanse. Against such attempts the Germans could and sometimes did use the powerful weapon of commercial blockade. But more often than not the kings were themselves dependent on the League for loans, financial support, and even military assistance.

clear-cut as they seem to be. History is, if not seamless, at least a web where breaches of the pattern conceal important strands of continuity. The declining power and strength of the Norwegian Kingdom, while superficially induced by the fortuitous accident of a royal house without male progeny, is better explained by more profound factors which were at work during a longer time span. Money, derived mainly from profitable trade, and the military or rather naval strength which money could buy, were the main foundations for the power which the Norwegian Kings could exert in the areas of the North Sea and the North Atlantic. Both those foundations were being eroded during the second half of the thirteenth century. The profitable Norwegian seaborne trade, particularly with England, was being challenged both by English merchants and by the rising Hanseatic commercial empire. Trade expansion was becoming capital-intensive as factories, bigger ships, and better storage facilities were required. Banking establishments in London and in the cities of Flanders and Northern Germany could provide capital funds which Norwegian merchants in Bergen and elsewhere lacked. As foreign merchants made inroads into Norwegian trade they also acquired instruments of political pressure, in the form of threats to blockade essential imports into Norway of grain. Against this the Norwegian traders could no longer rely on being backed by sea power. The armed force of the Vikings' longships, with their peasant soldiers, was increasingly being neutralised by professional and highly mobile horse-mounted land armies with better weapons such as the crossbow. As the maintenance of such land armies was beyond the capacity of impoverished Norwegian nobles, this development moreover made the country vulnerable to overland invasions from Sweden and Denmark.

1319–1536: Norway on the Defensive

To all appearances the Union between Sweden and Norway from 1319 was a personal union, at first with the infant King Magnus Eriksson as the only uniting factor. Norway was ruled by a Council of the Realm composed by nobles and church leaders. Insofar as they were concerned with foreign relations, their efforts went in two directions. Above all they fought to maintain their own powers against any attempts by the King to supplant them by awarding fiefs in Norway to foreign noblemen, or attempts to exploit Norwegian resources for his personal foreign policy ventures. Second came efforts to limit the Hanseatic League's control of Norwegian foreign trade – although here some of their number had divided loyalties on account of personal profits from commercial dealings with the Hanseatic merchants. In regard to the traditional western orientation of Norwegian foreign relations the King showed little interest in interfering with the Council's policies. Attempts to re-establish Norway's rights in parts of the former empire was, after all, also in the King's interest if they should result in income from taxation, or payment of Scotland's debts arising from the Perth treaty. But such attempts could be pursued only by diplomatic means, not backed up by armed force. The Council's diplomatic efforts in those directions were largely spent on supporting France's cause in the Hundred Years' War against England, in the somewhat forlorn hope that France could manage to influence her Scottish ally to pay up.

The Council's objections to royal foreign policy adventures came to a head when Ingebjørg, King Magnus' activist mother, decided to make a

grab for the province of Scania on the Swedish mainland. For better to protect Norwegian interests the Council then moved to appoint a regent for
Norway in the person of Haakon VI Magnusson, in 1355. A few years later
the Swedish nobles elected the German Duke Albrecht of Mecklenburgh as
King of Sweden. Denmark had in the meantime regained her former
strength under the new King Valdemar, who not only ejected the Swedes
from Scania but also secured control of the strategically important island of
Gotland in the Baltic. Haakon and his deposed father Magnus now threw
in their lot with Denmark with the hope of regaining the Swedish throne.
Haakon laid the foundation for a Danish-Norwegian dynasty by marrying
King Valdemar's daughter Margaret, and their son Olav Haakonsson acceded to the throne of both countries in 1380, taking also the title "rightful
heir to the Swedish throne" on coming of age five years later. When Olav
died in 1387 his clever and ambitious mother Margaret took the reins firmly in her own hands, steering towards nothing less than a triple union of
Denmark, Norway, and Sweden. This ambition was fulfilled when in 1397,
at a solemn meeting of clerical and temporal grandees in the city of Kalmar
in southern Sweden, she succeeded in getting her chosen heir prince Erik
of Pomerania crowned as King of all the three Scandinavian states.

In the realm of foreign policy the crucial issue from Queen Margaret's
reign onwards was relations with the increasingly powerful commercial
empire of the Hanseatic League. While Margaret tried to steer a middle
course between resistance and compromise, King Erik opted for a policy of
confrontation. Economic warfare followed during which the Hanse showed
their strength by blockading ports in Sweden and Norway. As Swedish
exports were particularly hard hit by those measures, the Swedish nobles
deposed Erik as King of Sweden in 1434. Although the Kalmar Union
maintained a formal existence until 1520, the *de facto* union from the middle of the 15th century onwards embraced only Denmark and Norway. The
defection of Sweden meant that Erik's successors made efforts to consolidate the rest of their kingdom by strengthening their control of Norway, in
part against attempts by the Swedish nobles to gain a foothold in Norwegian affairs. As long as those efforts could help to limit Hanseatic dominance of Norwegian trade, they had the support of the Norwegian Council
of the Realm.

The influence of the Hanseatic merchants had risen sharply from the
middle of the 13th century. They had a virtual monopoly on the importation of grain into Norway, and used this to gain a privileged position in all
spheres of Norwegian commerce, internal as well as external. It had been
estimated that, of a total population of 6-7000 in Bergen, Norway's principal port and trading centre, 2-3000 were German merchants. The Kings'
willingness to work with the Norwegian Council to stem Hanseatic power
was, however, limited by their need for financial support from Hanseatic

merchants in their attempt to extend their rule southwards, to the principality of Holstein. Another and more insidious effect of the Kings' interest in Norway was the gradual replacement of Norwegian members of the Council of the Realm by Danish nobles. The Council's weakness as defender of Norwegian sovereignty became evident when King Hans of Denmark-Norway in 1506 appointed his eldest son Christian to be Viceroy of Norway – a new title which served to demonstrate the unequal partnership within what was still formally a personal union of the two countries under one King.

Withdrawal from the British Isles

After the Perth treaty of 1266 Norway's hold on her former possessions in the British isles was limited to Shetland and the earldom of the Orkneys and Caithness, besides the claim for annual contributions from the Scottish King for the Hebrides and Man. The latter, as we have seen, was to remain an unsettled issue despite efforts by the Danish-Norwegian Kings to claim payment. From the viewpoint of the Scottish Kings, their non-fulfilment of the Perth treaty was a signal that sovereignty over the Hebrides and Man was but the first step towards the elimination of foreign inroads into the Scottish area. A logical next step was to take control of the mainland possession of the Earl of the Orkneys, Caithness, on the northern coast of Scotland, in 1374. Any attempt by the Earl of the Orkneys to resist a Scottish take-over of such an enclave would have been doomed to failure. Even in the Orkneys the Norwegian influence was clearly on the wane, as the Earl became more and more involved in Scottish politics.

Twice in the fifteenth century the Kings of Denmark and Norway – in constant need of money – tried to persuade the Scottish King to pay his dues in accordance with the Perth treaty. In 1426 James I of Scotland sent envoys to meet Norwegian negotiators in Bergen. The outcome was yet another affirmation of the terms of the treaty, against a Norwegian promise to cancel accumulated arrears. But again the Scottish King did not bother to pay the annual dues. The next, and the most determined, effort to extract from Scotland "the Annuals" was made by King Christian I. Christian was the first of the Oldenburg dynasty on the Danish throne, and he succeeded in expanding his power by regaining – temporarily – the Swedish throne as well as being made Duke of Schleswig and Holstein. But the resulting drain on his finances made him eager for new sources of income, and an alliance with King Charles VII of France, directed against England, produced a promise of French support for his demand that the Scottish King should resume payment of "the Annuals". The Scottish King James II, now at the peak of his power as a result of England's turmoil which was about to erupt in the "Wars of the Roses", had other ideas. During negotiations in 1460 the Scottish delegates proposed the marriage of their crown prince James to the Danish princess Margaret. The price was to be Norway's surrender of sovereignty over the Orkneys and Shetland, cancellation of "the Annuals", and a huge dowry. The negotiations were resumed in 1466 after the crown prince had acceded to the throne as James III of Scotland, and the final settlement was signed in 1468. The sovereignty over Shetland and the Orkneys was not ceded to the Scottish King. But Christian's inability to pay the enormous dowry forced him to mortgage the islands to Scotland instead.

Norwegian historians long tended to see the settlement of the marriage contract between the Danish princess and the Scottish King as an abject betrayal by a Danish King of vital Norwegian interests and rights.[6] Later assessments of the deal have been more dispassionate. As for writing off "the Annuals", they had been a dead letter for most of the two centuries that had passed since the Perth treaty. As far as the Orkneys were concerned, they had for a long time been permeated by Scottish influence, and by the middle of the fifteenth century were under Norwegian sovereignty in name only. Shetland was a more keenly felt loss, since the influence there of Norwegian language and culture was and would remain very strong. But the peace that followed the settlement helped to restore a flourishing trade across the North Sea. It is therefore possible to see the 1468 settlement as repeating the pattern of the Perth treaty. Rights of sovereignty that could not be enforced were being traded for peace and prosperous trade relations. The mortgage, moreover, was not at the time seen as the end of the story. Just as "the Annuals" had remained as a contractual obligation for two centuries, the mortgage remained on the books for possible redemption for at least two centuries thereafter. Perhaps the greatest historical significance of the settlement was as a symbol of Norway's decline: The Perth treaty had been a treaty entered into by the King of Norway in full knowledge of what he was doing. The 1468 marriage settlement, however, had been made by a Danish King without even nominal participation by the Norwegian Council of the Realm.

It is also possible to see King Christian's agreement to the marriage settlement of 1468 in the perspective of power politics. He needed powerful allies, in part in order to contain challenges by factions of Swedish nobles to his position in Sweden, but also, and perhaps mainly, to neutralise England's challenges to Danish and German trade in the North Sea and the North Atlantic. In the previous hundred years the English merchants had with considerable success made sharp inroads into the Icelandic trade in particular. With Scotland as an ally, and with the self-interest of the western Hanse on his side, Christian was now in a better position to assert his right as the sovereign of Iceland to control that trade and keep the English merchants at bay. From the viewpoint of Norwegian interests, however, this meant that the position of Bergen was diminished. Trade with Iceland had until then formally been the monopoly of Bergen, although this had increasingly become a dead letter, as it could not be enforced against the invasion of English merchants. Now the west German and Dutch merchants became free to trade directly with Iceland, bypassing Bergen.

The identification of Bergen's interests with those of Norway requires a qualification, however. We have seen that the merchants in Bergen were predominantly German and controlled by the German Baltic port of Lübeck, whereas the Danish King was in alliance with the western Hanse, meaning the German and Dutch North Sea ports. The maintenance of Bergen as a commercial centre nevertheless brought a modicum of benefits to Norway, which was lost when the ships of the western Hanse with the King's connivance bypassed Bergen. It is tempting to speculate on whether Norwegian interests would have been better served by a revival of the old commercial alliance with England, since the English merchants were less intent on monopolising trade by way of special privileges, and could have provided a counter-weight to the Hanse. But the King's dynastic and power political interests prevailed, and there England was the enemy.

2. Union with Denmark 1536–1814

Norway as a Danish Province?

In 1536 the Danish nobility put Christian III on the Danish throne, in defiance of the claims of his deposed uncle King Christian II. Being the preferred candidate of the nobles and the Danish Council of the Realm, Christian III had to meet most of their demands as formulated in the traditional accession charter which he had to sign. One of those demands was that

> Norway shall henceforth be and remain under the Crown of Denmark, the same as any of the other provinces, Jutland, Fünen, Zealand, or Scania, and it shall henceforth neither be nor be called a kingdom in itself.[1]

The legal validity of this "Norway paragraph" can be questioned. In formal treaties of 1544 and 1546, both related to the efforts to put an end to Christian II's persistent claims, Norway was still dealt with as the "Kingdom of Norway", without any mention of the "Norway paragraph". In practice, however, Norway was henceforth treated on a par with any other Danish province. While this may have strengthened the King's control over Norway, it abolished – at least for the time being – his claim to be King of Norway by hereditary right. Unlike Denmark, where the King had to be elected, Norway was well established as a hereditary kingdom, and this had heretofore strengthened the King's personal position against the nobility. That was now lost. Another important gain for the Danish nobles was that they now gained the same access to fiefs and important royal appointments in Norway as they enjoyed in Denmark. The Norwegian Council had not been consulted in these matters. In fact it had sidelined itself, being split down the middle between the Catholic archbishop of Nidaros with his followers, who presented themselves as the champions of Norwegian self-rule, and supporters of the Reformation as imposed by King Christian III.[2]

After such a big step down the ladder towards full dependency status it is legitimate to ask if the term "Norwegian foreign policy" has any meaning

Territorial changes 1600–1660

for the period that followed. To such a question there is no clear and simple answer. Evidently, the foreign policy which the King and the Danish Council pursued was primarily Danish, meaning that it was determined by Danish interests. But it is equally clear that many of the policy initiatives had their roots in interests common to the dual kingdom. The specifically Norwegian content of those interests obviously varied, but it is possible to distinguish two types of Norwegian interests that could be served by the King's foreign policy, even if for the sake of convenience one prefers to call it a Danish for-eign policy. First there were the policies which served to determine the long term situation of Norway as a state, always assuming that its demise as implied by the "Norway paragraph" was a temporary expedient. In that category fell policies which served to maintain Norway's status as a separate kingdom, and those which defined, preserved, or even expanded the territory clearly defined as Norwegian. Second came policies which in one way or another served the specific – mainly economic – interests of the King's Norwegian subjects. Both those categories need to be considered here as part and parcel of the historical development of Norway's foreign relations.

One interest common to both countries was the maintenance of sover-eignty over Greenland, Iceland, and the Faeroes, with accruing benefits for the merchants of Bergen. In that city the Hanseatic dominance was gradu-ally weakened during Christian IIIs reign. In a long series of negotiations the Hanseatic merchants sought formal confirmation of their pre-eminent position, but were step by step forced to acquiesce in a greater role and more rights for the Norwegian traders and merchants. The result was a sig-nificant growth of Norwegian seaborne trade and Norwegian exports, in which fish from North Norway was an especially profitable commodity. Closely linked with this commercial expansion was the active policy of Christian III's successors, Frederik II and especially Christian IV, in support of Norwegian efforts to assert sovereignty over the areas north of the arctic circle which today constitute the counties of Finnmark and Troms as well as the northern parts of the present county of Nordland. There were no internationally recognised borders in this area, and during the later middle ages both Sweden and Russia had exploited the weakness of the Norwegian state by extending their territorial claims. At stake was not only formal sovereignty, but also the right to tax and to control the trade of the Sami population – in some instances the Sami were being taxed by three diffe-rent kings! English and Dutch merchants were also active in the area.

From the middle of the sixteenth century Sweden pursued a particular-ly expansionist policy in the north, seeking not only to tax the Sami in the border areas but to extend Swedish control to the coastal regions. In the first instance the governors of Bergen and local officials led the struggle against the Swedish claims. But from the 1570s the King and the Danish Council took an active part, in the first instance by opposing Swedish attempts to have their claims written into treaties such as the peace treaties after the Nordic Seven Years' War 1563–1570. Swedish expansion took a new turn after the Russian emperor, conceding defeat after a long war with Sweden, in 1595 ceded to the Swedish King his claim to taxation rights westward from the Varanger peninsula. Christian IV, crowned King of Denmark and Norway in 1596, adopted from the start a forceful policy in defence of his kingdom's interests in the area. He delivered sharp protests against the Russian-Swedish treaty of the year before. He also complained to Queen Elisabeth I of England about the presence of English fishing boats off the coast of Finnmark, and he personally led expeditions by sea to the area, confiscating several of the offending boats. The network of the King's officials in the area was gradually strengthened, to enforce his sole right to tax the population of Finnmark.

The conflict between Christian IV and Sweden, mainly due to the disputes over rights in the north, grew more serious after Karl IX acceded to the Swedish throne. The Danish Council at first failed to support the King, and accepted Sweden's taxation rights along the coast of northern Norway. But when the Swedish King went further, and tried to establish territorial rights to the area, he was met with armed resistance from King Christian's strong navy. In 1611 Denmark-Norway declared war against Sweden, and in the peace settlement two years later Sweden accepted Norwegian sovereignty over the coastal areas in the north. Still the rights over the inland areas, including taxation rights, remained undecided for a long time, since the Finnmark area partly lacked an obvious natural border like that of the mountain ranges further west and south. The border between Sweden and Norway was in fact not finally determined until 1751. Then Sweden was under the threat of a Russian invasion, and the fear of an alliance between Denmark-Norway and Russia persuaded Sweden to agree to most of the claims made on Norway's behalf by the Danish King. Norway's land territory ultimately achieved its present delimitation when the border with Russia was settled in 1826.

Christian IV also proved to be a valiant defender of Norwegian offshore interests, and not only in the northern areas. As early as 1564 King Frederik II had used the expression "the Norwegian Sea" in complaints about the activities of English and Dutch ships. Behind that expression seems to have been a theory that, like the Danish Crown's dominium over the Baltic Sea, the Norwegian Crown could claim dominium over the northern ocean

Christian IV – a Good King for Norway?
Among the fourteen kings that ruled during the 434 years long union between Denmark and Norway, King Christian IV stands out in many ways. His rule was the longest – 60 years in all, from 1588
to 1648, and his energy and zest for life had no equals among either his predecessors or his successors.
He also paid more and on the whole benign attention to Norway, getting the bureaucracy on to a
firmer footing and more integrated into the central state apparatus. He visited Norway thirty times,
once incognito as a captain, on a voyage that took him along the whole coast as far as to the disputed
areas east of the Varanger peninsula. The main purpose was to survey and mark the King's sovereign
rights in the area. Christian IV's reputation as a 'bon viveur' was duly confirmed when he reached
Bergen and was invited by the Commandant of Bergen castle to a midsummer night party. The diary
of one of the other guests recorded that after drinking wine throughout the night, the boisterous
King "gaily broke all the windows as well as the baking oven." On the following day the party continued on the King's ship, with the guests being so well entertained that "few were capable of walking
home unaided".

35

– "dominium maris septentrionalis". Christian IV in his turn, by diploma-cy and by the use of the mighty Danish-Norwegian navy, fought against foreign whaling activities along the coast of Norway and right up to Spits-bergen, and claimed exclusive fishing rights within an apparently ill-defined distance from the shore. International maritime law at the time vacillated between defining territorial waters as being limited by the line of sight, the length of a gunshot, or one geographic mile which was then the equivalent of four nautical miles.

While Denmark-Norway through the sixteenth and seventeenth centu-ries could dominate the seas and coastal areas through naval power, Sweden commanded an increasingly powerful tool for expansion through her army. Already in the Nordic Seven Years' War the Swedish army seized a large chunk of central Norway including the county of Trøndelag, thus cutting Norway in half. But Norwegian army units counter-attacked, and in the peace settlement the King of Sweden had to give up any claim to those ter-ritories. In the 1640s a much stronger Swedish army, led by Karl X Gustav-us, inaugurated a series of military conflicts with Denmark-Norway with the ultimate aim of uniting the three kingdoms under the Swedish throne. In a period of less than twenty years, three wars were fought in which Sweden made considerable inroads into both Danish and Norwegian terri-tory. In the peace settlements that followed, although the Danish Council favoured ceding Norwegian territory rather than parts of Denmark, King Christian IV and his successor had different ideas, with the result that most of Norway remained intact. The King's policy was clearly motivated by a desire to preserve Norway as his hereditary kingdom, as such an indepen-dent power base put him in a stronger position against the feudal lords of the Danish Council. The Danish areas which were ceded to Sweden were rich agricultural districts on which the Danish nobles based much of their wealth and power. In this strengthened position the King of Denmark in 1660 established a royal autocracy wherein the King declared the two king-doms as belonging to him by divine right.

From 1660 until the end of the century the Scandinavian peninsula expe-rienced a period of relative peace. During the first decade of the eighteenth century, however, the Swedish King Karl XII embarked on a series of mili-tary campaigns to establish Sweden as the great power of northern and east-ern Europe. After initial successes in the Baltic area he was defeated by Russia, which now was in alliance with Denmark-Norway. Russia then took possession of Finland, while Russia's western allies occupied the Swedish possessions on the eastern and southern shores of the Baltic. Believing, as many of his predecessors, that Norwegians would rather be subjected to

BONDEBEVEPNING
1628

A Norwegian Army

Under the Union with Denmark, the duty of Norwegians to defend the realm still relied on the old Norwegian law of 1274, including the Leidang duty, although many escaped that duty through payment of a tax. Anticipating conflict with Sweden over that country's expansionist designs, King Christian IV undertook a revision of the old law, with updated requirements as to the type of armament the farmers had to possess. Yet the war against Sweden 1611–13 showed that a farmers' militia was an inferior force against well-trained and better armed Swedish forces. The international trend at that time was for increased use of professional mercenary troops, but that was a costly affair. In 1628 Christian IV therefore issued a law for the establishment of a national Norwegian conscript army of about 6 500 men, organised in companies led by foreign professional officers. The King's withdrawal from the Thirty Years' War (1618–48) postponed the implementation of the law. But in 1643 Sweden again went to war against Denmark, and Norway's defence forces were mobilised under the energetic leadership of the Danish Governor General Hannibal Sehested. The mainstay of the land forces were the young soldiers of the new Norwegian army, with the addition of a number of professional soldiers. The old Farmers' militia was employed as auxiliary troops. The main effort of the army went towards containing the greatest possible number of Swedish troops, without engaging in offensive operations. A Swedish incursion across the border, and into an often disputed region in the centre of the Scandinavian peninsula, was repulsed, but supply problems forced the Norwegians to withdraw from the area, and in the 1648 peace settlement the King ceded that region to Sweden, instead of the Danish lands which Sweden initially demanded.

Swedish than Danish rule, Karl XII in 1716 decided to march towards Norway. After a successful campaign against badly prepared defenders the Swedish army seized the capital city of Christiania, but a two month siege of the fortress Akershus failed to produce its surrender, and the invader had to withdraw after the Danish-Norwegian navy under the Norwegian admiral Peter Wessel destroyed the Swedish supply fleet. Two years later Karl XII again invaded Norway, but the campaign was cut short when the King himself was shot during the siege of the Norwegian border fortress of Frederikshald. Whether the fatal bullet came from a Swedish or Norwegian gun is still not entirely clear. The subsequent peace settlement brought no border adjustments, and this suggests that the borders between the three Scandinavian kingdoms were now on the way to becoming permanently

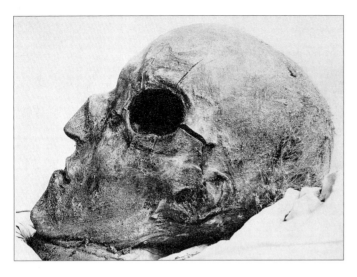

The Death of Sweden's Warrior King Karl XII

Sweden's century as a military great power began with the reign of Gustavus Adolphus (1611–32), and reached its apogee with Karl XII's initially successful campaigns in Eastern Europe. His march on Moscow 1708–9, however, like similar attempts by Napoleon and Hitler in later centuries, turned into a disaster. With Swedish power in sharp decline, and the economy in ruin, Karl in 1718 nevertheless managed to raise a large army, this time with Denmark-Norway as his target. In a two-pronged assault, one part of his army entered central Norway and laid siege to Trondheim, Norway's third most important city. Karl himself with the main force crossed into southern Norway, and invested the frontier fortress of Fredriksten. But on the eve of the final assault, the King was mortally hit by a bullet while inspecting his troops.

Military historians have since been engaged in a lively debate about who fired the deadly shot: was it one of his own soldiers, wishing to rid Sweden of the cause for her war-weary misery? The current theory, based on the findings of a pathological examination of the King's skull, suggests however that a grapeshot salvo fired from a Norwegian cannon was the cause of death.

established. In Norway the successful defence against the Swedish invaders was seen as a tribute to the reforms which had created a Norwegian army for the defence of the national territory, and this probably contributed to the growth of a consciousness of Norway as a separate nation.

In European history, the eighteenth century was a period of changing alliances and power alignments, with Russia, Great Britain, and France as the dominant players. In this turmoil the Oldenburg kings of Denmark-Norway preferred to err on the side of caution, aligning themselves *ad hoc* with one or the other great power only when necessary or advisable for short-term defensive reasons. The success of this balancing diplomacy kept the dual kingdom out of armed conflicts, and the resulting long peace provided good growth conditions for the foreign trade and shipping on which Norway was so heavily dependent. Fish, and increasingly timber, were the main Norwegian exports. Norwegian timber went first to the Netherlands and later to Great Britain as the principal customers, whereas Norwegian fish exports, in addition to supplying traditional customers in the continental North Sea ports, were finding new markets in the countries of the Mediterranean. The conditions for maritime trade tended to be determined by Britain as the major naval power, and the British Navigation Acts, which required that imports into Britain be carried either on British ships or the ships of the exporting country, were an important stimulus for the growth of a Norwegian merchant navy. A side effect of this was the establishment of a consular network whose members perforce worked to promote Norwegian trade and shipping interests even if they were Danes and received their instructions from Copenhagen.

Denmark-Norway during the Revolutionary and Napoleonic Wars

The second half of the eighteenth century marked a turn away from the southern orientation of Norway's foreign relations, determined by inter-Nordic relations and the dominance of the Hanse, back to the western and maritime orientation which had been so prevalent from the early middle ages to about the end of the thirteenth century. Seaborne trade and shipping led the way, and the prosperous development of both kinds of activity dictated a reasonably cooperative relationship with Great Britain. The period of wars and conflicts released by the American War of Independence and the French Revolution was to change this. In order to safeguard its trading interests, Denmark-Norway sought to reinforce its non-aligned position by entering into neutrality leagues, first with Russia and several other European states in 1780, and then with Sweden in 1794. The status and rights of neutrals were at the time ill-defined in international law, and more often than not determined by what each belligerent power found expedient in terms of its own interests. Neutral trade brought considerable profits, but the intensification of the war at sea towards the end of the century meant that neutral shipping was being squeezed by the efforts of both belligerents to block supplies to the enemy. This led the government in Copenhagen to the fateful decision to organise convoys of merchant vessels escorted by armed warships. Predictable clashes with British men-of-war ensued, and in 1800 Denmark-Norway re-joined Russia's Neutrality League in the hope that such a strong grouping could persuade the British to recognise the inviolability of neutral convoys. Britain, however, reacted instead by sending a powerful fleet to Copenhagen and, when the Prince Regent – soon to become King Frederik VII – refused an offer of a defensive alliance, subjected Copenhagen to a devastating bombardment from the sea.

The position of Denmark-Norway during the Napoleonic Wars brought into the open a fundamental dilemma of the dual kingdom. Strategically, and in terms of trade and economic interests, the main orientation of the two parts pointed in different directions. By force of geography Denmark's destiny, and in particular its security against foreign invasions, was linked with the Baltic and the Continent of Europe. Norway, also for reasons of geography, faced the North Sea and the North Atlantic, and depended on the sea for its livelihood. Just as Denmark could ill afford to incur the enmity of any dominant continental power, so Norway needed peaceful relations with the major sea powers. In the Napoleonic Wars France imposed a ban on British trade with continental ports, and enforced the ban by intercepting and taking as prizes any ships engaged in such trade. Britain, being dependent on overseas supplies, needed to retain Denmark-Norway as at least a cooperative neutral power, in order to have commercial access to the Baltic area. In such circumstances Denmark feared France more than she feared Britain, whereas Norway would have been better served by an alliance with Britain.

In 1807 the British decided to force the issue in view of the Danish Regent's vacillations. When Denmark-Norway still refused to come in on the side of Britain, Copenhagen was again attacked, and the entire Danish-Norwegian fleet was towed away to British ports. The Regent then concluded an alliance with France, and the stage was set for seven years of war in which Norway became increasingly isolated. British warships patrolled the straits of Kattegat and Skagerrak, intercepting ships that were bringing much needed supplies of grain and other victuals to Norway. Sweden, having joined the coalition against France, also became an enemy of Denmark-Norway. Swedish attempts to invade Norway were repulsed by the Norwegian army, but the two-front war against Sweden on land and Britain at sea, with the hardships it inflicted on the population, inevitably contributed to a feeling of having been left in the lurch by King Frederik and his government. To demonstrate its concern the Crown had established a Commission of Government in Christiania with Prince Christian August as its head. That Commission now demanded either a change of Danish foreign policy or a permission for Norway to seek a separate armistice with Britain and Sweden. At the same time influential circles in Norway began to entertain ideas of an autonomous Norway linked with Sweden by a common king. Similar ideas were afloat in Sweden, and gained ground after Russia in 1809 seized Sweden's Finnish province. To further such a development the Swedish nobles then elected Prince Christian August to be heir to the Swedish throne, with the hope that this would encourage the Norwegians to break with Denmark.

Events followed each other in rapid succession in those years. Christian August proved unwilling to use his position as head of the Government Commission in Norway and heir to the Swedish throne to foster a break-up of the union with Denmark, and after the Prince's sudden death in 1810 the Swedes elected the French General Jean Baptiste Bernadotte as heir to the throne under the name of Karl Johan. In Copenhagen the King's foreign policy advisers warned that the maintenance of the alliance with France might still arouse separatist sentiments in Norway. But the King's resentment at the behaviour of the British in 1801 and 1807, paired with a stubborn belief in the invincibility of Napoleon, made him impervious to such advice, although he did consent to giving the royal charter to the establishment of a university in Christiania. In the meantime Norway's situation had eased, as peace talks with Sweden got under way and the British had begun to issue licences for Norwegian ships carrying essential imports. Bernadotte now took up the idea of gaining Norway for Sweden as compensation for the probable loss of Finland, and he broke with Napoleon when the latter refused to support the plan. Russia also withdrew from the Napoleonic

King Karl XIV Johan: "… nobody has ever had a career like mine"

With those words the ageing monarch of Sweden and Norway described his life, shortly before his death in 1844. Born in 1763 as Jean Baptiste Bernadotte, the son of a French lawyer, he enlisted in the French army at the age of 17. Having declared his support of the French Revolution, he rose from Sub-Lieutenant to Brigadier-General in two years. Although he met Napoleon Bonaparte as early as 1797, it was not until the declaration of the Empire that he declared his full loyalty. Rewarded with an appointment as Marshal of the Empire, he then served Napoleon in various important positions, becoming Governor of the occupied Hanseatic towns in 1807.

The watershed came when the Swedish nobles elected him as Crown Prince and heir to the throne then held by the old, ill, and childless King Karl XIII. Bernadotte's old allegiance persuaded him to declare Sweden as at war with England, but when Napoleon in 1812 occupied the Swedish territories in northern Germany, Karl Johan – as was now his name – decided that the best way to further the interests of his new homeland was to side with Napoleon's enemies. Realising the futility of trying to regain Finland from the Russian occupants, he set as his aim to wrest Norway from Denmark. In order to ensure the full support of his new allies he agreed to engage with the Swedish army in the campaign against Napoleon, and took an active part in the battles that led up to the decisive allied victory at Leipzig in 1813. But he did not forget his ultimate aim, and after a swift campaign which drove the Danes out of their most valuable German province, the stage was set for the fateful treaty negotiated at Kiel on 14/15 January 1814, whereby Norway was transferred – nominally to the Swedish King, who lived in the shadows for another three years, but in reality to Karl XIV Johan. In 1818 Jean Baptiste Bernadotte could then formally and finally cap his rise from Sub-Lieutenant in the French army to the pinnacle position of King of Sweden and Norway.

coalition for reasons of its own, and in 1812 a princely deal was sealed and signed: the Russian Tsar Alexander promised his support to Karl Johan's plan to acquire Norway in return for Swedish acceptance of Russian sovereignty over Finland.

Napoleon's catastrophic campaign in Russia 1812–13 led to a scramble of European princes to join the campaign against France. In that stampede Karl Johan promised the active participation of the Swedish army against his erstwhile emperor, in return for which both Britain and Prussia promised to support his claim to Norway. It was now too late for the Danish King to change sides. A belated plea bargain for peace with the anti-Napoleonic coalition, with the cession of a large area of central Norway to Sweden, was turned down, and the British navy resumed its blockade of Denmark-Norway, causing near famine conditions in Norway. In the autumn of 1813, having participated in the defeat of Napoleon's army at Leipzig, Karl Johan marched towards Denmark, and the Danish King Frederik VI had no choice but to bow to the dictates of a Swedish Crown Prince backed by an overwhelming coalition of powers. On 14 January 1814 a treaty was signed in the North German town of Kiel whereby Norway was ceded "with full rights of ownership and sovereignty to the King of Sweden, constituting a Kingdom united with the Kingdom of Sweden". The former Norwegian possessions of Greenland, Iceland, and the Faeroes were not included in the deal – probably because the Swedish negotiators did not realise that they were historically linked with Norway.

The Norwegian Revolution of 1814

Events in Norway during 1814 reflect the state of Europe in the closing stages of the Napoleonic Wars: a Europe at the cross-currents of the waning surge of the ideas of the French Revolution and the rising trend of reaction and conservatism; a Europe over which the great powers were determined to impose peace and order. During that year the Norwegian nation would pass from being an integral part of the dual kingdom of Denmark-Norway, through eight months of what was to all intents and purposes sovereign independence, to becoming a part of the United Kingdoms of Norway and Sweden albeit with its own liberal-democratic constitution.

A basic principle of the international order prevailing at that time was the sanctity of treaties – in particular such treaties as were approved by the great powers. The Kiel Treaty, by which the King of Denmark ceded Norway to the King of Sweden, was not only approved but preordained by the great powers. A revolt against that treaty would hence appear to be doomed from the beginning. On the other hand, another hallowed principle of the traditional order was that of the legitimacy of princes and rulers. That principle was on the side of the Danish Royal House, against the upstart French General Jean-Baptiste Bernadotte who was instrumental in arranging the treaty and who, as Crown Prince Karl Johan, was about to succeed to the Swedish Throne. At any rate, if Karl Johan expected a tranquil transfer of Norway to the sovereignty of the King of Sweden, events were soon to prove him wrong.

The Kiel Treaty set in motion a political process where three different lines can be discerned. One of them pointed towards an attempt to restore the Danish-Norwegian union, albeit in a new form. Another veered towards accepting a union with Sweden, but as a personal union on the basis of full Norwegian autonomy. A third line aimed at a fully independent Norwegian kingdom. The two first lines were however not aired openly, leaving the option of a struggle for independence as the declared aim of all concerned. The leading figures in the process were, first of all, the Danish Prince Christian Frederik, the King's first cousin, who had been sent to Norway as *Stattholder* the year before. The King must have hoped at the outset that the Prince's presence in Norway would help to keep Norway within the union. But in the new situation brought about by the Kiel Treaty, Christian Frederik soon realised that unless he put himself at the vanguard of the independence movement he would lose all influence on events. To what extent or for how long he may have entertained a hidden agenda, ultimately aiming at Norway's reunion with Denmark, remains in dispute among historians. But outwardly at least he worked actively and with considerable enthusiasm to promote the cause of Norwegian independence.

In the realm of politics, the Prince's immediate plan was simply to assume the vacant Norwegian throne by virtue of his hereditary right as Prince of Denmark and Norway. His ascent should then be confirmed by a popular oath of allegiance. His aim, after all, was an insurrection, not a revolution. To lead a nation rising against an unjust treaty was not, in his view, irreconcilable with the established conservative ideology centred on the inalienable hereditary rights of the princes. This basically conservative phase of the Norwegian uprising turned out to be short-lived. The Prince was soon to learn that while the banner of Norwegian independence had strong support, the idea of a mere continuation of the state of unlimited monarchic rule did not. Meeting with 21 leading Norwegian notables in the middle of February, Prince Christian Frederik was informed that, while his policy of independence had their support, it would be necessary to convene a national assembly for the purpose of drafting a Constitution for the Kingdom. The Prince not only agreed to this; he also expressed his sudden conversion to the principle of popular sovereignty in the proclamation issued after the meeting: "The Norwegian people, released from their oath to King Frederik VI, and thus repossessed of the full right of a free and independent people itself to determine the constitution of its government", would henceforth assert and defend its sovereign independence. The Norwegian uprising thus entered its revolutionary phase.

The lack of opposition from the Prince to this revolutionary turn of events may seem surprising. But in fact he had no choice. The bourgeois elite assembled at the meeting was indispensable to the Prince's campaign for Norwegian independence. Despite allegations to the contrary by 19th century nationalist historians, the majority of the people had at that time no particular passion for independence. Their resentment against the King was first and foremost focussed on the economic hardship and starvation which his war policy had imposed on Norway. Their passion, therefore, was peace and a return to normalcy. It remained for the Prince and the nation's elite to convince them that independence and a less autocratic form of government was the best way to achieve those aims. Moreover, some members of the elite had their doubts about the benefits of sovereign independence. What kept them together was their desire for a liberal, constitutional monarchy under which their – and as they saw it, the nation's – interests could best be taken care of, regardless of the nationality of the King.

Working with Christian Frederik in those winter months were spokesmen of the Norwegian elite of businessmen and senior civil servants, led by such prominent persons as Count Wedel Jarlsberg and the rich merchant Carsten Anker. Count Wedel's aim had for some time been a union with Sweden on the basis of full equality between the two kingdoms. In essence this was a position based on a sober "Realpolitik" assessment of Norway's situation. Carsten Anker, having close connections with England, hoped for a status of full independence, possibly accompanied by some sort of special relationship with Great Britain. Britain was the key on at least two different counts: as the main customer for Norwegian exports, especially of timber, and as the principal naval power on whose benevolence Norwegian seaborne trade and shipping depended – as the deprivations and misery caused by the British blockade of Norway 1807–9 and 1813–14 had shown. Also, all who believed in an independent Norway looked to Great Britain as the only great power likely to have some sympathy for a freedom-loving people's demonstrated desire for independence.

For the time being, Christian Frederik as well as Count Wedel and Carsten Anker with their respective supporters could unite around the common aim, supported by the people with an almost euphoric enthusiasm, of working for the maximum degree of independence and self-determination for Norway. The main instrument for the achievement of that purpose would be a national assembly to provide the Kingdom of Norway with a Constitution. In the meantime the Norwegian army would be called on to defend or at least act as a deterrent against attempts by Karl Johan to impose his will on the people of Norway. With a Constitution as a *fait accompli* Norwegians would be better placed to safeguard Norway's right to self-government against the whims of present and future autocratic kings. As a first step towards mobilising the people in support of independence and constitution-making, all were now asked to assemble in churches throughout the country for an extraordinary day of prayer on 11 March. After all the adult males had been asked to swear a solemn oath "to uphold

Norway's independence and to wager life and blood for the beloved fatherland", the congregations then proceeded to appoint electors for the selection of delegates to a constitutional convention. In the meantime the Prince had embarked on an assiduous campaign to influence the great powers in favour of the Norwegian cause. The campaign had two clear aims: first to show that this was a genuine Norwegian popular movement and not the selfish intrigue of a Danish Prince, second to persuade them to drop their support for Karl Johan. So far, Karl Johan and his Swedish army had been an indispensable support for the campaign against Napoleon. Now, however, with the Corsican retreating everywhere, and with Karl Johan seemingly raising his ambitions towards succeeding Napoleon on the French throne, it might be time for the powers to reconsider the situation.

Initial results of the campaign gave few grounds for optimism. In recognition of Britain's key position an official delegation was sent to London to continue the work undertaken already by Carsten Anker. The aim was to provide the British government with a proper appreciation of the events in Norway and of the strong will of the people for independence. It was bound to be an uphill struggle. In an interview on 25 March with Lord Liverpool, the British Prime Minister, Carsten Anker had been informed in no uncertain terms that the best the Norwegians could hope for was British assistance in obtaining the best possible terms in the union with Sweden – and that was conditional on the removal of Christian Frederik from Norway. The British government naturally looked at the whole affair in terms of its own long term interests in north-eastern Europe. An important aim here was to retain free access to the Baltic, and for that purpose a regional balance of power, with no one power having a hegemony, seemed the best option. A reunion of Norway with Denmark would leave one power in control on both sides of the Baltic approaches, and therefore had to be prevented. A Scandinavian peninsula occupied by two independent but weak states would tend to be drawn into Russia's sphere of influence. Therefore a Norwegian-Swedish union would be the best alternative, but a weak union, with far-reaching Norwegian autonomy, would prevent Sweden from becoming too powerful.

On 27 April Lord Castlereagh told a Danish diplomat that "England, while having no reason to be satisfied with the [Swedish] Crown Prince, would still fulfil her obligation towards him." Swedish sovereignty over Norway was all part of a larger deal by which Russia had already acquired the Swedish province of Finland. For England to repudiate that arrangement was bound to have far-reaching consequences for the balance of power in Northern Europe. Yet there was considerable sympathy in England for the Norwegian cause, particularly among the Liberals. In the beginning of May the Whig leader Lord Grey, in a three-hour speech in the House of Lords, eloquently advocated a suspension of the blockade of Norway which had been reinstituted on 29 April by the government in deference to its allies. The proposition was dismissed in both Houses, but the strength of the Opposition was a significant factor in further modifying England's policy in the Norwegian matter. Already on 26 March the Prime Minister, Lord Liverpool, had indicated to a Norwegian envoy that if the Danish Prince Regent were dropped and the principle of a union with Sweden accepted, Norway could rely on English assistance in getting the best terms possible for that union. However, Norway's sovereign independence was not yet negotiable. The revolution had to run its course, including implementation of the people's right "itself to determine the constitution of its government".

The Constitutional Convention assembled on 10 April, and completed its task in five weeks. The resulting document, which with some amendments remains in force today as the Constitution of the Kingdom of Norway, enshrined what was the most liberal-democratic form of government in Europe at that time. It has for example been estimated that about 45 per cent of the adult male population were henceforth qualified for the right to vote. In comparison the British electorate after the Reform Bill of 1832 comprised only about ten per cent of adult males, and in Sweden the great reforms of 1866 would extend the right to vote to only five per cent. Otherwise the Constitution reflected the principle of the separation of powers, but granted extensive powers to the King and a relatively limited role for the Parliament – which would be named the "Storting" or Great Thing, "ting" or "thing" being the old Norse name for the law-making assemblies of the Viking Age.

The Convention's debates on the various paragraphs naturally centred on the form of government. Throughout those five weeks, however, the question of Norway's relations with other powers was either openly or indirectly under debate. The Convention had soon split into a majority "independence" party, whose most prominent spokesman was now Christian Magnus Falsen, and a minority "union" party, with Count Wedel as the natural leader of a group of patricians – large landowners, and rich businessmen mainly from the coastal towns of south-eastern Norway. The unionists saw the Constitution as a good foundation on which to establish a union of Sweden and Norway as two autonomous kingdoms under one king. They also distrusted the motives of Christian Frederik and the independence party, and suspected a reunion with Denmark to be their real aim. The independence party consisted of civil, ecclesiastical and military officials, and representatives of the free, strong and self-conscious farmer class which was such a distinctive characteristic of a country where feudalism had had little impact. While some of them viewed a possible reunion with Denmark without misgivings, the majority clearly sincerely hoped and believed in a Norway that could be sovereign and independent. As tersely put by one historian: "The independence party stood with a clear front against the union party, the ideals against the realities, the dream of an independent Norway against the possibility of its realisation."[3]

Behind the sometimes violent diatribes of the "independents" against the "unionists", we discern a deep distrust of Norway's Scandinavian neighbours and their ambitions to conquer or at least rule over Norway – ambitions which had dragged Norway into a succession of wars against Sweden, and more recently caused deprivations and outright famine through a royal foreign policy which disregarded Norwegian interests. The separatist and indeed isolationist sentiments engendered by that distrust were voiced with some eloquence by one of the members:

> Severe is the sky over Norway, and the climate is harsh: we live in a hyperborean corner of the globe, and nature has willed us to lack many of the advantages of milder lands. But nature, good within its apparent mercilessness, has clearly wanted to leave us compensation for such wants, and therefore seen to it that Norway's in some respects disadvantageous location should in other respects be most beneficial. The heavens have willed that this Kingdom, while it could not enjoy the fortunes of more fertile and powerful realms, should not either have part in their miseries and conflicts. Here we should remain, by the will of the heavens, as the pauper in his remote cottage, poorly provided, but content with so little, enjoying it in undisturbed peace, without the lusty pleasures of the great, but also untouched by their cabals, disputes, and concerns. Hence nature cut us off from the continent by an engulfing depth, a chasm, and protected the country with palisades of countless cliffs.
>
> But we transgressed the borders delimited by nature, and entered into an unnatural liaison with a Kingdom which could not but drag us into unnatural wars, involve us in misunderstandings with powers with which it was as unnecessary and strange as it was damaging for us to be in disagreement.[4]

Cleansed of its somewhat flowery prose, that speech pointed to two "lessons of history" which would form the basis of long-term trends in Norway's foreign relations: on the one hand isolationism, echoing George Washington's warning to the United States of America eighteen years earlier against entanglement in European power politics, and on the other the need for good relations with Great Britain.

Towards a New Union

On 17 May – still a date of great celebration in Norway as Constitution Day – the Convention first signed the Constitution with its 110 paragraphs,

The "Founding Fathers" of Modern Norway
Often referred to with some reverence as 'the men of Eidsvold', the 112 chosen delegates assembled on Carsten Anker's estate on 10 April 1814 were in many ways different from those seen at similar constitution-making assemblies during the revolutionary and Napoleonic period. They had been elected, directly or indirectly, by parish congregations all over the country, and one third of them were landowning peasants. The majority, however, were senior office-holders – civil servants, churchmen, and officers of the army and navy. Within five weeks they produced a constitution whose guiding principles were popular sovereignty and the separation of powers. The models that partly inspired the final product derived from such diverse predecessors as the American constitution of 1787, the French monarchic constitution of 1791, and the short-lived Batavian (1798) and Spanish (1812) constitutions. The liberal, if not radical, tenor of Norway's 17 May 1814 Constitution was reflected in such matters as the extent of the franchise and the single-chamber legislative Storting, the requirement of universal conscription for military service, and the ban against adding to the existing small number of families of noble rank.

and then proceeded to hoist the banner of full revolt against the European order by electing Christian Frederik as King of Norway. The events of that day can be seen as a brave act of defiance against the established European order. In fact it came to introduce the final drawn-out phase of the Norwegian revolution, that of resignation. Karl Johan was back in Sweden with his army, and demanded the immediate departure of Christian Frederik from Norway. By the middle of June the fledgling King had lost faith in the cause of sovereign independence, and the more sober-minded

48

of the nation's leaders were pondering how best to save as much as possible of the new Constitution. On this latter point, the arrival of the official envoys of the great powers in Christiania at the end of June provided considerable encouragement. Although for different reasons, neither of the great powers was disposed to foster a strong Norwegian-Swedish state. A loose union, wherein Norway could retain most of the new Constitution's limitations against the personal power of the King, could therefore be expected to receive their support. The King, however, would have to go, and by the middle of July King Christian Frederik was ready to accept the inevitability of his own resignation. But that now meant that sovereignty would revert to the people's representatives, in the Constitutional Convention. And for that assembly to be reconvened, its authority, and thereby the main framework of the Constitution which was its source, had to be accepted by the Swedish Crown. Through indirect negotiations, the parties came close to a compromise. But the final point – Sweden's insistence that, as a guarantee for Norwegian acquiescence in the Union, Swedish troops must occupy the two major fortress towns near the border – was unacceptable to Norway: after all that had been said and done since January, laying the country open to occupation by foreign troops would have been regarded as treason by the people. This meant war.

The country had been fully mobilised since the middle of June, the morale of the forces was very high, and preparedness in terms of munitions was as high as could be expected within the limits of the nation's general impoverishment – the people had in the meantime responded with enthusiasm to appeals for donations of gold, silver, food and clothing. The King abhorred war and did not believe that anything good could come of it. Yet there seemed no other way out. The people, largely uninformed about the complex diplomatic developments which had made sovereign independence an illusory aim, needed a war to be convinced – a war which Norway could not win. This the Council of Ministers understood, and they therefore in the end prevented Christian Frederik from proposing any further compromises in the matter of the border fortresses. But once war had broken out, on 26 July, they could not prevent the Commander-in-Chief from pursuing it with the aim of minimising destruction and losses.

On 6 August, having made considerable progress on the way to the Norwegian capital in the wake of the retreating Norwegian army, the Swedish Crown Prince through an emissary proposed a cease-fire which Christian Frederik was at once ready to accept. His ministers demurred, but when the Chief of Staff warned them that the Swedish army would reach the Capital very shortly, they saw no other option but to negotiate. During the dramatic negotiations that followed, the Council of Ministers insisted on the army carrying through at least one major battle before a final cease-fire, "for the honour of the nation and the army and in accordance with the spirit which prevails among the people". The King vacillated, gave orders to attack, but retracted the order half an hour later. The half-hearted way in which the brief campaign had been fought meant that the reality of defeat seemed only half-convincing in the eyes of the people. Suspicions of treason inevitably arose, and two generals had to go into hiding to escape the wrath of the soldiers and the people. Nevertheless, on 14 August three documents were signed in the little town of Moss on the eastern side of the Oslo fjord. One was an armistice agreement, one was a letter from Christian Frederik to the King of Sweden announcing his impending abdication. But the central document was a formal treaty later known as the Moss Convention.

By the Moss Convention of 14 August Christian Frederik surrendered his executive powers to the Council of Ministers, and promised to leave the country as soon as a new National Assembly could be convened. By that act, the accession of the Swedish King to the Norwegian throne was virtually assured, subject to formal ratification by the Storting – the new National Assembly. However, by that same instrument Karl Johan formally accepted what he had, in fact, already agreed to in practice by entering into negotiations with the Norwegian King and Council of Ministers: namely the principal validity of the Norwegian Constitution of 17 May 1814, an expression of the sovereignty of the people, subject only to alterations which would themselves be the subject of negotiations between the Swedish Crown Prince and the Norwegian Storting. Up until that time the official Swedish position had been – and logically had to be – that a treaty existed which had to be fulfilled, a treaty which recognised no other authority than that of Kings and their divine rights. Among the multiple reasons which motivated this acceptance of what Karl Johan before the summer had regarded as anathema, two stand out: First, his ambitions as a liberal alternative to a Bourbon restoration in France. Already on 12 July Madame de Staël, voice of the liberal French opposition, wrote to Karl Johan advising him to accept the Constitution which the Norwegians had just given themselves, and stated that their common interest in France now depended on his handling of the Norwegian matter. Second, a prolonged struggle in Scandinavia could further cool the waning enthusiasm of the great powers for supporting Karl Johan, particularly with the Vienna Congress about to be convened.

On the Norwegian side, the somewhat "phoney war" feeling that lingered in parts of the country meant that some of the delegates to the new National Assembly still refused to accept Union with Sweden, being so bound by the mandate of their electors. But they were in a dwindling minority, and on 20 October – the date of expiry of the armistice – only five delegates opposed the motion that Norway would unite with Sweden on conditions to be agreed upon. Then, having settled the terms of Union and incorporated the necessary changes into the Constitution, the Assembly on 4 November elected Karl XIII of Sweden as King of the self-governed realm of Norway. Thus ended Norway's *annus mirabilis*. Cast into the maelstrom of European power politics, fluctuating between the prospect of yet another subjugation under foreign rule and the heady chimera of sovereign independence, a union with Sweden on terms of autonomy and with her own liberal Constitution seems in retrospect to have been the best possible outcome.

3. The Swedish-Norwegian Union 1814–1905

The Formal Framework

The formal basis for the new Union was established in two documents. First came the Constitution as amended by the Norwegian Storting in extraordinary session in October – November 1814. Then came the Act of Union in the following year, which regulated a number of legalistic and procedural matters. Some of the amendments enacted in what became known as the "November Constitution" were of a more formal nature, necessitated by Norway's changed status from a separate and independent kingdom to a personal union with Sweden under one King. Of particular importance in that context was the position of the Norwegian Council of Ministers. Over and above each individual Minister's function as personal adviser to the King, as prescribed in the 17 May Constitution, the Council now assumed the status of a cabinet, sub-divided into two sections since the King would reside in Stockholm: the Cabinet in Christiania, chaired by a "*Stattholder*" or governor-general as the King's representative, and a Government Mission in Stockholm consisting of the Prime Minister and two other Ministers, to form part of a Combined Council of Ministers for consideration of matters of common interest to the two countries. There were also amendments of a partly symbolic nature, specifying among other things that Norway would have her own national bank, her own currency, and the right to her own national flag for commercial shipping.[1]

Other amendments of a more overarching nature had foreign policy implications, and had the clear purpose of limiting the powers of the King and strengthening the position of the Storting as the guardian of Norwegian autonomy within the Union. One amendment concerned the right to command and control the Norwegian army. Fearful that the King aimed to amalgamate the armies of the two countries for use in belligerent adventures, the Storting amended the relevant paragraphs to limit the King's right to free disposal of the Norwegian army and navy. In wars which could not be construed as defensive the consent of the Storting would in each case be required. The army was also divided between an "army of the line", which could be used abroad, and the territorial army which could only be used at home for national defence.

52

Another major amendment related more directly to the King's freedom of action in foreign affairs. Foreign policy was in those times almost invariably a royal prerogative, and the Norwegian 17 May Constitution went with the times by giving the monarch the right to "enter into and cancel alliances, receive and send envoys" – matters of diplomacy, in other words – without consulting the Cabinet. The King retained that right in the November Constitution. In Sweden the King was required to seek advice in such matters from a special "Ministerial Council" composed of the King, the Foreign Minister, and the Lord Chancellor. There was evidently no question of admitting any Norwegian Minister to that exclusive circle. However, the King's right "to declare war and conclude peace", which was a royal privilege according to the 17 May Constitution, would henceforth be subject to prior consultation also with the King's Norwegian Ministers through an "Extra-

ordinary Ministerial Council". A parallel limitation on the King's freedom of action had already been stipulated in the Swedish Reform Act of 1809, which shows that the legislative assemblies of both countries feared the consequences of an adventurous royal foreign policy. Nevertheless, while the King by those various stipulations had to seek the advice of Ministers, he did not need their consent. The final decision was his own to make. Norway's direct influence on the foreign policy of the Union was thus limited to advising the King on the crucial matters of declaring war and concluding peace. In addition the Storting could exercise a certain negative influence, by refusing to grant funds necessary for war-making purposes.

Norway under Karl XIV Johan

The period of war and blockade that finally came to an end in the autumn of 1814 had left Norway so impoverished that it could be said to teeter on the brink of bankruptcy. The necessary effort of establishing a national banking system, with a new currency, did not make things easier. It was in such circumstances bound to take time before some sort of financial stability could be attained. Low prices and exorbitant customs duties for the country's main export, timber, meant that while the markets' demand for the product remained high, the main merchants sank deeper and deeper into debt. Fish exports, particularly dried fish and herrings, fared better. Nor-

Karl Johan's Foreign Policy

Karl Johan's de facto take over of the Swedish throne in 1810 changed the course of Swedish foreign policy. Traditionally, Denmark-Norway and Russia had been seen as potential enemies, raising the fear of encirclement and a two-front war. But in 1812 Karl Johan allied himself with Russia against Napoleon, and in 1814 the Union with Norway secured Sweden's western frontier. In the following year Sweden also abandoned her last remaining possessions in Northern Germany, thus reducing the risk of involvement in Continental wars. The Swedish-Norwegian Union henceforth found itself in a central position in the power struggle between two great powers – England and Russia. Neutrality seemed the best answer: the Union's military weakness necessitated friendly relations with Russia, whereas economic and trade interests counselled close relations with England.

The Debt Settlement with Denmark

According to the 1814 Kiel Treaty the King of Norway assumed responsibility for Norway's share of Denmark/Norway's foreign debt. The Storting, while in principle willing to pay, demanded a settlement on an independent basis, without reference to the Kiel Treaty which Norway did not recognise. The Storting also requested that the King bring "Norway's right to Iceland, the Faeroes and Greenland" into the negotiations, and subsequently added – for good measure – the Danish possessions in the West Indies into the bargain as presumed joint property. Denmark however insisted on a settlement based on the Kiel Treaty, a position supported by the great powers, but with the rider that the King of Sweden, and not Norway, was the legal party. Karl Johan, in his turn, maintained that his right to Norway rested on his election as a constitutional monarch, not on the Kiel Treaty, and that he could not force the Norwegian parliament's hand in the matter. Pressure from the great powers, raising the threat of a commercial blockade, eventually forced Karl Johan to settle, and in 1819 a settlement with Denmark was arranged over the heads of the Norwegian Storting. That eliminated the debt as a foreign policy issue, but the settlement further aggravated the relations between Sweden and Norway, and between the King and the Storting.

way's merchant navy also suffered from the declining terms of trade, and its tonnage was reduced by almost a third in the fifteen years that followed.

On the international stage the end of Napoleon ushered in a long period of relative peace and stability. Karl Johan for his part seemed content to maintain a neutral stance, and concentrated on his main aim: to further the growing together of his two kingdoms into a strong and prosperous union. This meant that while there was no question of accepting any new limitations on the royal power in diplomacy and other matters of high politics, the King showed a benign attitude towards Norwegian efforts to have a greater say in matters of their own special interests. In that respect a major step forward was made in 1835, when it was enacted that a Norwegian Cabinet Minister would be admitted to the special "Ministerial Council" whenever issues of special relevance to Norway or matters of evident common interest to the two countries were being discussed. At about the same time Norway obtained that the appointment of consuls, a major part of whose task it was to look after Norwegian foreign trade and shipping interests, was transferred from the Swedish Council of Ministers to the Combined Council.

None of this affected the right of the monarch to make his own decisions regardless of the advice of Ministers. But it sharpened the Norwegian Ministers' vigilance in defending national interests, because they had to account to the Storting for the positions taken and the advice offered in such combined forums. One such case arose when it became known that the 1842 negotiations for a revision of the Sound Dues – the fees paid by ships passing through Øresund to and from the Baltic – had proceeded without Norwegian shipping interests being represented. The Storting reacted sharply, and threatened to impeach two members of the Cabinet Mission in Stockholm for dereliction of duty. The King defused the conflict by accepting that commercial treaties should henceforth be ratified in Combined Council.

Those advances in the direction of Norwegian influence on the management of Norway's foreign relations went hand in hand with a distinct upturn in her foreign trade and shipping. In the ten-year period from 1825 to 1835, while fish exports continued to prosper, timber exports grew by nearly 50 per cent, partly as a result of gaining a new market in France. The merchant navy in the same period grew from 1800 to 2300 ships. In the following years, further progress was made on both counts: Great Britain's new liberal regime under Lord Peel reduced the duties on timber imports from Northern and Eastern Europe. Moreover, Norwegian ships could take advantage of the Union with Sweden to carry also Swedish timber to Britain within the terms of the British Navigation Acts. In addition, the Norwegian merchant navy began to make inroads into the timber trade from the Baltic to France and the Netherlands.

On the whole, Karl Johan's reign was a period of progress towards financial solvency, and of consolidation of Norway's status as an autonomous entity within the United Kingdoms of Sweden and Norway. On the international stage, however, Norway was very much a subsidiary of Sweden. This was clearly demonstrated in the murky, in itself insignificant but nevertheless symbolic, "Bodø Affair". A group of English merchants had established a company in the town of Bodø in northern Norway, and got caught selling smuggled import goods. The merchants and their financial backers in the City of London then succeeded in getting the Foreign Office to support their claims to compensation on the basis of a fanciful version of the event. The Swedish Foreign Minister, in the words of an English historian, "indeed sympathised with the British view of North Norway as a kind of no-man's-land, where the rights of foreigners could not safely be left for determination by the native law courts."[2] The King, for his part, promised the British envoy that he would make his Norwegian Ministers "see reason", to which the envoy commented that "we recognised no separate government of Norway". The British

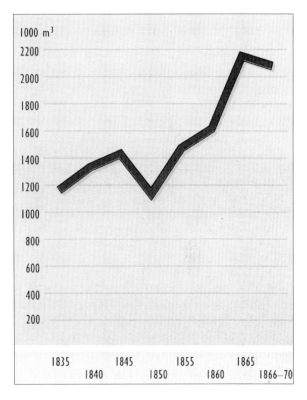

Norwegian timber exports
Next to fish, timber was Norway's most important export product. During the Napoleonic wars the blockades had effectively barred Norway from her most important markets, England and the Netherlands. Attempts to regain the British market after 1815 were hindered by a new customs regime which favoured Canadian and certain Baltic timber exports. Exorbitant duties on Norwegian timber, coupled with an inadequate supply of credit, produced crisis conditions for the old established Norwegian trading companies. Efforts to negotiate better terms of trade with Britain were to no avail, partly due to divergent Swedish and Norwegian interests. Not until the British Navigation Act of 1842 could the deadlock be broken, and in the meantime France had emerged as the most important market for Norwegian timber.

Russia's Support for Norwegian Autonomy

While at the outset looking askance at the Norwegian Constitution as alarmingly liberal, Russia had a clear foreign policy interest in preventing Sweden from forging a closer and thereby stronger union on the Scandinavian peninsula. Hence the reactionary Tsarist regime in Russia came to play the paradoxical role of guarantor of Norway's autonomy within the Union. Russia on several occasions indirectly supported Norway's resistance against Karl Johan's repeated attempts to merge the two countries. When the King in 1821 contemplated a 'coup d'etat' against the Storting's stubborn refusal to strengthen the bonds of union, the Russian Tsar sent a clear signal that this was unacceptable. Seven years later, when Karl Johan again became exasperated at Norwegian recalcitrance, Tsar Nicolay warned him that once the Prince had given the people a constitution he had the duty to abide by it! Finally, during the constitutional crisis of 1836, when the King wanted to dissolve the Storting on account of its demands for more influence, Russia again made clear her support for Norway's cause.

Government behaved as a big bully in the affair, threatening with economic sanctions against Sweden and Norway, and the Norwegian Government had to pay what in the circumstances was a large compensation.

Still those years also brought a victory of sorts for Norwegian sovereignty, with the final recognition by Russia of a clearly defined frontier between the Norwegian county of Finnmark and Russia's Finnish province. This largely uninhabited territory had for centuries been a "grey area" of unsolved claims and counter-claims, partly due to the nomadic lifestyle of the Sami with their reindeer herds, moving between summers on the coast and winters in the hinterland. But in 1826 the Russian Tsar, after some prevarication, agreed to a formal border treaty, whereby the western third of the "grey area" came under Norwegian sovereignty. The extent of Norway's mainland territory was thereby finally settled in the shape it now has, although this has not prevented occasional diplomatic skirmishes about rights for the Sami on both sides of the border. The division of the area was roughly the same as that proposed by a Norwegian border commission, and the remarkably accommodating attitude of the Russians has been explained in part by reference to the Russian Tsar's wish for friendly relations with Karl Johan.

Oscar I and Karl XV: Ambitions for a "Great Scandinavia"

In 1848, four years into King Oscar I's reign, the stability of the European states' system was rocked by the stirrings of revolutionary movements on the Continent. A desire for German unification led to uprisings against Danish rule in the German-speaking provinces of Schleswig and Holstein. The Prussians intervened to eject the Danish army from the area, and in this crisis King Oscar saw an opening for his ambition to add the Danish crown to his kingdoms, the Danish King Frederick VII having no direct heir. To further his aims Oscar promised immediate assistance to Denmark with 15 000 troops and a naval squadron. However, before going to war he was bound to consult an "Extraordinary Ministerial Council", and the possible use of Norwegian troops also required the consent of the Storting.

Common Sami areas

prior to the Norwegian–Russian border treaty of 1826

NORWAY

●Vardø

Neiden-
Siidaen

●Kirkenes

FINLAND

Pasvik-
Siidaen   Petsjenga-
Siidaen

RUSSIA

●Murmansk
●Kola (Malmis)

Unsettled Borders in the North

In the interior of the country north of the arctic circle, stretching roughly from the Lofoten area in the west to the eastern coast of the Kola Peninsula, the population consisted mainly of nomadic Sami who moved freely with their reindeer herds between winter pastures, then out to the coast, and back again. For centuries, the monarchs of Russia, Sweden, and Norway all claimed those territories as their own, mainly for the purpose of collecting taxes from the Sami. In 1595 a peace treaty between the Russian Tsar and the Swedish King divided the area between them, with Sweden gaining the exclusive right of tax collection westward from the Varanger peninsula. Through a peace settlement of 1613 between Sweden and Denmark-Norway, King Christian IV regained the coastal areas in the north for the Norwegian crown. But in the hinterland the borders remained ill-defined until settled between Norway and Sweden in 1751, and between Norway and Russia in 1809 (concerning the Grand Duchy of Finland) and 1826.

This looked like becoming a first test of Norway's influence on the foreign policy of the United Kingdoms. Several factors serve to explain why it did not turn out that way. First of all there was strong sympathy in Norway for Denmark's cause, not only on account of the strong cultural affinity produced by four centuries of close union between the two peoples, but also because Denmark was seen as a small country victim of aggression from a great (or would-be great) power. This was also the view of the majority in the Norwegian Cabinet, which moreover saw Denmark as a useful buffer against Scandinavia's involvement with German expansionism. A minority in the Cabinet took a clearly isolationist line, maintaining that the resources of a small country like Norway should be used for the country's own benefit instead of being spent on matters of European power politics in which it had no direct interest or influence. The Storting inclined towards that minority view, but since the King had gone out on a limb with his promises to Denmark, a ban on the use of Norwegian troops would have given a body

Norway and Sweden during the Crimean War

The Crimean War (1853–6) was caused by Russia's attempt to take control of the Black Sea and the exit to the Mediterranean. When Russian troops in July 1853 moved into the Danubian Principalities, the Turkish Sultan declared war against Russia, and in March of the following year England and France came in on Turkey's side. The Swedish-Norwegian Union as well as Denmark declared their neutrality in the conflict, but King Oscar I worked behind the scene to bring the Union into the war on the side of the Western powers. His aim was to see Russia's position in Northern Europe reduced, as this might open the way for the return of Finland and the Aaland Islands to Sweden. In support of his effort he resurrected the old idea of a Russian expansionist urge for ice-free ports on the coast of Finnmark, and in November 1855 he signed a treaty with England and France whereby the two powers guaranteed the territorial integrity of the dual kingdom against Russia.. The war remained focused on the Black Sea region, however, despite King Oscar's attempt to shift the attention of the powers to the northern theatre. In Norway the King's belligerent activity led to sharp confrontations with the government and the Storting. The Governor-General of Norway, Severin Løvenskiold, repeatedly warned the King against leading the countries to war, and in the end resigned from his post.

blow to the prestige of both the King and the United Kingdoms. Permission was therefore granted, and the necessary funds were allocated, but in the end all the effort that was required was the posting of 1100 Norwegian soldiers and a larger Swedish contingent to Northern Schleswig, to serve as peace-keeping forces during the transition from armistice to peace.

The Crimean War (1853–6) of Great Britain and France against Russia became the next test case for Norway's ability to influence the King's foreign policy. Officially the United Kingdoms maintained neutrality in the conflict, but King Oscar's aim was to enter the war in the hope of forcing Russia to give up Finland and the strategic Aaland Islands. This time the Norwegian government and the Storting were on their guard, and also refused to increase the budget for the military. In addition to their instinctive isolationism and fear of involvement in power politics, they were acutely aware that neutrality was a necessary condition for the prosperity and high earnings which the country's foreign trade and shipping was enjoying. Neutral trade with the belligerents, while often risky, now as always also brought considerable profits. The King then concluded the 1855 "November Treaty" by which Britain and France guaranteed the territorial integrity of the United Kingdoms against Russia. While ostensibly concluded for purely defensive purposes, the treaty could under certain circumstances drag Sweden and Norway into the war. Again the King submitted the treaty for Council approval as more or less a *fait accompli*, and the Norwegian government could do no more than register its strong disapproval. In the event, however, the war ended without Scandinavian intervention.

The efforts to seek control of the monarch's foreign political ambitions continued through the reign of Karl XV (1859–72). The first occasion arose when the German-Danish dispute over Schleswig-Holstein threatened to explode again in 1863. This time the King gave Denmark what amounted to a *carte blanche* to summon Swedish-Norwegian military assistance in case of an attack from Germany. The Swedish government, for internal political reasons, refrained from making an issue of it, but the Norwegian government expressed strong reservations against an intervention except as part of an international coalition that should include both France and Great Britain. The German troops launched an attack in 1864, but mediation from the great powers brought an early end to the war, without any need to call on the mobilised Swedish and Norwegian forces to intervene.

An additional explanation for the willingness of the Norwegian government and Storting to meet the King half way, in their eagerness to intervene in Denmark's disputes, is the impact of the popular movement termed "Scandinavianism" which periodically blossomed from about 1840 to the 1860s. Nurtured by a sense of Nordic uniqueness in ethnic, cultural, and political respects, and a wish to strengthen this community of closely related peoples in an era of great power dominance, this movement found strong support in academic and literary circles. For a time it could also be used by the nation's political elite – the roughly two thousand strong class of senior officials and senior civil and military servants – in favour of initiatives to strengthen the union with Sweden. Leading members of that elite class saw a fusion with the more conservative state of Sweden as a way to preserve their own power and influence against radical and nationalist trends. Others, however, saw the prospect of a Scandinavian confederation as a way to draw in Denmark as a counter-weight to Swedish dominance.

It should be noted that the political institutions of both countries essentially pursued the same aim in such disputes: the governments and parliaments wished to enjoy the economic prosperity which only peace and neutrality could bring, and therefore sought both separately and together to restrain the King's more adventurous ambitions. In this venture lay the seeds of a dilemma for Norwegian politicians: the road to control of the monarch's foreign policy seemed to go through a closer union between the two Kingdoms, whereby the political institutions could gain strength in unity. But that was still only a harbinger of future developments. For the time being, the important aim was to restrain the King's activism. And since the Ministerial Council could at best only advise the King, the most effective restraining instrument turned out to be parliamentary control of the purse strings. From 1869 the Storting used that instrument to strengthen budget allocations for the consular service to the detriment of funds for the diplomatic service. Here was a cause that served Norwegian foreign relations directly: the Norwegian merchant fleet from the middle of the century enjoyed a growth rate which can only be called phenomenal. Each decade from 1845 onwards saw nearly a doubling of the tonnage, with a clear trend towards bigger ships.

Historians who have looked at Norwegian foreign policy during the union with Sweden have had a tendency to see the efforts to influence the King's foreign policy as an expression of Norwegian foreign policy, without clarifying what foreign policy aims would be served by those efforts. It is

Henrik Ibsen and Scandinavianism

Henrik Ibsen was among the many writers and intellectuals who supported Scandinavianism during the 1860s. In 1863 he published the poem "En broder i nød" – A brother in need – in which he urged that Norway and Sweden stand by their obligation to give military assistance to Denmark in her struggle against Prussia. When war did break out between the two countries in 1864, however, few Norwegians favoured military intervention. Scandinavianism, it turned out, had little support beyond the capital city's elite.

important to keep in mind here that the wish to control the King's foreign policy did not mean a desire for an alternative foreign policy, but rather a basically isolationist desire for no foreign policy at all or – perhaps more precisely – a policy reflecting Thomas Jefferson's advice to the United States of America in his 1801 Inaugural Address as President: "Peace, commerce, and honest friendship with all nations, entangling alliances with none." And in the liberal-capitalist order this was to be obtained by minimal state interference in matters relating to external trade. Only when formal trade treaties were to be concluded, or when matters of customs duties or other import and export regulations were decided, did Norway have vital interests positively to protect or promote. As quoted by a Norwegian historian from a newspaper article in 1875: "Our fatherland is so situated that the great events in the outside world effect us but little and seldom. We are in that respect the balcony in the great world theatre ... This allows us in peace and quiet to deal with our own affairs."[3]

"No foreign policy" did not of course mean "no foreign relations". On the contrary, free trade and the expansion of shipping meant increased contact between Norwegians and the outside world as the century wore on. The long-term trend in Norway's orientation here showed a marked swing from south towards west – from Germany, with Denmark as the conduit, towards Britain. Norwegian exports to Great Britain were in the second half of the century two to three times greater than exports to Germany, and British traders were by far the most important customers for Norwegian shipping services. The cultural impact – in the widest sense of the word "culture" – of such contacts was particularly strong in commercial and industrial circles. Yet both the political elite and a wide spectrum of ordinary citizens also developed a clear affinity to English political culture and the parliamentary system of government, in spite of bad memories of Britain's hunger blockade during the Napoleonic wars. On the other hand, in academic circles as well as in the arts, German influence would remain the strongest until well into the next century, with Henrik Ibsen and Edvard Grieg as the most towering icons.

The Turning of the Tide

The 1870s were to mark the breakthrough for a national opposition against attempts to forge a closer union between the two Kingdoms. The change was heralded by an intense debate on proposals from a joint Swedish-Norwegian "Union Commission", appointed for the purpose of limiting the King's freedom of action in foreign policy. The Commission proposed that all foreign policy matters should henceforth be dealt with in a "Union Council of Ministers" composed of an equal number of Ministers from both countries. As the Ministers would be accountable to their respective parliamentary assemblies for the decisions, such a measure would go a long way towards effective control of the King's powers in foreign affairs. As a kind of *quid pro quo* the proposals relaxed somewhat the limitation on the King's right to use Norwegian armed forces abroad. The crunch came in the stipulation that the Foreign Minister should be Swedish, and hence would answer only to the Swedish parliament.

In the debate on the proposals in the Storting, in 1871, the supporters portrayed them as the fulfilment of long-standing demands for control of foreign affairs by the people's representatives, and sought to counter criticism of the retention of a Swedish Foreign Minister by pointing out that since a Union Parliament was not on the cards, the Foreign Minister had to be accountable to one of the national assemblies, which for practical reasons had to be the Swedish "Riksdag". But the opposition to the proposals was massive: the Union Council of Ministers was bound to become in effect a joint government for the two countries, and would in the fullness of time

61

lead to a Union parliament, ending up in a state union whereby "Norway's sovereignty, nationality, freedom and autonomy would founder, being the numerically weaker partner."[4] Those were the words of the parliamentarian Johan Sverdrup, who was then emerging as the leader of the national-democratic opposition. Under the impact of such emotions the proposals for union reform were resoundingly defeated.

With the question of procedural reform of the foreign policy process out of the way, and with no opportunities for foreign policy adventures that might tempt the King to deviate from the path of neutrality, Norway's foreign relations again became matters of trade and shipping. The increasingly extrovert economy of the country called for a trade policy of maximum freedom and minimal customs duties, which was perfectly in tune with the prevailing international trend of the second half of the nineteenth century. The abolition of such hindrances to free trade as the Sound Dues, which were a major source of income for Denmark, or the tonnage fees at the river entrances to Hamburg and Antwerp, required that the collecting state be compensated. Since Norwegian ships inevitably were heavily involved in maritime trade, Norway would have to pay a large part of the United Kingdoms' share of the compensation. This made it necessary to bring Norwegian representatives into the negotiations, and that meant another small step towards recognition of Norway as a sovereign and equal member of the Union. A similar situation arose during the long process of negotiations for a new trade treaty between the United Kingdoms and France. Here Norwegian shipping interests competed with both Swedish and Norwegian export interests, but the resulting compromise – a treaty signed in 1865 – favoured the Norwegian merchant navy.

On the broader question of commercial policy, the framework of the Union did not provide for a customs union. Norway's liberal trade policies contrasted with those of Sweden, with her protectionist traditions. The Swedish government, in its efforts to forge a closer Union, had long wished to legislate a harmonisation of the two countries' customs tariffs. Policy differences regarding both the wider issue of trading interests and the more specific one of the state's income from customs duties made this a thorny problem, however. Not until 1874, after Norway's own industrial development had diminished the fear of being overwhelmed by competition from the more advanced Swedish industry, was a law regulating trade between the two countries enacted by both parliaments. The result was not a customs union, but it went a long way towards establishing the United Kingdoms as a free trade area. This, as well as the subsequent institution for all three Scandinavian kingdoms of the gold standard, with the "krone" or crown as the basic unit of coinage, was a victory of sorts for the proponents of a closer Swedish-Norwegian Union. But the nationalist opposition, while it might lose some battles, was still determined to win the war. The victory they sought was the clearest possible separation of powers between the two states under one King. The question was where to draw the line.

The question of the extent of Norway's maritime territory, in the perspective of securing fisheries resources, has a long history. We have seen earlier how the Danish Kings in the sixteenth century sought to promote Norwegian interests by defining limits for foreign fishing boats' activities off Norway's shores. The nineteenth century brought important advances in that regard. In 1812 a document from the Chancery in Copenhagen established one geographic mile, defined as four nautical miles from the outermost islands or skerries, as Norway's territorial limit based on historical precedent. The complex indentation of the coastline, with its many fjords and islands, nevertheless made that limit hard to define and even harder to enforce. In the 1860s the government therefore determined that the whole of the Vestfjord area, a wide bay between the Lofoten string of islands and the mainland, was part of Norway's maritime territory. The subsequent expulsion of a French fishing vessel from the area produced a protest from the French government, but after a lengthy and detailed memorandum on the merits of Norway's case, penned by the Norwegian Prime Minister and loyally argued by the Swedish Foreign Minister, France – and subsequently also Great Britain – accepted the new line.

However, when the Norwegian government in the following year applied the principle of the straight line to another stretch of fjords and islands further south, the French government again protested, reiterating the common principle in international law that the limit should follow the indentations of the mainland coast. The protest also pointed out that the generally recognised extent of territorial limits was three and not four nautical miles. As the Norwegian government did not give in, and the French protest was left hanging, the "straight line" principle seemed to have made one more step towards becoming accepted internationally.

The Rise of the Storting

The desire of an increasingly strong opposition for more democracy, and the rising tide of nationalism, came together during the 1870s in the demand for the Cabinet to be made politically accountable to the Storting. Such a radical reform went contrary to the established system in the two Kingdoms, and ultimately contradicted the paragraph of the Norwegian Constitution which plainly stated that "The King himself selects his Council …" On paper the reform proposal rather innocuously stated a right of access for the Cabinet Ministers to the Storting. But the effect would be that the Cabinet could no longer pursue policies that the majority of the parliamentarians opposed. The King – now Oscar II, who succeeded his brother King Karl XV in 1872 – as well as his Norwegian Cabinet resolved to make a stand against the reform, and a major constitutional crisis was therefore unavoidable. When the King vetoed the reform for the third time, the majority in the Storting in 1884 promulgated the law, and impeached the Cabinet for failing to carry out the will of the people's representatives. The radical "leftist" grouping, now organised as a political party named "Venstre" – the left – won the day, and King Oscar II grudgingly had to appoint a new Cabinet selected from that party.

Among the great expectations with which the new Cabinet was met, three could be said to have a bearing on Norwegian foreign relations. First there was the formality that the Cabinet would now as a body be held answerable to the Storting also for its action – or indeed non-action – in matters of the foreign policy of the United Kingdoms. This would in due course almost inevitably lead to demands for an answerable Foreign Minister. Then there were the expectations regarding the substance of foreign policy. In continuation of the long-standing desire for Norwegian control of her shipping and trade relations with other countries, the 1891 election platform for the "Venstre" party demanded a Norwegian foreign service and a Norwegian consular service, as well as the right to conclude separate treaties with foreign powers. The latter demand bore fruit already in the following year, when a trade treaty between Norway and Spain was signed and ratified, followed by similar treaties with Switzerland, Belgium, and Portugal. Embedded in this move was the realisation that the trade policies of Sweden and Norway kept developing in different directions. Sweden was moving towards a more protectionist policy, whereas in Norway the principle of free trade still stood strong.

The question of a national consular service for Norway was well suited to become a profoundly divisive issue for the Union. The Norwegian merchant fleet was by the end of the 1880s three times the size of the Swedish one, and the third largest in the world. In line with that the Norwegian state contributed about two thirds of the budget for the Union's consular service. It was therefore not unreasonable that there should be dissatisfaction with an arrangement which meant that this service was led by a Foreign Minister answerable only to the Swedish parliament. The location of the consulates also took little account of the expansion of Norwegian shipping activity overseas, to North and South America, the West Indies, Asia, and Africa. Last but not least: the appointment of consuls, unlike the appointment of diplomatic envoys, was not within the reserved domain of the King, so there was no constitutional bar against establishing a separate Norwegian consular service.

For all these reasons a special Storting committee in 1892 proposed, and the Storting voted, the establishment of a separate Norwegian consular service. This began what has been called the "policy of the clenched fist". It said nothing about a Norwegian Foreign Minister as an ultimate goal. But such an outcome was clearly in the minds of many. The King and the Swedish government countered the decision with various compromise proposals, one of which would have opened the way to a Foreign Minister who was either Swedish or Norwegian. But the radical majority in the Storting was in no mood to give in, and the Norwegian Cabinet in 1895 simply decided to abolish the joint consular service. Sweden now threatened to use armed force against Norway unless the discussions were resumed on this and other issues concerning the affairs of the Union. In the face of this the Storting beat a somewhat ignominious retreat, and agreed to talks on the whole framework of the Union. Those talks however led nowhere, and reports suggesting that the Swedish King was trying to get the great powers to intervene against Norway did not improve the chances for a mutually acceptable solution.

The 1890s also saw a resurgence of Norwegian neutralism. In part this was the old wine of isolationism in new bottles, nourished by suspicions that the King's pro-German leanings might involve the United Kingdoms in foreign adventures against Norwegian interests. But the containing idealism was a new feature. The status of neutrality experienced remarkable growth during the nineteenth century. Relative peace and prosperity reigned in Europe, and economic liberalism favoured the expansion of trade without barriers of state interference. This, together with the rise of a neutral great power, the United States of America, provided a favourable climate for the development of a coherent legal neutrality doctrine. One important milestone was the Declaration of Paris in 1856, which consecrated the old but never before universally recognised rules for the protection of neutral trade in wartime: namely immunity from capture of enemy cargo on neutral ships and neutral cargo on enemy ships.

All three Scandinavian countries saw important advantages for their trade in the strengthened legal status of neutrality, although this was tempered on Sweden's part by an occasional hankering after a great power role. In Norway Johan Sverdrup, leader of the "Venstre" party and Prime Minister from 1884, had in 1883 formed an association of parliamentarians to promote the idea of neutrality. In 1898, in the course of preparations for the coming Hague conference on international law, the Storting urged King Oscar II to work for the neutralisation of the United Kingdoms. In the following year the new "Venstre" Prime Minister, Johannes Steen, used an Inter-Parliamentary Union conference in the Norwegian Capital to advocate a status of permanent neutrality for Sweden and Norway. Their geographic situation favoured such a solution. It would also, he thought, be in the common interest of the great powers if Scandinavia could be excluded from the contests of power politics. Of course, an internationally recognised status of permanent neutrality would also ease the burden of fulfilling the duties that accompanied the rights of neutrals. In 1900 all the Norwegian

Arming for the defence of Norway
With neutrality as the watchword, and an unwillingness to spend money on armed forces which the King might wish to use for foreign policy adventures, the Storting kept defence budgets at a minimum until the 1880s. But after Norway's 1895 retreat over the matter of a separate consular service, in the face of Swedish threats to use armed force, a period of strong rearmament began. The navy acquired four battleships and several smaller vessels, coastal defence forts and forts along the Swedish border were reinforced, and national control of the country's armed forces was strengthened. By the end of the decade this had provided Norway with a strong and modern defence capability in support of her claim to independence.

political parties – the formation of the "Venstre" party having been followed by the appearance of a conservative "right" or "Høyre" party and a Social-Democratic party – had permanent neutrality as part of their election platforms. Then, in 1902, a unanimous Storting asked the Cabinet to open negotiations for the permanent neutralisation of Sweden and Norway.

The lack of favourable responses from Sweden to this Norwegian foreign policy activism was bound to reinforce the wish for greater Norwegian independence in foreign affairs. But the aim, in practical politics, remained one of greater freedom to pursue national trade and shipping interests. Norway's most popular writer, poet, and political commentator at that time, Bjørnstierne Bjørnson, had put it in stark terms in a 1895 newspaper article: "We are aiming to do away with all politics through treaties of arbitration and neutrality, and to install our own consuls for our trade and shipping – fully managed by us, by a Foreign Ministry without a foreign policy."[5]

Towards Dissolution of the Union

In 1901 the Swedish government, imbued with a sense of impending crisis, proposed new negotiations about the arrangements for the consular service. A joint committee was appointed, which in 1903 put forward an agreed proposal based on separate consular services for the two countries. The relationship between the consuls and the foreign service of the United Kingdoms was to be determined by identical legislation. On the Norwegian side it now fell to a new Norwegian government to propose such legislation. This new government had been formed after the mainstream liberals had broken with the radical "Venstre" party and formed a coalition with the conservatives. Their proposals aimed to be non-provocative even while maintaining Norway's principal stand. The Swedish counter-proposals for the legislation, however, following the general trend towards merging the diplomatic and consular services, had the consuls subordinated to the Foreign Minister to a degree which Norway found unacceptable.

On 8 February 1905 the Norwegian Prime Minister put the matter before the Storting, and indicated that the Cabinet was prepared to take Norway out of the Union, if necessary. In the Storting debate different strategies were now proposed for dealing with the crisis. All of them would in all probability lead to a dissolution of the Union, assuming the King refused to sanction the proposed legislation. The Cabinet for various reasons found all those strategies to be too provocative, preferring instead a procedure which would put the consular issue on ice for the time being. But the crisis had now reached a point of no return, and a new government was formed under the premiership of the Bergen shipowner Christian Michelsen. His choice of strategy was for the Storting to enact the proposed legislation, and to leave the King with the choice of either sanctioning or refusing to sanction it. Then, as the King predictably refused to sanction the law as presented to him by the Norwegian Cabinet Mission in Stockholm, the Ministers in their turn refused to append their required counter-signatures, and tendered the resignation of the entire Cabinet. In a final twist to this legalistic minuet the King now refused to accept their demissions, stating the obvious fact that he would not be able to find another Norwegian Cabinet.

The final act for the Union came at an historic meeting of the Norwegian Storting on 7 June, 1905. Prime Minister Michelsen, taking his cue from the King's closing remark, submitted the following long-winded and constitutionally intricate proposal:

As all members of the Cabinet have resigned their functions, and His Majesty the King has declared himself unable to provide the country with a new government, whereby the constitutional monarchy has ceased to function, the Storting empowers the members of the demissioning Cabinet to exercise, until further notice, the functions assigned to the King in accordance with the Constitution of the Kingdom of Norway and the current laws – with the changes made necessary by virtue of the Union with Sweden under one King being dissolved due to the King having ceased to function as King of Norway.

Thus 91 years of Union between Norway and Sweden were brought to an end. In Sweden the outcome was met with resignation, in some quarters even with some relief, although others made belligerent noises and demanded armed intervention. It had not, on the whole, been an unhappy union, and for a long period it had seemed as if both countries were satisfied with an arrangement whereby the inequality of the two Kingdoms as regards size, wealth, and degree of development was compensated by a far-reaching equality of formal status. But the comparatively rapid progress made by Norway in terms of prosperity, industrial development, and above all in democratisation, lent strength to a cultural and political nationalism that was bound to collide with Swedish partly paternalistic, partly downright arrogant, feelings of superiority. From the 1860s onwards the degree of satisfaction with the state of Union was gradually being eroded by political disputes, and although dissolution of the Union was not consciously sought even by the most radical Norwegian leaders until the very last, there was, when the time came, no residual warmth between the two countries that could temper the conflicts.

4. The Challenges of Sovereignty

June–November 1905: Five Crucial Months

The unilateral termination of the Union by the Storting on 7 June 1905 plunged Norway inevitably into a foreign policy crisis. Two problems had to be confronted in the immediate aftermath of the decision: first that of arranging a "divorce settlement" with Sweden, and then the connected issue of recognition of the newly independent state by the great powers.[1] The twisted legal reasoning of the Storting's act of dissolution could hardly conceal that the decision, as the King declared in an address to the Storting on 10 June, was a revolutionary action in international law. Sharp Swedish reactions could be expected, and many thought the bitterness might lead to a war between the two countries. Why it did not come to that, is a question that has puzzled many international historians in their search for models of peaceful change.

One reason why the process of dissolution was achieved peacefully was the presence, on both sides of the border, of strong moderate voices. In Sweden the Social Democrats under their leader Hjalmar Branting took the lead in urging the government to show moderation. In Norway the Storting itself set the tone, as on the same day as it voted to terminate the Union it also offered the Norwegian throne to one of King Oscar's sons. The intention clearly was to sugar the bitter pill of secession, and King Oscar showed that he realised the purpose of the offer by rejecting it – but not before the other and equally important aim of the offer had been achieved: that of softening the impact of the revolutionary act in the eyes of the great powers, by indicating Norway's desire to remain a kingdom and not become a republic. Another conciliatory gesture from the Storting was a carefully phrased declaration of willingness to negotiate with Sweden about terms of settlement of the dissolution. A third step by Norway pre-empted a demand from the Swedish parliament that the voice of the people of Norway should be heard before Sweden would even discuss a dissolution of the Union. Norway's move was to announce a referendum on the 7 June decision, in order to demonstrate to international public opinion that the people supported the secession. The referendum was held on 13 August,

Christian Michelsen
Christian Michelsen (1857–1925), who led Norway out of the Union with Sweden in 1905, was a wealthy and successful shipowner from Bergen. He had joined the liberal 'Venstre' party in 1884, and entered the Storting in 1892. He played a prominent part in the struggle for a separate Norwegian consular service, but after the setback of 1895 he gradually distanced himself from the Venstre party's increasingly radical profile in social and economic policy. In January 1903 he launched an appeal for moderate and liberal forces to join hands around a programme for a more conservative economic policy, and a 'responsible' policy of national unity in the disputes with Sweden. This hastily built unionist party scored a great success in the elections that year, but its anti-radical platform became gradually overshadowed by the disputes with Sweden over the character of the Union. Michelsen took over as prime Minister in February 1905, and from then on he led his government and the country with a steady hand towards Norway's secession.

when 85 per cent of those entitled to vote – all male, of course – went to the polling stations. The outcome was not in doubt, but the size of the "yes" vote was astounding: 368 208, as against only 184 who voted against the secession. On top of that, over 250 000 women signed a separate declaration of support.

At the end of July the Swedish parliament formally declared that, since the Union rested on a mutually binding agreement between the two countries – the 1815 Act of Union – it could not be dissolved without the consent of the Swedish King and parliament. It then formulated a series of conditions which had to be fulfilled. Most of them were of a practical nature, aimed at preserving the few ties established through the Union such as free transit trade, or access for Swedish Sami to summer pastures in Norway. Those were easily settled when the negotiations got under way at the end of August, in the Swedish town of Karlstad near the border. But two Swedish demands were felt so onerous by the Norwegian delegates that they feared the secession might still end in war. Sweden insisted on the establishment of a demilitarised zone along the southern part of the frontier, with the consequent demolition of several border forts and fortifications on the Norwegian side. The Swedish demands were clearly intended partly to humiliate Norway, and partly to erase the insult to Sweden which the construction of those fortifications a few years earlier constituted. Norway's protest against the demands showed that they were in fact felt as a humiliation. But there was also an element of fear that Sweden then or in the coming years might be contemplating a war of revenge against Norway.

As neither delegation was willing to budge on the issue, the negotiations were interrupted to enable the delegates to consult with their governments. During the interval, both countries mobilised armies along the frontier – 23 000 soldiers on the Norwegian side and 50 000 on the Swedish side. The naval forces of the two countries were also brought to a high pitch of readiness. Tensions ran high, and public opinion in both countries was hardening against further concessions. When the delegates reconvened, their positions had not changed, and one of the Norwegian negotiators later said that he kept looking at his pocket watch to note the exact time for the outbreak of war. At this moment the great powers, instigated by Norway, intervened. Great Britain in particular made it clear to the Swedish government that it would have to moderate its position. A compromise solution was then worked out, which allowed Norway to retain intact two historic fortresses whose demolition had been included in the original Swedish demands. Also, the demilitarised zone was converted into a neutral zone on both sides of the frontier, in which no military activity was allowed as long as one or both countries were not at war against a third power. An agreement to that effect was given permanent validity unless abrogated by common consent – which in fact only happened as recently as in 1993. Thus, from being a humiliation of Norway, the zone could with some justification be said to have become a form of reciprocal guarantee against aggression.

This "implicit guarantee" was also the argument with which the government tried to appease the opponents when the agreement came up for ratification by the Storting in October. The humiliating aspect of the agreement was sharply attacked from the right as well as from the left. In the end, however, only 16 members voted against. The majority of 101 in favour hardly signified approval of the terms. But it was clear to them that the alternative was a war which Norway could not win, combined with condemnation by the great powers on whose goodwill Norway depended. The Storting's approval of the terms came about on 9 October, and four days later the Swedish parliament also gave its consent. Then, on 26 October, representatives of the two countries signed the five separate conventions that together formed the Karlstad Agreement, and on the same day the Swedish King abdicated the Norwegian throne "for himself and his family".

Sweden's acceptance of Norway's secession cleared the way to a recognition of Norway as a sovereign state by the great powers. Here Russia stole a march on the western powers. Already on 30 October the Russian foreign minister cabled to Kristiania that the Russian government recognised Norway as an independent state "in its entire territorial integrity". That extra phrase was not customary on such occasions, and suggests that Russia was eager to establish good relations as soon as possible, probably for two reasons: first because a divided and therefore weakened Scandinavia was seen to serve Russia's long-term interests, and second to seek to dispel possible fears of Russian expansionist designs. There is however no indication that this latter aim was obtained. It would take more than friendly gestures to eradicate ancient suspicions about the foreign policy aims of the enigmatic eastern great power. There was more satisfaction in Norwegian circles when the British envoy, Sir Arthur Herbert, on 3 November became the first foreign diplomat to present his credentials and establish residence in Kristiania, becoming by that fact the senior or "doyen" of the diplomatic corps accredited to the Norwegian government.

The crucial role played by the great powers, in assuring a peaceful outcome of the secession crisis, makes it necessary to look at the relevant powers' interests in the matter. To begin with, there was an interest common to all the European great powers in preserving peace in Scandinavia. There was more than enough unrest in other parts of the world – in Asia, and in Africa – in which the powers were involved. A war in what was normally a quiet corner of Europe would be most unwelcome. For the same reason, seeing that the dissolution of the Swedish-Norwegian Union was irreversible, the powers desired a rapid completion of the secession process, and an early solution of the issue of the governance of Norway, hopefully in the form of a monarchy since that was generally considered as a guarantor of stability. Ideally, Germany would have preferred the preservation of the Union. A relatively strong kingdom on the Scandinavian peninsula, under Swedish leadership, plus a weak and isolated Denmark, offered the most favourable conditions for strengthening German influence in the region. Great Britain also saw considerable advantage in a strong Scandinavia as a bastion against Russian expansion. For Russia, however, a weakened Sweden opened opportunities for strengthening Russian influence in the Baltic.

With Norway's secession an accomplished fact, and before the eventual formal recognition of the new state, the attention of the great powers had turned towards seeing how to make the best of it. First on the agenda was, as mentioned, the establishment of a monarchy in Norway. Second, and no less important, was the question of a suitable candidate for accession to the Norwegian throne. Here dynastic interests on the part of various royal households paired with political interests, as the kinship of the future king of Norway could influence the foreign policy orientation of the country. Although the era of absolutism was long gone, the formal role of the monarch in questions of foreign relations and defence was still considerable in most European kingdoms. And while his real power in those respects was diminished, it could still be important in a country like Norway which had little or no experience in international politics.

Republic or monarchy, and if the latter, which king, were hotly debated issues in Norway during the summer and autumn of 1905. The strength of republican sentiments may at first sight seem surprising, since Norway had always been a kingdom, and also since monarchy was still the prevalent form of government in Europe. The explanation seems to have been a widespread conviction that a republic was the more democratic form of government. But republicanism was also fed by a mixture of resentment of the foreign policy ambitions of the Swedish kings, and a more general desire to avoid becoming entangled in power politics through a future king's dynastic links. The monarchists, on the other hand, played on the fear of a republic becoming isolated, unstable, and without friends in the hostile world of great power rivalries. Such a country, standing alone, would need a military strength for its defence which Norway could not afford.

A clear under-current in the debate was the increasing likelihood that Prince Carl of Denmark would be invited to ascend the throne. One of his known assets was his position as the British King Edward VII's son-in-law, by his marriage to Princess Maud. This link to Great Britain was not shouted from the rooftops by the monarchists, since they shared the general aversion against entanglement in the diplomatic affairs of the great powers. But realism told them that a small country needed some form of reassurance for an uncertain and possibly turbulent future. And Norway's dependence on foreign trade and shipping made Britain an obvious choice. Britain's command of the seas in peacetime, and the superior strength of the Royal Navy in the seas surrounding Norway's long coastline, meant that Great Britain was both a valued friend in peacetime and a hoped-for friend in wartime.

The Danish government, the King of Denmark, and eventually also Prince Carl himself, wanted his accession to the Norwegian throne to be sanctioned by the people through a referendum. This was held on 12–13

A 1906 official photograph of Norway's new Royal Family, King Haakon VII, Queen Maud, and Crown Prince Olav.

November. Participation was slightly less than in the referendum on the secession, and the size of the majority was far below the near unanimity which had favoured the dissolution of the Union. But the outcome was clear enough, with only 21 per cent of the electorate casting a negative vote. Five days later the Storting formally elected Prince Carl to be King under the name of Haakon VII. The King, with the four years old Prince Olav on his arm, set foot on a sleet-covered pier in the capital of Kristiania on 25

November, and on 27 November he swore his solemn oath to uphold and defend the Constitution of the Kingdom of Norway. Only five months and twenty days had passed since the Storting had passed its "revolutionary" act of secession.

Charting a Foreign Policy Course

Seeing that the issue of monarchy or republic was tied in with the question of the general orientation of Norwegian foreign relations, it was natural that the first Foreign Minister of the sovereign state, Jørgen Løvland, should choose the main Storting debate on the future form of government to clarify his foreign policy programme. In a major speech on 26 October, 1905, Løvland outlined the two main lines to be pursued in the country's foreign policy. Stating his principal concern, he took as his point of departure the policy line previously advocated by the writer Bjørnstierne Bjørnson[2] and others:

> Looking at foreign relations, it is always stressed: we want no foreign policy. I can agree with that, provided one finds the proper limits for its meaning, namely that the task must be to keep us out of participation in combinations and alliances that can drag us into warlike adventures together with any of the European warrior states. That is of course what one wants. But the endeavour of maintaining and preserving neutrality – to remain neutral not only in wartime, but also in times of peace, to stay neutral towards the political combinations among the powers – that is a foreign policy of the utmost importance. [It] requires alertness, it requires daily watchfulness, and it requires influence.[3]

Løvland was on safe ground here, pursuing a tradition with long roots in Norwegians' distaste for international power politics, and which the 1814 experience of being traded from one to the other Scandinavian country had given added impetus. The Foreign Minister then went on to explain the second line of policy which the government proposed to follow:

> Then there is another foreign policy which must be pursued. No policy in present times plays a more important role in relations among nations than the one that must be our central concern: to secure to the utmost possible our international material relations. Trade, customs, and communications relations, secured by treaties, have since Bismarck's time become more and more prevalent in relations between the states. This is of the most essential interest for our country, being engaged in so many fields of economic activity [...] needing in some respects to live on exports, while in other respects being in need of imports. Not being economically self-sufficient, such inter-

These five men formed
Norway's delegation to
the negotiations about the
terms of settlement for
the dissolution of the
Swedish-Norwegian
Union. Number two from
the left is Jørgen Løvland,
who became Norway's
first Foreign Minister.

national connections through treaties and other means have for us the greatest significance. Here then is a foreign policy which the government of
sovereign Norway must conduct with all its strength and insight, and with
every support and assistance that can be obtained abroad.

In sum, what Løvland here advocated was the same policy course that
Thomas Jefferson had proposed for the young American nation nearly a
century earlier: active international trade relations, but no political alliances
that might drag the country into other peoples' wars. Such was the foundation of the classic American isolationism, which now also became enshrined as a cornerstone of classic Norwegian neutralism. The inspiration, in
both cases, can be found in the combination of a sense of geographical
remoteness from the arenas of European power conflicts, and a wish to be
left alone in order to get on with building a new nation.

Isolationism, or neutralism, is however a curious phenomenon. In its
more modern form of non–alignment it has been described variously as "a
tactical principle designed to extract the widest range of advantages from a
particular kind of power configuration".[4] Or, more bluntly, as "an informal,
unstated, unilateral alignment with unnamed powers".[5] This suggests that it
is necessary to look behind the facade in order to find if there is a tacit dimension. In American isolationism, as in Norwegian neutralism, that tacit
dimension lies in what yet another student of international relations has called "an optimistic degree of confidence in automatic protection".[6] In the
case of the United States, the safety of geographical remoteness was reinforced by the strength of the British navy, and the assumption that Britain

76

would act as America's first line of defence. The experience of Norway during the second half of the 19th century, when Norway's foreign trade and merchant shipping had flourished behind the shield of British naval power, suggests that this was also the case for Norway.

The Norwegian reluctance to get involved in diplomatic affairs of state, and her wish to devote her active participation in external relations to affairs of trade and shipping, was as we have seen well established before 1905. In that respect Løvland's foreign affairs programme merely confirmed a long-standing tradition. How deeply rooted that tradition was became clear in the Storting's debates on the budget for the foreign service during the winter of 1906. Since the secession Norway had maintained a skeleton of a foreign service, manned by the few experienced diplomats and consuls of Norwegian nationality who had served in the foreign service of the United Kingdoms. A senior member from the Liberal party now proposed nothing less than an alternative budget. Here the separation between the diplomatic and consular services was completely abolished, in order to signal that the country's economic interests should be the paramount field of activity. In the same vein went his proposals for a drastic reduction in the number of diplomatic missions in Europe and a corresponding increase in the number of consular stations overseas.

Although Løvland protested against such a radical reform, and managed to retain a few "pure" diplomatic missions, the outcome went a long way towards making the Norwegian foreign service the handmaiden of trade and shipping. A special feature was the large number of honorary consuls – prominent members of the business community in major ports, who got the honour of a consular title, but received no remuneration apart from a variety of fees exacted from the shipping companies and commercial firms that required their services. Their number rose to over 600 in the spate of less than a decade. The foreign service proper counted only fourteen consular envoys, and eight diplomatic envoys, with Norway's Minister to the Court of St. James' in London as the most important. The sum of those reforms served to reinforce Norway's determination to concentrate on the economic side of foreign relations, and to keep aloof from foreign policy in the narrow sense, even while maintaining a special relationship with Great Britain. For further evidence that this was so we have to look more closely at the national security dimension of Norwegian foreign policy in this formative period.

The Search for National Security

For the first few years after the dissolution of the Union, the only threat felt by Norway was that of a possible revanchist attack from Sweden. Today this is hard to imagine, and it is uncertain how widespread or strong that feeling can have been. But the evidence lies in the planning for a military defence of Norway against attack from across the border with Sweden. The permanent uncertainty about Russian intentions can explain part of that planning, but only a part. The fear of Russian expansionist urges, so widespread in Sweden at that time, was not generally shared in Norway. At any rate the Swedish threat served to justify the maintenance of a reasonable degree of military preparedness in those years, within the limited means available to a basically poor country. The main instrument for preserving Norway's national security was not her military defence, however. The isolationist desire to stay out of great power politics, and the belief that Norway's relative geographical remoteness from the flashpoints of continental Europe made that possible, suggested that security could be obtained by other than military means. An international treaty of guarantee, upheld by the presumed sanctity of international law, seemed the answer.

The occasion for seeking such a guarantee was provided by the existence, since 1855 and the Crimean War, of a treaty whereby the western great powers guaranteed Norway and Sweden against Russian aggression.[7] Since it was at least uncertain whether that treaty was still valid for either country, after the dissolution of the Union, the Norwegian government decided to seek its replacement by a wider treaty guaranteeing Norway's neutrality and territorial integrity. The initial proposals, worked out towards the end of 1906, was remarkable for its lack of realism: Norway wanted the four great powers – Great Britain, France, Germany, and Russia – each to recognise and promise to respect her neutrality. If Norway's integrity or independence was in danger, then one or more of those powers, if requested by Norway, would be pledged to come to her assistance. In return Norway would undertake an obligation to maintain a strict neutrality, and to prevent any violation of her territorial integrity. Norway nevertheless wanted to reserve her right to join with Sweden and/or Denmark in a joint neutrality defence. This meant, in fact, that Norway would hold all the cards, while the great powers would undertake obligations of which no one could predict the extent.

A couple of theoretical scenarios will show the illusory nature of what Norway here sought to obtain.[8] Assume that Germany violated Danish territory to achieve a better basis for a war at sea against Britain. Under the proposed treaty Britain would then be prevented from taking the seemingly obvious counter-measure of securing a stronghold on the Norwegian coast. If Britain nevertheless should choose to disregard the treaty and seize a naval base in southern Norway, then France, if requested by Norway, would have to come to the rescue against her British ally. Another example: if Russia should act to secure an ice-free port in northern Norway, in retaliation against Germany having closed the exits from the Baltic, then Russia's ally France would, if requested by Norway, be obliged to assist her against

A Royal Occasion – and a Slip of the Tongue

Marking the close relationship between Great Britain and the new Kingdom of Norway, King Edward was received in Kristiania on his official visit to his daughter and son-in-law in 1908. This picture shows that the fledgling Kingdom made an effort to muster some pomp and circumstance for the occasion.

Norway's dependence on Great Britain for her security could only be a tacit dimension in view of her official neutrality. In the summer of 1908, however, at a formal dinner on the occasion of a visit to Kristiania of ships of the British navy, Prime Minister Gunnar Knudsen during a speech let slip the following statement, as duly reported by the opposition press: "We trust [...] that there never will be trouble, and if there is, that we shall not be the cause of bringing you into it. But if the possible comes to pass, we shall place our trust in the British nation, mindful of the new link forged by our Queen."

The Prime Minister claimed that he had been misquoted – that his 'trust in the British nation' referred only to Britain's part in the Integrity Treaty, and that the reference to the Queen had come in a different part of the speech. The incident nevertheless served to underline the widespread impression of Norway's ultimate reliance on British naval power for her national security.

the Russian incursion. The central problem with the initial treaty draft was, briefly, that it had been formulated exclusively from the viewpoint of Norwegian interests, without taking into account the very real great power interests in Scandinavia.

A long drawn-out process of exchanges of notes and counter-proposals now followed, during which Norway step by step was forced to retreat from her initial stance. All that was left when the agreed Integrity Treaty was ready for signature in November 1907 was a pledge by the four great powers jointly to guarantee Norway's territorial integrity, and to provide whatever assistance they might find suitable for that purpose. There was no mention of Norway's neutrality. This meagre result was severely criticised in Norway at the time, and has tended to be regarded by later historians as a worthless scrap of paper or even worse. But such judgements ignore a silent but essential element of the treaty, which was present from the beginning: Norway's special relationship with Great Britain and British naval power in the North and Norwegian Seas. It was clear that, apart from the mentioned risk of Swedish revanchist ambitions, the only foreseeable threats to European peace and security with implications for Scandinavia was either Russian westward expansion or a war at sea between Germany and Great Britain. What would then be Norway's situation?

In the first of those two cases, any Russian threat against Norway would release a Norwegian call for British assistance under the treaty, which Britain would in her own interest respond to. In the second case, if Germany sought to strengthen her position through control of Denmark, Britain would need to secure a base on the southern coast of Norway. While this would obviously be undesirable in view of Norway's determination not to get involved in war, Norway would not be able to prevent it, nor would it be in Norway's interest to mount an all-out defence against it, as that would make Norway a *de facto* ally of Germany against Britain. Such a British incursion would in any case be of a temporary nature. There would also be a silver lining, since a British naval presence would at the same time secure Norway against a far more dangerous aggression from Germany. So the Integrity Treaty could be said to have served a triple purpose: first as a clear demonstration of Norway's intention to preserve neutrality in any future conflict in Northern Europe; second, as a great-power declaration of intent to leave Norway in peace; and, thirdly, as an instrument enabling Norway to call on British assistance if that declaration of intent should in the future be overtaken by circumstances.

Against those positive effects of the Integration Treaty must be weighed the negative effect it had on relations with Sweden. There is no shred of evidence that the treaty was or was meant to be directed against Sweden. In fact the initial proposal, in seeking an opening for joint Scandinavian defence against great power aggression, is a clear indication to the contrary. But the Swedes chose to interpret it – and particularly the fact that it explicitly covered also the neutral zone – as an affront, and tried in a variety of ways to put a stop to the whole project. Alternatively, Sweden sought to be included as one of the guaranteeing powers. An early suggestion that a great power guarantee might include Sweden as well, since the treaty project originated from the 1855 treaty covering both countries, was scornfully rejected by the Swedes: such guarantee would not only be an illusion, but a humiliation for a proud and independent nation such as Sweden. The Integrity Treaty seems to have been felt in Sweden as rubbing salt into the wound of the dissolution of the Union. And some Swedish circles even sought consolation for their wounded pride in portraying Norway as an upstart semi-independent country under British tutelage.

Norway thus made its mark as an independent actor in international affairs by a special combination of publicly declared neutralism and an implicit British "guarantee". At the bottom of that combination lay an isolationist feeling of insecurity, inspired by a view of power politics as a game ruled by the laws of the jungle. This feeling was also partly reflected in a major issue of internal politics at the time, that of the "concession laws". That issue arose because Norway, although a country poor in natural resources in

> ## Parliamentary control and the foreign service
>
> The strong position of the Storting, following the establishment of parliamentarism in 1884, was reflected in the management of the country's foreign affairs. Although the 1814 Constitution specified foreign relations as the King's prerogative, the Storting moved quickly in 1905 to assume both direct and indirect control. All important matters of foreign policy, unless surrounded with particular secrecy, would be dealt with by the King in Council, and the protocol of those deliberations were to be submitted for control by a special committee of the Storting. Above all, the Storting by its control of the purse strings held tight reins on the extent and composition of the foreign service. Considerations of economy were clearly present in the first budget for the foreign service, which allowed for only eight diplomatic envoys: In Stockholm, Copenhagen, London, Berlin, Paris, St. Petersburg, Washington D.C., and Buenos Aires. Consular envoys numbered 14, assigned to ports of particular importance for Norwegian shipping, including such overseas posts as Shanghai, Hong Kong, Yokohama, and New York. Most of the envoys had experience from the foreign service of the Swedish-Norwegian Union, but the most prestigious post, London, went to the famous polar explorer Fridtjof Nansen.

the traditional sense, had one asset of growing importance: rivers and waterfalls promising an abundance of energy in the form of hydro-electric power. Inside the country there was a scarcity of capital resources necessary to exploit those riches, and foreign investors had for some time shown that they were more than willing to step in, provided they could establish ownership of the waterways and thereby gain exclusive rights to develop new industries that needed an abundant supply of relatively cheap energy. The firm Norsk Hydro, still today Norway's biggest industrial concern, was established in 1905 to produce nitrates by a revolutionary new method. The capital was partly French and partly Swedish. Also, in 1906 the largest British aluminium producer indicated its eagerness to exploit Norwegian and Swedish hydro-electric energy resources.

At this stage Norwegian public opinion began to be alarmed at the pros-

Hydro-electric power, sometimes referred to as "white coal", was in many ways Norway's gateway to the modern industrialised world. This picture is from Rjukan, a small community in a narrow mountain valley whose mighty waterfall – seen here in full force while the tunnels to the power station are being cleaned – became the basis for the major industrial firm Norsk Hydro. The building in 1943 was the stage for the successful sabotage operation against the production of the "heavy water" used in Germany's attempt to develop an atomic bomb.

pect of an essential Norwegian natural resource being bought up and controlled by foreign capitalists. In the long run this could undermine the country's new-found independence. The government's instant reaction was to get the approval of the Storting for a law imposing a temporary ban on the sale, to foreign individuals as well as companies where the majority of shares was in foreign hands, of Norwegian waterways, mines, and forests. The purpose was to gain a necessary breathing space to work out more detailed rules and regulations governing ownership. A permanent law was then enacted in 1909. That "concession law" recognised the need for investment of private capital, in order to develop Norway's natural resources as the basis for a much needed industrialisation of the country. Traditional agriculture and fisheries had for some time been unable to absorb the increase in population, and Norwegians were emigrating to America in increasing numbers. The "white coal", as hydro-electric power was often called, could transform Norway into a comparatively rich country. The new law abolished the 1906 ban, but decreed a radical and highly controversial new principle as a condition for private interests' concession to purchase:

the rights to the waterways were to revert to the state after a period of at most 80 years. That condition was imposed on foreign and native capital alike, and the overtone of socialism implied in that measure made it a controversial issue also in internal politics. But the main motivation for the concession laws was the fear, widely felt across the whole political spectrum, of foreign capital becoming "an enemy within", ultimately making Norway the colony of richer and greater powers.

Building Fences

Both the Integrity Treaty and the concession laws should be seen as building protective fences around Norway's new status of independence and sovereignty. The same can be said for several other measures taken by the Norwegian government in the first decade after 1905. Some of those derived from the same inspiration as that underlying the Integrity Treaty, namely the belief that international law was a paramount means by which small and weak states could seek security. This was not a new idea for Norwegians: already in the 1880s and 1890s the Norwegian Storting had proposed international treaties of arbitration as the way to promote the peaceful settlement of conflicts between states. By concluding such treaties the parties agreed to have any dispute settled by a third and presumably neutral party. Suggestions that the United Kingdoms lead the way in concluding such treaties had however been rebuffed by the King and the Swedish government. The Storting was also active in the Inter-Parliamentary Union, where peace and arbitration stood high on the agenda. The high profile of the Storting in this field was one reason why the Swedish industrialist Alfred Nobel decided that the Nobel Peace Prize be awarded by a committee chosen by the Norwegian parliamentarians, unlike the other Nobel prizes which were awarded by the Swedish Academy.

Freed from the restraints of Swedish reluctance, Norway from 1905 onwards worked actively on two fronts to promote the principle of legal settlement of international disputes. Arbitration treaties were still high on the agenda, although a fair amount of second thoughts had crept in. The result was that most of the treaties concluded had an escape clause which excluded matters of decisive national importance from the arbitration process. Having met the real world, the parliamentarians had discovered the danger that important Norwegian economic interests might be at stake. A second front where Norway was active was measures to strengthen the position of neutrals, including the protection of neutral trade in wartime. The status of neutrals had made considerable advances since the middle of the 19th century, and at an international conference in the Hague in 1907 the rights and obligations of neutrals were codified in several conventions, subject to ratification by the legislatures of the contracting parties. This was a matter in which Norway's desire to strengthen the cause of international law went hand in hand with the country's economic interests.

Such was not the case with another fence-building effort undertaken at this time: the old issue of the limits of Norwegian maritime territory. As explained in an earlier chapter, the Norwegian position, on both the general limit of four nautical miles and the principle of straight lines across wide bays and inlets, had seemed on the way to being tacitly accepted by some major powers. This now proved to be an illusion. The first conflict arose with Sweden, concerning a small but rich lobster-catching area off the southern end of the frontier between the two countries. That conflict went to arbitration in 1907, and the decision three years later went against Norway. Far more serious was the dispute that arose when Great Britain in 1906 invited Norway to accede to the North Sea Convention of 1882, which decreed that the increasingly common three-mile limit would be applied by all the states concerned. Establishing a pattern which was to haunt their successors for a long time, the Norwegian government here got caught in a cross-fire of several conflicting interests. The pressure for a three mile limit from Britain, Norway's eventual protector, was supported in Norway by a small but growing and active lobby with overseas fishing interests. They feared that a continued Norwegian insistence on four miles might lead to exclusion of their boats from the outer limits of British and other territorial waters, in retaliation. Against that stood the interests of the local population, especially in northern Norway, which had strong support in the Storting. Fishing in coastal or near-coastal waters, with small boats and traditional methods, they felt their livelihood threatened by foreign trawlers sweeping over the rich offshore fishing grounds. They demanded not only the retention of the four mile limit, but an extension to nine or ten miles. Their cause gained strength through being seen as a matter of national self-assertion. This was David against Goliath, and the ensuing struggle threatened to become a permanent feature of Norwegian foreign relations, although neither Norway nor Great Britain was inclined to seek a confrontation for the time being.

Consolidation of the work of Norwegian independence, and nationalist self-assertion, were also the motives behind the efforts to "nationalise" northern Norway. Fearing a long-term erosion of national sovereignty in the area, through the nomadic cross-border movements of Swedish, Finnish, and Norwegian Sami, the government tried to restrict the traditional right of Swedish reindeer herds to seek summer pastures on the coast of Finnmark. Also, since the Sami and Finnish-speaking peoples in the area were seen as a potential fifth column, the government instituted a campaign to strengthen the position of Norwegian language and culture in schools and elsewhere, and to encourage farmers from the south to settle in the northern counties. Both national sovereignty and national security were seen to be at stake in the area unless the rights of foreigners and the influence of an

Norwegian fishing, sealing, and whaling in the Arctic area have always been of major importance to the national economy. This picture from about 1910 shows a sailing vessel which is probably seal-hunting off the coast of Spitzbergen. Note the look-out "barrel" on the mast, perched high up in order to spot shoals of seals or whales.

alien culture could be curbed. But racist views of the Sami as a primitive and inferior ethnic group also played a role.

Beyond wishing to consolidate Norwegian sovereignty and control over the national territory and adjoining waters, an expansionist streak also made its mark in this period of nation-building. The scarcity of natural resources on land had always pushed Norwegians to seek wealth outside national borders. Fishing, and hunting whales and seals in northern or arctic areas had long traditions, and had expanded in tandem with the development of bigger boats and improved equipment and methods. Whaling interests also stretched further afield, to the Southern Atlantic and the Antarctic. Gradually, in that age of imperialism, this led to a wish to secure the Norwegian presence through the acquisition of largely uninhabited land areas adjoining the fishing and hunting grounds. For the time being those efforts were on a fairly modest scale, such as the establishment of whaling stations in the Falklands area in agreement with the British. But clashes with Russia over Norwegian hunting and fishing activities in their territorial waters were an early harbinger that a Norwegian "arctic imperialism" would not pass unopposed.

Among Norway's interests in the arctic, Spitzbergen, or the Svalbard archipelago, had a special place. This "no-man's-land" was surrounded by rich fields for fishing, seal-hunting and whaling, and Norwegians tended to dominate among the nationals of many countries who were active in the

85

area. Already in the 1890s the Norwegian government had put out feelers to the Swedish government about claiming Norwegian sovereignty over Spitzbergen. That move came to nothing, and when the Norwegian Postal Authority sought international recognition of its maintenance of a post office on the islands, Russia protested. The discovery of important coal deposits on the main island around the turn of the century brought a new dimension to the issue. Norwegian coal companies were quick to seek claims, but American and British firms soon followed, backed by capital resources which the Norwegians could not match. The coal miners, however, were mostly Norwegians, and the presence of several hundred mine workers in a lawless "no-man's-land" soon made necessary the presence of some authority to uphold law and order. Norway was willing to undertake that task. But it soon became clear that both Russia and Sweden had strong reservations against this becoming the thin end of the wedge to establish Norwegian sovereignty over the archipelago. Through a long series of international conferences and exchanges of notes on the matter, a kind of Russian-Swedish-Norwegian condominium or joint authority emerged as a possible solution. But a major international Spitzbergen conference intended to finalise such an arrangement, which convened in Kristiania in the summer of 1914, got stalemated by Germany's demand to be included in any international arrangement of that kind. On that note the conference broke up, and the outbreak of the First World War gave the powers more important matters to attend to.

The nine years that followed Norway's dissolution of the union with Sweden stand as the first formative period for Norwegian foreign policy as an independent, sovereign state – a policy which I have chosen to call Norway's "classic neutralism". Its principal features, as publicly proclaimed by Jørgen Løvland, Norway's first Foreign Minister, turned out to be isolationism in regard to international power politics, combined with an active policy of promoting the nation's interests in foreign trade and shipping. Isolationism in its Norwegian variant closely resembled the American model originally enunciated by George Washington, in his "Farewell Address to the American Nation" on 17 September 1796, when he said that the "great rule of conduct for us in regard to foreign nations is, in extending our commercial relations to have with them as little political relations as possible." If anything, Løvland's variant was even stricter in that it lacked Washington's reserve position of allowing for "temporary alliances for extraordinary emergencies." Norway's reserve position was of a different kind. Behind the facade of non-alignment was the underlying but necessarily tacit assumption that in "extraordinary emergencies" Norway would have the protection of Great Britain, whose naval power ruled both the surrounding seas and the oceans where the ships of the Norwegian merchant navy sailed, and whose own national interest required that no other power should control the Norwegian coastline. The question, as the European war erupted in August 1914, was whether this double-barrelled neutralism would stand the test of a conflict between Great Britain and that other naval power facing the North Sea, namely Germany.

5. Norway in the First World War

"A cloudless sky"

Although relations among the European great powers were becoming increasingly turbulent during the first decade of the twentieth century, the Scandinavian states were able to continue to enjoy peaceful relations both among themselves and with the powers. Even Norwegian-Swedish relations took a turn for the better, as the bitterness of Norway's secession waned. A good omen was the joint neutrality rules issued by Sweden, Denmark, and Norway in December 1912. The status of neutrality, already strengthened by the Hague Conventions of 1907, had gained new ground through the 1909 Declaration of London, which further reinforced the protection accorded to neutral ships and neutral trade in wartime. Although the British government's proposal for ratification of the Declaration was defeated in the House of Lords, there seemed a good chance that its principles would govern the practice of the powers in a war at sea.

The heightened status of neutrality could not but confirm the wisdom of Norway's foreign policy course. The isolationist peacetime stance of neutralism shielded the country from entanglement in power politics, and left Norway free to pursue her economic interests in all directions. On the diplomatic front, the government's active support for international law as the best means for settling international disputes was generally uncontroversial. When a conflict arose between international law and Norway's national interests, as in the dispute over fishing limits, the government usually managed to defend the precedence of economic interests by portraying Norway as a special and deserving case. Here, after all, was a poor country with few natural resources: only three per cent arable land, 25 per cent forests, and the rest mountains. Only the export of fish, timber products, and the earnings of the merchant navy, enabled Norway to buy the necessary imports of food and coal. In case of war between the European great powers, Norway's declared neutrality, supplemented by the formal guarantee of the Integrity Treaty and the implicit reliance on Great Britain as the ultimate protector, would keep the country out of war. Even in a drawn-out conflict, in which the belligerents engaged in economic warfare, the increased protection of neutral trade and shipping which international law now provided promised to insure Norway's survival. All in all it seemed perfect good sense for Norway to continue to base her foreign relations on a combination of neutralism and the promotion of economic interests.

There was nevertheless, during those first years of Norwegian independence, one threatening scenario that from time to time made its appearance in Norwegian public debate. If the naval arms race between Germany and Britain should continue, this might trigger a naval war in the North Sea that could all too easily involve Norwegian territory. That prospect was brought home by the tensions between Germany on the one hand and France and Great Britain on the other, during the Second Moroccan Crisis in 1911. By coincidence the German High Sea Fleet was at that time conducting large-scale exercises along the Norwegian coast. The reaction in Norwegian political circles was to adopt a naval construction programme of the relatively very high sum of twenty million kroner. This followed the introduction into Norwegian defence planning of a possible hostile landing on the coast of southern Norway. As that crisis passed, however, Norway fell back on her primary assumption that any such major war would be avoided or, if not, that the great powers had some sort of tacit consensus, strengthened by the Integrity Treaty, not to involve Norway. This was also the reply from Prime Minister Gunnar Knudsen when, in February 1914, he was challenged by the leader of the Conservative Party on the question of defence expenditures. Besides, he added, "the sky, in world political terms, is now cloudless to a greater degree than for many years." Six months later Europe was at war.

Gunnar Knudsen – once referred to by a Danish newspaper as 'Norway's Bismarck' – was Prime Minister during the long reign of the Liberal 'Venstre' Party 1913–1920. He came into politics from a successful career in industry and shipping (hence his predilection for being portrayed as a man of the sea) before the turn of the century. His main political interest was in social reform and welfare issues. His approach to foreign policy was not particularly sophisticated, but his views reflected a strong admiration for Great Britain, where he had received his technical education, and whose leading position at sea had his great respect.

The First Test of Neutrality

The assassination of Austrian Crown Prince Franz Ferdinand in Sarajevo on the last Sunday in June, 1914, did not at first disturb the summer peace of the Norwegian capital Kristiania. The main event there that summer was the Jubilee Exhibition that marked the centenary of the 1814 Constitution. The war scare first hit Norway on 31 July 1914, with the news that Russia was mobilising its army in response to Austria-Hungary's declaration of war against Serbia. The next day the government issued a public declaration of its intention to remain neutral in the war that had just been declared. It also decided to man the coastal fortifications, and issued secret orders to the navy to be on the alert. On 2 August, after France and Germany had mobilised and Germany had declared war on Russia, the government decided on full mobilisation of the navy, and asked the President of the Storting to summon the parliamentarians to an emergency session. The question, in the minds of the Cabinet ministers, was of course whether Norway would be able to stay out of the conflict. And they all knew that the answer largely depended on whether Great Britain would enter the war against Germany. If that happened, then a German or a British attempt to seize naval bases on the Norwegian coast was a distinct possibility.

As it turned out, Germany at least for the time being seemed content to leave Norway to maintain her neutrality. In Britain, however, naval circles in particular had for some time been considering the possibility of securing a naval base in southern Norway in a maritime war against Germany. Rumours in the early days of August, about German pressure on one or more Nordic countries to adopt policies favourable to Germany, prompted British Foreign Secretary Edward Grey to cable the envoys at Brussels, the Hague, and Norway. They were instructed to inform the respective governments that Britain expected them to uphold their neutrality, and promised support if needed. With that reassurance the Norwegian Foreign Minister, Nils Claus Ihlen, could turn his attention to another actor whose stance seemed uncertain, namely Sweden. Norway and Sweden had already orally agreed on 29 July that the coming war must not lead to hostilities between them. This was followed a few days later by a Swedish offer of an alliance, with the proviso that Sweden was "willing to defend her neutrality on all sides, but that any collaboration with Russia is precluded. This in case Norway should consider joining England and on the further presumption of an Anglo-Russian association." The implied Swedish suspicion that Norway was leaning towards Britain had its parallel in Norwegian suspicions that Sweden was leaning towards Germany. Norway therefore replied that any agreement would have to be on the basis of absolute neutrality towards all great powers. The final outcome, announced on 8 August, was an agreement "to maintain separately and to the utmost the neutrality of the respective Kingdoms as against all the belligerent powers", and that the war should in no circumstances "lead to one Kingdom taking hostile measures against the other."[1]

With neutrality preserved, at least for the time being, Norway and the other neutral states of northern Europe were left to arrange their affairs as best they could under the circumstances. Since the most pressing problem for Norway was how to secure the necessary supplies of food and fuel, the government immediately issued a prohibition on the export of such goods. This was followed by the imposition of price controls, and the setting up of a "Food Commission", one of whose tasks was to undertake large-scale

Nils Claus Ihlen – Foreign Minister in Gunnar Knudsen's Liberal Ministry 1913–1920 – came like the Prime Minister from a successful career in business. But where Knudsen faced the country's problems with optimism and boundless energy, Ihlen conducted foreign policy with agility, subtlety, and an inclination for compromise which often led to temporary *ad hoc* adjustments instead of clear-cut solutions. His view of Norway's external relations was based on practical economics, well suited to a nation with considerable scepticism towards international 'high politics'. Educated in Switzerland he spoke German and French, and thus did not share the Prime Minister's Anglo-Saxon orientation.

imports of grain. These and other emergency measures were clearly taken in the widely shared expectation of a short war. In the main, Norway expected her foreign trade to continue more or less as usual, even though her main trading partners Germany and Britain were now at war with each other. The large Norwegian merchant navy operated all over the globe, but with a clear predominance of traffic to British and American ports. A very large part of that traffic, as well as ships carrying imports to Norway, passed within reach of the Royal Navy.

The unintended result of Britain's decision to try blockade purchases of Norwegian fish, to prevent its export to Germany: a massive pile-up of salted fish in Bergen harbour that the British did not want, and Norwegian consumers could not afford to buy due to inflated prices caused by a buyer – a Bergen businessman secretly acting for the British – with seemingly unlimited financial resources

In the first months of the war Britain was sufficiently concerned about opinion in the neutral countries – the United States in particular – not to interfere too much with ships on the way to Scandinavia or the Netherlands. Instead the British authorities tried persuading the shipping companies to have their ships call "voluntarily" at British ports for inspection. But vessels caught by British warships as blockade runners, or ships whose cargo while nominally destined for neutral ports were in fact on the way to Germany, were severely dealt with. The British government also tried to persuade Norway to set up a central import agency which would in fact, though not in form, be controlled by the government. But as the government shied away from any direct involvement which might make it a party to anti-German and hence unneutral trade restrictions, it was left to the shipping companies and export/import firms to handle directly all such arrangements with the British. This was, after all, the age of liberalism in which governments should interfere as little as possible with private business and commerce.

The first signs of a sharpening of the war at sea came when Germany already in August began laying minefields in the North Sea off the British coast. After initial protests the British then proceeded with minefields of their own. Properly surveyed and controlled, minefields could protect their own seaborne trade, and would also serve to convince neutral ships to call at British ports for guidance about secure shipping lanes. A more serious threat to traffic on the high seas appeared a few weeks later, when German submarines made their first forays into the North Sea, sinking several British cruisers. In a drastic countermove the British government on 2 November 1914 declared the whole of the North Sea a military area. All ships bound for the North Sea and crossing a line drawn from the Hebrides through the Faeroes to Iceland would do so at their own risk. The actual purpose of the measure came in the second part of the announcement: shipping to and from North Sea countries was advised to pass through the English Channel and the Straits of Dover, then north along the east coast of England to a point from which a safe route, through the minefields and on to Lindesnes on Norway's southernmost point, would be indicated. Again the measure clearly aimed at facilitating Britain's control of any trade that might reach the enemy through neutral ports.

As both cargo ships and passenger liners coming from overseas and bound for Norwegian ports normally passed to the north of the British Isles, Norway was in the forefront in the storm of neutral protests against this British declaration. With the assistance of the British Foreign Office, a number of Norwegian shipping companies then applied for and were granted dispensation allowing them to continue using the northern sea route – a clear admission that the danger to shipping in those waters was in fact negligible. The net effect of the "war area" declaration was therefore not very serious for Norwegian trade and shipping. More important, in the long run, was the manner in which the neutral states reacted to the measure. Attempts by Sweden and Denmark to form a united neutral protest front failed. First the United States, and then the Netherlands, declined to participate, and even the three Scandinavian countries experienced difficulties in presenting a common stance. The outcome was a fairly moderate communication in defence of neutral trade rights, addressed to all belligerents. The effort of the three governments to cooperate did however engender one sequel of symbolic importance, namely a meeting of the Kings of Sweden, Denmark and Norway at Malmø in December 1914. This was another clear sign that the bitter feelings caused by Norway's secession from the Union with Sweden were on the wane.

1915: Economic Warfare and the Diplomacy of Business

There is no doubt that the war made neutral trade and shipping increasingly profitable. Supplies needed for the conduct of war, and food for the civilian population, fetched higher prices when normal trade routes were cut and the war seemed increasingly likely to become a long one. Freight rates rose correspondingly, and more than the extra costs of war risk insurance for the ships. This was therefore a period of prosperity for Norway, as the demand increased for shipping services and for certain Norwegian export products, such as fish and metal ores which Germany needed. From 1915 onwards, however, Britain tightened its grip on Norway's trade by demanding effective guarantees against export or re-export to Germany in return for allowing essential Norwegian exports to go through or letting Norwegian ships bunker coal in British-controlled ports.

Germany's response to such blockade measures was to turn to submarine warfare as a means of hindering or hampering the importation by sea to Great Britain of essential supplies. On 4 February, 1915, Germany declared the waters around the British Isles as a *Kriegsgebiet* or war area, in which every enemy merchant ship would be destroyed even if it were not possible to assure the safety of passengers and crew. Neutral ships would also be at risk, both as "collateral damage" and because of alleged British misuse of neutral flags to cover their own ships. Apart from joining with Sweden and Denmark in an official protest, the reaction in Norwegian government and shipping circles was tempered by the conviction that the limited size of the German submarine fleet made the German threat somewhat illusory. Even the torpedoing of a Norwegian tanker by a German submarine on 19 February, in the English Channel, did not change that assessment.

Already in the autumn of 1914 it was clear that economic warfare was becoming a vicious circle, in that every new action from one belligerent was justified as being retaliation against the previous action by its enemy. Thus Germany's *Kriegsgebiet* declaration provided a welcome opportunity for another round of blockade measures from the main Entente powers Britain and France, as announced on 1 March 1915 and enshrined in a British "Order in Council" of 11 March. From now on those two powers would "hold themselves free to detain and take into port ships carrying goods of presumed enemy destination, ownership, or origin". Such ships, and their cargo, would then be dealt with by the Prize Courts. However, since the legal situation was at best unclear, the British authorities were hoping that, by deliberately arranging long and costly delays for the ships, they could persuade the shipowners to avoid carrying goods not approved and certified by the British as genuinely neutral imports. In reply to the Norwegian government's protest note, the British again proposed that Norway should set up an official, national import and export agency. Alternatively it was suggested that arrangements could be made with the principal shipping companies.

The Norwegian government must at this juncture have realised that economic warfare was there to stay, and that the degree of immunity which the neutrals had hoped to enjoy was a thing of the past. Already the country's economy was on the way to becoming divided, with one sector trading with Germany, whereas the rest would be forced to comply with the British blockade measures. And since Britain's ability to control Norway's imports gave them by far the strongest hold on the country's economy, the resulting bias would necessarily turn Norway into Britain's "neutral ally". For formal neutrality – the "facade", so to speak – to be preserved in such circumstances, it seemed essential to avoid any direct government involvement in any arrangement that favoured one or the other belligerent. Such a policy also tied in nicely with the prevailing economic liberalism of the era, which decreed that the state should as a principle interfere as little as possible with private industry and trade. The preferred option was hence to let individual firms, or associations linking firms within the same "branch" or field of industrial or commercial activity, deal directly with the British government while keeping the Norwegian authorities informed of the arrangements. The principle on which the arrangements were worked out was that the British would "ration" each firm's supply of raw materials and other essential imports, in direct proportion to that firm's willingness to cooperate in the British blockade of Germany. The greatest potential danger of such a system was that the British authorities, in order to satisfy themselves that such essentially private arrangements were carried out to the letter, demanded full and complete information about each firm's commercial dealings. And since knowledge is power, this opened the way to an extensive British penetration of Norwegian economic life, with long-term political implications.

Fish, Copper, and Sulphur

From Norway ... we receive important raw materials for our war industry and large amounts of foodstuffs for our civilian population and our army.[2]

That sentence from a German Foreign Ministry memorandum gives an indication of Germany's interest in keeping open the flow of goods from Norway. Among the products that Germany needed to import from Norway, fish, and copper or sulphur pyrites, were among the most important – pyrites being essential for the production of ammunition. As the British tightened their control of Norwegian foreign trade, the Germans were becoming increasingly worried about their imports. But since they lacked the means available to the British for exerting direct pressure on Norway, they were reduced to making use of diplomatic protests, accompanied by veiled threats of the use of armed force.

Fish and fish products were at the time of the First World War still Norway's major export, constituting about one quarter of the country's export earnings. The most important markets were Southern Europe and Latin

America, where the catholic requirement of fish on Friday was widely satisfied by such exotic fare as "bacalau" or other dried or salted cod dishes. The
other side of the coin was the fisheries industry's dependence on imports
from British or British-controlled sources of such essentials as coal or oil to
keep the boats running, and metal sheeting and olive oil for the sardine factories. From the first months of the war demand for Norwegian fish rose
sharply. With Germany in the forefront, foreign buyers went straight to the
source, bypassing the Norwegian middlemen and buying the fish "off the
hook". Price seemed to be a secondary consideration, and the fishermen
were soon basking in unprecedented prosperity.

The British government, however, was not pleased to see Germany
being fed by Norwegian fish caught with British tackle by boats running
on British fuel. But since Norway could hardly survive without fish exports,
and since export controls that extended to the individual fisherman could
not work, no easy solution was at hand. After lengthy discussions between
British and Norwegian authorities, an arrangement was agreed whereby
Britain would make blockade purchases of a major part of the Norwegian
catch through a Norwegian secret agent. The purchases began in February,
1916, and went on for about two months. Britain's part in the deal remained a well-kept secret, but the presence of a buyer with seemingly unlimited financial resources had an explosive effect on prices. Having spent eleven million pounds on buying masses of fish which they did not really
want, the British found this an experience not to be repeated – all the more
so since the Norwegian Provisioning Commission would only buy the fish
back from the British agent at prices which the Norwegian consumer could
afford.

After long and difficult negotiations, in which the Norwegian government in the end had to intervene directly in view of the national importance of the issue, a formal government to government agreement was signed on 5 August 1916. It was essentially patterned on the model of the private arrangements referred to above, making the exports to any country
dependent on that country supplying equivalent quantities of fuel, tackle
etc. But the agreement had two other features which required governmental participation: There would be a ban on fish exports to any one country
of more than 15 per cent of the total, and the British would only buy what
remained after domestic needs had been met at fixed prices. The Norwegian
government clearly feared German reactions when the export ban was
made public, and Foreign Minister Ihlen first sought to mollify them by
suggesting that Germany buy as much fish as possible in the ten day period before the export ban would come into effect. But when the German

government learnt about the 15 per cent clause they nearly hit the roof. Their formal protest declared the percentage agreement as blatantly unneutral, and alleged – without the burden of proof – that Germany would have been able to provide stores and supplies in return for a much larger share of the catch.

The conflict over Norway's export to Germany of pyrites coincided with the disputes over fish exports, but became rather more serious. An early proposal by the British envoy to Norway, Mansfeldt de Cardonnel Findlay, for a British purchase of Norwegian copper and nickel ores came to nothing. But Norway was heavily dependent on imports of finished copper products, particularly copper wire for the accelerated electrification of the country based on its abundant supply of hydro-electric power. Hence an agreement on the now familiar pattern whereby such import was made conditional on a ban on pyrites exports seemed the obvious solution. A statement by Foreign Minister Ihlen to the Storting in May 1915 showed a clear awareness of the potential seriousness of the issue, which was not just a matter of copper:

> Norway is now the only source which can supply Germany with the sulphur needed for the manufacture of ammunition, and our exports of pyrites have thus been enormously increased. The pyrites export to Germany, which used to average 3 000 tons monthly, rose in February to 25 000 tons, and in March to 28 000 tons. With a sulphuric content of 43 per cent this means 12 000 tons of sulphur, which is of the greatest importance to Germany. I understand that England is about to act in this matter.[3]

Part of the problem was that while practically all Norwegian pyrites also contained small amounts of copper, much of it had such infinitesimal amounts that it was uneconomical to extract it. This gave rise to a terminological problem which was to mar subsequent negotiations.

By the end of the year 1915 Britain's control of Norwegian imports of copper wire threatened to put a complete stop to Norway's electrification programme. Tough negotiations followed through the spring of 1916, as Norway tried to retain an opening for continued exports to Germany. The tone of the exchanges hardened during May, with Minister Findlay pointing out that the copper exported from Norway went into the making of shells which were causing death and disablement not only of the soldiers of Britain, but also of Norwegian sailors on ships destroyed by German submarines:

> The inflated price of Norwegian copper is, in fact, the price of blood – the blood of the friendly people to whom Norway would necessarily look for assistance in time of need, and on whom she depends, not only for the continuance of her present prosperity and independence, but for her existence as one of the foremost sea-faring nations of the world.[4]

The final agreement, confirmed by an exchange of notes at the end of August 1916, was on the face of it a simple deal based on a prohibition of the export of copper in any form unless the buyer provided an equivalent amount of refined copper products. The British would then immediately licence the export to Norway of several thousand tons of refined copper, in return for a first call on all present and future stocks of "pyrites containing copper". When Germany expressed concern about the export prohibition, Ihlen had assured them that only copper pyrites, subsequently defined as pyrites with a copper content of more than one half per cent, were involved – at least for the time being. Exports to Germany of pyrites with less than that amount of copper therefore continued, until the British Legation in mid-September made an emphatic protest, claiming that "all copper is extractable from these low-grade ores". There was also disagreement over the price to be paid for British pyrites purchases, and about the terms of the "first call" arrangement. In the meantime the exportation to Germany of low-grade pyrites continued, and fish exports to Germany also seemed to be well in excess of the 15 per cent allowed under the agreement. The Norwegian government was clearly not prepared to antagonise Germany at this juncture, since Norwegian-German relations were approaching a crisis on an issue concerning German submarine warfare.

The Submarine Conflict with Germany

The German submarine campaign against Britain, initiated in the spring of 1915, had until the summer of 1916 had little effect on maritime trade to the British Isles, and seemed to show special regard for neutral shipping. In August the lull was broken by an intensive campaign against shipping in the English Channel, and its success spurred the German Admiralty to press for similar concentrated assaults in other waters, noting by the way that the arming of British merchant ships made neutral ships a better target. One of the proposed areas was the arctic waters of the Barents and Norwegian Seas, which served as a transit area for war materials to Russia. Accordingly, three German submarines began operating there in September, with a resounding success from their standpoint: in a period of five days, ten ships were sunk, and all of them happened to be Norwegian. Inevitably, the media

drew the conclusion that German submarines were now singling out Norwegian ships as targets, as a reprisal for Norway's cooperation with the British blockade against Germany. Strident calls on the government to do something were voiced, fuelled by suspicions that the submarines had passed through Norwegian coastal waters on their way north.

The governments of the Entente powers had just before those events suggested to all neutral governments that submarines, due to their special character, ought to be excluded from the right of so-called "innocent passage" through neutral waters that other warships enjoyed. Norway's immediate reaction to the proposal had been one of marked scepticism: such a ban would antagonise Germany, and would in any case be unenforceable in view of the enormously long Norwegian coast and the ability of the submarines to pass submerged. But the newspaper campaign demanding action rose to new heights when it turned out that most of the crew of one of the sunken steamers had disappeared or perished from exposure. "The dead are calling! Where is the Norwegian government?" was the banner headline in one influential Kristiania daily on 10 October.

Both at the time and later, sober reflection should have shown that the sinking of so many Norwegian ships in the north could be explained without recourse to conspiracy theories. Above all, it was incontestable that Norwegian ships tended to predominate on the most dangerous routes, where freight rates were the highest. Also, since the belligerents were arming their merchant ships, the neutral ships were a less dangerous target for

A dramatic photo from the submarine campaign in Arctic waters in the autumn of 1916, taken by the captain of a German submarine as he scores a perfect hit on a Norwegian cargo vessel loaded with timber from Archangel.

the submarines to attack. Later research in German documents in fact has failed to find any suggestion of a special campaign against Norwegian shipping, let alone any indication of a connection between German submarine warfare and their complaints against Norway's biased trade policy. But rational arguments were of no avail in the heated atmosphere created by the shipping disasters, and on 13 October the government issued a Royal Decree banning submarines from Norwegian waters. Only in emergencies could they enter the territory, provided they did so in surface position and with the national flag showing.

The government must have expected German protests against the decree, but had hardly expected the storm that it released. Spurred by the German Admiralty's request to "raise the sharpest protest against this unneutral act", the German Minister in Kristiania was instructed to deliver a formal note of protest, and to demand that the decree be withdrawn. In this way the Norwegian government had manoeuvred itself into a position where it was squeezed between the Scylla of British blockade measures and the Charybdis of German threats. All the signs were that Norway was entering a phase of extreme difficulties, where the maintenance of neutrality itself would be at stake.

1916–17: A Winter of Crisis

Through its direct involvement in negotiating the agreements over fish and pyrites exports, the government had abandoned the previous policy line of letting private firms, either individually or through their branch associations, make their foreign trade arrangements without involving the government and thereby jeopardising its policy of neutrality. This new line meant that Germany could now plausibly accuse the Norwegian government of unneutral acts, and follow up with threats of reprisals. Britain and her allies, on the other hand, could threaten reprisals against the country as a whole unless the government saw to it that the agreements were carried out to the letter. In this game of threats and counter-threats, and reprisals and counter-reprisals, Britain had the stronger hand since she had the power to threaten Norway's survival. But the threat from Germany, with the possible prospect of a combination of extended submarine warfare against Norwegian shipping and aerial bombing of cities and industrial targets in southern Norway, was both more tangible and more immediate.

To understand the seriousness of the two-way crisis facing Norway in the autumn of 1916, it is necessary to look beyond the disputes over export quantities and even beyond the case of Norway. In the eyes of the belligerent parties Norway had become a test case for the principal methods by which economic warfare was to be pursued and the war possibly won. For Britain, allowing Norway to continue to export strategically important commodities would set a precedent which, if followed by other neutrals, would seriously endanger the prospect of forcing Germany to her knees through the blockade. For Germany, if one neutral country was allowed to get away with discriminatory measures against submarines, this would set a precedent which might jeopardise the use of the weapon increasingly seen as Germany's best, and probably only, means of severing Britain's lifeline of overseas seaborne imports.

Probably without realising how high the stakes were, the Norwegian government through the rest of the autumn tried, by vague compromise proposals and other dilatory diplomatic means, to stave off the looming crisis. With the dispute with Germany being the more acute one, Norway kept postponing the export stoppages demanded by Britain. Unknown to the government, however, Britain and France were at this time seriously debating whether to force Norway into the war, spurred by false rumours that Norwegian shipping might be about to be withdrawn from allied trade. On 29 October Sir Eyre Crowe, the senior official of the Foreign Office, submitted a memorandum to the Cabinet urging a firm line against Norway's failure to comply with Britain's demands. If this should lead to German aggression against Norway, forcing Norway into the war, this would be to Britain's advantage: it would close an important loophole in the blockade of Germany, and allow Britain the use of Norwegian waters and bases in the war at sea. This was a line that was also fully supported by the French government, whose main concern in the matter was securing their import of Norwegian nitrates for their ammunition industry. At the basis of the proposal lay one important assumption, however, namely that the British navy could secure Norwegian territory against a German invasion, and protect Norwegian shipping. And here the Admiralty was to provide conflicting but generally negative advice.

In spite of the cautionary advice from the naval authorities, Britain's diplomatic pressure on the Norwegian government continued. The Cabinet turned down a proposal from the British envoy for serving an outright ultimatum on the Norwegian government. But in December a new British government, headed by David Lloyd George, had come to power on the promise to pursue the war more effectively. One of their first decisions was to issue a new and more severe protest to Norway, threatening economic pressure of the strongest kind if Britain's demands were not fully met. Two memoranda, citing Norwegian violations of respectively the Fisheries and the Copper Agreements, were handed to the Norwegian envoy in London on 18 December. Four days later, as no immediate reply had come from the Norwegian government, Britain delivered her Christmas present to Norway in the shape of an immediate stoppage of coal deliveries – a measure which a British historian has called "probably the severest action undertaken by Britain against any neutral state during the First World War."[5] Its severity was further sharpened as Norway came to experience one of the coldest winters in memory.

The government now had to act, also because the crisis had created a storm of domestic criticism against it – resulting in the formation of a special Storting committee for foreign affairs to scrutinise government policy. A new Anglo-Norwegian exchange of diplomatic notes produced a compromise solution concerning the Fish Agreement. But on the issue of pyrites no compromise was possible, so in the middle of February Norway finally gave in and agreed to a complete cessation of pyrites exports to Germany, in return for a lifting of the coal embargo. Germany had by then already albeit reluctantly accepted this outcome, since Norway had in the meantime not only revised somewhat its submarine decree, but also promised a loan to Germany as well as export licences for certain other commodities. The Norwegian Foreign Minister's willingness, during the previous autumn, to stretch the terms of the agreements with the British in Germany's favour, must also have convinced the German authorities that the Norwegian government had done what it could to protect Germany's interests. Another factor which must have prompted both belligerent parties to seek an end to the crisis in their relations with Norway, was that the war at sea had entered a new phase with ominous implications for all concerned.

Unlimited Submarine Warfare and Norwegian Shipping

In spite of minefields laid by both belligerent parties, and the activities of German submarines, both neutral and allied shipping losses were moderate up until the summer of 1916. But after the German submarines intensified their operations in the autumn, losses began to rise sharply, and since allied merchant ships were increasingly equipped with cannons for their defence, neutral vessels were an easier target. For the Norwegian merchant navy, October marked a preliminary peak, with 49 ships lost, but the figure for November was still as high as 29, and for December it rose again to 35. Various schemes to reduce the losses, such as advice from the British Admiralty as to safe routes, or the institution of British naval protection for the daylight part of the voyage between Norway and the British Isles, seemed to have little effect, as in January 1917 40 ships were lost.

Then, on 1 February Germany declared unlimited submarine warfare against all vessels moving in a wide area around the British Isles and France. The eastern limit of the area touched the Norwegian coast, and in the north the area came up as far as the Faeroes. Germany's aim was clearly to deter all neutral ships from trade with British or French ports. Any such ships already in the danger area were given a limit of nine days to get out of there without being attacked. The initial reaction in Norwegian shipping circles

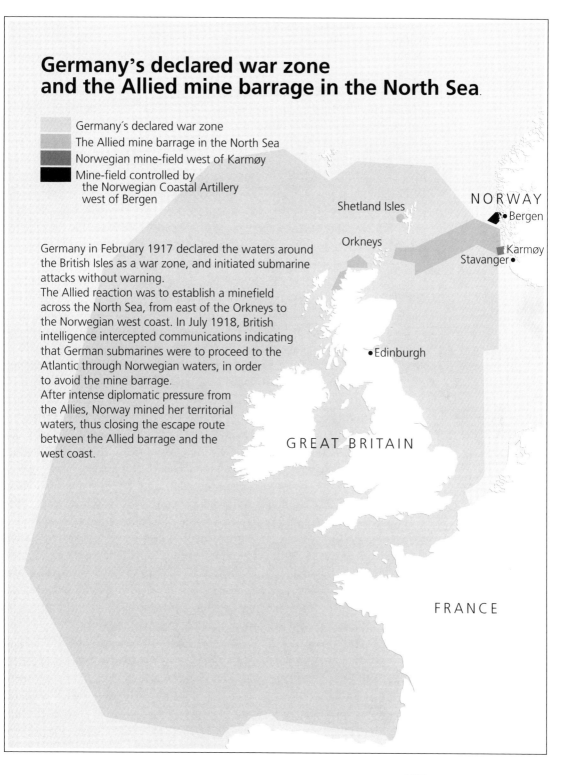

Germany's declared war zone and the Allied mine barrage in the North Sea.

Germany's declared war zone
The Allied mine barrage in the North Sea
Norwegian mine-field west of Karmøy
Mine-field controlled by
  the Norwegian Coastal Artillery
  west of Bergen

Shetland Isles

NORWAY
Bergen

Orkneys

Karmøy
Stavanger

Germany in February 1917 declared the waters around
the British Isles as a war zone, and initiated submarine
attacks without warning.
The Allied reaction was to establish a minefield
across the North Sea, from east of the Orkneys to
the Norwegian west coast. In July 1918, British
intelligence intercepted communications indicating
that German submarines were to proceed to the
Atlantic through Norwegian waters, in order
to avoid the mine barrage.
After intense diplomatic pressure from
the Allies, Norway mined her territorial
waters, thus closing the escape route
between the Allied barrage and the
west coast.

Edinburgh

GREAT BRITAIN

FRANCE

was hesitant: would the Germans really apply such extreme actions against neutral ships, and did they have a sufficient number of submarines to make the threat a real one? As the first week passed without any apparent increase in the number of ships sunk, many began to feel that this was another German bluff. The main hindrance to normal traffic between Norway and the British Isles hence appeared to be the British coal embargo and the disputes that caused it. The formal ending of that crisis, on 17 February, was therefore a matter of considerable relief also for Britain. From then on Norwegian ships began to resume their normal trading to British and French ports, including the crucially important service of transporting British coal to France.

This time the German submarine warfare was no half-empty threat, however. The figure of Norwegian ship losses in February was a moderate 29, but this was mainly due to the limited traffic in the first half of the month. The figure for March told a different tale, with as many as 52 ships lost. Harrowing tales of the sufferings caused by the crews attested to the ruthlessness of the submarine commanders, as they torpedoed ships without warning or regard for the survival of the sailors on board. Public opinion in Norway had until then been in a kind of a three-way split between anger at German sinkings of neutral Norwegian ships, annoyance at Britain's interference with Norwegian trade and shipping, and fury that their own government had let matters drift through rampant inflation, food shortages, and then a major crisis in relations with both belligerent parties. The new ferocity of Germany's submarine warfare now fed a growing hatred against all things German. As the German envoy recalled, describing the atmosphere in Kristiania as he left his post in the summer of 1917, "the unfriendly attitude of the people made us feel as if in enemy territory."[6]

The British authorities were from the start afraid that the unlimited German submarine warfare might well lead the neutrals to withdraw their ships from allied trades. After considering various alternatives, in secret consultations with the Norwegian government and shipping interests, a solution was found in a combined chartering and requisitioning arrangement: the British government would charter or, if necessary, requisition Norwegian ships for employment on less dangerous routes outside the declared war area. The dangerous North Sea trade would then be taken over by armed British steamers, which in addition would assure Norway's supply of coal from Britain. Fearful of Germany's reaction if it became known that the Norwegian government was behind such a deal, it was decided that the arrangement would take the form of an exchange of letters between the Norwegian Shipowners' Association and the British government. Also, since Germany could with justice denounce as unneutral a failure by the Norwegian government to stop a chartering arrangement, the formal take-over would be given the appearance of the British government requisitioning private

104

property in allied ports. There would then be carefully staged protests from the Norwegian government as well as from the ships' captains. This assured that this "tonnage agreement" did in fact remain Norway's best kept war secret.

In terms of Norwegian ships lost, April was another disaster month, with 43 vessels totalling about 100 000 gross tons sunk. But from May onwards the situation improved considerably. In terms of tonnage the losses declined to about 60 000 gross tons in June, and less than 50 000 tons monthly for the rest of the year. Still the loss of lives in that dreadful year 1917 was appallingly high: over 700 Norwegian sailors perished. However, the reduced rate of losses from May onwards seems to have been less due to the "tonnage agreement" than to the introduction of convoys. Long delayed by the conservatism of the British navy, the institution of the convoy system for sailings between the British Isles and Norway in April 1917 proved a great success.

The United States enters the War

In the wider perspective of the war, the main event following Germany's declaration of unlimited submarine warfare was the 2 April declaration by President Woodrow Wilson of a state of war between the United States and Germany. Although Wilson was careful to assert America's special position, by claiming to be merely "associated" and not allied with the "Entente" led by Britain and France, the British clearly had high hopes of America's contribution to the war against Germany. First there was the prospect that the blockade of Germany could be made watertight through the strict control of American supplies to Europe. Second was the hope that the United States Navy would cooperate in protecting the neutral countries of northern Europe against German aggression, thereby depriving those countries of the excuse that a total ban on their exports to Germany would expose them to German armed reprisals. Britain was at this time already seeking to meet Norwegian fears of German air attack, by offering fighter aircraft and anti-aircraft guns, but this could only be a stop-gap measure. The Norwegians were therefore advised to discuss the situation with the Americans. The Norwegian government, however, approached the whole issue of arms deliveries and assistance with extreme caution, for fear of compromising its already questionable neutrality.

The fear of German reprisals against Norway in the early summer of 1917 was not without foundation. Since April the German navy had contingency plans for war with Norway, in case Norway should abandon her formal neutrality and join with Britain. Rumours that this was about to happen recurred from time to time, often fuelled by incidents such as the capture of Norwegian ships by the German navy. The resulting worsening of German-Norwegian relations in its turn stimulated concern – or rather hopes – in British government circles that this might bring Norway into the war. The tension reached a high point in the middle of June, when the Norwegian police seized the German diplomatic courier Baron Rautenfels with his baggage full of an assortment of bombs and other explosives. The assumption of a connection between this and a number of mysterious explosions on board ships leaving Norwegian ports was inevitable. The excitement aroused by that event made even the German envoy fearful that Norway was on the brink of joining with the allies. In London at the same time, the War Cabinet seemed for the moment to agree that it would be an advantage if Norway could be brought into the war on their side. But the old doubts soon re-emerged, with the First Sea Lord making his concurrence dependent on an assurance of American naval assistance which, when sought, was not forthcoming. A special "Northern Neutrals Committee" was asked to study the situation, and their conclusion was that "the intervention of these countries even on the side of the Allies would on the whole not be an advantage to the Allies."[7]

Norway's more long-term concern, as this crisis with Germany blew over, was the effect that America's entry into the war might have on the country's imports. For the time being there seemed little reason for serious concern. Quite apart from the reluctance of the Americans to participate in a blockade which they had at least formally protested against while the United States were neutral, President Wilson himself seemed to regard Norway as a country that deserved more lenient treatment than the other neutral states. His instructions to the Exports Council in the middle of July 1917 was that he "wished to treat Norway very liberally in the granting of licences."[8] Still the Norwegian government decided to send a trade delegation to arrange a formal agreement with the United States government. As leader of the delegation the government had selected the world famous but somewhat headstrong polar explorer Fridtjof Nansen. His arrival in Washington was followed by a personal letter from Prime Minister Gunnar Knudsen to President Wilson, which – perhaps unfortunately – conveyed the impression that Norway was taking her position as a "most favourable nation" for granted.

Nansen's stay in Washington became a lengthy one. This was partly due to America's difficulty in working out a consistent export policy which her associates Britain and France found acceptable, and in establishing the machinery to carry it out. But worsening relations between an impatient Nansen and a procrastinating Foreign Minister Ihlen did their part. In spite of suggestions that drastic reductions in Norway's exports to Germany would be needed, Ihlen persisted with counter-proposals which the Americans at Britain's behest found quite unacceptable. As time went on, Norway's supply situation worsened, and in the Storting the opposition laid the full blame on the government for failing to reach an agreement with the Americans. Food rationing was finally instituted from 1 January 1918, after the United States had decided to publish the terms of their offer of an agreement. That was followed by Norway's publication of her counter-proposals, and in February a compromise seemed within reach. Still the British demanded clarification on several points: precision was needed, wrote Blockade Minister Lord Robert Cecil, since the "Norwegians are past masters in the art of bargaining".

The main reason for Ihlen's reluctance to accept the terms offered was of course his concern about relations with Germany. Judging from the protestations by Germany's new envoy to Norway, Admiral von Hintze, his government now feared that Norway's days of neutrality might be numbered. Germany therefore demanded a formal declaration, which was issued on 9 March 1918 and addressed to all the belligerents. Germany's fears were reflected in the crucial part of the declaration, where Norway undertook "to resist by force of arms any violation by any power or group of powers of her territorial rights, and to prevent the use of Norwegian territory as a base by any power whatever."[9] With that reassurance

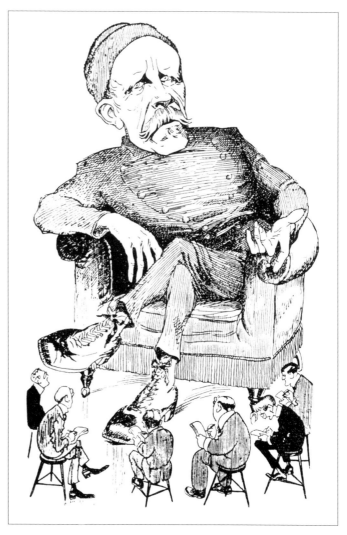

The government's decision to send the polar explorer Fridtjof Nansen to negotiate a trade agreement with the United States was clearly designed to exploit his famous name. This cartoon from a Norwegian magazine suggests that the editor may have suspected Nansen of having a somewhat inflated ego: the caption stated that Nansen "as Minister Extraordinary in America displays an enormous activity and is interviewed every day by a score of newspapers."

towards Germany, and after several more rounds of clarification of the text, Nansen signed the booksize US-Norwegian trade agreement on 30 April 1918. In the face of the growing scarcity of food and other commodities in Norway, it was high time. But it must also be said that Ihlen's persistence in the art of bargaining had resulted in much more favourable terms than those offered around Christmas time.

The North Sea Mine Barrage

Germany's fear, in the winter and spring of 1918, that Norway might have to surrender her neutrality and open her coastline to the operations of the British navy, was not as far-fetched as it may have seemed at the time. Although the loss of allied and neutral shipping due to German submarines had declined somewhat after the burst of activity following Germany's declaration of 1 February 1917, there was still concern in allied circles that the rate of sinkings might rise again, as the Germans increased the number of submarines and improved their operational tactics. Among the schemes for meeting such a threat, a plan hatched in the US Navy for a gigantic mine barrage right across the North Sea from Scotland to Norway was taking shape during the autumn of 1917. The effectiveness of such a barrage for preventing the exit of German submarines would be significantly improved if it became possible to close the loophole that the three-mile wide passage through Norwegian territorial waters would constitute. The allied navies had no faith in Norway's formal ban against such passage, so the only way would be to extend the mine barrage right up to the Norwegian coast. Furthermore, a base on Norway's west coast would be desirable for effectively patrolling the barrage. So, as the planning progressed, the allies were once more examining the whole question of Norwegian neutrality.

In the British Admiralty the need for a naval base in Norway was uppermost on their minds, but it would have to be obtained through Norway's voluntary consent. However, when Minister Findlay in late December was asked for his opinion, he was quite clear that Norway would never willingly agree, and would only give in to force or to a demonstration of overwhelming strength. That ended the quest for a naval base. The actual laying of the mine barrage began in March 1918, and the joint mine-laying operations of the British and American navies were not completed until October, when the number of mines had reached the astounding total of 70 263. The problem of the loophole through Norwegian maritime territory, however, loomed ever larger as the mining progressed, and on 7 August a sharp British note informed the Norwegian government that the closing of the passage could no longer be postponed. Within four days, the Norwegian authorities would either have to mine the passage themselves or allow the British to do it. Similar communications, although much milder in form and without the time limit, were presented by the other allied governments.

German-Norwegian relations had improved considerably after the skirmishes in the spring, and a new trade agreement was in fact about to be signed at the time when the allies presented their demands about mining. Rightly concerned about German reactions to what would in fact be an extension of an allied mine barrage into neutral waters, Ihlen again resorted to delaying tactics. His initial reply, as the four days' limit expired, was that the ban on the passage of submarines through her waters, and its enforcement, was Norway's own affair. His next step, after President Wilson had persuaded the British to avoid imposing any time limit, was to send identical notes to all the belligerents. Reporting certain recent cases where unidentified submarines had violated the Norwegian Submarine Decree, he requested all of them to investigate if any of their submarines had been involved. The British government replied with an admission of one violation; their allies replied in the negative; and the Germans did not reply at all. Then, on 14 September the much delayed trade agreement between Norway and Germany was signed. Two weeks later Ihlen informed the belligerents that in view of recent violations of the Norwegian Submarine Decree, the Norwegian government had decided to enforce the ban by way of a minefield in territorial waters, on the west coast just north of Stavanger.

This Norwegian mine-laying was hardly an act in strict accordance with neutrality. Notwithstanding the legal justifications that could be found, and the theoretical defence that could be constructed, these did not alter the fact that the mines were laid in direct conjunction with the allies' Northern Barrage. But the inevitable alternative of having the British laying the mines left Norway no choice if formal neutrality was to be maintained and an open conflict with Britain avoided. Earlier in the war Norway's mine-laying would almost certainly have provoked Germany into violent action. But in this late hour Germany's war effort was already ebbing. This, and Ihlen's diplomatic ruse, making the minefield appear as directed against Great Britain since only Britain admitted to the kind of violation which the mines were intended to stop, meant that Norway got away with nothing but muted German protests.

The First World War was the first testing time for the particular Norwegian brand of neutralism, fashioned and given substance through the less than ten years of peace that followed the break-up of the Union with Sweden. On the surface, at least, it had passed the test. Norway had not been drawn into the war, even while the fact of Norway's economic dependence on Great Britain had turned her into Britain's "neutral ally". Unwillingly, but compelled by necessity, she had become an accomplice in Britain's economic warfare against Germany. Combining that dependence on Britain with the preservation of neutrality had been possible since, in the nineteenth-century concept of neutrality, the state could remain neutral while the country's industry and commerce arranged their own foreign relations as best they could. But the two final years of the war had shown that for a small neutral state, such a division of responsibility became more difficult to uphold as central sectors of the economy were drawn into the tug-of-war between the belligerents. Also, the pervasive effect of foreign – in Norway's case British – control of the country's trade threatened to undermine its economic sovereignty in the long term. The question, therefore, was whether those lessons would be taken into account in policy planning for the future, or would recede into oblivion behind the facade of the successful maintenance of neutrality.

Besides, much of the lustre of neutrality itself had gone. From its pre-war status at the pinnacle of righteousness, the neutral had descended to become regarded by many as a spineless profiteer, a mercenary soul reaping wealth from the death and distress of those engaged in fighting a just war for the defence of humanity. Inside Norway the image of her neutrality was also marred by two dark shadows: on one side the rise of a class of "new rich" who profited from inflated export prices and freight rates, contrasting with the ordinary wage-earner whose income lagged behind the rampant inflation. On the other side there was the tragedy of the over two thousand sailors who had perished at sea while carrying essential supplies to Norway or earning foreign exchange for the shipping companies.

6. The Cross-Currents of the Inter-War Period

Introduction

For just over twenty years, while relative peace reigned in Europe following the prolonged nightmare of "la Grande Guerre", Norway was to go through the most turbulent period of her internal politics. External and domestic social forces, released by the turmoil of the war, competed to influence the direction in which Norwegian society was to develop. The quest for modernisation and industrialisation, of what was in many ways still an economically backward nation, clashed with the forces of socialism and communism that were in part released by the same quest. But modernisation also met resistance from the reactive forces of conservatism and nationalism, seeking to preserve the traditional values of an essentially primary-producing country from the influence of alien values. Eventually, and stimulated by the economic crisis of the thirties, some of those reactive forces were to seek refuge in proto-fascist or fascist movements. Although being ethnically exceptionally homogenous, Norway's nation-building project, begun in 1905 under the slogan "the new working-day", hence was to suffer many reverses. Deep social and political divisions emerged, and were only partly on the way to being overcome when the shadows of another European war began to loom towards the end of the 1930s.[1]

One aspect of the nation-building project that was actively pursued through the 1920s was that of asserting Norway's place as an equal partner in the Scandinavian triangle of independent states. The summit meetings of the three Kings and their government leaders during the war had broken much of the ice that remained between Norway and Sweden after the 1905 break-up of the Union. But the different approaches of the two countries to the problems of neutrality – Sweden's more dogmatic, legalist policy, in contrast to Norway's pragmatic "laissez-faire" line – had prevented closer political cooperation. There remained also in Sweden, especially in conservative circles, a hankering after a closer association or even federation of the Nordic countries in which Sweden could assert the leading role. Against that background it is not surprising that Norway should maintain a strong

111

scepticism towards Nordic cooperation schemes that went beyond clearly defined practical, functional limits.

In regard to Denmark, Norway's self-assertion was played out mainly in the cultural field. The four hundred years of the Danish-Norwegian kingdom had left a legacy of pervasive cultural affinity, as demonstrated by a more-or-less common language and literature, which the 19th century movement to revive Norway's own cultural heritage had dented but could not displace. Norway's cultural nation-building project began in this respect with a 1917 language reform to bring the written language closer to the spoken idiom. Next came the replacement of Danish-inspired place-names with names of historical origin, which in 1925 gave the capital Kristiania back its ancient name of Oslo. The movement was climaxed in a drawn-out process wherein Norway sought and finally obtained the transfer from the Danish National Archives of material concerning Norwegian history during the union period.

Norway's self-assertion in regard to her Scandinavian neighbours coincided with, and reinforced, her wider cultural re-orientation from Germany to Great Britain and eventually also the United States. With Denmark and to a smaller extent Sweden as conduits, Germany had dominated Norway's cultural links with Europe. But the public's reaction to German submarine warfare against Norwegian merchant ships during the First World War had produced a wave of anti-German feelings, subsequently re-awakened and magnified by the emergence of Nazi Germany. The image of Britain and the United States as the champions of democracy and national self-determination, on the other hand, had been strengthened by their victory and by their lead in creating the League of Nations. Pro-British feelings, already firmly based on admiration for Britain as a model of parliamentary democracy as well as on the close maritime links, were also reinforced by Britain's image as the linchpin of opposition to the spread of totalitarian ideas in Europe in the inter-war period. In regard to the United States, the links created by the massive emigration of Norwegians both before and after the turn of the century engendered admiration for the freedom, enterprise, and dynamism of the New World.

In foreign policy, we found in chapter four that the initial, formative years were marked by two principal guidelines: isolationism/neutralism in regard to great power politics, and active promotion of the nation's economic interests at home and abroad. The question was whether the end of the war would mean a return to the unfinished business of that programme, or whether the experience of the war would alter the aims of Norwegian foreign policy, or the means toward those aims. The legacy of the First World War seemed to suggest that neutrality, although severely challenged, had stood the test of keeping the country out of the war. In the words of Christian Fredrik Michelet, who took over as Foreign Minister when the long-serving Liberal cabinet of Gunnar Knudsen and Nils Claus Ihlen in the summer of 1920 gave way to a Conservative government:

> Neutrality has hitherto been regarded as so to speak an unwritten clause of the Constitution of the Kingdom of Norway; neutrality has been a state maxim, a state principle, independent of changing governments and changing Storting, a principle with deep roots in the entire Norwegian people. It can be said that neutrality has been for us one of the bright spots of the war.[2]

As for the hidden dimension of that neutralism, the implicit reliance on Great Britain as the ultimate protector of Norway's territorial integrity, the experience of the war had not made it necessary to play that particular card. But the war had amply demonstrated Norway's economic dependence on Britain in times of crisis. All this seemed to confirm that the country's foreign relations, and the foreign service which was to handle those relations, should continue to keep aloof from power politics and concentrate on the promotion of economic interests. Consolidating the nation's sovereignty over its territory, and expanding its sphere of interest as regards fisheries, whaling, and sealing, formed part and parcel of those interests, and would presumably continue, albeit with some caution as regards possible conflict with British interests. This chapter will deal first with the efforts to expand and protect Norway's economic interests, before turning to the evolution of Norwegian neutralism after the First World War.

Foreign Policy in a Changed Environment

On the domestic front, the many foreign policy problems that Norway experienced from 1916 onwards had led to criticism of the government's handling of the country's foreign relations, outside as well as inside the Storting. Increasing demands for greater parliamentary control and influence over policy forced the government in January 1917 to agree to a special "select committee" being instituted as a forum for consultation about external affairs. The committee could be called to meet at any time and its sessions would be secret. Among the seventeen members of that body would be representatives of all the political parties. In 1922 that arrangement was made permanent through the institution of a parliamentary committee for foreign affairs, which in the following year was merged with the committee for constitutional affairs. This latter committee was the Storting's instrument for dealing with formal issues of foreign relations such as the conclusion of treaties.

The Storting's influence on the formulation and management of the nation's foreign policy was also greatly strengthened by the fact that, beginning with the Liberal Party's loss of its majority in the 1918 election, the

113

entire inter-war period was marked by frequently changing minority governments. From the summer of 1920 to the spring of 1935 Norway had nine cabinets, none of which lasted for more than two years. Their weak parliamentary basis meant that in particular the Storting's committee for foreign affairs obtained a decisive voice in the way the nation's foreign relations were determined and conducted.

For the Ministry of Foreign Affairs and the foreign service, the increased workload resulting from the war meant an expansion of the personnel and the budgets. Much of that expansion was meant to be temporary, however, in the advent of a return to "normalcy". But as the situation at the end of the war showed little resemblance to pre-war conditions, reforms were needed. The established separation between the diplomatic and consular services, and with it the assumption that diplomacy, or "high politics", could be left to itself whereas matters of trade and shipping needed to be dealt with by consular representatives, had become increasingly difficult to uphold. In 1920 a reform commission for the foreign service was appointed, and its proposals portended radical changes. The Ministry of Foreign Affairs, and the diplomatic and consular services, were to be merged into one service, and recruitment to the service should be based on uniform criteria. For the Ministry the commission proposed a re-organisation into three departments – one for political and commercial affairs, one for legal affairs, and one administrative department. The department for political and commercial affairs would then be subdivided on geographical lines, since political and trade relations with any one country tended to merge. The commission also proposed a new post as permanent secretary or secretary general to coordinate the work of the three departments and serve as the Foreign Minister's closest adviser.

The commission justified the radical nature of its reform proposals by pointing to one essential lesson of the wartime experience:

> One thing which the world war has shown beyond doubt, is that Norway also has political interests, interests of the highest importance for the whole nation as they concern our freedom and sovereignty, the nation's dignity and position among the peoples, as well as our entire economic life. [...] Even in peacetime conditions there is an ongoing game of political interests to which the small nations have to devote their close attention.[3]

The reform of the Foreign Ministry followed in the main the commission's proposals. Norway's commercial relations were to benefit from the reorganisation, in that the geographical "bureaux" were able to develop expert knowledge of the countries and issues they dealt with. Political relations, however, were to suffer from subsequent reorganisations whereby major issues transcending geographical borders were transferred to separate bureaux: one for Arctic-Antarctic matters, one for League of Nations affairs, from 1929, and then, in 1934, a bureau for political affairs. This meant in fact a reversal to the old division between political-diplomatic and economic-commercial affairs. That development was completed with the establishment, in 1938, of a department for political affairs. Formally that department was placed on an equal footing with a department for economic and commercial affairs, but weak leadership and insufficient coordination by the permanent secretary meant that Norway drifted towards the looming European crisis without the benefit of leadership and guidance from experienced diplomats.

Internationally, the environment in which Norway had to operate had also undergone great changes. After "the war to end all wars", and notwithstanding the danger of a wave of revolutions, a new international order seemed in sight. The League of Nations, foreshadowed in President Wilson's "Fourteen Points" for the peace settlement, was based on the liberal belief that there was a necessary connection between national self-determination and democratic institutions. Once the new system was in place, international stability based on justice would prevail. Of more immediate interest to Norway was the fact that Germany, having lost the war, and Russia, now in the shape of the Soviet Union and ravaged by revolution and civil war, had – at least in the short term – disappeared as potential threats to Norwegian security. The western powers seemed favourably disposed towards Norway in view of the services to the Entente of her merchant navy. The Norwegian government also felt that the enormous losses of Norwegian shipping entitled the country to some compensation as part of the peace settlement. Proposals by Norway's envoy in Paris to secure an expansion of territory at the expense of Russia and/or Finland, and his more fanciful idea to acquire a share of the German colonies in Africa, got nowhere. But Norway had another aim in mind.

The Protection and Expansion of Economic Interests

Norway's "Arctic Imperialism"

Norway's main aim as part of the peace settlement was to obtain sovereignty over the Svalbard archipelago. The British coal embargo against Norway at the end of 1916 had brought home to the authorities that Svalbard, in addition to its value as a base area for fishing, whaling and sealing, could also provide Norway with her own supply of coal. Norwegian businessmen, awash with profits from wartime trade and shipping, had already purchased the coal-mines developed on Spitzbergen by the American industrialist J.M. Longyear. So, after some wavering, Foreign Minister Ihlen instructed the Norwegian delegation to the Paris Peace Conference to seek to obtain sovereignty over Svalbard.

115

Norwegian territorial claims in the Arctic in the inter-war period

North Pole

ARCTIC OCEAN

Kara Sea

Thule

Franz Josef Land
(Soviet Union/Russia)

BAFFIN
BAY

Novaya Zemlya
(Soviet Union/Russia)

80°

Longyearbyen

Spitsbergen

BARENTS
SEA

Greenland
(Denmark)

GREENLAND
SEA

Bear Island

Godthåb

Murmansk

70°

Jan Mayen

Tromsø

Arkangelsk

NORWEGIAN
SEA

Denmark Strait

Arctic Circle

Reykjavik Iceland

Davis Strait

A Successful Norwegian territorial claims
in the Arctic in the inter-war years

B Official Norwegian claims on the
east coast of Greenland.

Helsinki

St. Petersburg

Moscow

NORWAY

60°

Stockholm

Oslo

The omens seemed favourable: France had already signalled a positive attitude, and US Secretary of State Robert Lansing was known to favour Norway's request, albeit with some reservations intending to preserve equal access for nationals of other countries to exploit the natural resources of the islands. The third of the victorious great powers, Italy, had no interest in the matter, but was willing to support Norway's claim. Britain's attitude was more uncertain, and seemed for a time to be veering towards a solution under the new "mandate" system, which essentially meant that Norway would only be holding the archipelago "in trust" for the international community. Sweden, not unexpectedly, wished primarily to see Svalbard remain a "terra nullius", although a mandate arrangement might be acceptable. But in view of the emerging great power consensus in favour of the Norwegian claim, the Swedish government gave up its opposition. Denmark, however, in signalling her acquiescence, seized the opportunity to extract a verbal promise that Norway would not object to pending Danish claims for sovereignty over the whole of Greenland.

In July 1919 a proposed treaty text was worked out in consultation with the great powers, and approved in draft form by the Supreme Council of the Paris Peace Conference in September. It proclaimed Norway's "full and unrestricted sovereignty" over the archipelago, but appended two important reservations. Nationals of the states signatory to the treaty would enjoy equal rights to exploit the economic resources of the area, and the islands were not to be used for "warlike purposes". The formal treaty was signed by Norway on 9 February 1920, and during the next five years was acceded to by all of 45 other states.

In recognition of his assiduous work for Norway's claim, Norway's envoy Wedel Jarlsberg had been hailed as a national hero when he brought the treaty text to Kristiania in September 1919. The government gave a dinner in his honour, and in his speech he expressed his deeper feelings about the significance of the acquisition of Svalbard:

> We should not forget that Norway was once a mighty realm. The urge to go forth and expand rises and ebbs in waves of long duration. Now begins the ascent. [...] Norway has the same right as greater lands to expand the borders of her national life. There are new and fertile fields to be tilled, we must work for a great and greater Norway.[4]

His words met with mixed reactions in the Norwegian press. But his message would not go unheeded in the years that followed. There was also an apparent lesson drawn from the success of the claim to Svalbard: by granting Norway's sovereignty over the archipelago, the great powers seemed to have accepted an underlying contention for the Norwegian claim, which was that the common interests of the international community would be best served by granting territorial control over a disputed area to a small power. In that way the area in question would be eliminated as a source of conflict among greater powers, while the small power controlling the area would be more likely to heed the conditions imposed on its control by the international community.

Both the Arctic Ocean and the Antarctic had before the war been marked out as natural areas of expansion for Norwegian fisheries or for whale and seal catching. With the Svalbard archipelago secured, the Norwegian fishing and seal-catching communities sought further afield, in the first instance to the waters further east where their activities had met with little or no competition before the First World War. This time, however, the situation turned out to be different. A more assertive Soviet Union in 1921 extended its

117

Minister Fredrik Wedel Jarlsberg, Norway's long-serving envoy to France (and reputed to have one of the best 'cuisines' in Paris), worked assiduously to secure territorial and other gains for his country in the peace settlement after the First World War. Although he had hoped for more, it was undoubtedly with great satisfaction that on 9 February 1920 he took his seat in the Salon de l'Horloge of the French Ministry of Foreign Affairs, to put his signature to the treaty whereby sovereignty over Svalbard was awarded to Norway.

fisheries limit to twelve miles, thereby excluding Norwegian sealers from their best catching areas in the White Sea. Thus began a period of conflict marked by Soviet seizures of Norwegian boats alternating with Norwegian – and British – efforts to reassert what they regarded as their traditional rights. In Norway's case this culminated in the dispatch, in 1922, of a naval vessel to patrol the area west of Novaya Zemlya right up to the previous limit of four miles. The conflict abated after the Norwegian sealing companies arranged to purchase concessions to catch seals within the disputed area, and was solved for the remainder of the inter-war period as part of a comprehensive Soviet-Norwegian settlement in 1926, to which we shall return.

More serious in the long term was the Soviet decree of 1926, which declared all islands in a sector from the continental Soviet Union northwards to the North Pole to be Soviet territory. This would include Franz Joseph Land east of Svalbard, where Norway had for long carried on extensive seal-catching activities. Statistics for the entire period 1865 to 1928 show the area as having been visited by 110 Norwegian expeditions and only 12 Russian ones. The Norwegian government delivered a written protest note against the decree, but of course to no avail. The sector principle for territorial claims was not entirely new: Canada had applied it one year before to lay claim to all the islands between Canada and the North Pole, including the Sverdrup islands which, like so many of the islands and territories in the Arctic, had been discovered and explored by Norwegian polar explorers. On that occasion the Norwegian government evidently decided

118

that a protest would be a futile gesture. But while recognising Canadian sovereignty over the area the Foreign Ministry made it clear that this in no way implied acceptance of the sector principle.

This far Norwegian Arctic policy had the appearance of a defensive retreat rather than an exercise in imperialism. One explanation for that is the diminishing importance of seal-catching, except for a few isolated coastal communities. Sealing interests were nevertheless one of the factors leading to Norway's 1929 annexation of the small volcanic island of Jan Mayen north of Iceland. The initial impulse for that act seems however to have been the island's importance for meteorological observations particularly related to fisheries – in fact the first, partial, annexation was declared by the Norwegian Institute of Meteorology. A third and more defensive reason was the fear that other nations might get there first and shut out the Norwegians.

The Greenland Affair

A much clearer example of Norwegian arctic imperialism in the inter-war period is the Greenland affair – the only occasion on which Norway laid claim to territory which was internationally recognised as belonging to another state. As suggested by Foreign Minister Ihlen's 1919 oral disclaimer of any objection to Danish sovereignty over Greenland, Norway was generally satisfied with the fishing and sealing rights which she had long enjoyed in the area. But in 1921 Denmark not only officially declared her full sovereignty over Greenland, including the large parts of the island hitherto regarded as *terra nullius*, but also issued a decree which declared the coastal waters all round Greenland as formally closed to all ships. Although a bilateral arrangement three years later safeguarded the traditional Norwegian rights to catch seals in the area, the Norwegian fisheries were bound to suffer. What really exacerbated the conflict, however, were the deep historic and nationalist overtones. The Norwegians might have forgiven, but had not forgotten, the fact that Greenland together with Iceland and the Faeroes was ancient Norwegian land, part of the Norwegian medieval "empire", and had been arrogated to Denmark by the 1814 Kiel Treaty without Norway's voice being heard. As the future Prime Minister J.L. Mowinckel explained:

> In order to understand this, and justly and objectively to comprehend Norwegian opinion and thinking, it is necessary to view and judge the whole issue in national and historic terms. [...] The loss of the Norwegian realm's outlying possessions – Iceland, Greenland, and the Faeroes – in 1814, and especially the way that loss occurred, has always pained and angered the minds of Norwegians.[5]

119

Five Norwegians with imperialist aspirations have here staked their claim to an area of Eastern Greenland "on behalf of H.M. King Haakon VII" on 27 June 1931, by hoisting the Norwegian flag. Two weeks later the government, after some vacillation, put their stamp of approval on the annexation.

The wave of Norwegian nationalist resentment caused by Denmark's action was further reinforced by memories of the Danish King's appropriation of Norwegian church property during the Reformation, and Denmark's refusal to hand over to Norway archive material concerning Norway from the union period. In the initial stage the dispute might still have been solved through a negotiated arrangement which secured Norway's economic

interests. But as Denmark forced the issue of sovereignty in ways which seemed to preclude such a negotiated settlement, the dispute appeared to have
reached the point of no return. Norway, in a fit of national fervour, now
contested even the Danish sovereignty claim over East Greenland.

As a temporary expedient, the two countries decided that both would
continue their economic activities on Greenland more or less as before,
pending further negotiations. An awkward aspect of Norway's position in
the matter was that while she contested sovereignty over East Greenland,
the main economic interest centred on facilities for fishing boats in the
south-western part of the island. Yet the nationalist mood and the activities
of various pressure groups now led to an intense Norwegian activity in the
eastern part, including a series of expeditions and the construction of huts.
Then, in 1930, the Norwegian government accorded policing authority to
leaders of the expeditions, to which Denmark retaliated by giving policing
authority to the leader of a planned major scientific expedition to the area.
Pressure from institutions like the Arctic Council for a Norwegian annexation of East Greenland was mounting, and at the end of June 1931 the current leader of a Norwegian expedition declared a private occupation of part
of the area. Under the influence of nationalist fervour, pressure from activist
groups, and – somewhat surprising – advice from the country's experts in
international law, the government caved in and declared an official annexation of the occupied area.

The Norwegian government, formed by the Farmers' Party shortly
before, had in the meantime been moving towards an agreement to submit
the issue to the International Court of Justice. The annexation deadlocked
any such proposal, at least for the time being, and the confrontation continued to fester for another year. But in the end the two countries agreed
to submit the matter to arbitration by the International Court. On 5 April,
1933, the Hague Court delivered its decision. It condemned the Norwegian
occupation as illegal, and thereby reaffirmed Denmark's complete sovereignty over the whole of Greenland.

Norway's action in the Greenland affair, seen in retrospect, was clearly an
aberration in more ways than one. For one thing it represented a deviation
from established Norwegian policy in arctic affairs. While being clearly
expansive in the economic sense, motivated by the need to find new and
better sources of livelihood for the coastal population of northern and western Norway, the policy had so far been marked by caution and a defensi-
ve/reactive stance in regard to annexation of territory. The other sense in
which it was an aberration, was the way in which pressure groups, newspapers and public opinion had combined to push weak minority governments
into positions which not only went contrary to Norway's traditional line of
support for international law, but also conflicted with the guidelines set
down by the Storting. The majority in the committee for foreign affairs,

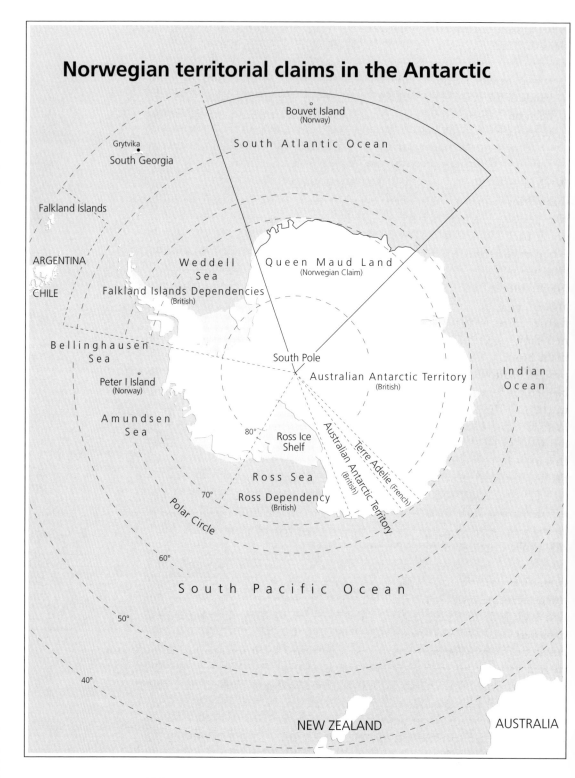

Norwegian territorial claims in the Antarctic

Bouvet Island
(Norway)

South Atlantic Ocean

Grytvika
South Georgia

Falkland Islands

ARGENTINA

CHILE

Weddell
Sea

Falkland Islands Dependencies
(British)

Queen Maud Land
(Norwegian Claim)

Bellinghausen
Sea

South Pole

Australian Antarctic Territory
(British)

Indian
Ocean

Peter I Island
(Norway)

Amundsen
Sea

80°

Ross Ice
Shelf

Australian Antarctic Territory
(British)

Terre Adelie (French)

Ross Sea

70°

Ross Dependency
(British)

Polar Circle

60°

South Pacific Ocean

50°

40°

NEW ZEALAND

AUSTRALIA

reflecting on the situation following the Hague Court's decision, made it clear that such events must never be repeated:

> It must be completely excluded that important decisions are taken out of the hands of the responsible authorities, that loose agitation replaces calm deliberation and objective discussion, and that actions are taken behind the Storting's back.[6]

Norway turns to the Antarctic

While the economic importance of the seal-catch was gradually diminishing, Norwegian whaling experienced a steady growth during the inter-war period. Catching whales along the Norwegian coast had traditions going back to the Middle Ages. But from the 1870s technological change – bigger boats and harpoon development – opened the way to Norwegian whaling in more distant waters, at first around Iceland and the Faeroes, Newfoundland, and Svalbard. As exploitation overtaxed the resources in one area – due to ignorance as well as a lack of concern – the whalers sought further afield, and by the start of the new century Norwegian whalers turned their attention towards the South Atlantic and Antarctic waters. The main product was whale oil, extracted by boiling the blubber. At first this process had to be done on land stations, and the first such station was established on South Georgia in the British Falklands dependency in 1903. But in the following year a Norwegian company began to experiment with a factory ship, a kind of "floating boiler". Still, stations or bases on land were required, and for this Norway sought and obtained concessions from Great Britain, which claimed sovereignty over all territory in a wide sector from the Falklands all the way to the South Pole.

After the First World War whaling in Antarctic waters expanded rapidly, as big factory ships took over. Britain led the way in claiming sovereignty in the area, beginning with the so-called Ross Dependency on the Pacific side of the Antarctic in 1923. Norway now began to fear that such annexations might lead to the exclusion of her whalers, not only from landing rights, but also from operating in ever expanding territorial waters around the annexed territories. As such annexations tended to be based on who first had discovered and explored the areas, and seeing that Norwegian explorers such as Roald Amundsen had been among the pioneers in the Antarctic, Norway began to search for unclaimed territory. The first Norwegian annexation was the tiny Bouvet Island between South Africa and the Antarctic, in 1928. This was at first disputed by Britain, but finally recognised by the British government on condition that Norway agreed to institute regulations and limitations on her whaling activity. In 1929 Norway went further, and acquired a foothold in the South Pacific by claiming the small Peter I Island. But an attempt by a Norwegian expedition to occupy an area on the Antarctic itself, situated within a sector which an Imperial Conference shortly before had declared as a British sphere of interest, raised a storm of protest in British and South African media.

A new phase of the race for Antarctic possessions began when Britain in 1933 claimed a very large sector – nearly one third of the total Antarctic – on the Indian Ocean side, to be administered by Australia. The Norwegian government did not officially dispute the British claim. In return the British Foreign Office in an exchange of notes showed a clear understanding of Norway's indicated "special interests" in the so far unclaimed sector between the Australian and the Falklands sectors.[7] For the time being the Norwegian government did not pursue this matter, partly because Anglo-Norwegian relations were in a delicate state, due to the conflict over Norwegian fisheries limits that we shall return to. But in December 1938 the Norwegian government became aware that a secret German expedition was on its way to the Antarctic. Norway now had to act quickly, and on 14 January the government by Royal Decree declared the entire sector between the Falklands Dependency and the Australian Dependency – about one-fifth of the Antarctic – as Norwegian territory. Germany, and the Soviet Union, rejected the Norwegian claim, and the United States and Chile expressed reservations with regard to their eventual rights in the area. The British government, however, to whom Norway at the same time gave its approval of the 1933 Australian Dependency, officially recognised the annexation. An Anglo-Norwegian "modus vivendi" was thus established for the Antarctic, putting an end to a long period of dispute, and perhaps indicating that Britain had come to regard Norway as a more amenable neighbour than other possible claimants.

The Conflict with Britain over Fishing Limits

While the disputes with Britain in the Antarctic never reached serious proportions, the age-old conflict over the extent of the fishing limits along the Norwegian coast came to constitute a serious threat to Anglo-Norwegian relations from the early 1920s onward. As we have seen in previous chapters, two principal questions were involved: first whether Norway would be able to maintain a four mile as opposed to the more generally acceptable three mile limit, and, secondly, how the border was to be drawn across wide bays and inlets: should it go straight across, or should it follow the intricate indentations of the coastline? The seriousness of the conflict reflected the importance of fisheries to the Norwegian economy. Fish products made up about one quarter of the total value of the country's exports. Fishing was also the main livelihood for a majority of the one-third of the population that lived in scattered communities along the coast. A further dimension to the conflict was its deeper nature as a struggle between conservatism and modernisation. Most Norwegian fishermen stuck to the traditional ways,

124

fishing from small boats in coastal or near-coastal waters, and enjoying variously feast or famine according to whether the seasonal influx of fish was good, bad, or failed. From their viewpoint the big ocean-going trawlers of Britain and other European countries were scavengers, overtaxing the resources and charging roughshod through the nets and lines of the local fishermen.

In 1923 a series of collisions between foreign trawlers and Norwegian fishermen, and several arrests of trawlers fishing inside the four mile limit, produced a British request for negotiations on the fishing limits. In return for a restriction to three miles Britain was prepared to accept the wide bays of Vestfjord and Varangerfjord as Norwegian territory. The Liberal Mowinckel government now agreed to negotiate on that basis, hoping to achieve a regulation of trawler activity on the rich fishing grounds outside territorial waters as an additional British concession. A compromise proposal was worked out, but the British government found it went too far towards meeting Norwegian desires. Instead the British suggested negotiations on the basis of the old North Sea Convention, which had twice before been firmly rejected by Norway. This time the Mowinckel government agreed, and their compliant attitude during the negotiations that followed resulted in a protocol which a Norwegian historian has termed "a massive breakthrough for British interests and standpoints, and a corresponding curtailment or elimination of the traditional rights of the Norwegian coastal population." The British envoy subsequently wrote that the proposal "appeared to me so advantageous to British interests that I had the honour to recommend that a determined effort be made to conclude an agreement on these lines with as little delay as possible."[8]

In spite of massive protests from fisheries interests and the Ministries of Trade and Justice, the government again agreed to negotiate. The result apparently took even less notice of Norwegian interests than the draft proposal, but still the government recommended to a closed session of the Storting that the agreement be approved. But when the major features leaked to one of the main newspapers they aroused a storm of disapproval. Thereafter the extended committee for foreign and constitutional affairs unanimously rejected the proposed agreement.

During the years that followed Norway reverted to her pre-war stance, which was that each state had the right to establish, within reasonable limits, the extent and configuration of its maritime territory, limited only by the acquired rights of other states. A commission of experts was appointed, and their report mainly favoured retention of the four mile limit. But they were unable to agree about from which base line the four miles should be measured – from the mainland, from the inhabited islands, or from islets and skerries submerged at high tides? As the Storting and the minority government could not agree either, the matter kept being postponed, while confrontations continued between British trawlers and the Norwegian coast guard. The crisis came to a head in 1934, when a British naval vessel was sent to Norway with secret instructions to use force if necessary to prevent British trawlers being arrested in areas that Britain did not recognise as territorial waters. No incidents occurred, but in 1935 the Labour Party came to power, and the new Foreign Minister, Halvdan Koht, favoured an expansive interpretation of the base line principle. This was then enacted into law. The British government now officially threatened Norway with naval reprisals. But new British proposals revealed that they were retreating somewhat from their previous positions, and a "modus vivendi" was eventually reached, an important feature of which was that some of the best fishing grounds outside territorial waters were established as trawler-free areas.

While the conflict with Britain had thus lost its acute character before the outbreak of the Second World War, the wider issue of the extent of the Norwegian fishing limits was to remain unsolved until settled – in Norway's favour – by the International Court of Justice in 1951. The long duration of the conflict, and the impossibility of reaching a negotiated settlement, reflects on the one side the importance of the fisheries to the Norwegian economy, but also the strong concern to preserve the continued existence of many scattered and isolated communities along the coast of northern Norway. The people there saw no alternative to their traditional way of life, with fishing in coastal waters as the mainstay. In the county of Finnmark as many as 86 per cent of the male population over the age of 15 were engaged in fishing, and they had neither the inclination nor the resources of capital to engage in industrial fishing with trawlers and more modern methods.

On the British side the fisheries were also important to the national economy, but fishing there mainly meant deep sea fishing with trawlers. Giving in to Norwegian demands for extended fishing limits and restrictions on trawler activity would create a dangerous precedent for similar demands from other countries with similarly rich offshore fishing grounds. But there was another, strategic, reason for Britain's intransigence: British naval power was closely tied to the greatest possible freedom to operate in international waters. Any extension of the maritime territory of other states meant a limitation of Britain's ability to exert her power and influence. All this made Norway into something of a test case for Britain. In some ways Norway may also have appeared as a convenient test case, considering the disparity of power. But when push came to shove it turned out that Britain flinched from using naked power against a small and friendly neighbour across the North Sea.

126

Managing an Extrovert Economy

As a country dependent for over one third of its gross national product on external trade, Norway hoped for a speedy return to normal trade patterns after the serious dislocations caused by the economic warfare of the First World War. This did not happen over night. The blockade of Germany, one of Norway's two main trading partners, continued for another year, and trade with Russia, although less important, was stopped when the western powers declared a blockade during that country's civil war. But Germany regained her position as an exporter to Norway remarkably quickly, although she continued to lag behind Britain as a market for Norwegian exports. Towards the Soviet Union Norway was quick to follow the British lead in concluding a trade agreement in 1921, thus reopening that market for Norwegian fish products. A normalisation of relations with the Soviet Union was also desired in order to get that country's government formally to acknowledge Norwegian sovereignty over Svalbard. But here again Norway found it advisable to await Britain's *de jure* recognition, which came about in 1924.

For Norwegian fish exports, however, the catholic countries of western and southern Europe were very important customers. Spain and Portugal in particular had before the war bought two thirds of the export of salted and dried cod. But in 1917 Norway had for public health reasons instituted a temporary prohibition on the importation and sale of alcoholic beverages with more than twelve per cent alcohol, and in 1918 a referendum made that prohibition permanent. Both the government and Storting seem naively to have assumed that what came to be called "the wine countries" would still continue to buy Norwegian fish. They were in for a rude awakening: the French protested, and Portugal and Spain decided to impose maximal customs tariffs on salted and dried cod of Norwegian origin. With France, whose main wine exports to Norway were not hit by the prohibition, the problem was solved in 1921 by Norway having to accept a large import quota of cognac and fortified wines. A year later Norway had to concede similarly large quotas of sherry and comparable wines for Spain. Then, as Portugal held out for even greater concessions, Norway caved in and cancelled the prohibition against fortified wines entirely.

In spite of the time and effort given by the government, the Storting, and the foreign service to the maintenance of fisheries and fish exports, the role of fish and fish products in the export trade was decreasing through the inter-war period. Together with whale oil, with which fish was combined in the export statistics, and which was also on the decrease as resources were depleted through uncontrolled exploitation, their share was reduced from about fourteen to just under ten per cent. Another traditional export, that of timber and pulp and paper products, was also declining. Instead, mining and chemical products, mostly in raw or semi-processed form, had by 1935 become the most important export commodity group.

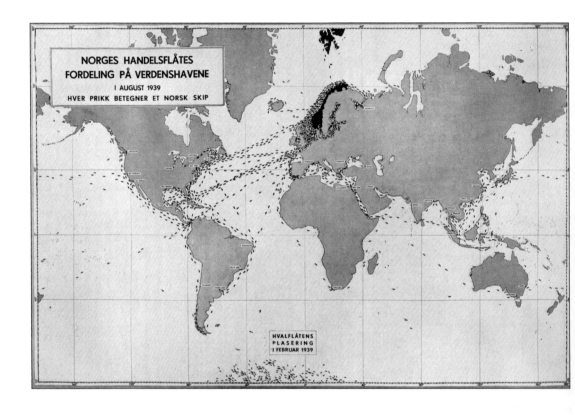

NORGES HANDELSFLÅTES
FORDELING PÅ VERDENSHAVENE
I AUGUST 1939
HVER PRIKK BETEGNER ET NORSK SKIP

HVALFLÅTENS
PLASERING
I FEBRUAR 1939

This map drawing appeared in a publication just before the war from the Norwegian Shipowners' Association. Aiming to impress on the Norwegian public the importance of the merchant navy, the map purports to show the worldwide distribution of the merchant fleet in August 1939. Each dot is supposed to mark one ship.

The one factor that kept Norway's balance of payments from being in permanent huge deficit was, in the inter-war period even more than before, the earnings of the merchant navy. Having been slow in converting from sail to steam before the First World War, and after losing nearly 800 ships during the war, Norwegian shipping made a remarkable recovery. While the total number of ships increased only slightly, the total tonnage nearly doubled from 1920 to 1939, to 4,4 million gross tons – seven per cent of the total world tonnage. This made the Norwegian merchant navy the fourth largest in the world, surpassed only by Britain, the United States, and Japan. It was also the most modern, since the growth was not based on the purchase of older ships but on new and purpose-built ships. About two thirds of the vessels were motor ships, not steamships. A third notable feature was the high proportion of large and modern tankers. And whereas half the world's tanker tonnage was tied to the large oil companies, the Norwegian tanker fleet, which accounted for over 18 per cent, was owned by independent shipowners.

Evidently, Norway's own foreign trade was unable to provide employment for more than a fraction of her merchant navy. Hence most of the ships traded between foreign ports, which meant valuable foreign currency earnings. The merchant navy thus represented between 30 and 40 per cent of the nation's export earnings. The growth and importance of the merchant navy, not just as a foreign currency earner, but also as a source of employment during the crisis years of the 1930s, was not due to government policy, but to the foresight and enterprise of Norwegian shipowners.

A New Internationalism?

As noted earlier, neutrality – with more than a tinge of isolationism – seemed firmly established as the basis of Norway's declared foreign policy course as the war ended. This was soon to be challenged, however, as the victorious powers at the Versailles peace conference decided to establish an international organisation for peace and security called the League of Nations. Initial reaction in Norway to the plan was markedly positive. It was seen as creating a forum where the world community of civilised states would work to eliminate war and promote international law as the basis for solving conflicts between nations. The Scandinavian states also in a joint note to the French government expressed the hope that the widest possible number of states would be invited to take part in drawing up the framework for the new organisation.

None of the Scandinavian countries was, however, invited to take part in that process. Only in the final stage were they, together with the other neutral European states, on short notice invited to present their views. In a joint statement they presented the vision of a world where relations between states were to the greatest possible extent governed by the rule of law. They also wanted a greater say for the smaller states in the League. In a special statement the Norwegian representative advocated an international arbitration regime in which all previously declared limits on the jurisdiction of the arbitration courts were to be abolished. Although politely received, none of those suggested amendments were allowed to disturb the framework as already decided by the victorious powers.

Somewhat more problematic than the place accorded to international law in the new organisation, was the implication of the draft charter – or Covenant, as the biblically inspired American President had chosen to call it – that membership of the League would be incompatible with neutrality. The burden of economic and military sanctions, to be imposed by the League against states starting wars of aggression, was in principle to be shared among the member states, and it would obviously be unfair to allow some states simply to opt out of such an obligation. In practice, however, it was assumed that the burden of participating in military action against an aggressor would be carried by the great powers. The smaller powers might, on request and after consultation, have to grant free passage to forces engaged in such action, and would be obliged to take part in a blockade or other economic sanctions imposed by the League. But seen from Norway's corner of Europe the danger of such involvement seemed fairly remote.

In the end, when Norway's accession to the League of Nations came up for official approval in 1920, a unanimous government and a massive majority of the Storting were in favour. The Labour Party voted against, mainly because the new organisation neither outlawed war nor demanded complete disarmament, but also because their ideological kinsmen, the Soviet Union, and the new Germany with its socialist government, were excluded. The wish for the widest possible membership of the League was shared by all in Norway. But it was widely assumed that Britain and the United States, which also advocated such a "universalist" stance, would in due course prevail over France's opposition against admitting Germany to the League. More importantly, those in favour of Norway's membership, while regretting the shortcomings of the League of Nations as regards the role accorded to international law and to the minor powers, still saw it as a major step towards a better organised international society where the ideals of democracy and the rule of law would gradually replace power politics and wars. In the meantime Norway's membership would ensure that Norway remained linked with Great Britain, the principal power in the League, and also the power whose parliamentary democracy the Norwegians admired and on whose naval strength Norway was dependent for her security and economic well-being.

The structure of the League of Nations represented in many ways a compromise between the traditional dominance of the great powers in international politics and the growing influence of minor powers. The strengthened status of neutrality during the half-century preceding the First World War, as reflected in the active participation of the smaller states in the Hague Peace Conferences of 1899 and 1907, and the Wilsonian ideal of national self-determination, had laid the groundwork for a more democratic structure. The League was hence composed in the first instance of an Assembly in which each member nation would participate on a basis of equality. Then there was the Council, where the great powers would be permanent members, but where at least four other states elected on rotation by the Assembly would also sit. Except for purely procedural matters, all decisions by the League had to be unanimous.

The League thus gave the minor powers an unprecedented opening for their voices to be heard on matters of international politics. Like many others, Norway did not hesitate to make use of that opportunity. Based on what has been called a "small-state philosophy", which saw the minor powers as guardians of higher moral standards in the conduct of international affairs, Norway's representatives in the League organs became strident advocates of the role of international law in solving disputes between nations. "Right instead of might" was the watchword. The reign of what Foreign Minister Løvland in 1905 had referred to as "the European warrior states" should give way to an international order in which conflicts would be

130

resolved in an orderly and peaceful manner, like in the democratic states of western civilisation. As a "satisfied" *status quo* state, with no traditional or natural enemies in its neighbourhood, and no explosive internal cleavages that might threaten its integrity and cohesion, Norway's spokesmen in the Assembly seemed to suggest that all would be well "if only the others were like us".[9] As J.L. Mowinckel, one of the towering figures in the small circle of the Norwegian foreign policy establishment, said in reporting back to the Storting from an Assembly session,

> no one can suspect us of having any selfish or special aims or interests. It is known that we for our part speak from a quite objective love of peace, and from a belief that there is among the peoples a growing feeling of what is right.[10]

Christian L. Lange, another prominent Norwegian internationalist, who combined his position as delegate to the League with his work as Secretary General of the Inter-Parliamentary Union, saw Norway's secure geographical position as a natural basis for an active and positive peace policy: the only kind of conflict in which Norway was likely to be involved would be of an economic or legal nature, eminently suited for solutions based on international law. Without much regard or understanding of the situations of countries less fortunately placed or with greater international responsibilities, Norway, as well as the other Scandinavian states, hence persisted in lecturing the others about their obligation to solve their disputes by peaceful, legal, means. As part of that campaign, one of the first causes championed by Norway was that of establishing a firm basis for the International Court of Justice, and widening its jurisdiction. When the great powers persisted in their reluctance to submit their disputes to the Court, Christian Lange used the forum of the League to appeal to the peoples of the great powers over the heads of their reluctant leaders. For disputes outside the Court's jurisdiction Norway advocated the widest possible use of mediation and arbitration.

But what about disputes that could not be solved by legal or other peaceful means? It was perfectly clear that the League Covenant required Norway to participate in economic sanctions against any state declared to be an aggressor, and even to grant passage for troops taking part in military sanctions on behalf of the League of Nations. This was a cause for concern in view of Norway's geographic closeness to the two "pariah" great powers Germany and the Soviet Union. Would this not in fact make Norway a member of a western alliance against those two powers? When Norway nevertheless joined the League, it was with the clear understanding that it would not be long before Germany, and in due course also the Soviet Union, would be invited to join. Then the League would have taken a major step towards Norway's cherished ideal of universality of membership, and

131

would lose its character as an alliance of the victors directed against the losers in the War. Moreover, each widening of the membership would make it all the more difficult for a country like Norway to "stick out like a sore thumb" by refusing to join the club.

On the whole, most Norwegians probably shared the widespread assumption at the time that the horrible experience of the First World War, and the apparent determination of the great powers to make the League of Nations a real instrument for peace, meant that the sanctions paragraphs of the Covenant would serve as an effective deterrent against any major war. The actual use of sanctions, and Norway's involvement in them, seemed a fairly remote prospect.

The international situation through the 1920s seemed to confirm the wisdom of those assumptions. An important milestone was The Locarno Treaties of 1925, which guaranteed the frontiers of Belgium and France against German attack and cleared the path to Germany's membership of the League. In the words of one of the most distinguished historians of this period of European history:

The Locarno agreements gave new hope that the League of Nations might assume the role which Wilson had expected of it and that, in spite of the bitterness of the post-war years, a new international order in Europe might be attainable.[11]

The years 1924–1925 also brought an important improvement in Norway's relations with the Soviet Union. In February 1924 Norway officially recognised the government of the Union of Soviet Socialist Republics as the legal authority of the Union, at the same time as the Soviet Union officially recognised Norway's sovereignty over Svalbard and became a signatory to the 1920 Svalbard Treaty. In December 1925 a detailed trade and shipping agreement could then be concluded. Together with extended arbitration treaties with Sweden, in 1925, with Denmark, in 1926, and with Finland, in 1927, Norway's relations with her neighbours now appeared well established. Another sign that Norway regarded her security situation as threat-free was the abrogation, in 1924, of the 1907 Integrity Treaty with the great powers. Among the other motives behind Norway's initiative in that respect were feelings that the treaty was "an unfortunate and perhaps dangerous hangover from the era of great power rivalries" as well as "incompatible with Norway's dignity as an independent state".[12]

Seeing no threat to her national security, the Norwegian foreign policy leadership does not seem to have considered the possible effects of the abrogation of the Integrity Treaty on the British-Norwegian security relationship. The assumption that Norway would remain protected by British naval power had always been unspoken. It had now also become unquestioned.

132

In 1926 the Liberal Mowinckel government proposed far-reaching cuts of the country's already modest military and naval forces. When the Admiralty Staff tried to convince the government that Norway might still be exposed to an attack from the sea, on account of the strategic importance of certain areas, Mowinckel commented that only Great Britain had the capability for such attacks. And since Britain in her own interest would see to it that no other power gained a foothold on the Norwegian coast, all that mattered was for Norway to maintain good relations with Britain. The clear implication was that the country's armed forces had no significant role to play.

The "new internationalism", which in the years between the two world wars came to supplement – but not dispel – Norway's "classic neutralism", was sufficiently different from Løvland's 1905 recipe to deserve being nominated as marking a second formative period in the evolution of Norway's foreign policy doctrine. Although its ideological basis was inherited from Norwegians' advocacy, in the closing decades of the Swedish-Norwegian union, of international law as the principal instrument for solving disputes among nations, the self-confident activism of Norway's official spokesmen as they propagated such views in the League of Nations and other suitable forums was new. It is hardly too far-fetched to see here another resemblance to the ideal also presented by George Washington in his "Farewell Address", seeing it as "worthy of a free, enlightened [...] nation to give to mankind the magnanimous and too novel example of a people always guided by an exalted justice and benevolence." Yet this "new internationalism" was of a purely verbal nature: speeches and declarations in favour of a greater role for international law, or advocating international disarmament, were cost-free for a state which itself was not a party to disputes over territorial claims, and which saw no external threats requiring the maintenance of significant military strength. In such circumstances there seemed to be nothing to prevent the slow drift back into neutralism and isolationism.

Carl Joachim Hambro came from a career as a journalist to become a leading figure in Norwegian politics and especially in foreign affairs. A member of the Storting from the Conservative Party 'Høyre', he became chairman of the Committee on Foreign Affairs in 1925, President of the Storting and Norwegian delegate to the League of Nations in 1926, and President of the League Assembly in 1939. He was a man of strong opinions and expressed them freely. His advocacy of the cause of small states and criticism of the behaviour of great powers made him very unpopular in British government circles right from the years of the First World War, when he lambasted Britain's blockade measures against Norway as well as the policy towards Ireland.

The 1930s: The Clouds darken

In spite of the recurring turbulence in internal politics, causing social and labour unrest, the long-term trend in the Norwegian economy during the inter-war period was one of growth. Although Norway could no more than

133

other countries escape the effects of the world economic crisis from 1929, their impact in terms of the Gross National Product was fairly short-lived. After the bad year of 1931, the economy by 1934 was back to its pre-crisis level except for a continuing high rate of unemployment. Worst hit was the agricultural sector, and in 1935 that provided the basis for the so-called "crisis deal" between the Labour Party and the Farmers' Party for state intervention *inter alia* to stabilise food prices. The Labour Party which now came to power had shed its revolutionary garb in favour of a pragmatic, reformist programme, and had gained 40 per cent of the votes in the 1933 general election.

In foreign and security policy the big question was whether Labour would persist in its anti-military stance. Seeing the armed forces – not entirely without reason – as a handy instrument for the ruling classes in their defence against socialism, Labour advocated international disarmament, and wished to set an example for the world by reducing the armed forces to a kind of neutrality guard. The Labour Party had few illusions about the potential danger to European peace and security presented by Hitler's coming to power in Germany in 1933. But their answer was to call for the widest possible international solidarity, the Soviet Union included, against fascism wherever it appeared.

By the time the Labour government took over, the League of Nations system had already suffered its first defeat as an instrument for the deterrence or punishment of aggression. The Japanese invasion and conquest of Manchuria in 1931–2 was a special case in many ways, in that a great power member of the League had gone to war against another member. Norway at that time represented the Scandinavian states in the League Council, and the Scandinavians naturally condemned the Japanese aggression and called on the League to demand an immediate cease-fire. Norway also proposed that sanctions should be applied against whichever party refused to comply with the call for a cease-fire. The only member of the League with a capability to act forcefully in that part of the world was Great Britain. But as she could not act alone, and since the United States limited itself to a diplomatic protest, the final outcome was a moral condemnation of the Japanese aggression. The official Norwegian reaction to this demonstration of the League's weakness showed a certain understanding of the realities of power politics behind the inability of the great powers to act. Over time, however, it could not but reinforce Norway's traditional distrust of great power politics.

The Labour government, with the decidedly un-revolutionary Johan Nygaardsvold as Prime Minister, took over on 20 March 1935. By than it was clear that another international crisis, this time nearer to Europe, was brewing. Mussolini's Italy was about to realise her long-standing plan to conquer Ethiopia, having secured what amounted to a green light from the French government. On 17 March Haile Selassie's government had appealed to the League for action. After interminable debates and attempts to mediate between the parties, tempered by the desire of Britain and France to keep Italy as a partner in an anti-German front, Italy launched her attack on Ethiopia on 3 October. Four days later the League unanimously condemned Italy's aggression. With a 50-4 majority the League Assembly subsequently confirmed the imposition of limited economic sanctions – Italy's oil imports being the most notable exception. In Norway the question now was whether the government would uphold Labour's traditional anti-League stance, manifested as recently as the year before in a proposal that Norway should withdraw from membership. However, the strong-willed new Foreign Minister, the internationally renowned historian Halvdan Koht, had throughout dissented from the party line on the issue. In a speech to the Assembly he now declared Norway's active support for sanctions, and her readiness to suffer the economic consequences. But he warned that "if the League of Nations should prove unable both to prevent the war and to restore peace, then this would force us to consider in what kind of position the League would then find itself – we would have to ask ourselves what future it could then have."[13]

Before the end of 1935 that situation had already arisen. Italy pursued her successful military campaign in Ethiopia, and Britain was not prepared to proceed to military sanctions on her own. As Foreign Secretary Sir Samuel Hoare declared to the House of Commons:

We alone have taken these military precautions. There is the British fleet in the Mediterranean, there are British reinforcements in Egypt, in Malta and Aden. Not a ship, not a machine, not a man has been moved by any other member State.[14]

Halvdan Koht early became active in politics and the peace movement while pursuing a distinguished career as a historian. He became Foreign Minister when Johan Nygaardsvold formed his minority Labour government in 1935, and for five years attempted to put into practice his aspirations about the smaller states of Europe playing a mediating role in the burgeoning conflicts among the great powers. During the fateful months in the spring and summer of 1940 he was a tower of strength for the King and the government, firmly opposing any compromise with the Germans. But his leading position in the government marked him as a scapegoat for the failure to prepare for a German invasion, and being identified with Norway's policy of neutrality, he had to go when relations with the British ally had to be placed on a new footing from the autumn of 1940.

With France unwilling to proceed with sanctions, the French and the British then put together the notorious Hoare-Laval plan which rewarded Italy with about two-thirds of the territory of Ethiopia, and left her to conquer the rest. By May 1936 it was all over, and the League could cancel its sanctions.

The obvious conclusion from the Ethiopian affair, drawn by a vast majority in Norway, was that the League of Nations had suffered a massive and possibly fatal defeat as an instrument of collective security. Many drew a

135

second conclusion, to the effect that Norway's obligations under the sanctions paragraphs of the League Covenant were now positively dangerous, as they risked involving Norway in a war between the great powers. This re-awakening of the isolationist impulse set the stage for a development which through the next two years gradually was to bring the country to within an inch of its traditional neutralist stance. This development had wide support right across the political spectrum. Nor was the flight from sanctions limited to Norway: a joint declaration from the seven small Northern European states in the so-called "Oslo" group – the four Nordic states plus the three Benelux countries – in July 1936 declared that they no longer would consider themselves bound by the obligations of Article 16 of the Covenant of the League.

A small group, led by intellectuals within the Labour Party, drew different conclusions from the international events. Having observed the ominous trends in Hitler's policy in Germany, beginning with Germany's withdrawal from the League in 1933 and soon followed by decisive moves towards German rearmament, they feared that Europe was drifting towards a war between the western great powers and the fascist states. In such a war Norway might also become involved. Norway ought therefore to work to strengthen the League system, together with Great Britain, and possibly also the Soviet Union which had joined the League of Nations in 1934. Foreign Minister Koht sympathised with parts of that programme, in that he resisted moves towards an early and definitive breach of Norway's obligations towards the League system. But he shared much of the cynical majority view that the policies of the great powers were dictated by their own national power interests, with little regard for the interests of small states. Moreover, after touring the capitals of Eastern Europe, including Moscow, at Easter time 1936, he drew the depressing conclusion that even the smaller states were coming to the belief that only an armed encirclement could deter Nazi Germany from aggression against her neighbours. This, he told the Storting, was nothing but a return to the old power politics.

Koht's alternative – his "active peace policy" – was a combination of general disarmament and a revival of the League system as a forum for consultations and an instrument for conciliation and mediation. Sanctions were useless as long as the great powers were unwilling to apply them to the full, and also dangerous, since economic sanctions could lead to military sanctions, which would be the old-fashioned power politics under a new name. Koht was hence a strong supporter of the policy that led Norway and the other "Oslo states" to make participation in sanctions entirely voluntary. Still he resisted a formal return to Norwegian neutrality, since this would be incompatible with membership of the League. Koht has later claimed that membership of the League meant being on the side of the "good guys" – the western powers and the Soviet Union, against the "bad guys" – the fascist powers that had by now left the League. But it is clear that his purpose in retaining membership was to have a forum for promoting his "active peace policy". This became apparent in the League deliberations during the Spanish Civil War in 1937. Apart from active participation in the policy of non-intervention, he made determined efforts to get the League Council to demand a cease-fire, to be followed by a supervised referendum where the Spanish people could state what form of government they wanted. When those efforts failed, and as substantial Norwegian trade and shipping interests in Spain were suffering, Norway in the summer of 1938 made a deal with Franco-Spain. Although the government strenuously denied it, this in fact amounted to a recognition of Spain's fascist regime.

The purely nominal character of Norway's membership of the League was made clear when the Storting on 31 May 1938 unanimously approved a resolution whereby the country declared "its right to observe a complete and unconditional neutrality in any war which it does not itself approve as an action of the League of Nations". If Norway's "new internationalism" initially had seemed to open the door for a more active engagement in international politics, that door was now closed, however softly. While Norway's delegates to the League would continue their verbal appeals to the great powers to act to settle international disputes by peaceful means, Norway herself had by the middle of 1938 completed her return to neutralism. What remained to be seen was whether threats of war nearer to home, in the shape of an increasingly aggressive Nazi Germany, would change the course of Norwegian security policy.

7. War Comes to Norway

Introduction

Norway's retreat from the League system, and her return to isolationism, was primarily motivated by a fear of getting involved in other peoples' wars. This was coupled with a belief, echoing that which had been so eloquently expressed by George Washington in his Farewell Address to the American nation in 1796, that the country's "detached and distant situation" enabled Norway to avoid such involvement. Although never expressed in public, the attitude strongly resembled George Washington's rhetorical question to his people: "Why, by interweaving our destiny with that of any part of Europe, entangle our peace and prosperity in the toils of European ambition, rivalship, humor, or caprice?" To most Norwegians, Europe was foreign territory, and the rise of the fascist powers in Italy, Germany and Spain, and the failure of the western great powers to stop them, meant that Europe was sinking into barbarism.

But what if Norway should herself be attacked, either because of the strategic value of her territory and coastline or because of the economic value of her natural resources? The consensus was that this was an unlikely eventuality. The experience of the First World War suggested that while Norwegian trade and shipping might be severely affected in a war between Germany and Great Britain, it would still be possible for Norway to steer some kind of neutral course between the belligerents' conflicting demands. There was more dispute about the need for armed forces to defend against violations of neutrality, minor encroachments, or other incidents that could start a vicious circle – the "war by accident" syndrome. We have seen that the Labour Party by 1935 had begun to move away from its total anti-military stance, albeit slowly. This was mainly due to its effort to achieve and retain credibility as a party of government, although, as we have noted, a minority of party intellectuals and foreign policy oriented persons favoured maintaining a certain measure of armed force as a "neutrality guard". The Labour party group in the Storting still looked askance at the military. Their suspicions that the armed forces were partly geared towards intervention against unrest among the workers were confirmed when the Defence Minister from their own party in 1936 discovered the General Staff's plans for mobilisation against internal social or political unrest.

Norwegian Reactions to Munich

The Nygaardsvold government, and Foreign Minister Koht in particular, were clearly concerned by the increasingly aggressive stance of the fascist powers from 1936 onwards. Their recipe for breaking the trend towards a major European conflict, however, remained the same as before: general disarmament, no forming of blocs or opposing alliances, and conference diplomacy for a peaceful settlement of disputes with due regard to international law. In the summer of 1938 Koht introduced a new element in his "active peace policy", in the form of a proposal for mediation by the smaller powers. As the other "Oslo states" were dubious about its prospects, it came to nothing. Then, as the crisis over Czechoslovakia came to a head in September, Koht proposed a Nordic initiative, with reference to Article 11 of the Covenant which gave the League a right to take steps to assure the peace. But the other Nordic states feared this might eventually lead to proposals for sanctions, which would put the "Oslo states" on the spot. The initiative was finally watered down to a resolution expressing a "sincere hope" that none of the parties would resort to force. It is difficult to avoid the impression that these initiatives were as much meant for home consumption as intended to influence the course of events.

The German occupation of the Sudeten parts of Czechoslovakia, on 1 October, did nothing to dispel fears of Hitler-Germany's expansionist plans. But the solution of the crisis, whereby four great powers, including Great Britain, had here connived at the partial dismemberment of a small and highly respected League member, met with a distinctly mixed reaction in Norway. On one side stood Carl Joachim Hambro, President of the Storting and chairman of its committee for foreign affairs. Arising from his well-known attitude of championing the cause of the small states, while condemning great power policies, he took this occasion to fire a broadside against Neville Chamberlain in particular for condoning "an act of violence without parallel in human history".[1] He did not, however, draw the logical conclusion, since that would have meant encouraging the powers to take up arms and start a European war. The majority attitude in Norway, on the other hand, was one of relief that war had been avoided, and one in which sympathy for Czechoslovakia was tempered by sanguine hopes that that country would now be safe within its new borders. Many proposed that Chamberlain should be awarded the Nobel Peace Prize, a suggestion that triggered new outbursts from Hambro, this time against the "moral cowardice which tied their [the small powers'] tongue when the great powers violated right and fairness, treaties and promises".

Inevitably, the euphoria of "peace in our time" would in due course fade behind the realisation that "appeasement" did nothing to stem Nazi–Germany's push for greater "Lebensraum". Koht himself was ambivalent about the Munich deal. His relief that a major war had been avoided was clouded by a realistic fear that it had been just a matter of buying time. And when Hitler in March 1939 occupied the rest of Czechoslovakia, he seems to have come to the conclusion that a European war was coming, and was not far away. Attention then turned inevitably to the question of Norway's national security.

National Defence and the British "Guarantee"

In 1937, 1938, and especially 1939, the Labour government had agreed to fairly substantial extraordinary budget allocations for defence. This was a response to increasingly dire warnings from the military authorities about the miserable state of the country's armed forces. The Commander-in-Chief of the Army in the autumn of 1937 had described the army as without comparison the worst trained and most poorly equipped in the whole of Europe. The Admiralty Staff painted a similar picture as regards the navy, and emphasised the consequent danger that Norway might be unable to prevent acts of war within her maritime territory, whether in the form of one party's warships attacking its enemy's ships, or if Germany should seek to obtain naval bases on the Norwegian coast. But the only political party which showed some enthusiasm for the demands of the military was the Conservative "Høyre" Party. The other major opposition party, the Liberals, or "Venstre", supported the government's line. With former Prime Minister J.L. Mowinckel as their principal spokesman on foreign affairs, the Liberals did not share Labour's ideological aversion to the military. Instead, they put their faith in the traditional protection which British naval superiority in the North Sea provided against incursions from any other power such as Germany. As late as in May 1939, at a secret session of the Storting, Mowinckel claimed that with its much weaker navy now than in the First World War, Germany could not hope to maintain an air or naval base on the Norwegian coast against British naval power. In this view he was supported by no less an authority than the Commander-in-Chief of the Navy, Admiral Henry Diesen. In a newspaper interview earlier that year he said that anyone wishing to seize a point on the coast had to be master of the seas, and if he was then he had no need to do so. That danger was therefore "highly exaggerated".

Such faith in the British navy was clearly the kind of sentiment that, if publicly expressed by the government, would jeopardise Norway's neutral stance towards the prospective belligerents. Koht therefore was careful not to give either of them any grounds to suspect that Norway was leaning

140

The minelayer *Olav Tryggvason* was the only major new ship acquired by the superannuated Norwegian navy in the 1930s. She was briefly the focus of attention when Foreign Minister Koht wished to send her to protect Norwegian merchant vessels during the Spanish Civil War – a proposal which had to be withdrawn due to opposition in the Storting.

towards the other side. When Hitler at the end of April 1939 offered to conclude non-aggression treaties with the Scandinavian states, Norway, unlike Denmark, firmly rejected the proposal. At the same time Koht put off a planned visit to London, fearing that it would be seen as a move towards establishing a special relationship with Great Britain. There can be no doubt that Koht regarded Germany as the main threat to peace, and that, if Norway should be forced into the war, then she would have to come in on the side of Britain. But the bottom line for Koht seems to have been that he was reasonably confident that Norway would be able to preserve her neutrality. In a conversation with British envoy Sir Cecil Dormer on 26 April 1939, Dormer asked Koht how he envisaged an eventual German threat to Norway. Koht intimated that it would not come as an assault without warning, but rather in the shape of an ultimatum, threatening an attack from the air if Norway refused to yield to a German demand for a base on the coast. To a further question about what Norway would reply to that, Koht refused to be drawn, but said that the answer was perfectly clear in his head. It is safe to assume that the answer would have been to reject the ultimatum and call for help from Great Britain. But this was all rather hypothetical in the light of Koht's final remark, to the effect that he thought military developments had made it unnecessary for belligerents to secure bases in Norway.[2]

The belief that Germany had neither the intention nor the ability to challenge British naval supremacy in the North Sea by seizing bases in Norway was apparently held also in Britain. It was not until the British Legation in Oslo, from autumn 1938 onwards, began to send reports suggesting Norwegian doubts on that score, that the British began to take a closer interest in Norway's situation. Sir Laurence Collier, head of the Northern Department in the Foreign Office, noted in March 1939 that such Norwegian doubts, while disturbing, were groundless:

> The assumption of the "defeatists" – that this country would not defend Norway against Germany – is of course wrong; and a glance at the map ought to show them that we could never allow so vital a strategic position for attack on Great Britain to fall into German hands without a fight.[3]

Through the summer of 1939, as the Foreign Office began to fear that Norwegian lack of confidence in British protection might start Norway's slide down the slippery slope towards subservience to Germany, discussion turned to the question of offering some reassurance. In the middle of September, after war had broken out, Dormer did assure Koht in confidence that Britain would regard a German attack on Norway as an attack on herself. But while Germany immediately responded to Norway's 4 September declaration of neutrality with an assurance of respect, the British government took this opportunity to present a draft trade agreement that Koht saw as a first move towards involving Norway in economic warfare against Germany. The linkage between an assurance of British protection and demands for Norwegian cooperation in economic warfare, we now know, was also present in the discussions in London that preceded Dormer's declaration. And here lies the key to Koht's over-riding concern during the seven months after the outbreak of the European war: he did not fear that Germany in and of itself would need or wish to involve Norway in the war. But if Great Britain should force Norway into concessions that seriously damaged Germany's interests, then Germany might retaliate and thus release a vicious circle with Norway as the victim.

The Noose is Tightened

On the face of it, events during the autumn and winter 1939–1940 served to strengthen Koht's perception. In discussions about large-scale British chartering of Norwegian ships, which the Norwegian government again as in 1917 left to the Norwegian shipowners, but still monitored closely, the British according to Koht twice uttered veiled threats about a coal stoppage. Various British blockade measures also caused annoyance, as did British foot-dragging over the war trade agreement which Norway demanded in return for the shipping agreement. The outbreak of the Winter War between the Soviet Union and Finland on 30 November for a time diverted the attention of the Norwegian government towards possible threats of a spill-over effect on northern Norway. A report from the Legation in Berlin referred to allegations coming from senior officials in the German foreign ministry, to the effect that ice-free ports in Finnmark were next on the list as soon as the Russians had secured their gains in Finland. Norway consequently strengthened her defensive preparations in the north. The Liberal Party's foreign policy spokesman, J.L. Mowinckel, speaking at a secret session of the committee for foreign affairs, also suggested an approach to the British on the subject of the Soviet menace, since "while Britain unfortunately cannot assist Finland due to that country's geographical situation, we are thank God so situated that Britain very easily and quickly can help us." In his sharp rejection of that idea Koht again complained about the constant pressure from Britain's economic warfare:

> There can be no doubt that if we approached England about such a matter, then England would in her turn put forward demands that would go far beyond our neutrality, both political and military demands – an alliance in fact. It is possible that we may at some stage have to do that, but we must then be fully aware of the consequences that would follow. I will therefore for my part advise against any diplomatic move in relation to England before we might be in a situation where it becomes necessary.[4]

More was to come as the British and French governments around Christmas time began to consider military measures which, while seemingly intended to give help to the Finns, in fact would bring both Sweden and Norway into the war. The focus of allied attention was the presumed vital German need for Swedish iron ore for their munitions industry. The ore mines were in northern Sweden, and since the Gulf of Bothnia was ice-covered during the winter, most of the ore was transported by rail to Narvik on the Norwegian coast and shipped from there. Winston Churchill, who in September had joined Chamberlain's government as First Lord of the Admiralty, was proposing laying mines on the Norwegian coast in order to force Germany's maritime transport of Swedish iron ore from Narvik into the open sea. But this plan was gradually being overshadowed first by French schemes to send an allied expeditionary force to northern Finland – which would open a theatre of war well away from French territory – and then, at the end of December 1939, by a plan which appeared to combine aid to Finland with seizure of the supply route for iron ore. The idea was to persuade Norway and Sweden to grant passage for a force which would land at Narvik, proceed to the Kiruna ore mines, and then eventually to Finland.

While that plan was being worked out, the British government continued to press for new limitations of Norwegian exports to Germany. In the meantime, also, Norwegian neutrality was being challenged by the sinking of two British and one Greek merchant ships along the Norwegian coast. Investigations as to whether the sinkings had occurred inside or outside territorial waters, and whether caused by mines or torpedoes, took their time. But on 6 January 1940 a sharp British note to the Norwegian government

This modern and highly efficient loading pier at Narvik was the main export outlet for Swedish iron ore, which was brought there by train from the Kiruna mines. From a somewhat exaggerated estimate of the importance of Swedish iron ore to the German armaments industry, the western powers in the late autumn of 1939 accelerated their planning for the stoppage of that supply line.

claimed that since all three sinkings were in their view caused by torpedoes from German submarines, this meant that Germany had in fact brought the war into Norwegian maritime territory. Britain would therefore hold herself free to extend her own naval operations into those same waters. In an emphatic protest, the Norwegian government declared that any such action by the British navy would be a flagrant violation of international law. In a telegram to King George VI King Haakon urged him to use his influence to prevent such action. The British government, in a second memorandum, backed down from its harsh line, but returned to a line which Winston Churchill in a radio address shortly before had presaged: Britain was fighting for the cause of all free peoples against Nazi aggression, and could not allow the smaller neutral countries to tie her hands in the struggle against an enemy which far more ruthlessly violated neutral rights. At the same time the memorandum made it clear that the iron ore was the crux of the matter.

In Norway this incident once again brought to the fore the question of Britain's real intentions towards Norway. Before Christmas Koht had conceded that while the British demands would have the effect of forcing Norway out of her neutrality, he did not think Britain directly wished to involve Norway in the war. Now, at a secret session of the Storting on 8 January, Koht went one step further:

I must admit that I cannot rid myself of the suspicion that the British government in effect has set as its purpose to drive us into the war. They

144

keep saying that we can remain neutral, but demand at the same time that
we help the allies against Germany. That was the portent of the demand for
an embargo against Germany, and for military assistance against the Soviet
Union. But to use Norwegian territory for actual acts of war would more
than anything be a violation of our neutrality, and we must protest and
defend against this to the best of our ability.[5]

In retrospect it is not difficult to see how Koht could have come to that
conclusion. The distant coolness that characterised British-Norwegian relations at that time barred Koht from insight into a fundamental ambivalence in Britain's intentions towards Norway. Taken as a whole the
Chamberlain government, needing time, and believing time was on their
side, had no desire to accelerate Europe's descent into full-scale war. As a
global power Great Britain feared most of all a three-front war in which
Japan, Italy and Germany were all ranged against her. Driving Norway and
Scandinavia into the war would also dangerously alienate opinion in the
Dominions and the United States, whose support Britain would need.
Against that stood Winston Churchill, with his urgings to seize the initiative and not let small nations "tie our hands when we are fighting for their
rights and freedom", and Britain's French ally, pressuring for action that
would deflect Germany's attention away from the western front.

It is only in the light of this ambivalence that we can understand the drift
of Anglo-French decision-making during the remaining weeks before
9 April. On 5 February the French-British Supreme War Council agreed in
principle to a plan to send a large expeditionary force to Scandinavia. On
the assumption that Sweden and Norway would give their consent,
100-150 000 troops – almost none of whom had any experience of winter
warfare! – would be involved over a couple of months, starting in March.
The main force, disguised as "volunteers", would land at Narvik, proceeding
from there along the railway line to the ore mines and on to the Swedish
Baltic port of Luleå. Other forces would occupy ports in southern Norway
as a defensive move against German counter-moves, or be held in readiness
to defend Sweden. As the ostensible purpose was to help Finland, in response to an appeal from the Finnish government, Prime Minister Chamberlain
thought the Scandinavian governments might protest but would not oppose the operation. This must surely be ranked as one of the most hare-brai-
ned schemes of the Second World War. However, as the Finnish forces at the
end of February were nearing collapse, the Finnish government was leaning
towards opening negotiations with Russia rather than issuing an appeal for
western help which at best would come too late. Sweden and Norway still
showed no willingness to agree to the passage of troops, and the Norwegian
government bluntly declared that it did not wish to be dragged into the
European war and turn Norway into a battlefield for a great power strug-

gle. In an act of some desperation the British War Cabinet nevertheless on 12 March decided to send a small force to land at Narvik, "provided it could do so without serious fighting". It turned out to be too late: a few hours afterwards Finland signed an armistice with the Soviet Union.

But what about Germany?

Being under fairly constant pressure – or perhaps rather bullying – from Great Britain, and having at least from November onwards to face the additional threat that Soviet expansion into Finland presented, the Norwegian government undoubtedly felt during that winter that the danger of becoming involved in war was increasing. On 9 January 1940 the Defence Minister gave a full statement to a secret session of the Storting about the state of the country's defence, fully admitting its many shortcomings. The army had put in place a modest preparedness in the shape of neutrality guard units in southern Norway. In northern Norway the Finnish–Russian war had resulted in the call-up of all army units in the area, and in moving north a large part of the mostly outdated ships that made up the Norwegian navy. Both the army and navy air forces had been more or less fully mobilised over the whole country, but the modern aircraft that would have made them into reasonably effective instruments of defence were not due to be delivered until late in the spring. The fairly massive extra funds for the military – three times the regular defence budget – had only been allotted for the budget year 1939–1940, and new aircraft had for the most part to be imported from factories whose order books were already full.

With attention being focused on Britain's various demands, as well as fears of a spill-over effect from the Winter War, it is hardly surprising that any possible German threat to Norway was absent from the discussion, except in the shape of likely reprisals if pressure from the western powers should force Norway into concessions that seriously affected vital German interests. The consensus of opinion in many ways paralleled the situation in the First World War: Norway's best hope of avoiding war was to maintain at least the volume of trade with Germany that corresponded with Germany's expressed minimum requirements, and resist British demands that openly and clearly conflicted with the status of neutrality. Isolated military voices had from 1937 onwards expressed fears that Germany's growing air strength presented a serious challenge to the presumed British control of the North Sea, and that this made possible a scenario in which Germany could threaten Norway from the air, or even be in a position to seize a naval and air base in south-western Norway. But the latter possibility was generally discounted as a purely temporary occurrence, quickly neutralised by British counter-moves.

However, while British blockade measures were openly reported and discussed, and rumours flourished about allied plans for action in Scandinavia on account of the Winter War, nothing of any substance leaked out from Berlin about German planning. A theory, according to which the German navy would need to establish itself on the Norwegian coast in order to be able to operate effectively against Britain's navy and maritime trade, had been propagated by the German naval officer Wolfgang Wegener in a book published in 1929. But no one in Norway, or for that matter in Britain, was aware that the head of the German navy, *Grossadmiral* Erich Raeder, from early autumn 1939 was trying to foist that idea on Hitler. In December Raeder got unexpected assistance for his effort in the person of Vidkun Quisling, leader of the Norwegian Nazi Party *Nasjonal Samling* and Defence Minister in the Farmers' Party government 1931–33. Quisling's pro-German leanings and activities were of course well-known in Norway, but his clumsiness as a politician as well as his party's lack of success in the elections made it hard to take him quite seriously. But Raeder, and then Hitler, concluded after meetings with him in Berlin in mid-December that he might be useful to them. Quisling's claim that there existed secret arrangements for an eventual British occupation of Norway was the perfect lead-in for Raeder to warn Hitler about the dire consequences to Germany if Britain should get control of the Norwegian coast. In Quisling's mind this could best be prevented by Germany helping him and his party to stage a political *coup d'etat*. But Raeder, Hitler, and the German military were already thinking in terms of a forceful alternative. An initial staff study was transformed into operational planning at the end of January, code-named *Weserübung* – Exercise Weser.

General Staff archives everywhere are full of plans, or contingency plans, which never left the drawing boards. This might possibly also have become the fate of the Weser plan if it were not for two or three coincidental developments. First of all Hitler's main plan and interest, if not obsession, was still the massive lightning offensive across western Continental Europe that would result in the fall of France and, hopefully, a peace deal with Great Britain. That operation was during the winter repeatedly postponed, due to bad weather and other hindrances, which meant that Hitler was in need of some other daring and successful venture in order to prove to the German people his genius as a leader. Exercise Weser could fit that bill. Secondly, an incident in the war at sea occurred which brought Norway into full international focus – the Altmark affair. The 'Altmark' was a German naval auxiliary ship, on its way back to Germany from a naval action in the South Atlantic with a number of British sailors on board as prisoners. To escape from pursuing British naval vessels, the ship for the last leg of its voyage sought the shelter of Norwegian territorial waters, but on 16 February a British destroyer entered the fjord against protests from two torpedo boats of the Norwegian navy, boarded the German ship, and liberated the prisoners.

The *Altmark*, seen here in the Norwegian fjord where she was attacked by ships of the British navy and had to surrender her prisoners, was a German navy auxiliary ship. Although the Norwegian government's handling of her passage through Norwegian waters was flawed, the action by British destroyers was a flagrant violation of Norwegian neutrality. Hitler's fury, against the British action as well as against Norway for failing to prevent it, was probably a factor in his decision to accelerate planning for the invasion of Norway.

In the spate of protests and counter-protests from the three involved countries that followed, a number of intricate issues of international law were raised, about which it is enough to say that while none of the countries involved emerged blameless, Norway as the weaker part got the brunt of the fury. Hitler apparently was enraged both at the impertinence of the British action and the failure of the Norwegians to defend their neutrality. He now gave orders for the planning of Exercise Weser to be accelerated, and in the first week of March operational orders were drawn up for an occupation of Denmark and Norway. The motive was three-fold. In addition to Raeder's original argument about the need to improve the strategic position of the German navy and air force against Britain, two points of a more defensive nature were made. Germany had to forestall a British move to take control of the Norwegian coast, and also protect her supply of Swedish iron ore. The plan for Norway envisaged a simultaneous landing at eight of the principal cities and ports, from Oslo all the way to Narvik in the north, on the assumption that complete surprise and a show of overwhelming force would convince the Norwegians not to offer resistance.

Both rumours and hard intelligence had by then convinced the German leadership that Britain and France were preparing to act in Scandinavia. The Finnish-Soviet armistice of 12 March, however, brought those preparations to an end. As Hitler's chief of staff noted in his diary, that armistice had deprived Britain, and thereby also Germany, of the political basis for action in Scandinavia. But Exercise Weser remained on the agenda, and on 26 March Raeder, while admitting that the danger of a British landing in Norway was no longer acute, maintained that the basic picture had not changed.

148

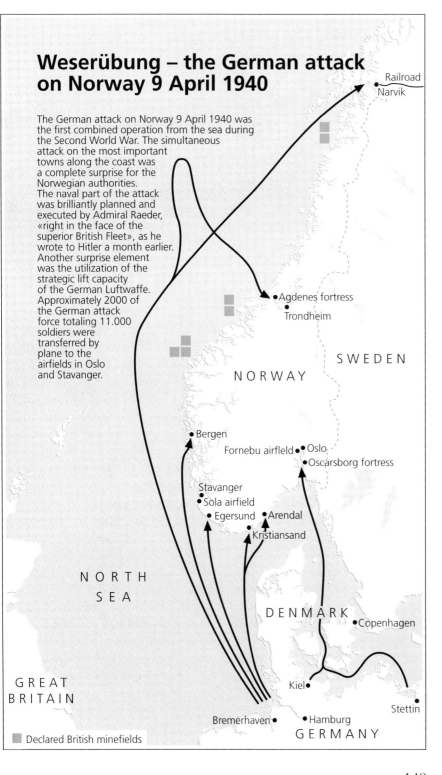

Weserübung – the German attack on Norway 9 April 1940

The German attack on Norway 9 April 1940 was the first combined operation from the sea during the Second World War. The simultaneous attack on the most important towns along the coast was a complete surprise for the Norwegian authorities. The naval part of the attack was brilliantly planned and executed by Admiral Raeder, «right in the face of the superior British Fleet», as he wrote to Hitler a month earlier. Another surprise element was the utilization of the strategic lift capacity of the German Luftwaffe. Approximately 2000 of the German attack force totaling 11.000 soldiers were transferred by plane to the airfields in Oslo and Stavanger.

Railroad
Narvik

Agdenes fortress
Trondheim

SWEDEN

NORWAY

Bergen

Fornebu airfleld Oslo
Oscarsborg fortress

Stavanger
Sola airfield
Egersund Arendal
Kristiansand

NORTH
SEA

DENMARK
Copenhagen

GREAT
BRITAIN

Kiel

Stettin

Bremerhaven Hamburg
GERMANY

Declared British minefields

The British were bound to continue seeking control of Norwegian coastal waters in order to hinder the German iron ore traffic from Narvik. "Sooner or later" Germany would therefore have to carry out their invasion, and since the forces were now being assembled, it should be sooner rather than later. Accordingly, on 2 April Hitler ordered the occupation of Denmark and Norway to begin on 9 April. Within hours the first supply ships left port, steaming for the most distant invasion targets in the far north.

The Onslaught

In the Norwegian capital the authorities, having no inkling of the German plans and preparations, were still mired in their conviction that only some further drastic western pressure or action could trigger violent German aggression against Norway. To stave off such an escalatory spiral the government on 2 February had secretly communicated to the British government its willingness to act on an earlier British proposal for mine-laying at certain points on the coast, as a preventive measure against German submarines' abuse of Norwegian maritime territory. Here again the experience of Norwegian neutrality in the First World War provided the pattern. But as nothing was actually done, and since France and Britain faced mounting pressure at home for some resolute initiative to break the passivity of their "phoney war", their Supreme War Council at the end of March took the fateful decision to proceed with their own mine-laying in Norwegian waters. Unaware of the German plans, they did not on balance expect that such a relatively modest move would provoke any major German retaliation. Some minor forces would nevertheless be held in readiness if it should become necessary to forestall German landings on the western coast of Norway.

In the night of 7–8 April the British navy accordingly laid two minefields on the coast, in flagrant violation of Norwegian neutrality. In a communication to the Norwegian government the action – foreshadowed in a diplomatic note three days earlier – was explained as intended to stop iron ore transports to Germany. In Oslo tension now rose to new heights, and the Storting spent most of the day of 8 April debating the terms of the Norwegian protest note to the western allies. The fear of German retaliatory aggression was strongly present, fed by rumours and unsubstantiated diplomatic reports during the previous couple of days about military and naval activities in German ports. But no "hard" intelligence was available which singled out Norway as a target, and no one seems to have considered that the German plans might have taken on a life of their own, independent of any western provocation. Germany had thus already by the first days of April achieved strategic surprise for Exercise Weser. It remained to be seen whether the German forces on the way to Norway would also achieve tac-

The state-of-the-art German cruiser *Blücher* had a crucial role in the German invasion, as she carried the key personnel for the assault on the Norwegian capital and the seizure of the government. The success of the fortress Oscarsborg in sinking her gave the King, the government and the Storting time to move to the interior of the country.

tical surprise – a seemingly essential requirement, since Raeder himself was fully aware of the risk of carrying out such an operation against the superior naval power of Great Britain. The British, however, were prey to prejudices of their own, and interpreted all the spotty intelligence reports of German naval movements, from the morning of 7 April onwards, as preparations for a break-out into the Atlantic. Not before the afternoon of 8 April did it occur to the British Admiralty that some of those forces were on their way to Narvik.[6]

In Oslo the government had hastily been assembled in the early hours of 9 April, on the first news that foreign warships were entering Norwegian waters. Some counter-measures were taken, including mobilisation of those parts of the army that could be readied at fairly short notice. Otherwise the Ministers seem to have relied on the navy and the coastal forts to take action in accordance with standing orders for neutrality defence. With the means at their disposal this proved quite inadequate, with one vital exception: the fortress Oscarsborg at the entrance to Oslo sank the cruiser "Blücher" which led the forces charged with seizing the capital, thus delaying the German assault sufficiently to allow the King, the government and the Storting time to escape into the interior of the country. The government had by then already firmly rejected the ultimatum presented at 4.30 in the morning by the German envoy. This meant war, but could the Norwegian armed forces mount any effective resistance? And could the British provide sufficient assistance? Doubts were clearly present on both scores, and by dawn on 10 April despair was beginning to take hold, both within the government and in the General Staff. But after a meeting that afternoon with the German envoy, during which the Germans foolishly put forward a demand from Hitler that Vidkun Quisling be asked to form a new government, King Haakon told his Ministers that he would abdicate rather than

THE IRON COMES BACK

The really good cartoons – like this one by the British cartoonist Low – have no need for explanatory text. But Low's text demonstrates the misconception that it was Norwegian iron ore that was exported to Germany.

appoint such a government. The government rallied round the King's decision to fight on, and replaced the vacillating Commanding General with General Otto Ruge, who favoured resistance even against all odds.

As far as foreign policy was concerned, the German assault left only one course open: to try to secure effective military assistance from Great Britain and other enemies of Germany. At first this was left to General Ruge. But the British forces sent to Norway proved quite inadequate to lend sufficient strength to Ruge's effort to stem the German advance in southern Norway. At sea, instead of trying to exert a stranglehold on the German forces by cutting their sea lines of communication in the Skagerrak and the southern North Sea, which would have meant exposing their warships to attacks from the strong German Luftwaffe, the Admiralty moved all British surface ships north to the Norwegian Sea. After four weeks, on 3 May, southern Norway had to be abandoned to the invader, while in northern Norway the Norwegian army, with assistance from British, French, and Polish troops, had managed to hold the lines of defence north of Narvik.

Koht, together with Defence Minister Birger Ljungberg, now went to London and Paris to appeal for more help, while the King and the government went north to the Tromsø area. The two ministers found no lack of promises from the western powers, but the Blitzkrieg German offensive on the Continent from 10 May inevitably meant that the campaign in Norway slipped further down the scale of allied priorities. The allied effort in northern Norway was also hamstrung by a mutual lack of trust at the level of command, and by their unfamiliarity with the terrain and the climate. The re-conquest of Narvik, on 28 May, turned out to be nothing but a prelude to the withdrawal of all allied forces from Norway. That left the King and the government with no other option than to abandon the armed struggle on Norwegian soil.

After much soul-searching the King and his government in the afternoon of 7 June prepared to go into exile rather than surrender the cause of Norwegian independence. Before that decision was made, an incident occurred which in itself was a remarkable post-script to Norway's collapsed policy of national security. Having summoned the British envoy to a meeting on 30 May in order to find out what the plans and intentions of the allies were, Prime Minister Nygaardsvold, furious at the hapless diplomat's inevitable prevarications, began to lose his temper: "I said that we had believed England in her own interest would have done what could be done to evict the Germans from Norway, but we have so far been bitterly disappointed."[7] Having drifted into the crisis in an almost fatalistic commitment to the neutrality of the past, Norway had thus suffered what Henry Kissinger once wrote about the combination of disadvantages that results if a neutral state makes its defence dependent on the assistance of other powers: concern about its neutrality prevents such a state from making joint defence preparations with the presumed protector, while the expectation of outside assistance reduces the need for a national defence preparedness.

8. In the Wartime Alliance

Introduction

The Norwegian government which left the homeland on 7 June for an uncertain exile carried a heavy burden. Its foreign policy had been destroyed by the German invasion on 9 April, and the end of the armed struggle on Norwegian soil after a two-month campaign meant that its defence policy was also in ruins. The government was further aware that its decision to seek refuge abroad could lead to its final, fatal failure. In leaving the national territory, the government inevitably left itself open to the accusation of having abandoned a people faced with foreign occupation. Seeking refuge in Britain also meant joining with an ally who many Norwegians felt was at least partly to blame for dragging the country into war; an ally whose assistance during the campaign had been woefully inadequate; and who, moreover, might well turn out to be the losing side in the war. That was the long term danger.[1]

But even if Britain should pull through, the King and the government might still turn out to be losers: the short term danger was that skilful enemy propaganda could exploit the government's political liabilities to turn the Norwegian people away from their exiled leaders and towards some internal regime willing to seek a *modus vivendi* with the occupant. Then the government would become exiles in every pejorative sense of the term: an émigré clique cut off from the people of Norway and consequently of little or no use to a fighting alliance. This was a real danger during the summer of 1940, as parliamentary leaders and Storting members who had remained at home seemed to bow to the pressure of the German *Reichskommissar*, Josef Terboven, for the dismissal of the King and his government and the institution of an alternative government. But King Haakon's firm refusal to countenance even a temporary arrangement on those lines, combined with Terboven's unwillingness to compromise on the selection of members for his so-called "council of the realm", ended that critical phase. Instead, Terboven in September had to appoint what was called a "Council of Commissioner Ministers", consisting mainly of members of Quisling's nazi party, and entirely subject to the control of the *Reichskommissariat*.

The bright side of the balance sheet was that the government in exile also brought with them some important assets. First of all, with the King firmly on its side, the government's legal and constitutional status was beyond doubt. And the authority of the King and government to represent their country abroad was never questioned either by allied or – at least not openly – by neutral states. Regarding assets of a more material kind, the Norwegian government had one important advantage in being financially independent of the allies. Having secured control over most of Norway's overseas merchant navy – about four million tons of modern tankers and cargo ships – the Norwegian government could not only make a considerable contribution to the allied war effort, but could also be sure that its activities abroad would be self-financed. Further financial security was provided by the Bank of Norway's gold reserves which had been shipped abroad during the campaign in Norway.

King Haakon's unflinching and active support for the government in exile was a major asset for Norway's role in the Alliance. His radio speeches to his people – although he was not a good speaker and never got rid of his Danish accent – made him the principal symbol of Norway's continued struggle for freedom, and boosted morale in the occupied country.

As the home country was occupied, it was clear that Norway's contribution to the war effort could not be based on large manpower resources. The manpower employed in the merchant navy would obviously have to be reserved for allied maritime transport. As far as the Norwegian armed forces were concerned, only small elements of the navy and air force had managed to escape to Britain with the government. Any further addition to manpower would have to come through refugees from the home country. Yet the Norwegian government was determined from the first moment to establish and maintain its own armed forces on land, sea and air as recognisably Norwegian elements of the allied forces. On this basis the first Norwegian naval squadron was formed on 30 June 1940, based at Rosyth. Also in June 1940 the Norwegian government decided that the officers and men of the Norwegian air forces, instead of simply enlisting in the Royal Air Force in Britain, should be sent to Canada for training in a newly established Norwegian training centre there.

A preliminary statement of the Norwegian government's intentions in the military sector was put on paper by the Defence Ministry on 10 July 1940, in an aide-mémoire submitted to the British authorities. In the introductory sentence, this document stated that "It is the intention of the Norwegian government to continue the fight outside Norway in collaboration with our allies and so far as our means will permit until final victory."[2] In the section on the army the document stated that registration of Norwegians of military age had already been effected by Norwegian consulates in the United Kingdom. "The intention is to call up those between the ages of 21 and 35 who are passed fit for service by the medical committee, and

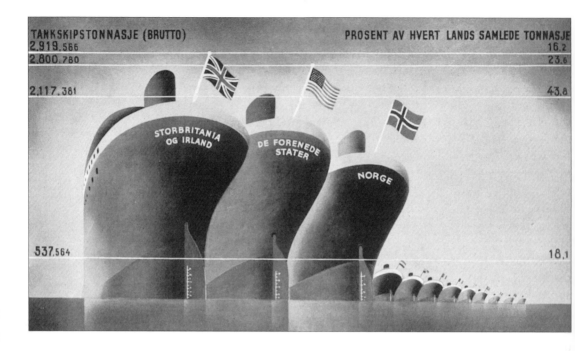

TANKSKIPSTONNASJE (BRUTTO)   PROSENT AV HVERT LANDS SAMLEDE TONNASJE

2.919.566   16.2
2.800.780   23.6
2.117.381   43.8

STORBRITANIA OG IRLAND
DE FORENEDE STATER
NORGE

537.564   18.1

The large and modern Norwegian tanker fleet was an essential asset to Allied war transport. British government sources in the spring of 1942 estimated that 40 per cent of the oil and petrol brought to the British Isles was carried by Norwegian tankers.

to organise Norwegian units which – having acquired the necessary training – can join British forces in Home Defence, and which, when the time is opportune, can join possible expeditionary forces for the purpose of regaining Norway, or complete other tasks towards the same end." For the air forces the Norwegian government announced their decision to "form special squadrons of their own personnel with the intention of fighting alongside the allies for the same purpose mentioned in regard to the units belonging to the army." Similar tasks were specified for the Norwegian naval units.

On the basis of that programme, and relying on the increase in manpower provided by refugees from the home country, Norway gradually built up on British soil a navy of about 50 ships, an air force with two squadrons of fighters and two squadrons of coastal command aircraft, and several smalle army units. The total number of men in the Norwegian armed forces based in the United Kingdom never attained significant numbers when seen in the larger perspective of the Alliance. From a total of about 2500 men in the autumn of 1940, the figure rose to about 15 000 by May 1945, not counting the approximately 13 000 Norwegian troops then having been trained in Sweden. But it is necessary to remember that throughout the war the Norwegian merchant navy, with its requirement of 25–30 000 sailors, always had first call on the available manpower resources.

Shaping an Alliance Policy

Having staked Norway's future as an independent and sovereign state on a victory for the Grand Alliance, of which she was now a member, the government's foreign policy became to all intents identical with its alliance policy. Moreover, it soon became clear that Norway's place in the Alliance would not only be determined by what it could effectively contribute to the war effort: it would also depend to a large extent on how the Norwegian government organised that contribution; in other words how the Norwegian government determined its posture in the Alliance, and in particular its attitude to Norway's major ally, Great Britain. Anglo-Norwegian relations in the summer of 1940 have been characterised by one well-placed observer as "profoundly unhappy". Many problems, often serious ones, had arisen between the two countries after Britain went to war in September 1939, and relations during the campaign in Norway had revealed a basic lack of mutual trust between the two governments. The British probably felt that the Norwegian government was mentally entrenched in its neutral past and lacked the necessary will or ability to participate in the war alliance in an active way. On the Norwegian side there were many who felt that the British regarded Norway as a pawn in the great power game, potentially useful but with little intrinsic value.

The initiative for an improvement in Anglo-Norwegian relations would naturally have to come from the Norwegian side. Such initiatives could come through action, by Norwegians in exile making an energetic effort to contribute, with all the means at their disposal, to the war against the common enemy. But, as we have seen, the means were modest apart from the Norwegian merchant navy. Efforts to improve Anglo-Norwegian relations would therefore have to be initiated at the political level; and throughout the summer of 1940 Norwegians in London were searching for ways to demonstrate that Norway had broken with her neutral past and had found her place as an ally. This process of laying the political groundwork for Norway's role in the Alliance took the form of a debate which lasted well into the autumn of 1940.

In that debate, three alternative courses were outlined. The first alternative was represented by the Foreign Minister, Halvdan Koht. In the summer of 1940, his attitude to Norway's place in the Alliance was dominated by his view that Norway's future independence depended on not one but two great powers. First, naturally, there was Britain. Koht from the beginning advocated active cooperation and close association with Britain, and made several important moves to that end during the summer of 1940, such as establishing collaboration in intelligence matters. However, Koht's willingness to cooperate closely with Britain was tempered by his lack of confidence in a British or allied victory in the war. If the war should end in a compromise peace, Norway's fate would also depend on the attitudes of other great powers, particularly the Soviet Union. In any case, Norway's geographical position in an area where the interests of the great powers overlapped, made it a matter of common sense to take into account the interests of more than one of these powers. On the assumption that the Soviet Union's major interest in Norway was that the country should remain free of domination by any other great power, Koht was anxious to manifest Norway's sovereign status in the Alliance. In his view, Norway's best policy was to maintain active practical cooperation with Britain, while retaining a clearly independent profile.

Dissatisfaction with Koht's policy was to appear from two quarters. One line of dissent appeared within the government, from two of Koht's cabinet colleagues. The two ministers in question were not from the Labour Party, and had been brought into the government in early June 1940 in an effort to widen its political base. Their proposals for an alliance policy advocated what might be termed traditional Norwegian attitudes to foreign relations – particularly relations with great powers. There was the old emphasis on seeking formal written guarantees or treaties, whereby Norwegian rights would be jealously guarded and secured and the corresponding duties and obligations of Great Britain could also be specified. It was an approach that reflected Norway's traditional and deep-seated small power resentment of great power politics. But it was a line of policy which hardly offered any solution to the immediate problem of establishing a positive relationship with a great power ally which was then fighting with its back against the wall.

Another alternative for Norway's alliance policy was put forward in a letter to the government from five prominent Norwegian intellectuals who had accompanied the government into exile. Chiefly inspired by an historian and expert in international affairs, Arne Ording, that letter took as a point of departure that Norway, by refusing the German ultimatum on 9 April, had *de facto* become Britain's ally. Norway's destiny was therefore linked with that of Great Britain, and with the war which the British now seemed determined to pursue to the end – a war that would have to assume the character of a revolutionary and ideological struggle against Germany and all that Nazism stood for. In such a war the nations which had refused to capitulate and which still had their free governments, like Norway, could play an important and active role. Moreover: "If the Norwegian government does its utmost to utilise its material and moral resources in the common cause, Norway's cause will stand all the stronger in the future peace settlement". A central part of their argument was that Norway could only hope to safeguard her independence and protect her national rights during the war through active and effective support for Britain and the common cause.

If the British government is convinced that the Norwegian government will do its utmost, then Norway's authority will be respected and Norway will

158

at least to some extent be taken into the councils of the Alliance. But if the British government thinks that the Norwegian government is lukewarm towards the struggle; is unreliable; or goes its own ways; then sooner or later the British authorities will end up by pushing our own military and administrative authorities aside.[3]

Referring to Koht's concern for Norway's relations with the Soviet Union, the letter stated that Norway could not have her ally's enemy as a friend. It would therefore be foolhardy to let distant and uncertain promises of Soviet political support interfere with the close cooperation needed with Britain.

What was at issue between Koht and the authors of that letter was not whether Norway should be an active ally. There was no disagreement that Norway should both protect her independent rights within the Alliance and at the same time cooperate actively in the common cause. The question was more one of priorities. Koht wished to emphasise Norway's independence and long-term rights while engaged in active cooperation with Britain. The policy proposed by the authors of the letter gave first priority to active and positive cooperation with Britain, seeing that as the best way of assuring Norwegian independence and rights in the long run. The various disputes which led to Koht's resignation as Foreign Minister, in November 1940, were therefore not so much a matter of the government wanting a change of policy, but rather of a felt need for a change of emphasis, and above all of attitude, towards the wartime Alliance. But as Koht was also identified with Norway's pre-war neutralism, his resignation came to symbolise that the Norwegian government had broken with its neutral past. And the new Foreign Minister, Trygve Lie, was both by temperament and conviction determined to show a new spirit of cooperation.

By the end of the year 1940 the Norwegian government had still to formalise its alliance relationship with Britain. Negotiations for a military agreement with Britain had begun in August 1940, with the *aide-mémoire* of 10 July as its basis. In the first drafts for a formal agreement the nature of the Alliance was only briefly touched upon in the introductory passages. After taking over as Foreign Minister, however, Trygve Lie suggested adding a political clause in the introduction to the effect that the two powers should declare their agreement that one of the aims of the war was the complete liberation of Norway from German domination. This was accepted by the British government, and the agreement was signed on 28 May 1941. It stated that the Norwegian armed forces were to be employed either in the defence of the United Kingdom or for the re-conquest of Norway. The agreement also left the operational control of the Norwegian forces to the British High Command, in its capacity as Allied High Command. But through its detailed provisions the agreement secured that the Norwegian forces would form nationally identifiable units – Norwegian air squadrons,

Trygve Lie replaced Halvdan Koht as Foreign Minister at the end of 1940, with a programme of close cooperation with the British in order to strengthen Norway's position in the Alliance. He quickly established cordial relations with Britain's Foreign Secretary Anthony Eden, while Crown Princess Märtha in Washington became a good friend of President Roosevelt. This picture of the three of them was taken at the opening ceremony for a British-Norwegian Institute in London.

Norwegian warships with Norwegian crews and flying the Norwegian flag, and Norwegian army units.

Alliance Cooperation in Practice

By the time the Anglo-Norwegian military agreement was signed at the end of May 1941, patterns of practical cooperation had already developed. Of primary importance was the use made of the Norwegian merchant navy in allied war transport. By the time the Germans invaded Norway, a large part of the Norwegian merchant navy was already working for Britain under chartering agreements negotiated between the British government and Norwegian shipowners since September–October 1939. Those ships could then continue to sail more or less as before. But after April 1940 the administration of this fleet, as well as the ships which had previously been employed in other trades and had gone over to the allied cause after the invasion, became the concern of the Norwegian government. During the campaign in Norway the government through a formal Order in Council had requisitioned the merchant fleet for the duration of the war. A "Norwegian Shipping and Trade Mission" was shortly afterwards established in London, and that organisation – better known by its cable address, Nortraship – functioned for most practical purposes as a state shipping company, subject in policy matters to the Norwegian Ministry of Shipping.

Generally, the policy of the Norwegian government regarding the utilisation of the merchant navy was to cooperate as closely as possible with

160

British and allied shipping authorities, without undue insistence on retaining national control at all levels. Here, as in many other aspects of alliance cooperation, the Norwegian government accepted that alliance warfare had to be pursued with a high degree of unified control, unhampered by too many concessions to national self-determination. On the other hand, the Norwegian government spared no pains to secure the protection of Norwegian interests in such matters as rates of pay for sailors – generally better than pay on British vessels, although considerably lower than equivalent rates on American ships; the allocation of allied ships between high risk and low risk routes; and securing charter rates that were sufficiently high to meet Norway's wartime economic needs abroad.

By putting positive and open cooperation first, and national self-interests second, the Norwegian government showed its determination to avoid the sort of inter-allied conflict that could give the British government reason to want to take over the administration of the Norwegian merchant navy. Ideas of such a take-over were mooted by the British on a couple of occasions: first in April 1940, when uncertainty about the attitude of the Norwegian government led to suggestions that the Norwegian fleet ought to be put under the British flag; and again in the spring of 1941 when Chancellor of the Exchequer Sir Kingsley Wood suggested a larger British role in the control of the Norwegian merchant navy, with freights being paid in sterling. Both attempts were rejected. As Prime Minister Johan Nygaardsvold put it in a letter in May 1941: "That the government should retain a good measure of control over this fleet has always been seen as most important for our cause and for the future of the country. Nobody knows how long this will last. Naturally, as allies we must take our share of the sacrifice, but I do think that we ought to have sufficient influence to administer our losses ourselves."[4]

The exiled government's need to be not only the guardian but also the visible guardian of Norwegian interests was particularly important in terms of its relations with the people in the occupied country. Enemy and collaborationist propaganda missed no opportunity to portray the Norwegian government in exile as an émigré clique which had sold Norway's interests to the western powers, and hence existed only as a pawn in allied hands. Thus every allied war-like activity in occupied Norway, be it bombing, sabotage, or raids on the coast, was presented as demonstrating the failure of the Norwegian government to prevent, or even its active connivance in, acts which destroyed Norwegian property and even Norwegian lives. Aware of this danger at the beginning of the war, the government was reluctant to engage in activities which would extend the war into Norwegian territory. This however meant that the British agencies concerned with activities inside occupied territory began to act independently of the Norwegian government. Individual Norwegians would be consulted or would even take part in such actions, but the government was often kept in the dark.

This was obviously a development fraught with dangerous consequences in the long run. During 1941, British agencies such as the Special Operations Executive (SOE) and the Directorate of Combined Operations showed an increasing interest in activities behind enemy lines in Norway. But the Norwegian government was hampered in its efforts to control this development through lack of a clear war policy of its own for actions on Norwegian territory. Basically, the government's choice, in this as in other alliance matters, was between cooperating to the fullest possible extent and in that way seeking to obtain influence on decisions, or protesting in defence of independence and sovereign rights. During 1941 the government tried both alternatives at intervals. But whereas cooperation with the SOE carried the risk of saddling the government with responsibility for acts which it did not condone, protests were on the other hand rendered ineffective by the lack of a constructive alternative policy.

The German attack on the Soviet Union in June 1941 ushered in an era of active British planning for operations, large and small, on the Norwegian coast. The most ambitious of these plans, for massive joint Anglo-Russian landings in northern Norway, had to be put aside due to lack of British resources for such large-scale undertakings. Instead the Chiefs of Staff in the middle of October, at Churchill's urging, requested the planning staff to consider plans for something approaching guerrilla warfare on the Norwegian coast, through small raids, the landing of arms and personnel, and so on. Guidelines agreed between SOE and Trygve Lie established that the Norwegian authorities would have no objection to small-scale raids that were not considered likely to lead to any serious unrest in Norway. Some of the plans being considered by the Chiefs of Staff during November 1941, however, envisaged raids of up to nine thousand men. It was only at the insistence of the Admiralty that two raids carried out between Christmas and New Year in 1941 – against Vaagsøy in western Norway, and Lofoten in northern Norway – were on a smaller scale than that. They were nevertheless sufficient to provoke serious German reprisals against the civilian population.

The Norwegian government had not been consulted about those raids. Around New Year 1942 they therefore decided to demand a general review of Anglo-Norwegian cooperation in the military field. This demand coincided with the final stages of an internal Norwegian debate about the organisation of Norway's military and defence set-up in exile. The outcome of that was a thorough reform in which the three separate service commands were subordinated to a new Defence High Command, whose main mission would be to ensure better cooperation with the British, particularly as regards planning for the liberation of Norway. The British Chiefs of Staff now agreed to a Norwegian proposal for setting up a joint Anglo-Norwegian planning committee. Another committee, concerned with planning and controlling current operations behind enemy lines in Norway, was set up jointly by the SOE and the relevant branch of the Norwegian High Command. In 1942 the Defence High Command also initiated closer cooperation with allied air forces in the selection of targets for bombing in occupied Norway. Thus the government effectively abandoned its previous policy of making isolated protests against specific bombing attacks in favour of a policy of constructive collaboration. By providing full information on Norwegian industries, and by helping to define targets or target systems suitable for bomber attacks, the Defence High Command sought to eliminate other targets which a closer examination suggested ought to be spared, or which could more profitably – or with less loss of civilian lives – be destroyed through sabotage.

The Government's "Atlantic Policy"

This remarkably pragmatic approach to alliance relations with a great power, just described, was a far cry from Norway's traditional attitude to small state/great power relationships. An even more striking departure from established foreign policy "credos" was soon to appear. The ideological underpinnings for the development of mutual trust between Norway and Great Britain, and for the gradual improvement of cooperation even in the military sphere, was the radical – not to say revolutionary – change of foreign policy direction which the exiled government undertook from the end of 1940 onwards. Known as the government's "Atlantic policy", it was a concept with profound implications not only for Norway, but in the long run also for post-war western security. While the process that led to the 1949 North Atlantic Treaty had its immediate origin in initiatives taken by British Foreign Secretary Ernest Bevin around the end of 1947, the *idea* of North Atlantic defence cooperation antedates Bevin's initiative by almost exactly seven years. The origin of the suggestion that the nations bordering on the North Atlantic had vital defence interests in common, and therefore ought to act together in peacetime for the protection of those interests, lies in ideas first put forward by Trygve Lie to representatives of the British Foreign Office at the end of 1940, and later developed into Norway's wartime "Atlantic policy".

Lie's first public intimation of Norway's long-term Atlantic security interests was made in a broadcast speech to Norway on 15 December 1940. Barely eight months had then passed since the German occupation of Norway, an event which both the Norwegians and the western powers had been unable to prevent. Naturally, therefore, the direct motivation behind Trygve Lie's idea was to prevent a future repetition of that catastrophe. Yet the more timeless aspect of the proposal, the idea that nations separated by vast oceans had closely connected security interests requiring mutual protection, was a radical innovation. And it was this aspect which quickly became the centrepiece of Norwegian wartime foreign policy planning. Signalling a complete breach with Norway's non-aligned past, Lie's speech stressed the need for post-war cooperation with nations sharing the same ideals and aspirations – primarily the United Kingdom and the United States – in order to safeguard the security of the western world.

The Foreign Minister's speech was deliberately vague about forms of cooperation: speaking of the war-time Alliance "which our allies and all progressive forces of the world are endeavouring to build up and strengthen", he went on to say that this endeavour would in its turn

> provide the basis for a cooperation which can and must endure after the war: a political cooperation to secure our national freedom and remove the danger of assaults by arrogant and tyrannical aggressors, and an economic cooperation providing social security and preventing the destruction of our economies and our welfare.

Only between the lines can one here discern the far-reaching proposals for post-war military cooperation which the Foreign Minister was at the same time putting forward in private conversations with officials of the British Foreign Office: proposals pointing towards an alliance for mutual security covering the North Atlantic and embracing Britain, Norway, the United States, Iceland and the Faeroes. For the post-war world, Lie here envisaged nothing less than a joint defence arrangement with naval and military bases in the territories concerned.

Although post-war problems were hardly uppermost in British minds in those desperate times, the immediate reactions among British Foreign Office officials were distinctly favourable to Lie's ideas. They naturally welcomed the implied rejection of neutrality and isolation as a viable policy for the smaller European states in the future. And some saw the idea of a network of bases as being of particular interest. Thus Assistant Under-Secretary Sir Orme Sargent was inspired to put on paper the following long-term perspective:

> One of the major post-war problems will be to enable this country to maintain its position vis-à-vis the Continent of Europe, and it is already fairly evident that the failure of France will render the cooperation of the United States essential for this purpose. May not the extension of M. Lie's ideas offer a practical means of achieving this cooperation? Just as there would be, according to M. Lie's suggestion, British and Norwegian [sic] bases in Norway, there might be similar Anglo-American bases in Portugal, Iceland and even Dakar, and at the same time American bases in Irish ports and even in British ports.[5]

Trygve Lie (left) stands as the exponent of Norway's change of foreign policy course from neutralism to active engagement in international power politics. A law graduate from Oslo University, he was legal adviser to the Federation of Trade Unions before joining Nygaardsvold's government as Minister of Justice in 1935. He was Minister of Supply when in November, 1940, he took over from Halvdan Koht as Foreign Minister. An ambitious man of action rather than a man of ideas, he had a knack of surrounding himself with able advisers. His own contribution to the policy change was his enthusiastic determination to put all Norway's cards on the alliance with Great Britain. Together with professor Arnold Ræstad and professor Wilhelm Keilhau, the historian Arne Ording (right) had the leading role in the 'brains trust' of Norwegian academics that gave shape and long term purpose to the 'Atlantic policy' of the government in exile. Ording had before the war been one of the leaders of a group of communist intellectuals which in 1936 joined the Labour Party. His expertise as an analyst of international relations then brought him into the public eye as a valued writer and speaker on contemporary foreign affairs. In London he combined his work as policy adviser to the government with providing a regular series of commentaries on the progress of the war to the BBC's Norwegian service. After the war he continued as political adviser to the Foreign Ministry while holding a Chair of International History at Oslo University, until ill health forced him to take early retirement.

Sargent was not alone in realising that the present salvation and future security of Western Europe hinged on the active engagement of the power of the United States. As seen by Lie's adviser and the chief architect of his policies, Arne Ording, a central concern behind the "Atlantic policy" was in fact to attempt "to nail the Anglo-Saxon great powers to their responsibilities in

165

In this excerpt from Sir Cecil Dormer's farewell dispatch as Minister to the Norwegian government, attention is focused on Trygve Lie's informal suggestion about offering base rights in Norway to Britain and the United States after the war. Trygve Lie may have spoken "off the record", since that particular idea had not been cleared with the Cabinet, and the proposal was not repeated. But the dispatch clearly stimulated the interest and goodwill of the British Foreign Office toward Norway's "conversion" from isolationism to active engagement in international security affairs.

THIS DOCUMENT IS THE PROPERTY OF HIS BRITANNIC MAJESTY'S GOVERNMENT

SCANDINAVIA AND BALTIC STATES.   April 1, 1941.

CONFIDENTIAL.   SECTION 1.

[N 1307/87/30]   ARCHIVES   Copy No.

Sir C. Dormer to Mr. Eden.—(Received April 1.)

British Legation to Norway,
March 28, 1941.

Sir,
    THERE is one recent development in Norwegian foreign policy which seems to me to hold out possibilities of such exceptional importance that I beg permission to draw attention to it once again before I relinquish my appointment as His Majesty's Minister to that country. I refer to the question of Great Britain and the United States being invited after the war to keep naval and air bases in Norway.
    In his first broadcast, on replacing M. Koht at the Ministry for Foreign Affairs, M. Lie intimated, as I reported at the time, that the Norwegian Government were discarding their former policy of pinning their fortunes to the Scandinavian *bloc*, and that they intended henceforth to align themselves with the great democracies of the West. This, indeed, represented a *volte*-face. Whatever faults the present Norwegian Government may possess, they did not hesitate, once they rid themselves of M. Koht's influence, to recognise the hollow pretence and utter failure of their once-boasted policy of inter-Scandinavian co-operation and of strict neutrality in the affairs of Europe. That chapter of history is, I feel, too familiar to our minds for it to be necessary to describe the sequel of shocks which "Scandinavian co-operation" suffered during the course of the past three or four years. The great thing is that M. Lie says that he is now convinced that the policy of neutrality was wrong, and that in future, for the security of Norway and the peace of Europe, it is essential to keep open the highway of the Atlantic, and that that can only be done by the establishment of bases in Norway, the Faroes, Iceland and Greenland. He thinks that the three States should exercise their responsibility jointly, though Norway, be it said in parenthesis, would like to have the Faroes.

Europe". For the time being, American neutrality of course barred any active exploration of these ideas with the leaders in Washington. Lie nevertheless in April 1941 took the opportunity of a talk with the US Minister to the Norwegian government to acquaint a representative of the American government with his thinking. Drawing a parallel between Norway's current importance to British maritime defence and her future importance to American strategic interests, the message he sought to convey was that in the age of fast, long-range aircraft the United States could no longer afford to be indifferent to the question of who controlled the Norwegian coastline. Hence his proposal that "the nations bordering on the North Atlantic should seek an arrangement or a plan for the future security and protection of the North Atlantic area."

    Two months later Lie had occasion to explain his views to a House of Commons audience at Westminster. Referring to his proposed security arrangement as "an Atlantic Association", he emphasised the need to have

166

control of the seas as a key motive. But he also projected such a grouping as a possible nucleus for a collective security scheme: by starting with "the nations that have not only fought together, but also belong together because they have not only common interests but also a common ideal in life and politics", such a group would have a more realistic basis than the pre-war League of Nations.

Encouraged by the favourable albeit unofficial reaction of Foreign Office officials to his ideas, Lie in the autumn of 1941 took his proposals a major step further. In a lecture to a Royal Institute of International Affairs audience at Oxford, later reworked into an article in *The Times* after consultations with his Cabinet colleagues and others, Lie came closer to identifying some central aspects of the post-war international order which Norway would like to see established. He stressed at the outset, as a lesson of Norway's history as a maritime nation, "that the sea does not divide but links together. [...]We are an Atlantic nation, and we do want, above all, a strong, organised collaboration between the two great Atlantic Powers, the British Empire and the United States of America."[6]

More specifically, Lie looked forward to an agreement on Eastern Atlantic defence with Britain, the United States and Canada, also covering Greenland and Iceland. He was convinced that Norway, after the war, would wish to be an active participant in such an arrangement, a conviction not shared by all his countrymen: already Lie had confessed to British officials that some of his Cabinet colleagues as well as other influential Norwegians lagged behind in their understanding of the realities of international politics.

Among Lie's British interlocutors, too, the positive reactions to the "Atlantic policy" were tempered by scepticism as to its practicability. But the cautious official attitude of the British had much to do with the uncertainties surrounding the war aims of their new great power ally, the Soviet Union. Senior officials warned that Lie's "Atlantic policy" was "precisely the sort of post-war planning which Stalin is so anxious to discuss with us", and if he were to hear "that we, and possibly also the United States, were discussing it with the Norwegians without his being informed there would be the devil to pay."[7] There was also concern that Stalin's post-war aims might include ice-free ports in North Norway. British Foreign Secretary Anthony Eden therefore advised Lie to proceed with caution. However, during Eden's talks with Stalin late in December 1941, no such Russian claims were put forward. On the contrary, Stalin's "spheres of influence" thinking appeared to envisage both a British-centred military alliance in north-western Europe and British naval bases in Norway and Denmark, as a counterpart to territorial adjustments and security arrangements for the Soviet Union along its western frontiers. Encouraged by this, the British Foreign Office in the winter of 1942 moved closer towards approval in principle of

In this article in "The Times" 14 November 1941 Trygve Lie gave his first public presentation of the Norwegian government's 'Atlantic Policy'. The publication was preceded by consultation with Cabinet colleagues and political advisers, and by a lecture to a Chatham House audience at Oxford. There were mixed feelings in Norwegian circles about the strong commitment to postwar military cooperation, and the discussions that led up to the official governmental policy declaration half a year later, stressed the need also for global security cooperation, adding Norway's desire for good relations with her Soviet neighbour.

5

A COMMUNITY OF NATIONS

◆

PLANS FOR A LASTING PEACE AFTER VICTORY

THE BANKRUPTCY OF NEUTRALITY

By Hr. Trygve Lie, Foreign Minister of Norway

Intimate international cooperation will be needed after the war in the political, military, and economic fields. Norway has no frontier problems, and no desire or territorial expansion. But the Norwegian people have been convinced that he policy of neutrality is bankrupt. The first question is with whom shall we cooperate?

Happily our strategic position, our economic interests, our ideals, and our way of life" all point in the same direction. There has not been the conflict etween ideological and strategic considerations which has shown itself in the ther Northern countries; there has been ntimate collaboration between Norway nd her neighbours in the years preceding he war, and it is, naturally, our desire to aintain the relations of good neighbourness. I should also like to stress the fact at Norway has lived on friendly, neighourly terms with Russia for many undreds of years.

A FORGOTTEN FACT

In view of these traditions of peace the erman invasion of Norway came as a omplete surprise to the Norwegian population. During the war 1914-18 Norway d succeeded, politically speaking, in feguarding her neutrality, but none the ss she rendered great services to the llied cause. We lost about 2,000 sailors d nearly 1,000 ships; a loss representg 49.7 per cent. of the total Norwegian erchant fleet on July 1, 1914, while the ritish losses were relatively lower. This as forgotten all too quickly, and our pe is that the common suffering this me will make cooperation lasting. As Atlantic people we want above all a rong organiz... ...tween

The most important basis for extended international cooperation in the future is an amicable relationship between the British Empire, the United States, Soviet Russia, and China. But this time such movements must be organized to ensure practical results. We have all discussed the reasons why the League of Nations did not succeed in carrying out the tasks assigned to it. It would have been possible to use the League machinery against Italian and German aggression if the leading Powers in the League had seriously wanted to do so. Countries adopted, however, a short-sighted policy of self-interest, and in an atmosphere of pacific public opinion nobody was willing to run any risk. This produced an inevitable disillusionment and a critical attitude towards the idea of a community of nations.

PLANNED ECONOMY

It is therefore essential that the new international cooperation should be built upon firm and safe ground. Since we are at war it would be natural to start with military collaboration. After the war the allied countries will have important policing duties to perform in common, especially in relation to Germany, though much will depend on what sort of Germany we shall have to deal with. The Atlantic Charter, which has been approved by all the allied Governments, lays down that unilateral disarmament of Germany shall be enforced during the period immediately following the war, but that the German people shall not be starved. For a shorter or a longer period it will, in any case, be necessary to keep Germany under military occupation, and here the allied forces will have a common task. Such military cooperation, however, should be developed to continue in the f...

natural to think of the defence of the Atlantic and strongly to emphasize our desire to see the United States participating in this task. Military and political questions being closely connected, we must also work together in the political tasks which will have to be tackled after the war; not least in connexion with the peace settlement. The inter-allied conferences which have taken place recently have created the beginnings of a common political machinery. They might perhaps be developed into a real Inter-Allied Committee holding regular meetings and having, so far as possible, executive powers.

Such an organization would be only provisional. In the interval there will be time to discuss plans for an extended form of cooperation, either in the form of a new League of Nations or a federal body. It is, however, very important that no country should be forced to join such an organization whether by pressure from outside or in any other way. As a preliminary, reconstruction work must be carried on internationally, and no new body should be founded except on a demand from the people of all countries. It might be difficult to induce people who have carried on a long struggle for their national freedom to give up, so to say, part of their sovereignty. It should, on the other hand, be much easier to make them accept concrete proposals understood by all to be necessary, as, for example, military cooperation.

THE PLACE OF NORWAY

The details of future economic cooperation must be governed by certain simple facts. One is that political stability is impossible without international economic collaboration; and the other is that the world will certainly not return to the old liberal economic system. The war has made necessary in all countries a national planned economy under the direction of the State; and in the years immediately following we shall be faced with tremendous tasks of economic reconstruction. The first will be to supply the whole European continent with consumption goods for which there will be an urgent need; the next, to supply them with the means of production, to make it possible to start the wheels turning again. This second task should be carried out according to a common plan, so that each country, so far as possible, can restart the economic activity most suited to it. Thus a step will have been taken towards an international planned economy, and afterwards will come the regulation of markets and common plans for opening up new markets. Here is a much more important matter than the access to raw materials of which so much has been heard.

In Norway we have our special task within the planned economy of the future. Norwegian shipping has never received subsidies in any form; it has, on the contrary, been heavily taxed. If, nevertheless, it has been able ...

a post-war security arrangement based on a system of military and naval bases as being "one of the few ideas of a post-war order which seem to have practical value and which have a chance of gaining general acceptance." But the British Cabinet was still not prepared to take a stand on post-war security schemes in the absence of anything like a consensus among the three great powers now leading the Alliance. And Roosevelt, in particular, seemed averse to any "spheres of influence" arrangements.

In the meantime Lie and his advisers had continued to propagate their ideas, with markedly positive response from the Foreign Ministers of the Netherlands and Belgian governments in exile. By May 1942 the internal Norwegian debate on the proposals had reached the stage where a full Cabinet consensus seemed within reach. Some concessions had to be made, to "universalists" who looked forward to a new and better League of Nations, and to advocates of closer cooperation at the regional Nordic level. But the resulting official document, entitled "Principal Features of Norwegian Foreign Policy", showed that the Cabinet fully endorsed the "Atlantic policy" as the central feature of Norway's long-term security aims:

> Until it becomes possible to create an effective and universal League of Nations, Norway will be compelled to seek security in regional arrangements. Norway, therefore, desires binding and obligatory military agreements concerning the defence of the North Atlantic, and she is anxious that Sweden should be a party to these agreements. The Norwegian government would also look with satisfaction upon the adherence of Denmark, the Netherlands, Belgium and France to the system. The Norwegian government desires that the military cooperation shall be developed as far as possible in the course of the war itself. The Norwegian government desires to initiate negotiations even now regarding this future military cooperation.[8]

It should again be stressed that the central motive for Norway's "Atlantic policy" so far was not to create a bulwark against Soviet expansion, but rather to take Norway out of its pre-war isolation and prevent a repetition of Germany's aggressive policies. By May 1942, however, and for a variety of reasons, no policy statement would have been complete without consideration of the relationship with the Soviet Union, and the Norwegian government went on record with a strong endorsement of closer relations and cooperation with the USSR. Speculations about Soviet designs on North Norway were denounced as groundless, but the official policy document seemed to recognise a legitimate Soviet security interest in the far north:

> During this war, Northern Norway has been one of the starting points for the German attack upon the Soviet Union. Provided that there is friendly cooperation between the Soviet Union and the Western Powers, the Soviet government will be positively interested in the development of the defence of Northern Norway. Should relations between the Soviet Union and the Western Powers be hostile, the position of Northern Norway would be much more complicated. Norway will, therefore, do her utmost to prevent such a conflict from arising.

In sum, this document made clear both Norway's post-war security aims and her basic dilemma at the crossroads of western and Soviet strategic interests. This dilemma was more succinctly recorded in the diary of Lie's adviser, Arne Ording, later that year, when he speculated about the possible ramifications of future military cooperation:

We may find ourselves faced with the following choice: either to provide bases only for the British and the Americans, which the Russians may see as a threat, or to give them also to the Russians, which will create both strategic and internal problems. Or to adopt a new neutrality line, this time balancing between the western powers and Russia in the same way as we previously, with tragic and well-known results, tried to balance between Germany and the western powers.[9]

Atlanticism to the Back Burner

In many ways the "Main Principles of Norwegian Foreign Policy" document from May 1942 came to represent a climax in the development of Norway's "Atlantic policy". From then on, as the post-war planning of Britain and the other great powers got into its stride, Norway's role as the initiator of new policy approaches was coming to an end. Henceforth the prime necessity became one of adjusting to policy developments determined by the great powers. To some extent, the Norwegian government also had to face the problem of internal dissenting opinions, as well as a revival of interest in closer Nordic cooperation. In liberal and conservative Norwegian circles outside the government, the isolationist impulse was not yet dead. From the United States, the Norwegian conservative leader Carl Joachim Hambro attempted to re-establish the old distinction between the cynicism of the great powers and the moral superiority of small states, and warned against a peace settlement dictated by the "Big Four". Regarding Scandinavia, Swedish advocates of a Nordic federation during 1942 and 1943 found the time opportune for renewed calls in favour of Nordic unity after the war. As the Norwegian over-reaction against the idea showed, the attempt could hardly have come at a worse time. For just as the Swedes could only discuss Nordic unity on the basis of complete neutrality as between the great powers, the Norwegians could only discuss it within the framework of cooperation with the allies. For either of them to discuss Nordic unity on any other basis would mean sowing seeds of doubt about the firmness of their current policies.

In the autumn of 1942, Anthony Eden tried to extract from the British government some sort of commitment to an Atlantic defence system. Both the Netherlands and Belgian Foreign Ministers were now on record as supporters of the idea of tying Great Britain and the United States into a western post-war security system. And the Dutch Foreign Minister Eelco van Kleffens, after a visit to the United States, claimed to have found much positive interest for the idea among American leaders. Prompted by this widening support, Eden in October 1942 proposed to the War Cabinet to instruct the British Ambassador in Washington to discuss the idea with the State Department, and to express general British support for the political content

170

of this projected defence system. But the consensus of the War Cabinet was opposed to even such a limited commitment on the part of Britain, and the outcome was a request that the Foreign Office first develop the broader lines of British and international post-war security. The resulting memorandum, entitled "The Four-Power Plan", gave primary emphasis to the emerging American ideas of a universal system of post-war security and cooperation, dominated by the great powers. Regional defence systems had their place: "In particular, it is to be hoped that in North-Western Europe special agreements will be made whereby it will be possible for Great Britain and possibly the United States to establish naval and air bases in the territories of the various powers bordering on the North Sea ..."[10] But regionalism seemed by now to have been relegated to a somewhat subsidiary concept.

These new signals were also received in the Norwegian Foreign Ministry. In November 1942 Arne Ording noted in his diary that "we must now put the main emphasis on the United Nations." And in March 1943, during Trygve Lie's first visit to Washington, Sumner Welles, then Under-Secretary of State, told him that regional defence arrangements would have to await the establishment of a global security system. It was best to start with the greater framework in order to avoid the controversies that could easily arise if one started at the other end. Welles also led Lie to understand that the United States and Britain would primarily be interested in links with a unified Nordic group. Similar conclusions could be drawn from Winston Churchill's first public statement on the post-war international order. In a radio speech on 21 March 1943 he projected a vision of groupings of small states with strong links to the major powers on whom would rest the overall responsibility for the maintenance of peace. However, while the Norwegian Foreign Ministry clearly saw the need for an alteration of priorities in its foreign policy, the uncertain contours of the great powers' plans for the post-war world during most of 1943 precluded any major restatement of the main policy lines.

In January 1944, the change of emphasis in Norwegian foreign policy for the post-war world was publicly stated both in a major speech by the Foreign Minister and in a parallel article in *The Observer* by Arne Ording. First priority was now clearly given to the universalist concept of the United Nations. And this was done, as Lie admitted to the Foreign Office, in order to conform to the views of Great Britain and the United States. An Atlantic regional arrangement was still stated as most likely to provide the maximum degree of security for Norway in the post-war world. But this now took second place to the global scheme of four-power cooperation, and was moreover made dependent on the goodwill, or at least lack of opposition, of the Soviet Union. As Lie put it, "Norway's interests would be best served by an agreement embracing the countries bordering on the

North Atlantic, on condition that it was subordinated to an international organisation and was accompanied by an extension of our good relations with the Soviet Union."[11] This, then, was the general order of priority applied by the Norwegian government in its approach to the organisation of peace during the remainder of the war. But the new proviso regarding relations with the Soviet Union points to the final and major development in Norwegian war-time foreign policy: the emerging problematic "special relationship" between Norway and its new great power neighbour to the east.

Planning for the Liberation

An important purpose behind the government's efforts to gain the trust of the British authorities was to secure a voice in the planning for the liberation of the home country, in order to ensure that Norwegian interests were safeguarded – and that the exiled government could stand forth as the visible guardian of those interests. For a time in 1941 and early 1942 the omens were not good: Churchill was pressing for an early invasion in the north which, if it came about, was bound to become a risky and extremely bloody affair that would bring enormous sufferings for the people of Norway. Fortunately his military leaders were able to stand firm against the idea – operation "Jupiter", as Churchill had named it. As the western allies then turned to North Africa as the target for a landing that could serve as a prelude to entering Italy, while building up forces for a massive invasion across the English Channel, the Norwegian authorities could begin to concentrate on more long term planning for the liberation of Norway. Those plans had to take into account both military and civilian aspects. The liberation would have to be a military operation, even if the German forces should decide not to offer armed resistance. But the Norwegian government had to make sure that the interests of the civilian population were taken care of. Law and order had to be secured in the liberated parts of the country, and supplies of food and other necessities would have to be provided.

A first question concerned what contribution the Norwegian forces could make to the operations. Given Norway's limited manpower resources, it was evident that any military operation for the liberation of Norway would have to be mainly an allied effort. Norway's contribution, as envisaged by the Defence High Command, would have two main components: first, the Norwegian Secret Military Organisation inside the country, estimated at a strength of about thirty thousand men; and second, the Norwegian forces in Britain. The "Home Forces" were thought to be sufficiently trained and equipped to be able to play an important part in creating confusion behind the German lines after an allied landing had taken place, as well as maintaining law and order in areas recently liberated. The Norwegian land forces in Britain were reorganised to form liaison units attached to all the different staffs and units of the allied liberation forces, so as to ensure adequate regard for Norwegian interests and satisfactory relations between the allied forces and the civilian population. The government's aim was to provide for the earliest possible transfer of power from the military to Norwegian civilian authorities. Negotiations in May 1943 led to a preliminary agreement between Norway and Britain on the principles to be followed.

The allied plans for the liberation of Europe, as revealed to the Norwegians in the autumn of 1943, appeared highly inadequate and unsatisfactory from the Norwegian point of view. Since the "Jupiter" plans were abandoned, Norway had clearly become a strategic backwater in regard to the military plans of the western allies. In spite of what Churchill had maintained, the allied staffs could not see Norway as a step on the road to the final defeat of Germany. The liberation of Norway was therefore becoming, in military terms, a diversion from the main campaign. And in the allied planning organs there was a natural tendency to reduce to a minimum the resources to be spent in such an outlying theatre. As a result, the Norwegian government began to fear that the liberation of the home country might be long delayed. Even if the Germans in Norway should decide to surrender without offering resistance, it looked as if there might be a delay of several weeks before a small allied force could arrive to take over control. Moreover, this force would most likely be concentrated in southern Norway, leaving northern Norway virtually a no-man's-land.

The Soviets Enter the Stage

While the western allies in the beginning of 1944 were building up forces for the final assault on the continent, the Red Army was advancing westward, not only into Poland but also towards Finland, Norway's neighbour in the far north. And after Finland, what? Would the Germans continue their retreat, and would the Soviets pursue them into Norway? With such prospects, and in view of the allied failure to allocate troops which might prevent leaving northern Norway as a military vacuum within easy reach of Soviet armed forces, the Norwegian government in the spring of 1944 resolved to initiate closer cooperation with the Soviet Union. And by April 1944 the decision was taken to approach the Soviet government about a separate liberation agreement, in case Soviet troops came to participate in the re-conquest of Norway. In this the Norwegian government acted against the advice of the British Foreign Office, which feared that such an approach might constitute a virtual invitation to Soviet forces to undertake operations on Norwegian territory. In the opinion of the Norwegian government, however, the prospect of Russian forces operating in Norway without any agreement regulating their relations with the Norwegian civilian population or the Norwegian authorities, seemed the more dangerous alternative. Obviously the Soviet government greatly welcomed the Norwegian approaches, and an agreement, in terms identical with those already agreed with the British and American governments, was signed on 16 May 1944.

The May 1944 agreements concerning the liberation of Norway marked the formal entry of the two future super-powers, the United States and the Soviet Union, as active factors of influence on Norwegian foreign relations. So far the United States had seemed more or less content with leaving Norwegian wartime affairs in the hands of the British. But the rise of American dominance over the conduct of the war, and hence also in alliance affairs, meant that Norway increasingly had to take into account the views and attitudes emanating from Washington. In their management of relations with the United States the government benefited from the personal relationship that developed between Crown Princess Märtha, who lived with her children in the Washington area throughout the war, and President Franklin Delano Roosevelt – a relationship which greatly facilitated Crown Prince Olav's access to the President. On the whole, US–Norwegian relations evolved without serious problems.

In fact the only really serious problem arose when Roosevelt in the winter of 1943 tried to bring Norway into his efforts to establish a basis for workable post-war east-west relations. A mainstay of his ideas to deflect possible Soviet demands for territorial expansion was the creation of a network of internationalised ports and bases at strategic points, to be administered under joint great power control. In view of the Soviet Union's presumed need for ice-free ports with direct access to the Atlantic, Roosevelt took the opportunity of a meeting with Trygve Lie in March 1943 to suggest the Norwegian coast as the ideal location for one or two such ports. Trygve Lie was predictably horrified, and alarm bells were set off on suspicion that the idea might have originated in demands put forward by the Soviets. Apparently reassured that the notion was a product of Roosevelt's fertile mind, the government soon calmed down.[12] But age-old fears that the Soviet Union had its eyes on northern Norway slumbered in the back of their minds, and events in 1944 were to bring them to the fore again.

The impact of the Soviet Union as a factor in the foreign policy calculations of the Norwegian government did not come out of the blue in 1944. In fact, ever since the autumn of 1942 the Soviet Union had been showing an increasing interest in Norwegian foreign policy guidelines. And in April 1943, while enquiring of the Norwegian Finance Minister whether there were any new developments in Norway's "Atlantic policy", the Soviet ambassador to the Norwegian government in exile said that "Norway

It was after some hesitation, and against the advice of the British Foreign Office, that the Norwegian government signed a liberation agreement with the Soviet Union equal to that made with Great Britain and the United States. The agreement provided a framework for limiting the jurisdiction of Allied military commanders during the re-conquest of Norway. The government viewed the possible presence of the Red Army in Norway with some concern, but decided that a presence regulated by a formal agreement would be better than having Soviet forces simply marching into northern Norway in hot pursuit of retiring Germans. Here Soviet ambassador Victor Lebedev (left) and Trygve Lie (right) sign the agreement. In the middle Prime Minister Nygaardsvold.

should be aware that in order to obtain her security aims, it was not only necessary to be in agreement with the western powers. One should, in addition, make sure of a good relationship with the Soviet Union, which was also a power with Atlantic interests."[13] But the major impetus for Norway's increasing attentiveness to Soviet interests in the north was provided by the prospect that the Red Army, following Finland's eventual withdrawal from the war, might become the first allied liberation troops on Norwegian territory. It was this prospect, and the lack of interest on the part of the western powers in providing allied liberation forces to counter-balance the possible presence of Soviet troops in North Norway, that lay behind a series of cooperative approaches towards the Soviet Union in the spring of 1944, culminating in the invitation to sign a liberation agreement simultaneously with similar agreements with the western powers.

Old suspicions of Soviet expansionist aims acquired a new lease on life, however, when it turned out that the Soviet Union refused to respond to Norwegian and allied urgings to follow up the liberation agreement with the necessary joint planning for operations in the north. Soviet troops entered Norwegian territory in pursuit of the German forces on 18 October 1944. Only in the evening of that day did Molotov inform the Norwegian ambassador that they would welcome the participation of Norwegian forces in the operation. Three weeks later Trygve Lie arrived in Moscow, and the talks that ensued proceeded in a friendly atmosphere. However, the possibility of establishing bilateral relations and closer cooperation on a more permanent basis was wrecked by Molotov: having summoned Trygve Lie to a midnight meeting in the Kremlin, on the eve of his departure, Molotov presented demands for a revision of the Svalbard Treaty and the cession of Bear Island to the Soviet Union. His proposals turned on a claim for equal status with Norway in exploiting the economic resources of Svalbard, but he also hinted at strategic considerations regarding freer access to the Atlantic. As described by Lie – possibly with dramatics added – Molotov in front of a map put his clenched fist first on the Dardanelles and then on the Baltic approaches, declaring "here we are shut in, and here. Only in the north is there an opening, but this war has shown that the line of communication with Northern Russia can be cut or hindered. This must not happen again."[14]

The immediate effect of Molotov's brusque tactics was to pulverise the prospects of a cordial relationship being established in the north. The presence of Soviet troops on Norwegian territory in Finnmark, initially welcomed by the Norwegian government in an official statement on 26 October as "a further manifestation of the friendship between our two countries", was henceforth bound to serve as a reminder that Soviet aims and Norwegian territorial sovereignty in the Arctic might be at cross-purposes. During the winter and spring of 1945 the Norwegian government embarked on a diplomatic exercise to try to stave off the Soviet demands over Svalbard. Allusions were made to the fact that any revision of the Svalbard Treaty would require the consent of all the signatories. But Soviet reactions to Norway's approaches, in this as in other matters concerning the high north, showed a clear preference for conducting Soviet-Norwegian relations on a strictly bilateral basis, excluding any involvement of the western great powers before agreement had been reached with Norway.

Norway's handling of the Svalbard affair that winter revealed a split between those – primarily Trygve Lie and Minister of Justice Terje Wold, actively supported by Rolf Andvord, the ambassador in Moscow, as well as some of the government's senior advisers – who were willing to go to great lengths to meet Soviet requirements, and the Prime Minister and a couple of other ministers, who wanted to postpone the whole matter until the war had ended and the Storting could be consulted. Trygve Lie's line, which from the outset was also based on a strategy of keeping the issue as a strictly bilateral Soviet-Norwegian matter, with Norway keeping the initiative, prevailed, to Molotov's evident satisfaction. When Norway's western allies were not consulted, this was presumably partly due to disappointment at their lack of interest and support regarding Norwegian concerns about Soviet aims in the north. But there was also a fear that the western powers could then "take over" and settle the affair with an eye only to great power interests in the area. The government thus ended up with a formal proposal, dated 9 April 1945, for a joint Soviet-Norwegian militarisation of the archipelago which, if the Soviets had jumped to it, would in practice have ended Norwegian sovereignty over the islands. Fortunately for the government, the Soviet Union put the affair on ice, either because they wanted more or because at that time – April 1945 – they had bigger and more urgent end-of-war issues to deal with. Be that as it may, Molotov's demands inevitably produced shock waves that were to reverberate far into the post-war period.

One reason why Trygve Lie and the government caved in to Soviet pressure to the extent they did was their distinct impression that neither Great Britain nor the United States was willing to act on Norway's concern by providing forces and other forms of assistance for the liberation of Norway, and thus establish a western military presence as a deterrent against possible Soviet ambitions. This lack of interest on the part of the western allies was no doubt in part a result of having no forces to spare for operations in the far north which would not contribute to a speedier defeat of Germany. They also claimed to be convinced that the Soviet Union had no expansionist plans in northern Norway, and that a sudden appearance of western forces in the area would lead to misunderstandings and incidents which might trigger the very development that Norway wished to prevent. In fact, recent revelations from Soviet archives show that elements within the Soviet military and Foreign Ministry in the summer of 1945 did entertain ideas about using the Soviet presence in the province of Finnmark as a lever to propose "joint cooperation about strengthening the defence of northern Norway, constructing army, naval, and air bases, strategic railways etc.", and eventually "to raise the question of correcting our land frontier with Norway to our advantage."[15] But the political decision-makers in the Kremlin evidently turned them down, and in the event the Soviet troops withdrew peacefully from the area in September, after seeing that the western liberation forces which came to Norway after 8 May had also been pulled out.

The American preference for a universalist "United Nations" approach to post-war security; Norway's concern about Soviet war aims in the high north and the refusal of the western powers to share that concern; and the apparent western disinterest in Norway's fear that the 350 000-strong undefeated German forces in the country might attempt a violent "last stand" – all this was bound to affect the mood of the Norwegian government in the last year of the war. The main result was that the government in the course of 1944 passed from an early restatement of its Atlantic policy preferences, through a period of accommodation to Soviet interests, to an attitude of detachment from international politics. From the autumn of 1944 until the end of the war, the prevailing mood among the exiled leaders was one of disillusionment with the western powers, and deep suspicion of the aims of Soviet policy in the north. With such a fundamental uncertainty about the future direction of Norwegian foreign policy, it is hardly surprising that the belated British attempts during 1944 to regenerate interest in Atlantic security schemes should fall on stony ground as far as Norway was concerned. The time for Norway's open commitment to collective Western defence arrangements had passed. Instead, Norway seemed on the way to fulfilling the pessimism of a Foreign Office instruction to the British ambassadors to Norway and Sweden in June 1943. Explaining why the British government was reluctant to take sides in the persistent disputes over the merits or otherwise of Nordic union after the war, this instruction went on to say: "We must not forget that Norway was an ardent neutral until she was invaded by Germany, and that she is a belligerent in spite of herself. There is no reason to suppose that she will not resume the mentality of neutralism as soon as the war is over, notwithstanding the preachings of Monsieur Lie to the contrary."[16] Nordic union, however, seemed an unlikely prospect, after the troublesome wartime relations between the two neighbours on the Scandinavian peninsula.

The Trouble With Sweden

Throughout the Second World War Norway's relations with Sweden were beset with problems. Some were more or less inevitable, arising from Sweden's efforts to preserve her neutrality while being surrounded by neighbours whose situations were quite different: Norway being a member of the Grand Alliance even while the home country was occupied, Denmark being in a sort of half-way house between neutrality and occupation, Finland being a co-belligerent of Germany. For Norway, Sweden was important throughout the war as a potential sanctuary for refugees, and as a conduit for communication between the government and the resistance movement. The more than 1600 kilometres long frontier between the two countries was impossible to control for the German police and troops in Norway, and this "safety valve" gave the Norwegian resistance movement an advantage which most other resistance movements did not have, provided that the Swedish authorities were willing to cooperate. Norway had no wish to see Sweden jeopardise her neutrality status – in other words risk serious German reprisals or armed attack – but clearly hoped that the Swedish government would stretch their definition of neutrality in Norway's favour.

Relations got off to a bad start: on 12 April 1940 King Haakon, pursued by German aircraft which had just bombed a small village where he had stayed over night, sought refuge in a hotel on the Swedish side of the border. He left Swedish territory half an hour later, after a message from Stockholm to the effect that he might not be allowed to return to Norway, and risked being interned. Swedish Cabinet Ministers' diaries, later published, have revealed that the Swedish Prime Minister had wanted to intern him at once.[17] The same diaries also give glimpses of a condescending attitude towards Norway's military effort in a campaign that tended to be seen as a purely British-German affair, with the Norwegian government being regarded as Britain's "puppet". During the campaign various incidents occurred in which Swedish authorities held back supplies to the Norwegian forces, even while allowing the transit through Sweden of German supplies and personnel. A protest note from the Norwegian envoy was curtly dismissed with the statement by the Swedish Foreign Minister that Sweden did what she could for Norway, and "what she did not do she could not do."[18] There was also the matter of the so-called "Narvik Plan", by which the Germans should be persuaded to leave Norwegian territory north of Narvik unoccupied, with the demarcation line supervised by Swedish troops. Although grasped as a last straw by the Norwegian government, in the final days of the campaign, the idea originated in Swedish quarters as a way of ensuring an opening towards the west, to be achieved if necessary against the wishes of the Norwegian government.

On the official level the Swedish envoy, on instructions from Stockholm, stayed behind in Oslo after the invasion instead of accompanying the government to which he was accredited. Direct contact was left in the hands of a junior diplomat, but when the King and government went into exile he also stayed behind, in fact leaving Sweden's official representation with the Norwegian government unattended. Then, instead of reassessing the situation after the Norwegian government established itself as a fully recognised ally of Great Britain, Sweden persisted in regarding the government in exile as a constitutional fiction, or at best as a "quantité negligeable". When the Norwegian envoy in Stockholm died, Sweden refused to accept his appointed successor as a fully accredited representative, whereas the Quisling regime was as late as in 1944 spoken of by the Swedish Foreign Minister as "the government". The Swedish government studiously avoided concluding any formal agreements with the government in exile, and formal notes delivered by Norway's chargé d'affaires were mostly not answered in writing. Couriers carrying messages between the Norwegian government and the resistance movement, and agents crossing into Sweden after missions behind enemy lines, were occasionally arrested or turned back.

It is difficult to avoid the impression that the Swedish government during those first three years, in the expectation of a German victory in the war, regarded the King of Norway and his government as doomed to perdition. Not until late in 1943, when the fortunes of war had turned against Germany, were full diplomatic relations between the Norwegian and Swedish governments restored. The change of policy which ensued also owed much to mounting internal criticism of the Swedish government's handling of affairs relating to Norway. Public opinion in Sweden had shown an increasing sympathy for Norway's cause which Swedish press censorship could not in the long run entirely suppress. Britain's pro-Swedish envoy in Stockholm had a point when he at one stage characterised Swedish-Norwegian relations as having "two facets. There were the relations between the Swedish government and the Norwegian government in exile and there were the relations between the two countries as countries."[19] The most important result of the 1943 change of policy was to allow the establishment of so-called "health camps" for Norwegian refugees of military age, as a first stage in the formation of lightly armed and equipped Norwegian military units. Gradually expanded, those units in due course became an important factor in Norway's preparation of forces destined to enter Norway and ensure an orderly transition from war to peace.

During the summer and autumn of 1944 the western allies put increasing pressure on the Swedish government to put an end to all concessions to Germany. In that connection Trygve Lie decided to accept a formal invitation to visit Sweden for talks. The talks broke much of the ice that had beset the relationship, among other things by giving the impression that the Swedish government would be prepared to assist with military means if necessary to assure an orderly end of the German occupation. The prospect of Swedish troops as liberators of Norway was viewed with some distaste by the Norwegian government, but as the end of the war approached, and as the western allies had few or no forces available for the event that the German forces in Norway should refuse to capitulate, Swedish assistance might become necessary.

In April 1945, as General Eisenhower began to fear that the German forces might attempt a last stand either in southern Germany or in "Festung Norwegen", the Norwegian government formally appealed to the Swedish government to mobilise their army in order to convince the German command that prolonged armed resistance would be futile. The answer from Sweden was a curt refusal, stating that their own information from Norway, through contacts within the Resistance leadership there, clearly indicated that a Swedish mobilisation would have the opposite effect of what the Norwegian government seemed to think. That answer, and the implication that Sweden was a better judge of the situation than Norway's own government, put relations back on ice. In fact the Swedish government was shortly afterwards pressed to agree to receive an allied military mission to discuss contingency plans for an eventual allied campaign to liberate Norway through Swedish territory, and with Swedish assistance. But that was overtaken by the decision by the German command in Norway, on the day after the capitulation of the German forces on the continent, to accept the allied terms for surrender.

Norway in the Grand Alliance: A Balance-Sheet

On 31 May 1945 Prime Minister Nygaardsvold and most of the members of his government returned to the country that they had left almost to a day five years earlier. They had gone into exile as a government in profound despair, alienated from a people which seemed to be turning their backs on them, weighed down by the burden of a failed foreign and defence policy, and linked in destiny to weak allies retreating before a seemingly invincible enemy. They returned as a worthy and respected partner of a mighty and victorious alliance; as unchallenged leaders of a nation united; and at the helm of a functioning government apparatus, armed forces of all three services numbering about 27 000 men, and a severely decimated but still powerful merchant navy. How had it all been possible? The first answer is the obvious one: the victory of Norway's great power partners in the Grand Alliance made it possible. However, a minor power in a great power alliance may also suffer defeat in victory. In this case the allied victory was also Norway's victory. On the whole, and despite the disappointing lack of western allied support in the preparation for the liberation of the homeland, the five wartime years of Norway's active participation in power politics and alliance cooperation has to be summed up as a positive experience. A final contributing factor was of course the peaceful and orderly surrender of the German occupation forces.

Norway's alliance relationship was primarily a British-Norwegian affair. In fact, the close relations with Great Britain as Norway's principal ally left a legacy approaching a very cordial "special relationship". It had not all been plain sailing: as we have seen, relations varied over time as well as among the different sectors in which Norway and the allies cooperated. The explanation for these variations may be found in a multitude of different factors, ranging from the relative weight of the Norwegian contributions to the war effort in the different sectors to matters of individual personal relations among the Norwegians and the British who attempted to work together. Thus, in matters relating to the Resistance movement or to clandestine actions inside Norway, Anglo-Norwegian cooperation was essential, and was also achieved after the initial difficulties had been overcome. In the field of maritime war transport also, where Norway's contribution was a vital one, there were few serious problems. On a more practical level, relations between the British and Norwegian navies and between the respective air forces, where it was mainly a question of working together on a day-to-day operational basis, relations could hardly have been better.

Such a satisfactory alliance relationship was not a foregone conclusion. Above all, a great power such as Britain and a small state such as Norway were not, and in fact could not be, fighting the same war. Whereas Britain had to seek the accommodation of a multitude of different interests, many of a global nature, Norway's war aim was essentially a simple one: the liber-

181

ation of Norway from foreign occupation, and the restoration, *mutatis mutandis*, of conditions as they existed before the war. In addition, both countries in the summer of 1940 carried a ballast of recent history in which mutual trust was not a noticeable element. And although no doubt most of the Norwegians who came to Britain in the war years sensed a community of outlook and interests with the British, they were most definitely in a foreign country, trying to speak a foreign language. For this was the 1940s. Before 1940 the average Norwegian cabinet minister was far less familiar with Whitehall than today's average Norwegian housewife is familiar with Oxford Street. And whereas English tourists in Norway today have the impression that every schoolboy speaks fluent English, at least one Norwegian cabinet minister during the war had to rely on his fluency in French, while another undertook an intensive study of English. When Trygve Lie took over as Norwegian Foreign Minister in November 1940, the Foreign Office, in a biographical sketch which was otherwise very favourable, thought it necessary to remark that Lie's English was "not very good" and that Mrs Lie and their two daughters spoke only Norwegian. There were therefore practical as well as political difficulties to be overcome before satisfactory relations could be established.

The most important single factor in that process, breaking the ice and laying the foundation for cordial Anglo-Norwegian relations during the war, was no doubt the new departure in Norwegian foreign policy which Trygve Lie and his collaborators initiated. And while the "regional alliance" overtones of the "Atlantic policy" concept got pushed to the back burner during the second half of the war, due to American dislike of "old world" alliance politics and preference for a "universalist" approach, the idea of a trans-Atlantic security community was not dead. Similarly, Norway's return to formal non-alignment in 1945 did not signify a return to pre-war policy. The basic premise of Norway's "Atlantic policy" – a realisation that neither large nor small European nations would in the future be able to opt out of the international power game – remained in force, despite a recurring nostalgia for times past when Norway had seemed able to keep out of other nations' quarrels. Moreover, the disillusionment towards the western powers may have concealed, but could not displace, a strong counter-current of practical and functional ties developing from the wartime association, whether in the form of arrangements concerning British supplies and training for Norwegian forces or through Norway's commitment to participation in the Allied occupation of Germany. Such arrangements, while devoid of a formalised security policy superstructure, preserved the central element of the nation's security "lesson" from the war: the conviction that in order to preserve Norway's independence in case of assault by a major power, allies would be needed, and that military cooperation could not be left to improvisation.

9. From War to Cold War

A New Start

The celebration of freedom from foreign occupation, which began in the evening of 7 May 1945 even though the undefeated German troops in Norway did not officially capitulate until the next day, seemed to have no end. From 9 May onwards scattered contingents of allied and Norwegian forces arrived; on 13 May Crown Prince Olav and a delegation of government ministers came to Oslo; on 31 May the Prime Minister and the rest of the government; and then, on 7 June, exactly five years to the day since leaving for exile, King Haakon VII made his triumphant entry into the capital. Interspersed with various less momentous events that also were causes for celebration, the festive atmosphere lasted through the whole of the summer. It nearly got out of hand. The new Prime Minister, the Labour Party's new leader Einar Gerhardsen, on 1 August told the Allied Commander-in-Chief that one of his main tasks was now to get the people back to work!

On the whole, and notwithstanding the rapturous acclaim given to the military parade in Oslo on "Allied Forces Day", 30 June, what the people celebrated was their own victory. And in that victory the heroes were those of the Resistance. The government, the administration, the armed forces, and all the others returning from exile, were a fading minority compared to the mass of the population which had lived in an occupied country and which now saw themselves and their Resistance leaders as the real victors. This introspective mood was also reinforced by the principal task now facing the nation, which was to re-establish democratic institutions on the basis of the new national unity forged by the war, and to re-build the economy for future prosperity. In an unprecedented move, representatives of all the political parties had in the final stages of the war agreed on a joint political programme for post-war Norway, inspired by a feeling that the old party-political divisions had lost much of their meaning. One reflection of that feeling was the attempt, during the summer of 1945, to merge the Labour and Communist parties.

That "joint programme" also set the tone for Norwegian foreign policy in the first post-war years. The – characteristically brief – passage devoted to foreign and defence policy in that document stressed Norway's intention to make "a positive contribution towards the effort to construct an international security system based on international law", and to work to "safeguard the rights of small nations". Those were statements that might as well have been put forward before the war, with the possible exception of the word "security". A more radical innovation was the passage which stated that the country's defence would "build on the experiences of the war years" in order both to protect the country and "fulfil our international military obligations". Both passages were however open to a variety of possible interpretations, and it remained for practical policy-making to show which course Norway would take. A first tentative answer was given in Norway's embrace of the new United Nations organisation.[1]

As a member of the Grand Alliance, Norway had during the war participated in the preparatory work for the new international organisation, and was also present at the San Francisco conference which during May and June 1945 hammered out the UN Charter. There the Norwegian delegation had distinguished itself by a clearly "realist" acceptance of the predominant position of the great powers as bearers of the main responsibility for international peace and security. In particular, Norway pointedly refused to participate in the efforts of the group of small states, led by Australia's Foreign Minister Herbert Evatt, to eliminate the great powers' veto in the Security Council. In the debates at San Francisco Norway stressed that the veto issue should be seen, not as a legal question but as one of "political engineering": drawing a parallel to the requirement of unanimity for the election of Popes in the Catholic church, the argument was that "the rule of unanimity among the great powers meant that they must collaborate, even though they might at times disagree, until they reached a peaceful solution."[2] This acceptance of a privileged position for the great powers was on the other hand accompanied by support for a series of amendments designed to safeguard the rights of small states. Another echo of Norway's traditional approach to international politics was the delegation's efforts to strengthen the position of the International Court of Justice, which would henceforth be the principal judicial organ of the UN. Norway had wished to make its jurisdiction compulsory, meaning that the Court would have an automatic right to consider a dispute brought by one member against another. At the same time, Norway actually proposed an amendment, subsequently written into the Charter, authorising the Security Council to enforce the decisions of the Court. In sum, therefore, Norway demonstrated a remarkable willingness to endow the new organisation with "teeth" so as to make it more effective than its inter-war predecessor.

The emphasis on great power unity underlying the establishment of the United Nations – a lesson learnt from the powerlessness of the more "democratic" structure of the League of Nations – was evidently rooted in

184

a common view of the need for great power cooperation if global security was to be preserved. But there was also in many quarters, and certainly in Norway, a belief in the probability that the "Big Four", having kept together in the Grand Alliance, would somehow manage to work together also in peacetime. Norway, having already signalled her willingness to accept fairly extensive international commitments through her "Atlantic policy", seemed in the spring and summer of 1945 ready to transfer that willingness to the United Nations. The Norwegian desire – and belief – appears to have been that post-war security stood a good chance of being assured, if a framework acceptable to the great powers could be realised without being watered down by small-state fears and demands for "sovereign equality" at all costs.

"Bridge-building" and the Svalbard Issue

Behind the belief that the "Big Four" would be able to cooperate after the war there was, of course, the realisation that without the power of veto the Soviet Union would stay out of the UN and take care of its security interests by other means. With the shadow of Soviet manifest or suspected expansionist aims in the high north, Norway clearly had a vested interest in supporting an organisational framework that was acceptable to the Soviet Union. This also helps to explain why the Norwegian delegation at San Francisco made no contribution to the discussions about the regional security arrangements provided for under the UN Charter. A "western bloc" or "Atlantic association" had ceased to be a practical possibility for all sorts of reasons: the Soviets would see it as a hostile "ganging up" against them, the United States was pathologically averse to old-style regional alliances, Britain was too weak to shoulder the burden of European security, and Norway was determined to avoid any provocation of her Russian neighbour. The solution, for Norway, was to hark back to the somewhat pious hope first expressed in the summer of 1942 of serving as "the link and the bridge for a trustful cooperation between the Soviet Union and the Atlantic powers."[3]

Although the term "bridge-building" was seldom used officially in descriptions of the country's foreign policy after the war, the more neutralist-minded commentators, as well as others who were simply uninterested in foreign affairs, took to it like fish to water. Common to all, however, seems to have been a wish that Norway should avoid involvement in quarrels between the great powers and get on with tasks that were nearer at hand. When the years 1945–48 in Norwegian historiography have got stuck with the label "bridge-building policy", this may say something about a desire, among the first historians of the period, to show the policy in a positive light. Later accounts have been fairly unanimous in describing the main tenor of Norwegian foreign policy during those years as one of disengagement from international affairs. Even in the United Nations, which in fre-

Halvard Lange served as Norway's Foreign Minister from 1946 until 1965, and thus had a profound influence on the country's foreign and security policy, especially its relations with the Atlantic Alliance. A convinced internationalist from his student days, the horrors of the First World War first made him join the ranks of the pacifists, and then the moderate Social Democratic Party. In the 1930s he abandoned pacifism and advocated a collective security solution through the League of Nations. His views on becoming Foreign Minister were well suited to Norway's general policy of non-alignment and support for the United Nations, and his support for Norway's choice of an Atlantic solution for its security problem was the result of a gradual process during 1948. Thereafter he became a staunch supporter of NATO and of Norway's active membership of the Alliance.

quent official policy declarations was described as "the cornerstone of Norwegian foreign policy", Norway demonstrated a consistent tendency to abstain from taking a position whenever the great powers were divided on an issue. When Norway in 1946 also declared that she was not a candidate for election as a non-permanent member of the first Security Council, an Oslo newspaper was in no doubt that this reflected a wish to avoid having to take sides. Arne Ording, who stayed on as adviser when Halvard Lange took over from Trygve Lie as Foreign Minister, apparently said of the policy that "it is all right to crawl under the table once in a while, but one should not take up residence there". Halvard Lange himself later quoted that statement as probably the best and briefest characterisation of Norway's problem during those years.[4]

The American ambassador to Norway in December 1945 summed up his impression of the country's foreign policy in three terse points: "1. Pro-UK-US to the greatest extent she dares. 2. Pro-Soviet to the extent she must. 3. Pro-UNO to the greatest extent she can."[5] The resulting low profile taken by Norway was primarily due to fears of provoking the Soviet Union. An early example of that was the handling of an invitation for Winston Churchill to visit Norway in 1946. The purpose was to honour the great wartime leader of the victorious Grand Alliance, of which Norway had been a modest member. But after Churchill held his famous March 1946 "iron curtain" speech in Fulton, Missouri, the government got cold feet. Since the invitation to Churchill had come from King Haakon, an outright cancellation was impossible, and an attempt to get the British Foreign Office to persuade Churchill to find an excuse not to come was sharply rebuffed. The King himself then saved the day by a personal letter to Churchill, in which he explained that the timing was inconvenient – to which Churchill replied that he did not mind postponing the visit until such time as the situation got better – or perhaps much worse!

An important reason behind this concern about Soviet reactions was Molotov's resurrection of the Svalbard issue. The first indication that the Soviet Union had not forgotten the affair came in February 1946, in the form of a message from Molotov through the Norwegian envoy in Moscow that it was time to put the matter on the agenda again. Halvard Lange, who had succeeded Trygve Lie as Foreign Minister when the latter had shortly beforehand become the first Secretary General of the United Nations, cautiously consulted his colleagues in the government. Less burdened by the onus of previous policy, and free of the pressure of the presence of the Red Army on Norwegian soil, the new government clearly hoped the problem would go away. The ambassador was therefore told that if Molotov should again bring up the issue, his answer might be that in the changed circumstances brought about by the two countries' membership of the United Nations, the question of joint bases ought to be dealt with in accordance with the paragraphs in the UN Charter concerning armed forces and military bases to be made available to the world organisation. Ambassador Andvord, however, who had had a leading role in the 1944–45 handling of the matter, persuaded Lange and the government that since the Soviets saw Svalbard as a purely bilateral matter for the two countries, it was best to say nothing and hope that particular dog would go back to sleep.

The Paris Peace Conference in the summer of 1946, where all the members of the Grand Alliance met to discuss the peace treaties with Germany's five wartime associates, was the first opportunity for Molotov to meet Norway's new Foreign Minister. Although the meeting was reasonably friendly – or as friendly as any meeting with Molotov could be – his first words to Lange was a reminder that the Svalbard issue was still unsolved. On the Norwegian side the issue had been discussed by the Storting in closed sessions in the summer of 1945, while Soviet troops were still present in Finnmark. Trygve Lie, not surprisingly, had then vigorously defended the government's handling of the issue, including the offer of 9 April 1945 to negotiate about a joint defence of the islands. Although some of the parliamentarians had misgivings, Lie apparently interpreted the consensus as one of support for his conduct of the affair, as well as for his intention to pursue the same line if the Soviets should reopen the issue.

When Molotov then reopened the matter in Paris, and actually proposed to have negotiations during the UN General Assembly's sessions that autumn, a special cabinet committee was put together. This resulted in a brief for Lange to propose negotiations on a new basis, centred on a revision of the Svalbard Treaty itself. But when Lange in New York met Trygve Lie and others involved in the wartime handling of the affair, he was urged to seek new instructions based on a return to Norway's 9 April 1945 proposals. A divided government tried to work out a compromise which more or less left the vacillating Foreign Minister with a free hand. In the end, Lange met Molotov accompanied by Terje Wold, now chairman of the Storting's foreign affairs committee, who as Minister of Justice in London had been the principal advocate for "appeasing" the Russians over Svalbard. While agreeing to consider the meeting as talks rather than negotiations, Molotov must have been pleased to find that Lange was prepared to take the 1945 proposals as the basis. He voiced no objections to the Norwegian

187

Einar Gerhardsen, here in front of the microphones on his arrival as the first NATO head of government to visit the Soviet Union, was Norway's Labour Prime Minister from 1945 to 1965 except for two short intervals. He was a strong leader, but with a particularly well-developed sense of the mood of the party, the voters, and public opinion. In foreign policy his instinctive sympathy for Nordic cooperation did not prevent him from fully supporting the decision to join NATO, but during the 1950s his lack of enthusiasm for armaments and the military made him interested in seeking openings for East-West detente. His visit to Moscow in 1955 was an early effort in that direction.

proposals concerning joint Soviet-Norwegian defence of the archipelago, but made it clear that Bear Island could still be an issue. The Soviets would also want equality of status concerning exploitation of the coal resources on the islands. The talks ended with an agreement that formal negotiations should start early in 1947.

Back in Oslo the government's "hard-liners", led by Defence Minister Jens Christian Hauge and supported by Prime Minister Gerhardsen, now took the matter to hand. A meeting between Gerhardsen, Hauge and Lange produced an agreement that meant a complete reversal of the position agreed with Molotov: Norway would declare her willingness to discuss economic questions relating to Svalbard, but considered the issue of joint defence as bypassed by the recent proposals put forward by the Soviet Union at the UN about general disarmament. In spite of determined opposition from the "appeasers", this time represented by Arne Ording and other senior officials of the Foreign Ministry, this was the line which the government during January and February 1947 got the foreign affairs committee to agree to, and which the Storting then sanctioned at a closed meeting with a resounding majority. Only the eleven Communist members voted against. The decision was then communicated to the Soviet Union, and although the message was couched in exquisite diplomatic language, it can be assumed that the senior officials waited with bated breath for the explosion. The reaction in Moscow was dead silence!

Norway's nearly disastrous handling of the Svalbard affair in 1944–45 can only be explained by a mixture of deep-seated fears of Russian/Soviet ex-

188

pansionist aims in the high north, and a failure to understand the relative unimportance of Svalbard in the over-all picture of Soviet foreign policy. No one in the Norwegian government – with the possible exception of the Prime Minister – seems to have considered at least the possibility that Molotov's demands were simply a trial balloon, to test how far Norway's cooperative stance from early 1944 could be stretched in a situation where the Red Army had a foothold on Norwegian soil. Such a theory could then have been tested through the use of delaying tactics, for which the Norwegian government had one particularly good card: the fact that the Svalbard Treaty was a multilateral treaty, to which over 40 states including the western great powers were parties. Any change of that treaty could therefore never be a bilateral Soviet-Norwegian affair, but would according to international law require virtually endless correspondence and discussions with the other signatories. Of this the Russians were perfectly well aware: at the meeting in the Kremlin Molotov had stated that it was their intention "to take the matter up in due course with the other Allied signatories to the Treaty."

The Norwegian government, from an ill-conceived determination to somehow "keep the initiative", instead chose a different course. It more or less invited the Soviets to press on with their demands, and also steered them towards a concentration on the military and security aspects of the affair. It is more understandable that the government in 1946 found it difficult to backtrack from the disastrous 9 April 1945 offer to the Soviets, taking into account the pressure exerted on behalf of that offer by its authors. The position of Halvard Lange, the new Foreign Minister, was an unenviable one. As he himself exclaimed to the British ambassador in January 1947: "How could any Norwegian Foreign Minister have agreed to this, and how can I get us out of it?"[6] In his 30 January statement to the foreign affairs committee he defended his rejection of the "joint defence" concept. To discuss the defence of a part of Norwegian territory with an individual foreign state would have conflicted with Norway's established foreign policy, he said. In other words, a return to the 1945 Svalbard offer would not have been bridge-building – it would have meant going a long way towards choosing the Soviet side in the burgeoning Cold War.

The Spanish Question

As if the thorny Svalbard issue was not enough, another urgent matter landed on the desk of the harassed Halvard Lange within a few days of his taking over as Foreign Minister. The Spanish question, like the Svalbard issue, was a matter inherited from previous governments. But there the similarity ended. Norway's relations with Spain had been abnormal ever since the outbreak of the Spanish Civil War in 1936, although the Nygaardsvold gov-

ernment just before the war – on 31 March 1939 – had swallowed the bitter pill and officially recognised the Franco regime. Norway's export trade
and shipping had only begun to resume their potentially important and
profitable activities, however, when war came to Norway. During the war
the Norwegian government in exile maintained its diplomatic representation in Madrid, but the Franco government, although it did nothing at the
official level, sent no envoy to the Norwegian government in London. Spain
even indicated an intention to recognise the Quisling regime and break
relations with the legitimate Norwegian government, but was persuaded to
refrain from doing so. The peculiar one-sided relationship continued into
the post-war period, as Spain came under increasing international pressure
to get rid of Franco's fascist dictatorship. Public opinion in several European
countries demanded that their governments break relations with Spain, and
the Norwegian delegation was one of the activists behind a February 1946
resolution from the United Nations General Assembly, which in somewhat
veiled language encouraged the member states to act in the spirit of earlier
decisions not to admit Spain to the UN.

In France and Great Britain, like in Norway, the trade unions and the
Communist and Socialist parties were in the forefront of the campaign
against the Franco regime. By the end of February 1946 both the French
and British governments seemed on the point of breaking relations, perhaps
even organising a follow-up through international action by way of the UN
Security Council. Rumour had it that even the United States might support some such action. In Norway a flood of resolutions from trade unions
as well as from the general public demanded action by the government. The
Oslo dock-workers on 6 March decided to boycott ships trading with
Spain, and on the same day the Storting was the scene for a heated debate
provoked by a question from a Communist representative. The government
was clearly reluctant towards the idea of Norway acting alone. An isolated
Norwegian breach of relations would have no effect on the situation in
Spain, and would cause considerable harm to Norwegian trade and shipping interests that were in the process of establishing themselves in the
Spanish market. But the motion voted by the Storting, proposed by a
prominent member of the government's own Labour Party, while it left the
government some freedom of action, amounted to a clear expectation of
some initiative from Norway.

During the summer and autumn of 1946, while the pressure on the government continued, Lange consulted the British and other European governments about the prospects of some joint international action. The
answers must have strengthened his conviction that even diplomatic pressure on a wide front would only produce a siege mentality inside Spain,
since there was no Spanish opposition either on the inside or among the
Spaniards in exile with sufficient strength to offer a viable alternative regi-

me. Demands on the domestic front for Norwegian initiatives still led the
government to work actively for some joint UN action beyond purely verbal condemnations. In the meantime the Spanish government had evidently determined that Norway was a leader in the offensive against them. A
propaganda campaign in Spanish newspapers was tailored to present Norway as an enemy of the Spanish people, and in January 1947 the Spanish
government went one step further, threatening to shut out Norwegian ships
from Spanish ports. This was followed by a demand for the accreditation of
a Spanish envoy to the Norwegian government. The anti-Spanish opposition had by then weakened considerably, and its demand now focused on
maintaining trade and diplomatic relations with Spain at the reduced level
where they had been ever since the war: in other words, no normalisation
of relations. The government, however, seeing that Norway was by then the
only state outside the eastern bloc without a trade agreement with Spain,
feared the loss of the entire Spanish market for Norwegian shipping and
trade. After long and difficult discussions with the opposition, which still
included the left wing of the Labour Party, the government won through.
On 22 March 1947 the Storting, against the votes of the Communist
representatives plus two Labour members, voted to establish normal trade
relations with Spain. Two months later Halvard Lange got the agreement of
the Storting's committee for foreign affairs to accept the accreditation of a
Spanish chargé d'affaires, stressing that the diplomat in question would have
his residence in Copenhagen!

Although Norway's policy in the Spanish question ended with a full
retreat from the hard-line stance with which it began, the country's fundamental aversion to the kind of regime that Franco represented did not
abate. When Norway accepted Spain's membership of the United Nations,
in 1955, it was as part and parcel of a compromise to break the east-west
deadlock over the admission of new members. Norway had always supported the principle of universality of membership both in the League of
Nations and in the UN. So when the Soviet Union proposed a deal whereby 16 candidate states – all except Outer Mongolia and Japan – would be
admitted, Norway no longer saw any reason to oppose Spanish membership. Yet membership of NATO was a different matter altogether, even
though the Alliance already contained countries like Portugal, Greece, and
Turkey, that were hardly representative of the democratic ideal that NATO
professed. Here Norway drew a firm line and, with her veto power in
reserve, more or less single-handedly and against a fair amount of pressure
from her major allies prevented Spain's membership until after Franco's
death in 1975 and the subsequent restoration of the Spanish democratic
monarchy.

There was very little disagreement in Norway about the country's attitude to the Franco regime. The hot dispute during 1946 centred on what

191

to do about it. Halvard Lange, the government, and the more level-headed members of the Storting, all realised that only massive and long-term international pressure, if anything, had any hope of producing a change in the governance of Spain. For Norway to try to "go it alone", thinking that she could serve as a "spearhead" which others would follow, was clearly an illusion. Yet the massive demands during the spring and summer of 1946 were evidently based on that illusion. One reason for giving so much space to the affair here is the fact that – as will be seen later – the vision of Norway as a "spearhead" or "vanguard" for international action on ethical or moral grounds would get a new lease on life from the 1970s. This suggests that such a role for Norway, and the belief in it, has deep-seated roots in the Norwegian psyche.

The Demise of "Bridge-building"

Earlier in this chapter it has been stated that Norway's "bridge-building" during the first post-war years consisted mainly of keeping the lowest possible profile in matters of serious dispute between the Soviet Union and the western great powers. The clearest exception to that general trend was Norway's activity during the Paris Peace Conference in the summer of 1946. In many ways the Norwegian policy line there represented a continuation of the line taken at San Francisco the year before. The Paris conference was clearly designed so that while the small states would be heard, the decisions would be up to the great powers. As could be expected, most of the small states – again led by Australia's Foreign Minister Herbert Evatt – tried to gang up against such great power dominance. Again, Norway stood out in her support of the great powers, dismissing as unrealistic the wish of smalle states to apply democratic voting rules to international relations. It was necessary to take into account the great differences in power and responsibility, and if the smaller states were not willing to accept that fact, then their policy would be based on an illusion, and they might end up losing all influence. The peace of the world depended on establishing trustful cooperation among the great powers, and it would serve no purpose to construct a principal antagonism between great and small powers.

The great power/small state dispute dominated the first two weeks of the conference. At issue was the procedural framework proposed by the four great powers together. When the small-state caucus objected to the privileged position of the great powers, the United States and Great Britain tried to meet them part of the way whereas the Soviet Union stood firm on the original proposals. Hence the battle seemed to pit the small states against the Soviets, whereas Norway and to some extent France worked for compromises that might satisfy the Soviet Union. However, after some initial success in bridging differences, the conference soon split into two camps, aided

192

in some way by Soviet unwillingness or inability to acknowledge the efforts of Norway and France to act as honest brokers. Molotov meticulously noted the stance of the Norwegian delegation, and praised its initial attitude. But he soon reverted to the traditional Soviet position whereby states were either with them or against them. Increasingly the western great powers began to apply the same principle. Although the mediating role played by France prevented a break-up of the conference during the struggle between Jugoslavia and Italy over Trieste, Norway's modest bridge-building efforts in the end satisfied no one.

Halvard Lange's first public policy statement on becoming Foreign Minister in February 1946 was a strong affirmation of Norway's non-aligned stance. "As a loyal member of the United Nations we must do what we can towards strengthening the mutual trust among the nations on which that organisation depends, and hence cooperate with all, without participating in the formation of any bloc."[7] At international conferences like the Paris Peace Conference, and at the UN, the aim of the latter part of that programme could somehow be pursued by either not voting at all in controversial questions, or by voting now with the eastern group, now with the western powers. Even so, the progressive worsening of the east-west relationship meant that Norway risked falling between two stools, as both the Soviets and the western powers increasingly expected Norway to "declare herself". There was a clear tone of exasperation in the outburst by Britain's generally pro-Norwegian ambassador Sir Laurence Collier, in April 1947, that both the government and the people had "an increasing tendency to bury their heads in the snow in the hope of avoiding entanglement in the struggle between the Great Powers."[8] This balancing act met its first serious test after the American Secretary of State George C. Marshall in June 1947 announced his plan for US assistance to the economic recovery of war-ravaged Europe.

Since later accounts of this period have tended to emphasise the "aid" aspect of the Marshall Plan, it is important to keep in mind that it also contained a political programme. The participating countries were expected to join in a fairly comprehensive organised cooperation, shaped on the lines of free trade. But already before such terms had been spelt out, most of the potential recipients assumed that there would be certain political strings attached to the offer of aid. It is against that background that the initial Norwegian reactions to the Marshall Plan must be seen. A joint European reconstruction plan based on American dollar aid could all too easily develop into an economic and political bloc formation. Halvard Lange's initial reaction was that if Norway could afford to keep out of it, that would be the best option. Although Norway had a hard currency problem, it seemed much less severe than that of most other European countries, and might be solved by outright currency loans. The political aspects were therefore uppermost in the minds of the government, since it was assumed that the Soviet Union would not join. There was also the concern that the principle of the state-regulated "planned economy", which was at the base of the Labour government's reconstruction policy, could not survive against the economic liberalism advocated by the United States.

Norway, together with the other two Scandinavian countries, still accepted the French-British invitation to a conference to elaborate the framework for an organisation of cooperation. One reason reflected a lingering hope that bridge-building might still work: if the cooperation could be anchored in the United Nations Economic Commission for Europe, then the Eastern European countries might join, in which case the Scandinavians might play a mediating role. But behind it all was the stark realisation, expressed in a memorandum by Arne Ording, that to stay outside "would be a demonstrative alignment with the eastern bloc." At the conference Norway worked to limit the scope of the planned cooperation, in favour of what has been called a "shopping-list approach", probably hoping that Britain's Labour government would support a framework of the least possible interference in the economic policies of participating countries. This might also make it easier for some Eastern European countries to join later, although the Soviet Union clearly was putting pressure on them to stay out. But when the Americans intervened to specify certain conditions for their aid, the "shopping-list approach" fell by the wayside. At the same time the Norwegian government began to realise that the country's hard currency problem was far greater than anticipated. The resulting dilemma was to permeate the process by which the government through the winter tried to reach a final decision on whether to join the permanent Marshall Plan organisation. But the worsening East-West climate, highlighted through the break-up of the conference of the great power Foreign Ministers in December 1947 and the Communist take-over in Czechoslovakia in February 1948, made it clear that Norway's foreign policy balancing act had to stop. It was not, after all, a question of choosing sides. Being ideologically, economically, and culturally a western country, Norway had only one option when fence-sitting was no longer possible.

Seen in retrospect, Norway's "low-profile" foreign policy during the "bridge-building" years can hardly be judged a success. The Soviet Union as well as the western great powers realised that Norway for all sorts of reasons was a western country, and that if push came to shove she would join the group led by the Anglo-Saxon powers. As seen from the Kremlin, a Norwegian balancing act hence lacked credibility. The only foreign policy course that could satisfy the Soviet Union was one which followed its lead on specific issues. For a while during 1945 and 1946 Moscow appears to have had hopes that admiration and sympathy, which the Soviet Union enjoyed by virtue of its war record, might lead Norway into closer political and even military association with its eastern great power neighbour, and not only in relation to Svalbard. This at least is the impression left by Soviet Foreign Ministry documents that recently have become available. In the summer of 1947, however, presumably partly due to Norway's rejection of the Svalbard demands, the Soviet ambassador to Norway had changed his tune: he now saw Norway's bridge-building rhetoric as "only a cover for increasingly strong political and military links with England."[9] By that time western patience with Norway's balancing act was also coming to an end, although few policy-makers were as bad-tempered as George Kennan, the Director of the US State Department's Policy Planning Staff, who in an analysis from September 1947 denounced the Scandinavians as "pathologically timorous about the Russians".[10]

Judged in the light of information available to Norwegian policy-makers at the time, however, and the circumstances then prevailing, Norway had good reasons to avoid alienating the Soviet Union: she was facing an overwhelmingly powerful neighbour, in a part of the world that might become an area of East-West confrontation due to Soviet designs on Svalbard and US-British bases on Iceland and Greenland. In a wider context it also made sense to avoid or at least postpone the creation of a situation where the Soviets, faced with a bloc of wartime allies "ganging up" against them, would revert to a siege mentality. In addition to all that came political uncertainties about the United States as a leader of the free world, in view of its unrestrained capitalist system, its overwhelming economic strength, and its latent isolationism. Most Norwegians felt more at ease with the idea of British leadership, and in the Norwegian Labour government many shared British Foreign Secretary Ernest Bevin's wish that a third way might be found between what he in his colourful prose called "the red tooth and claw of American capitalism and the Communist dictatorship of Soviet Russia".[11]

The Western Security Connection

When the balancing act of Norway's bridge-building lost credibility, a major reason was the unspoken assumption of western protection that lay behind the low-key but still visible counter-current of functional defence and security links with Great Britain. In September 1946 the Labour government presented to the Storting its first plan for the reconstruction of the armed forces after the war, the so-called Three Year Plan. The introduction to the plan pointed to the obvious need for the country's defence policy to be in tune with its foreign policy and the international situation. By that time Norway's foreign policy doctrine was firmly locked on support for the United Nations. The Defence Ministry, however, had to take into account that adequate defence cannot be improvised, and "responsible authorities cannot disregard the fact that there exists today a certain tension between the great powers – in particular between the western great powers and the Soviet Union". The United Nations could not by itself guarantee the peace, and gave no security to the smaller countries in any conflict between the great powers. Defence preparedness was therefore necessary, especially for a country with an exposed strategic location in a border area between east and west, since "armed conflict between great powers could conceivably be prefaced by actions against larger or smaller areas of our territory." The first necessity was a defensive capability which would serve notice to the world that any attack would be resisted. However,

> It is difficult to imagine that Norway should have to defend herself against assault without having allies, and it is necessary to realise that Norway with her limited military and economic resources could not alone resist for any length of time against superior military power. But Norway's armed forces must be able to hold on alone until we get effective assistance from those who might become our allies.[12]

Those potential allies were of course not named. But only a few months earlier the Storting had approved a secret proposition from the government for the purchase of 300 million kroner's worth of armaments for the three-year period. The supplier of the armaments was Great Britain. Indeed, Norway's dependence on Britain as a source of military supplies was so clear that the Defence Ministry, in proposing the purchases, could hardly pretend that the issue of foreign policy implications was irrelevant. But in admitting that this could be raised as an issue, the Ministry promptly moved to dismiss it: firstly, Britain was the only country willing to sell, for example, naval vessels; secondly, "we must buy where we can pay" – an oblique allusion to Norway's foreign currency situation with a surfeit of pounds and shortages of dollars and Swedish kroner. "Besides," the Ministry asserted, "the purchase of materiel carries no commitment towards military cooperation. In that respect Norway stands as freely after as before the purchase".

Only one member of the Storting questioned those assumptions during the debate on the appropriations. The spokesman for the Communist Party was clearly concerned to see the nation's armed forces linked so strongly with the arms and technical equipment of one particular foreign power. He saw Norway becoming dangerously dependent on Britain for military supplies, and referred also to the various schemes by which many Norwegian officers were being trained in the United Kingdom. He might have added to his list the recent decision to have a Norwegian army brigade serve under British command in the Allied occupation forces in Germany, but he did not – nor did he register his dissent by voting against the appropriations. During the parliamentary debate on the Three Year Plan, a few

Norway's strong commit-
ment to non-alignment
and support for the
United Nations in the
immediate aftermath of
World War II did not pre-
vent the maintenance of
functional military and
defence links with her
wartime ally Great
Britain. The most visible
link was the presence of a
Norwegian brigade as part
of the British Army on
the Rhine during the
occupation of Germany.

months later, the one representative who raised the issue of functional ties
to potential allies was again the same spokesman for the Communists. In
amplification of his earlier remarks he again pointed to the risk of becoming
dependent on the supplier of arms and equipment, a dependence which

> is not compatible with the foreign policy which the people wish to see con-
> ducted. Our people desire to have a policy which prevents the forming of
> any bloc and bars the association of our country with any such bloc. We will
> ourselves decide on which side to fight, if it should become necessary – with-
> out being dependent on one specific country's deliveries of arms or techni-
> cal and political training of our officers.[13]

The other deputies, who gave their unanimous approval to the arms purchases as well as to the concept underlying the Three Year Plan, were hardly unaware of their foreign policy implications. Their approval may therefore be taken as approval of the unspoken assumption that if Norway should
be attacked, then the source of military supplies would also be in the vanguard of her unnamed potential allies. This assumption of British assistance
in the event of aggression from any other great power was, after all, forty
years old. And the five years of close military cooperation in the wartime
alliance had served to reinforce the underlying assumption by creating a
multitude of personal and functional links between the armed forces of

197

Norway and Great Britain. The main difference between the inter-war and the post-war period was that British assistance, backed by American strength, was no longer taken for granted as being sufficiently motivated by Britain's own interests alone. It was now realised that Norway's own defences would have to bear the brunt of any attack, until western assistance could be organised and brought into action.

The carefully phrased assumptions of the Three Year Plan were to remain unchanged as the basis for the subsequent defence budgets. In the debate on the defence budget for the fiscal year 1948 (July 1947 – June 1948) the Defence Minister in June 1947 quoted from the Three Year Plan, and said that the same basis continued to apply "since the situation has not changed in its fundamentals". At the same time, the Under-Secretary in the Defence Ministry put on paper a long memorandum with a somewhat different tenor. That document made it perfectly clear that "those who might become our allies" were in fact the western great powers, but went on to raise the question whether the simple assumption of such assistance was still sufficient, without some more definitive reciprocal measures from Norway's side. Would such external assistance be provided in the possibly very short time that Norway's own defence could hold an enemy at bay? The gist of that memorandum was clearly that more concrete preparatory measures were necessary to ensure that the assistance would come in time and be effective.

Scandinavian or North Atlantic Alliance?

The catalyst for the process which in the course of fourteen months – from the end of January 1948 to the end of March 1949 – was to bring about a complete break with Norway's official foreign policy line, was British Foreign Secretary Bevin's proposal, on 22 January 1948, for a Western Union. Norway was not on Bevin's list of invitations to such an organisation, and initial Norwegian reactions at the official level were extremely reserved. The Prime Minister himself stressed that Bevin's speech provided no occasion whatsoever for any decision on participation by Norway in any kind of bloc or security association. But the non-socialist opposition, and activist circles within the ruling Labour party, were showing signs of impatience. In the defence budget for the fiscal year 1949, presented in January 1948, the government again asserted that the assumptions behind the Three Year Plan, and the assessment of the international situation on which it was based, retained their validity. The budget document nevertheless referred to the recent increase of tensions between the great powers which had caused the Foreign Minister in his December statement to the Storting to foreshadow the possibility of a future policy revision. In tune with that the Defence Ministry intimated that plans were being prepared for extraordinary measures "if it should seem desirable and economically possible to increase the nation's preparedness against sudden aggression and to speed up our readiness for mobilisation."

Dramatic events now followed each other in rapid succession. First came the Communist take-over in Czechoslovakia on 25 February, an occurrence which made a strong impression since that country was seen in Norway as another "bridge-builder" between east and west. Then came the report that the Soviet Union was "offering" Finland a pact of friendship and cooperation, presumably akin to the pacts already made with Eastern European states which had pushed them down the slope towards satellite status. Worse still, that report came accompanied by rumours that Norway was next on the list of such "invitations". Norway's initial reaction was a fairly dramatic increase

In February 1948 President Benes of Czechoslovakia (left) was forced to appoint the Communist leader Clement Gottwald (right) as Prime Minister and head of a Communist-dominated government. The coup in Czechoslovakia – a country seen by many Norwegians as a fellow 'bridge-builder' between East and West – was a major influence in bringing about a reorientation of Norwegian security policy towards alignment with the West.

of her defence preparedness, particularly in northern Norway. In March 1948 the Storting approved an extraordinary expenditure of 100 million kroner for such purposes, and authorised the call-up of extra personnel.

These extraordinary defence measures were the most visible indication that a national security crisis might be approaching. In the meantime Defence Minister Hauge had on his own quietly undertaken a major new initiative towards a clarification of the possibilities of western assistance: on 17 February, following a previous conversation with the United States' military attaché, he called the US naval and air attachés to his office and "raised numerous questions re possibilities and probable character of American assistance to Norway in case of war". According to the embassy report he

asked what place Norway might have in American air strategy, what aid might be expected in early stages of war, and whether, where, and at what stages in such emergency US would want to establish air, sea and land bases in Norway. He placed considerable emphasis on Norway's role in guided missile warfare. Hauge gave definite impression he hoped obtain some form of American commitment to aid Norway should war occur.[14]

This was followed by Foreign Minister Lange's official enquiry to the

199

Jens Christian Hauge emerged as the leader of the military resistance in 1942, at the age of 27, and became Minister of Defence when Einar Gerhardsen formed his Labour government in 1945. He was a staunch advocate of close cooperation with the western great powers, and was instrumental in convincing the Prime Minister and the rest of the government to join the Atlantic Alliance. His somewhat ruthless manner made enemies among the military as well as among his Cabinet colleagues, and he left his post at the beginning of 1952. He then had a brief spell as Minister of Justice in 1955, but remained throughout an influential figure behind the scenes in Norwegian politics.

ambassadors of Britain and the United States in Oslo on 8 March, about what help Norway could expect if attacked. Three days later British Foreign Secretary Bevin made an urgent request to Washington for negotiations about trans-Atlantic security cooperation "before Norway goes under". The case of Norway thus became one of the triggers for the process which began with the so-called Pentagon talks, continued with the Washington security talks, and ended up with the formation of the Atlantic Alliance.

The gist of the various reactions from the western powers to Lange's 8 March enquiry about possible military support must have been encouraging in one respect: they seemed to suggest that Norway was of sufficient importance to western defence to serve as a trip-wire for western action in case of Soviet aggression. But to the extent that the Norwegian government had hoped for more concrete assurances of assistance, they were disappointed. The official reply to Defence Minister Hauge's questions to the US service attachés, when it finally came through in the middle of June, could hardly be called encouraging. The brief cablegram merely stated that the "Role of Norway in US defence plans necessarily dependent upon over-all strategy", which would again depend on whatever collective measures might be developed by the United States and Western Europe, and on Norway's eventual participation in such measures. The message ended with a pointed reminder that "US strategic concepts are beyond the purview of armed forces attachés". Even a passage on supplies of armaments did not go beyond a promise that this would be "sympathetically considered". The British had even less to offer.

In April Foreign Minister Lange gave the public a glimpse of some of the soul-searching which he had undertaken since the beginning of the year. The impression he gave was that if Norway should consider joining any form of regional security scheme, then a Scandinavian solution would be his preferred alternative, possibly in some kind of association with Great Britain. Within weeks of Lange's speech Swedish Foreign Minister Östen Undén, fearing that Norway was adrift away from non-alignment and towards a western security arrangement, initiated talks which in the end persuaded the Norwegian government to explore the possibility of a Scandinavian solution to the security of the region. The issue of Scandinavian defence cooperation henceforth came to dominate the political agenda during the remainder of 1948. A Scandinavian alternative clearly had strong appeal. Among politicians, particularly in the Labour Party, it appeared as "the lesser evil" if it really became necessary for Norway to seek external support for her security. It would also be easier to swallow for a public entrenched in the image of Norway as a non-aligned country that still put its trust in the United Nations. For the government, however, the question was which alternative could provide sufficient security "guarantees": a Scandinavian defence pact, or an Atlantic security scheme?

To make a long story short, the former alternative fell through mainly because the Norwegian government found its likely effect as a deterrent against attack insufficient, in view of Norway's exposed strategic situation. An expert "Scandinavian Defence Committee", which had begun its work in the middle of October, presented its report on 14 January 1949, and on the crucial question of deterrence, the Committee said:

Sweden's firmly neutralist Foreign Minister Östen Undén, seen here (on the left) in conversation with Halvard Lange, tried very hard during 1948 to prevent Norway 'going west' and to persuade Norway as well as Denmark to join with Sweden in a non-aligned defence union.

> The preventive effect of a defence association can generally be said to depend on how an attacker judges the ability of the association to defend itself. Since prepared cooperation increases the total war strength, a Scandinavian Defence Association whose members have shown in words and in action their will to common defence against attack, can be expected to a certain extent to have a preventive effect and to constitute some guarantee against isolated actions. Such a defence association cannot however by itself be considered sufficient to forestall an isolated or coup-de-main attack ...

Having raised this question mark regarding the credibility of an isolated Scandinavian alliance as a deterrent, the Committee went on to state that:

> On the whole it needs to be strongly emphasised that a defence association, or any otherwise constituted prepared cooperation among the three Scandinavian countries, does not exclude the necessity for outside assistance. In peacetime, assistance will be required for the build-up and modernisation of armed forces. If they were to be attacked, armed assistance would be needed already in the initial phase.[15]

One reason why the Scandinavian alternative had much support was that it might be seen as less provocative by the Soviet Union. The "Soviet threat" was clearly in everyone's mind during this period, although it was hardly ever spoken about. Sweden attempted to raise the issue indirectly, mainly through muted warnings about the likelihood of Soviet reprisals against Finland if the other Scandinavian countries became linked with a Western bloc. In that connection it is worth noting that the Swedish Ministers during the Scandinavian negotiations repeatedly, and in spite of Norwegian assurances to the contrary, claimed that allied military bases would be an inevitable consequence of any Scandinavian association with a Western alliance. However, so far as it is possible to ascertain from the available Soviet evidence, the Russians were firmly convinced that a Scandinavian defence union, even if nominally non-aligned, would still become linked with a Western bloc.[16]

The Road to NATO

At the official level, little was said during this "Scandinavian" phase about the alternative of an Atlantic security scheme, which in the autumn became a strong contender for Norwegian preferences. But on 10 December 1948 Lange gave a first indication that Norway might have to seek a solution to her security problem in a wider framework if the Scandinavian alternative should fail to provide a satisfactory answer. Not until the Foreign Minister made a major policy declaration to the Storting on 27 January 1949, however, was the public officially informed about the contemplated alternative to a Scandinavian defence pact. Lange revealed the differences of opinion which had emerged during the negotiations between Norway, Sweden and Denmark concerning the very nature of the proposed defence pact, and stated that in Norway's view such a pact, even if not connected by treaty to any larger regional security system, must "in character and content" rest on the idea of "regional collaboration within an area large enough to constitute a factor of real power".

One week later, the Foreign Minister returned to the Storting to inform them that the negotiations for a Scandinavian defence pact had failed, and that the Cabinet would now investigate the conditions of an eventual invitation to participate in the discussion about an Atlantic Treaty. A high-powered delegation, led by the Foreign Minister himself, would therefore go on a fact-finding mission to Washington and London. High on the list of matters to be discussed was the question, raised by the Soviet ambassador just before their departure, of allied military bases in Norway.

It was on 29 January, in the midst of the final discussions about the Scandinavian alternative, that the Soviet ambassador in Oslo, in a surprise démarche, asked whether Norway intended to join the Atlantic alliance, and, if so, whether this would mean bases in Norway for foreign air and naval forces. Norway's reply was to formulate the so-called "bases policy", in the form of a unilateral declaration that Norway "will not open bases for the armed forces of foreign countries unless attacked or threatened with aggression." Such bases were in fact right from the beginning clearly unacceptable to Norway, both for internal political reasons and from a desire to avoid provoking the Soviet Union, and this had been made clear on principle to the American ambassador already in the summer of 1948. Replies to a preliminary enquiry through the Norwegian ambassadors in Washington and London in December had then suggested that such bases would not be required. Seeking high-level assurances, Lange in Washington now asked his interlocutors in the State Department whether such bases would be required under the Atlantic Pact. The answer was still negative as far as the United States was concerned. Whether the future Atlantic Council might at some stage propose that Norway provide certain "facilities" was a different matter: it would then be up to Norway to decide.

As the Scandinavian alternative still had strong support in the Storting and in the Labour Party, Lange was also to enquire about possible western support for that alternative. The clear conclusion was that a Scandinavian defence pact, if it should be both formally and in reality without links to the western powers, could not count on any political or material support. In his official statement to the Storting, on 24 February, the Foreign Minister then reviewed the progress made by the western powers towards the formation of an Atlantic Alliance, stressing the joint determination to have any such arrangement conform with the "regional arrangements" as defined in the Charter of the United Nations. He made it clear that it was a matter of Norway's own free choice whether to join such a Treaty or not. But the Cabinet's advice was that Norway should participate in the security cooperation of democratic peoples which was being planned, and that Norway should aim at participation even in the preparatory discussions which were under way.

The Storting debated and approved Norway's participation in the preparatory talks in early March. At the end of March the government then formally proposed, and the Storting approved, Norway's signature and ratification of the North Atlantic Treaty. It is therefore particularly in those two parliamentary debates that we can expect to find a representative cross-section of opinion on whether the decisions made were perceived as a major turning-point in Norwegian foreign policy. The developments reviewed in the foregoing pages certainly constitute a *prima facie* case for considering Norway's abandonment of her post-war universalist, United Nations-oriented policy of non-alignment, in favour of membership in a regional defence alliance with the western great powers, as a decisive change of course. Did the Storting, and public opinion as reflected through its members, see it that way?

An initial conclusion from a study of the two March 1949 parliamentary debates is that there was general agreement about the crucial importance of Norway's impending accession to the North Atlantic Treaty. Several speakers ranked it with the great turning-points of modern Norwegian history: 1814, with the secession from Denmark and the enactment of the Constitution, and 1905, when Norway broke away from the Union with Sweden to become a fully independent Kingdom. On a different and less rhetorical level, however, supporters and opponents of Norway's membership in the Atlantic Alliance viewed the decision in widely different perspectives. The opponents, the Communists and a few Labour members, while suggesting that the government had manoeuvred so as to make the Storting's decision a formality, strongly warned against the decision as constituting a major departure from the Norwegian foreign policy tradition of support for the United Nations, friendly relations with the Soviet neighbour, and firm opposition to dividing the world into military blocs. The supporters, on the other hand, stressed the lesson of 1940 about the futility of isolated Norwegian neutrality, and pointed to Norway's wartime "Atlantic policy" as the tradition which would henceforth be pursued through membership in the North Atlantic Alliance. Many of those who spoke in favour of the decision presented it as a supplement and reinforcement of Norway's post-war support of the United Nations, and emphasised Norway's security commitments under the United Nations as being more far-reaching and supra-national in character than the obligations inherent in the North Atlantic Treaty.

As to the more precise nature of the commitment which Norway would incur through membership of the Atlantic Alliance, the opponents laid great emphasis on the country's strategic location as a frontier state in relation to the Soviet Union. Notwithstanding the Treaty's apparent safeguards for the national sovereignty of the member states, and in spite of the government's recent assurance that there would be no foreign bases on Norwegian territory in peacetime, the Communist deputies forecast the gradual conversion of Norway into a base area and a stepping-stone for an American knock-out blow against the Soviet Union with atomic bombs. Most of the supporters, on the other hand, emphasised the deterrence aspect of the Treaty, seeing it as an expression of mutual solidarity which would make it clear that Norway would not have to stand alone in the face of aggression. This assurance of external assistance was particularly important since Norway was nearing the limit of her ability to devote national resources to armed defence. The Alliance, far from committing Norway to accelerated rearmament, would in fact provide military assistance on very reasonable terms, and there was a clear assumption that the economic reconstruction of Europe would continue to have priority over rearmament. The supporters also rejected as unfounded the opponents' allegation that Norway was destined to become the advance bastion of a Western Alliance directed against the Soviet Union, or a forward base for American nuclear bombers.

To sum up, the solid majority which supported Norway's accession to the North Atlantic Treaty, while agreeing about the great significance of the decision, described its importance mainly in terms of the deterrent value of such a formal expression of mutual solidarity. There was accordingly no suggestion that Norway's defence policy would change, except for the expectation of supplies of arms and equipment on reasonable terms. Nor was there any suggestion from the supporters that the foundations or basic orientation of Norway's security policy had changed. Perhaps the most perspicacious comment came from a source not previously credited with special insight into foreign policy: Jakob Lothe, parliamentary leader of the Liberal "Venstre" party, stated that the collaboration with the western powers, which Norway had entered into after the German invasion in 1940, "had in a way been maintained up to this day, and it was now about to be given firmer shape".[17] By her signature of the

Halvard Lange signs the North Atlantic Treaty on behalf of Norway during the formal ceremony in Washington D.C. 4 April 1949. Although Great Britain ever since 1905 had figured as an 'implicit guarantor' of Norway's security, that signature demonstrated that the country for the first time in its history as a sovereign and independent state had joined a peacetime defence alliance.

North Atlantic Treaty on 4 April 1949, Norway had basically confirmed her long-standing but hitherto unspoken reliance on support from a friendly western power, as a fall-back position if her security and independence should come under threat from any other power. What had changed – beside the replacement of Great Britain by the United States as the principal protecting power – was, first and foremost, that such support would no longer rest on the shaky basis of a tacit assumption. From now on it would be backed by a formal and explicit guarantee that an armed attack against Norway would be considered as an attack against all the Treaty partners.

10. On NATO's Northern Frontline

Introduction

L ooking back from 1949 it is possible to discern three formative periods in the development of Norway's foreign policy as an independent, sovereign state. The first one, the period from 1905 to the First World War, clarified the basis of Norway's so to speak "classic" neutralism: an isolationist stance of disengagement from international power politics, combined with an active policy in defence of the country's foreign trade and shipping interests. A second formative period may be discerned during the inter-war period, when Norway's membership of the League of Nations provided a new forum for her somewhat moralistic advocacy of international law as the "civilised" way of settling international disputes. Both those periods could build on traditions established during the foregoing century: the isolationist impulse, brought into the open after the great powers in 1814 handed Norway over from Denmark to Sweden, and the "fin-de-siècle" quest for permanent neutralisation paired with the promotion of arbitration treaties. Fundamental to both periods was a firm conviction that the survival and prosperity of small states required progress towards fulfilment of a somewhat dialectic process – *pace* Hegel – whereby the thesis of international anarchy, and its antithesis of great power dominance, could be replaced by the synthesis of a better organised world based on international law. The third formative period is the one from 1940 to 1949 which has been reviewed in the foregoing chapters: the break-through of an active internationalism, perhaps best described as the transition from being an onlooker to becoming an active participant in international power politics.

The initial impulse for that transition was an outside intervention, in the shape of the German invasion 9 April 1940. It was however followed up by a conscious and deliberate decision by the King and the government, made in Tromsø at the end of the Norwegian Campaign, to link their destiny with a great power ally, and further developed through the government's choice of a policy of close and active cooperation within the framework of the Grand Alliance. It has to be noted, though, that this choice of policy was made against some dissenting voices both within the government and in

206

influential circles at home. Even more important, it was made in the absence of a parliamentary or other forum that could be said to represent a cross-section of public opinion. A heavy question mark hence remained with regard to the long-term survival of the new policy. In fact the first post-war years, during which the emphasis was on non-alignment, suggested that Norwegian public opinion had yet to be convinced that the country ought to commit itself to an active engagement in power politics. Although this did not mean a return to status quo, since non-alignment was coupled with a strong under-current of military links with Great Britain, the stance was at least one of an uneasy balance between neutralism and alignment. Then, in a mixture of pressure from external events and conscious domestic initiatives, Norway in 1949 renewed her commitment to an alliance dominated by the western great powers.

The question to be kept in mind, as Norway embarked on her new "career" as a committed member of a peacetime security alliance, is whether 1949 marked a decisive turning-point, or whether it was an essentially temporary response to external events, pending a return to "normalcy".[1] During the first twelve months after Norway's signature of the North Atlantic Treaty, official statements to enlighten the public about the new and firmer shape of western collective security continued to stress its nature as a *political* commitment towards mutual assistance, with Norway at the receiving end. This formal commitment alone, it was claimed, had already caused a certain easing of international tensions. In addition, much stress was laid on expected benefits from the Mutual Defence Assistance Program, in terms of military supplies to be provided by the United States under a bilateral agreement as approved by the Storting in January 1950. Nothing was said about the US insistence on an "integrated defence" as a condition for assistance – in the Norwegian text of the agreement, "integrated" was translated as "coordinated". Norway was moreover exempted from the required reciprocal assistance in the form of base rights, due to her "no foreign bases" policy. All this, together with assurances that there would be no expectation of a level of rearmament efforts which might endanger economic reconstruction and political stability, may have convinced the government that Norway's security at least for the moment was adequately taken care of through the open and formal commitment to an alliance backed by the enormous resources of the United States and its atomic bomb. Deterrence – in this early phase of the Cold War perhaps better described by the French term "dissuasion" – was the name of the game. For all the European signatories, in fact, the North Atlantic Treaty had served its purpose by giving them the necessary confidence to go on re-building their economies and strengthening their political stability without fear of being undermined or overwhelmed by the threat of communism.

But what about a "worst case scenario" in which the Soviets might still

Norway's strategic position may appear peripheral on ordinary maps of Europe. But a polar projection of the globe seen from the top shows that the shortest flying distance between the heartlands of the United States and the Soviet Union goes across the northern part of Norway, thereby underlining the country's exposed situation in an East-West conflict.

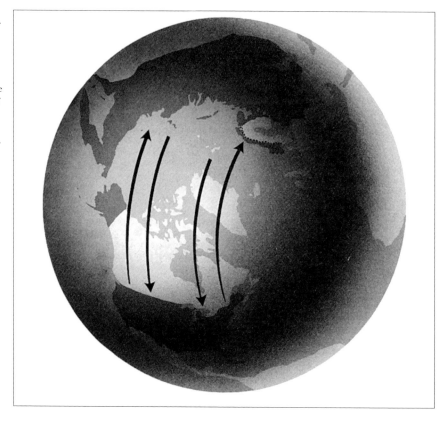

be tempted to use their military power against a defenceless country on the remote outskirts of the Alliance? Would Norway's great power allies then be prepared to send their soldiers to – as a sceptical French newspaper headline put it much later – "die for Nordkyn" (Nordkyn being the northernmost point on the Norwegian mainland)?[2] The government seemed to think so. As the Defence Minister suggested, in a September 1949 speech to the Oslo Students' Union, Norway's membership in the Alliance had removed "even the theoretical possibility" of an isolated attack on Norway. And in a major war it would be "very important to the countries of the Atlantic Pact to deprive the attacker of the possibility of enjoying the advantages offered by our strategic location".[3] Eight months later, defending his first budget proposal under the Treaty, which would have the effect of reducing Norway's annual defence expenditure by ten per cent, he said to the Storting: "Common defence and common planning means to us that other, stronger, countries prepare to utilise some of their military resources for the defence of our country and our part of the world. I should like to stress that. Only that kind of common defence and common planning will be acceptable to a country like ours."[4] Since Defence Minister Jens Christian Hauge had a clearer realisation – and fewer qualms – than his colleagues about the mutual character of Norway's alliance commitment, it is safe to assume that his words were meant to reassure the many who still feared the uncertain long term costs and benefits of alliance membership.

In other words, as long as Norway on her own did what little she could to maintain and improve her own defences, it seems to have been assumed that beyond the general deterrent effect of the Alliance, should that fail, western assistance would be forthcoming as being in the great power allies' own interest. This was not all that different from the assumption of "automatic" protection which had been the bottom line of Norway's national security since 1905. Judging by an opinion poll from July 1949, in which 63 per cent of those interviewed said that joining the Atlantic Pact had increased Norway's security, it was the positive variant of that assumption which prevailed. But among the 25 per cent who thought Norway's security was diminished, or unchanged, one could also find the old somewhat cynical small-state view of the great powers acting solely from their own power interests. Halvdan Koht, arguing in the autumn of 1940 against seeking formal political assurances that the liberation of Norway would be part of Britain's war aims, was an earlier exponent of that view when he stated that "the peace settlement will be decided by power considerations and interests whether or not one has such an agreement."[5] One of the most prominent opponents of Norway joining the North Atlantic Alliance in 1949, the writer Sigurd Evensmo, put it this way: "When a great power finds it in its own interest to intervene for the "protection" of the small ones, it will do so without any treaty. If they see no such interest they will not intervene, regardless of treaty obligations."[6]

In the Shadow of the Central Front

The North Atlantic Treaty, as signed on 4 April 1949 and generally referred to as NAT in US diplomatic correspondence at the time, could best be described as a fairly traditional reassurance treaty: a political guarantee that the western European democracies, in case of aggression from the Soviet Union in any form, would have the backing of the enormous resources and the atomic weapons of the United States. Little was said about exactly how that backing would be provided if the worst came to the worst.[7] Deterrence was very much a matter of psychology and perception, and any speculation about the military capabilities – or lack of them – that could be mustered if the balloon went up could only give the game away. That was also the gist of the advice given in the spring of 1949 by the British Chiefs of Staff to their American opposite numbers, when considering what to tell the Norwegians about the defence of their country:

The Norwegians should be told that they cannot plan on any direct air or land assistance from the Allies, at any rate, in the early stages of a war; they can rely on the Allied Navies keeping open one line of sea communications whilst the Norwegians are still fighting; it would be unwise to base their plans on the assumption that Swedish neutrality will be respected; their forces are far too limited to defend anything but one small area of Norway and that even to insure this everything possible should be done to expedite their planned expansion and re-equipment; the Norwegians should decide now the area to be defended.[8]

The "one small area" which could be defended was limited to the region around Stavanger on the west coast.

The inability of the allies to defend not only Norway but the major part of the European continent by conventional military means only began to be taken seriously after the outbreak of the Korean War. Widely taken as a signal that the Communist bloc was ready if necessary to use military force to achieve its political aims, the North Korean invasion of South Korea became the impulse for transforming the political treaty into a mutual security organisation for collective defence, with a high degree of military integration as the ultimate purpose. Defence Minister Hauge did not mince his words when he outlined to the Storting the consequences of that transformation, in December 1951:

> For the principle of common defence to become a reality, a number of things in the military field will be required which the countries have not been used to in peacetime. It presupposes a common strategy and common defence plans. It requires joint military commanders and joint military institutions with the responsibility – the power – to organise the defence on the basis of those common plans. Common defence requires a concentration on tasks that are important from an overall viewpoint. This involves organising joint military forces as well as a division of labour among member states, cutting across national borders and traditions [...] It is perhaps putting it too mildly to say that this is unusual. It is revolutionary for all the countries – as much for others as for us [...][9]

Two sets of formulae would henceforth determine the course of Norwegian security policy. In relation to the Soviet Union, the "deterrence" obtained through membership of the Atlantic Alliance would be paired with efforts of "reassurance" that such membership was strictly for defensive purposes. Conversely, in relation to the Alliance, the acceptance of "integration" as necessary to secure allied assistance would be accompanied by a careful "screening" against allied activities that could be construed – by neutralist sections of the public, by Norway's neutral neighbours, or by the

Soviets – as provocatively offensive. In that way Norway also hoped to preserve NATO's northern flank as a low-tension area. The effort to steer a steady course that took account of so many different parameters was bound to involve a series of balancing acts, in which the litmus test would be whether the action contemplated would improve Norway's national security in a long-term perspective.

In practical terms the first priority for Norway as for the other European members of the Alliance was, as Arne Ording had put it 1940, to "nail the Anglo-Saxon powers to their responsibilities in Europe". The challenge for Norway was further to convince the major allies that the defence of NATO's northern flank was essential to the security of the whole Alliance. The means to that end had three constituent elements: first came the need to provide the allies with "stakes" in the defence of the area – stakes that would create or reinforce that allied self-interest which would ultimately be the only reliable motivation for substantial support. The area in this respect was not limited to the Norwegian mainland, but included the surrounding seas which were the Soviet navy's principal exits to the Atlantic and to the sea lanes of communication between the United States and Western Europe. Second was the need to build up Norway's own defence capability to withstand the initial phases of an attack, in order to gain the necessary time for the organisation of effective allied support. Third came those practical preparations – facilities, logistics, and training – which would ensure that no part of that necessary time would be wasted. All three elements were equally important, and had to go hand in hand – the first one to ensure allied willingness to assist; the other two to ensure their ability to do so.

A clear conclusion from the Korean War was the need to build up NATO's conventional force strength. The United States, in spite of its heavy commitment of forces in South Korea, was prepared to station considerable forces also in Europe, as a temporary measure, on condition that the European NATO countries proceeded apace with their rearmament. Norway could not escape from doing her part, although she could with some success plead for special consideration due to a weak economy. The defence budget's share of the Gross National Product rose from 2,5 per cent, in 1950, to 5,6 per cent in 1954. Norway also accepted a wide measure of integration as part of the collective defence effort. An army brigade, which had served as Norway's share in the occupation of Germany, became part of the joint allied defence of the European continent, until it was withdrawn in 1954 in order to strengthen the defence of northern Norway. Norway also agreed to cut the size of her own navy in the expectation that the British and US navies would provide the necessary protection at sea – a policy which had to be reversed in the 1960s, when that expectation no longer held.

One area where Norway could and did provide an important service to the whole of the Alliance was maritime transport. With a merchant navy that grew from about six million gross tons in 1950 to three times that figure towards the end of the 1960s, of which about one half were tankers, Norwegian ships could have a crucial role to play in NATO's trans-Atlantic sea lines of communications. It was therefore only natural that Norway should not only join NATO's Planning Board for Ocean Shipping when it was formed in 1950, but also become a member of its Executive Committee. Taking its cue from the wartime Nortraship organisation, the Storting in 1952 approved arrangements that would enable the government to requisition the use of the merchant fleet in an emergency.

An important step towards Norway's integration in NATO's defence was the decision, in March 1951, to establish the headquarters for NATO's Northern Command – AFNORTH – in Oslo. At Hauge's urgings a British Admiral became the first Commander-in-Chief, with an American Air Force General as his Air Deputy: this supposedly secured both a link to Britain's Royal Navy and – as Hauge later put it – "a hook in the nose of the US Air Force." Although concerns were voiced about whether AFNORTH might in fact amount to a foreign base, the government clearly saw this as an important first step in what was to become Norway's long and hard struggle to get the Alliance to take the defence of NATO's northern flank seriously. Further efforts in that direction would soon come up against the balancing act just referred to, however, as the government had to contend not only with Soviet reactions but also with mounting internal opposition against the pace of Norway's military integration into the Alliance. The opposition came from two quarters: a residual neutralism, which on the left was reinforced by anti-American sentiments, and a "national-conservative" opposition that could be found especially among the Conservatives and the Agrarians. The latter were more clearly isolationist in their insistence on national self-determination, and wanted to turn the clock back to the days when the North Atlantic Treaty was just that – a political reassurance treaty, without the "O" for Organisation.

The first exercise of Norway's "balancing act" was Defence Minister Hauge's re-definition of the "no foreign bases" policy in February 1951. The militarisation of the Alliance following the outbreak of the Korean war produced a need for practical steps to make common defence possible, including joint exercises to acquaint armed forces' personnel with terrain and conditions in the various countries where they might have to operate. Hauge's statement spelling out the precise contents of the bases policy stressed two points: nothing in the original declaration precluded arrangements giving access for foreign forces on joint exercises, or for brief visits by allied aircraft or naval ships. Furthermore, the policy could not prevent Norway from constructing her military installations so as to be able to accommodate and support allied forces that might in a crisis be transferred to the country to assist in its defence. Nothing in that clarification could be said

212

to contradict the words of the 1949 declaration. Yet some dissenting voices alleged that it contravened its spirit, since it opened for the pre-stocking of arms and equipment for allied forces. And where would one draw the line between "short-term visits" and temporary stationing of foreign forces?

Throughout the 1950s massive amounts of arms and equipment flowed into the country through the US Military Assistance programme, and NATO's infrastructure programme provided huge funds for the construction of airfields and other installations. Still the allied military missions in Norway took a very critical view of the state of the country's armed forces, citing inadequacies of national service training, the poor quality of the army officers, and especially the lack of a corps of long-service non-commissioned officers which was the backbone of their own armies. They also bemoaned the highly unsatisfactory supply and logistics organisation. The government in fact tried to lengthen the period of service for the conscripts from 12 to at least 18 months, but determined resistance both within the government and in the Storting forced them to compromise on 16 months for the army and 18 months for the navy and the air force.

The ambitious targets set by NATO for European rearmament were soon to prove unrealistic. The only other way to build up a reasonably credible European deterrent against the assumed superior strength in conventional forces of the Soviet Union and its satellites was to allow the rearmament of Western Germany. In the countries occupied by Germany during the war this prospect was clearly distasteful, and nowhere more so than in Norway. Yet the Norwegian government was badly placed to protest in view of its own weak defence effort, and swallowed the bitter pill with the assurance that a stronger defence of western Germany would help to close the southern entrances to Denmark and the northern flank of NATO. The build-up of German armed forces was bound to take time, however, and in the meantime the combined drain on American military resources of the war in Korea and the military assistance to Europe made it almost inevitable that nuclear weapons would have to make up for Europe's military weakness.

In 1954 the Eisenhower administration publicly announced the doctrine of "massive retaliation", and later that year NATO then embraced the inclusion of nuclear weapons into its arsenal. This predictably had the effect of easing the pressure on Norway as well as the other European NATO members to keep on strengthening their conventional forces. It also, at least for a time, made it more difficult for Norway to argue for an allied commitment of forces to the defence of the northern flank: "massive retaliation", if indeed it had any meaning, had to mean that an attack against Norway would release the full force of NATO's nuclear potential. By the end of the 1950s, however, while the Soviet buildup on the northern front was continuing, the credibility of that strategy was beginning to wear thin:

Would NATO, or the Americans, really release a full-scale nuclear Armageddon in response to, for example, a limited Soviet offensive to take control over the Norwegian border provinces in the north, in order to expand its operational base towards the North Atlantic? Such a "limited war" perspective gained some ground after the Kennedy administration came to power in the United States. And the most vulnerable areas would then be NATO's flanks, not least the weakly defended northern flank.

This "limited war" perspective lay behind the gradual transition from "massive retaliation" to a "flexible response" strategy during the 1960s. Some new and more mobile allied force elements, at least partly designed to "show the flag" in such places as the high north, were formed, mainly the ACE (Allied Command Europe) Mobile Force, and the STANAVFOR-LANT or Standing Naval Force Atlantic. A regular pattern of major NATO exercises on the northern flank was also established. Such measures were important as a demonstration of NATO solidarity and concern. But certain Soviet activities in the north were equally telling demonstrations of Norway's vulnerability: in June 1968 a major Soviet military exercise on the Kola Peninsula climaxed in a sudden demonstrative deployment of an armoured division along the Norwegian border, guns pointing westward. The same year saw the first of several major Soviet fleet exercises in the Norwegian Sea, suggesting a capacity to prevent allied reinforcements from reaching Norway by sea in a crisis. The prospect of a successful defence of Norwegian territory against a Soviet attack thus seemed increasingly doubtful as the Cold War entered its third decade. The United States was bogged down in the war in Vietnam, the British remained reluctant to undertake commitments in the high north, and the growing German navy's capabilities were limited to the southern North Sea.

Norway's "Self-imposed Restraints"

There was no lack of ambivalences in Norway's posture in NATO during the 1950s. Each new step towards defence integration was accompanied by much soul-searching, in which the military necessity of strengthening the country's defence had to be weighed against the risk of a political backlash from the many sceptics. The latter's main banner was the "no foreign bases policy" which, although generally accepted as an eminently sensible basic principle of Norwegian national security, was nevertheless subject to interpretation in either a restrictive or a liberal direction.

The anti-integrationists won a victory of sorts already in 1952. NATO's principal weakness in the early years was the lack of an adequate air defence, particularly on the northern flank. The US Air Force was willing and able to remedy that to some extent by stationing considerable forces in the area, but such stationing required base rights in Norway, whose publicly declared policy did not allow it, and/or in Denmark, whose more muted stance pointed in the same direction. Caught in a vice between the military need to provide adequate air defence and a fear of the political consequences if the "bases policy" should be abandoned, the government in vain tried a compromise whereby US air forces might be stationed in the British Isles or in Denmark, but with frequent rotation visits to Norwegian air bases. In the end Prime Minister Oscar Torp, who in November 1951 had had to take over from Einar Gerhardsen, decided to test the strength of the opposition in the Storting's committee for foreign affairs. The outcome, a clear reaffirmation of the bases policy, may well have been influenced by the unease caused by a simultaneous and related allied demand, for wartime facilities at two Norwegian air bases for bombers and escort aircraft of the US Strategic Air Command. As that request was limited to wartime use it did not conflict with the ban against peacetime stationing of allied forces, and was in fact granted later that year. The discomfort still felt in Norwegian circles, however, stemmed from the fear of becoming a target in a nuclear exchange between the Strategic Air Command and its Soviet equivalent.

Towards the end of the 1950s Norway made another big step towards limiting her integration into NATO's defence plans. The fear of nuclear war, and of Norway becoming involved in it, became an active concern as the development of medium- and short-range tactical nuclear weapons presaged their introduction into the armoury of

Oscar Torp was the leader of the Norwegian Labour Party from 1923, and was Defence Minister in the government in exile 1942–45, carrying out a major restructuring and rejuvenation of the military leadership. After the war he served for a while as Minister of Supply and Reconstruction, and then as leader of the Party in the Storting until becoming Prime Minister 1951. When Gerhardsen returned as PM in 1955, Torp became President of the Storting. He was throughout a firm supporter of Norway's alliance commitments.

the European armed forces. The military's argument that the Norwegian armed forces deserved to be equipped with the same weapons as would be used against them, cut very little ice against the increasing pressure from public opinion for a ban on such weapons, and in 1957 the Labour Party conference adopted a proposal from the floor that nuclear weapons must not be introduced into Norway. Later that year Einar Gerhardsen, who had come back as Prime Minister in January 1955, took a NATO summit meeting by surprise with a speech urging a postponement of the issue of placing medium-range nuclear missiles in Europe, adding that Norway had no intention of storing nuclear warheads or building missile bases on her soil.

The government later tried to reassure the Alliance by making it clear that the ban on nuclear weapons might at any time be reconsidered, if warranted by changed circumstances, and by tacitly allowing for the fact that allied forces coming to Norway's assistance in a crisis might be equipped

The question of nuclear weapons was a hot issue in Norwegian debates on foreign and defence policy from the middle of the 1950s. While the government wavered, the military, and NATO, clearly hoped that Norway would accept nuclear weapons in the country's armed forces, and the introduction of the short-range tactical missile 'Honest John' – which was so-called 'dual capable' as it could if necessary carry a conventional warhead – symbolised the dilemma. This picture shows the missile being installed at an army base in northern Norway. The campaign against nuclear weapons won through, and the missiles were withdrawn.

with nuclear weapons. Norway, moreover, never dissociated herself from NATO's established doctrine of relying on nuclear weapons as a last resort, and accepted a number of the implications of that reliance, such as the establishment of communications facilities for NATO's nuclear forces.[10] But Norway's profile in NATO – and Denmark's, for that matter – was henceforth clearly marked as a member state with reservations. In the meantime another self-imposed restriction had been added: as a further effort to allay Moscow's alleged fear of northern Norway becoming a springboard for aggression, the Norwegian government imposed special limits on the movement of allied aircraft and warships in the north. Although the limits varied over time, the effect was to make Norwegian territory within about 250 kilometres of the Soviet border a "no-go" area for NATO forces. As with all the "self-imposed restraints", however, this one also applied only in peacetime or, more precisely, "so long as Norway is not attacked or threatened with aggression", as the 1949 bases declaration put it.

When Norway's struggle to raise allied concerns about the defence of the northern flank remained generally fruitless through the 1950s, the principal cause was not "self-imposed restraints" or the internal anti-integrationist opposition, but rather the slow build-up of NATO's conventional military strength in Europe, and the concentration of attention on the problems of the central front. Although Eisenhower during his brief time as Supreme Allied Commander Europe entertained an idea about building up strength on the flanks to counter a Soviet assault in the centre, the prevailing strategy viewed the Continent of Europe as the main battlefield. It was therefore not uncommon to hear the northern flank being spoken of as "the forgotten flank of NATO". When Norway nevertheless, and in spite of her self-imposed restraints, remained an important ally, one reason was buried in the hidden field of intelligence cooperation.

Norway's Role in Western Intelligence

Apart from Turkey, who joined the Alliance in 1952, Norway was the only European NATO member with a common border with the Soviet Union. So from the early 1950s Norway became an area of major and rapidly increasing interest for the Americans as a platform for intelligence collection. Over and above the general lack of any precise information about the military capability of the Soviet Union, American and allied interest was becoming increasingly focused on the Soviet north-west as a base area for the Soviet Navy and for Soviet long-range bombers, as well as a promising route for an American strategic bombing offensive against the heart of Russia. Modest initial efforts by the fledgling Norwegian Intelligence Service (NIS) to establish listening posts near the frontier, eavesdropping on Soviet military and naval communications, caught the attention of American intelligence agencies in 1952, resulting in a formal NORUSA agreement on intelligence cooperation two years later.[11] From then on an abundant supply of money and sophisticated technical equipment enabled the NIS to build and expand their stations in the north, even while insisting on Norwegian control of the operations as well as manning the stations with Norwegian personnel. Soon their activities came to include also electronic intelligence, locating, identifying and assessing the capabilities of Soviet radar stations in the area, largely to make possible the mapping of "gaps" through which allied aircraft could penetrate on their way to their targets. Norway's own interest in the activity was two-fold: there was an obvious need for the Norwegian military to have a clear picture of Soviet military and naval strength and activities in that border region, and to have early warning of movements that might have threatening implications. But an accurate picture of Soviet capabilities in their North-western Military District would also enable the Norwegian authorities to influence allied estimates of the threat to the northern flank, and consequently their strategic planning. An NIS assessment from October 1956 stated that

> Norway's position as a warning area for the Western Great Powers – North Norway especially for the US and Canada, South Norway for the United Kingdom – ensures that the Western interest in expanding the electronic intelligence effort in Norway is very strong. [...] There is today also the very real situation that Norway is needed as a warning platform for the United

217

States not only in the opening stages of an eventual war, but also for the duration of belligerent activities. This engenders a strongly increased American interest in Norwegian territory remaining unoccupied, on condition that Norwegian warning efforts are maintained at an acceptable level.[12]

The Americans hence continued to urge further expansion of the listening stations in the north, to which the Cabinet Defence and Security Committee agreed. Prime Minister Einar Gerhardsen, who otherwise was beginning to have second thoughts about Norway's integration into allied and particularly American military activities, concurred that "one should in principle take a positive attitude whenever Norway on account of its geographical situation could be of particular service to the common defence through such clearly defensive measures."[13]

Signals intelligence was not confined to the efforts of land-based stations. The NIS also ran boats in the Barents Sea masquerading as fishing vessels but equipped with a variety of listening and detection devices – from 1976 also with a purpose-built intelligence ship. Signals intelligence collection by air was on the other hand mainly the province of the United States and Great Britain. In addition to American reconnaissance aircraft based on Greenland, US and British aircraft from 1952 showed an increasing interest in utilising Norwegian air bases as staging posts for flights along Russia's arctic coastline. As this was construed as being within the category of visits and exercises allowed under the "bases policy", the Norwegian government let it go on as long as it was within manageable limits, and did not involve violation of Soviet territory. But by the end of 1958 the frequency of such allied reconnaissance flights, and a justified fear that this might lead to "incidents" between allied aircraft and Soviet fighter aircraft in the border area, convinced the NIS chief and the government that the activity was getting out of hand. Their conviction was confirmed by a Soviet protest delivered to the Norwegian ambassador in Moscow in January 1959, upon which the government publicly announced that allied aircraft would not be cleared for overflights of Norwegian territory east of 24 degrees longitude.

The Soviet protest note of January 1959 did not mention anything about allied overflights of Soviet territory, although it is now known that U-2 spyplanes, operating from a base in Western Germany, on at least one occasion in 1957 had penetrated into Soviet airspace in the north before turning into Norwegian airspace. A new Soviet protest, a mere three weeks after the first one, raised the stakes: this time Nikita Khrushchev himself raised the issue, referring to an American aircraft coming from Norway which had infringed Soviet territory. What had in fact happened was that a U-2 aircraft, after two such planes had visited Bodø air base for "meteorological observation flights" over international waters, allegedly had wandered into Soviet airspace on its way back to its base in Turkey. The Norwegian authorities were now on the alert, although they did not wish to stop what were perfectly legitimate flights over international waters from Norwegian bases, and decided to allow only a limited number of the long lists of allied requests that had just been tabled. Before the end of 1959 new and even longer request lists were submitted by the British and US air forces, this time accompanied by information to the Chief of NIS that the purpose of the flights, which would be over international waters, was to gather electronic intelligence data about Soviet missiles. After a discussion in the Cabinet Defence and Security Committee, the Prime Minister's decision was recorded as follows in the minutes:

> The Prime Minister agreed that Norway could make a valuable contribution through the control and warning system being built up in northern Norway, and that this was an activity which the Soviet Union could not object to. He further stated that no great consequence could be attached to allied overflights of Norway without landing. Flights that departed from Norwegian airfields, on the other hand, could be permitted from time to time but only within strict limits.[14]

However, on 1 May 1960 a U-2 aircraft was shot down over Soviet territory. It had left its base at Peshawar in Pakistan, and after entering Soviet airspace had overflown the missile testing base at Tyuratam in Kazakhstan before setting course for its next main target, the missile base at Plesetsk south of Archangel. The flight ended near Sverdlovsk, apparently because the aircraft was disabled or de-stabilised by the shock-wave from a ground-to-air missile exploding near the tail. The pilot, Gary Powers, bailed out, was taken prisoner, and it was revealed that he was on his way to Bodø in North Norway.

The downing of Gary Powers and his U-2 had a series of grave political repercussions, of which the most spectacular was of course Khrushchev's break-up of his summit meeting with President Eisenhower in Paris shortly afterwards. That story is well known. Here we shall review briefly the consequences of the affair for Norway's relations with the two super-powers. The Soviet reaction to Norway's involvement in the U-2 mission was sharp, and took the form of oral statements from Khrushchev himself as well as from Defence Minister Malinovski, topped up by an official protest note on 13 May. There were threats of retaliatory strikes against Norway, claiming the "right to initiate any measure we like against these bases and airfields, and we can hit these bases so that nothing is left of them."[15] There were repercussions also on Norwegian-US relations, with a Norwegian protest against unwarranted use of a Norwegian air base for a flight violating Soviet airspace – although the Norwegian government's anger at the Americans was somewhat tempered by a suspicion that the Norwegian intelligence chief had known more than he was willing to admit about the operation. At any

In August 1964 Khrustchev visited Norway. In his memoirs he somewhat arrogantly described being received by King Olav: "We were taken to a palace which looked nothing like a palace. There was nothing royal about it ... We were received at the door by a man in a khaki-coloured uniform ... Suddenly I realised that this was the King. He could easily have been mistaken for the gardener." Two months later Khrustchev was ousted from power.

rate the Soviet government seemed reasonably satisfied by Norway's protest to Washington, but returned to the attack after a US RB-47 reconnaissance aircraft was shot down by Soviet fighter planes near the coast of the Kola Peninsula shortly afterwards. Although the US plane was shot down over international waters, the Soviets claimed it was violating Soviet airspace, and accused Norway of being in various ways involved in the flight.

In addition to its expanding effort in the fields of communications intelligence and electronic intelligence, the Norwegian Intelligence Service during the 1950s and 1960s also developed a network of shipping agents – mostly officers of the large Norwegian merchant navy, many of whose ships trafficked ports in the Soviet Union, the eastern European countries, and even China (Norway having been one of the first western countries to recognise the Communist regime of Mao). With a little bit of training, equipped with state of the art cameras and telelenses, and being briefed and debriefed by experienced intelligence officers, they observed and photographed anything of potential military interest that could be seen from the vantage point of their moving platforms. Started on a modest scale in the 1950s, this activity during the 1960s brought back thousands of film strips each year for scrutiny by the NIS and allied services. Photographic intelligence was also carried out by Norwegian military aircraft flying along the Soviet border with on-board cameras set at an oblique angle. In the early 1950s the NIS even experimented with an activity closer to the "cloak and dagger" image of espionage, by sending agents across the Finnish and Norwegian frontier to observe military targets in Northern Russia.[16] Although all their agents of the 17–18 one-man or two-man expeditions made it back to safety, the intelligence output was hardly worth the risks involved. That the experiment continued for a couple of years still says something about western intelligence's desperate need for accurate information about what went on behind the Iron Curtain in those early years.

Among the results from the NIS' intelligence collection and analysis was a clear indication that the northern regions of Russia were taking on an increasing importance for the Soviet military. The Soviet Northern Fleet was expanding, and new bases for its increasing number of submarines were being built to exploit the advantages of an area with ice-free inlets and free access to the North Atlantic Ocean. The Barents Sea was also used as a testing ground for new types of submarines, as the Soviets were experimenting with nuclear-powered boats and sea-launched missiles with conventional and later nuclear warheads. As early as January 1958 the CIA Chief of Station in Oslo expressed serious concern about the increased pace of the Soviet build-up not only of the air forces in the region but also of the Northern Fleet. In a memorandum for the NIS Chief he characterised the roughly 100 submarines of that fleet, many of them new and very long-range, as the greatest potential single threat to Atlantic shipping in wartime. Although assessments of that threat varied over time, the role of submarines in western and particularly American strategic planning became increasingly important through the 1960s. And as the bases on the Kola Peninsula provided Soviet submarines with free access to the Atlantic, the US Navy had an obvious interest in keeping tabs on their movements.

Both the US Navy and the Norwegian Defence Research Establishment

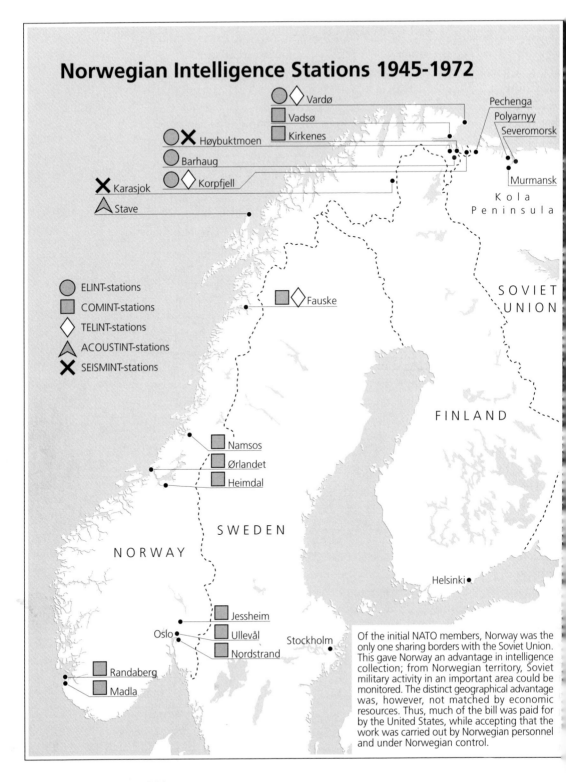

Norwegian Intelligence Stations 1945-1972

Vardø
Vadsø
Kirkenes
Høybuktmoen
Barhaug
Karasjok
Korpfjell
Stave

Pechenga
Polyarnyy
Severomorsk
Murmansk
K o l a
P e n i n s u l a

- ⬤ ELINT-stations
- ⬛ COMINT-stations
- ◇ TELINT-stations
- ▲ ACOUSTINT-stations
- ✕ SEISMINT-stations

Fauske

S O V I E T
U N I O N

F I N L A N D

Namsos
Ørlandet
Heimdal

S W E D E N

N O R W A Y

Helsinki

Jessheim
Oslo
Ulleval
Nordstrand
Stockholm

Randaberg
Madla

Of the initial NATO members, Norway was the only one sharing borders with the Soviet Union. This gave Norway an advantage in intelligence collection; from Norwegian territory, Soviet military activity in an important area could be monitored. The distinct geographical advantage was, however, not matched by economic resources. Thus, much of the bill was paid for by the United States, while accepting that the work was carried out by Norwegian personnel and under Norwegian control.

had from the end of the 1950s been experimenting with systems for acoustic detection and identification of submarines and their movements. And in 1964 an array of under-water hydrophones, connected to a cable terminating at a small naval station at Andøya in North Norway, became operational. Continually improved, extended, and complemented by specially equipped long-range surveillance aircraft for pin-point location of detected boats, that system soon became the chief means of keeping tabs on the movements and operational pattern of the increasingly sophisticated and powerful Soviet nuclear-powered ballistic missile submarines, as they passed through the Norwegian Sea on their way to and from the Atlantic Ocean. In the words of US ambassador to Norway Philip. K. Crowe, reporting to Washington in 1972, "Norwegian cooperation in the military and intelligence fields is of considerable strategic importance to us in keeping watch on the growing Soviet naval and submarine threat from the Murmansk area [...]."[17]

In the meantime the Soviets had turned Novaya Zemlya into a main testing area for nuclear weapons, and developed Plesetsk south of Archangel as the first major launch site for inter-continental ballistic missiles. The monitoring of Soviet nuclear tests became an active concern for the NIS from the late 1950s, stimulated not only by the Americans and the British, but also by Norwegian concerns about radioactive fall-out. From 1964 onwards the NIS also became engaged in the surveillance of Soviet satellite activities, with a new station built at Fauske near Bodø. Satellites were then being developed not only for photo reconnaissance but also for the collection of communication and electronic intelligence, and the new station was particularly well placed to monitor satellites in polar orbit. As the Plesetsk base also became a launch site for Soviet Inter-Continental Ballistic Missiles (ICBM), the monitoring of those activities was soon added to the tasks of the Fauske station. northern Norway's importance as an intelligence collection site thus kept increasing.

The apparent contrast between Norway's refusal to accept the stationing of allied armed forces and the storage of nuclear weapons in the country, and her willing and active partnership with the United States in intelligence matters, requires an explanation. One obvious answer is that intelligence collection by Norwegian personnel under Norwegian control, and mostly carried out from Norwegian territory, was seen as an essentially defensive activity. It is significant that the archives of the Soviet Ministry of Foreign Affairs, recently becoming accessible, reveal a remarkable lack of complaints about Norwegian intelligence activity. Sharp protests were reserved for instances of US intelligence activity involving Norway, such as the U-2 incident. It is also necessary to consider the alternative to a nationally controlled NIS: an extensive intelligence activity by the allied great powers themselves on or around Norwegian territory, in which consideration for the Norwegian "low-tension profile" would have had to yield to urgent

With a common border with the Soviet Union Norway came to play an important role in the collection of intelligence about military activities in the North-western Military District of the USSR. These two radar and intelligence stations at Vardø looked straight across the waters of the Barents Sea to the Kola Peninsula.

needs for Western knowledge about the enemy's constantly increasing military activity in the North. The geo-strategic focal point which Norwegian and especially northern Norwegian areas represented during the Cold War was an established fact, independent of Norwegian policy. For this reason, a Norwegian intelligence service, in close cooperation with allied powers but under Norwegian control, was both the best alternative and the best Norwegian contribution to the Western alliance's common defence.

As regards the not very widespread but highly vocal internal opposition against Norway's increasing integration into allied – and especially American – military activities, intelligence work had the advantage of being an entirely secret activity, different from the highly visible presence from time to time of allied aircraft and naval ships. Considering the left-wing clamour at the occasional reports or revelations about intelligence projects, which were said to be undermining the bases policy or – even worse – making Norway an accomplice in US preparations for nuclear warfare, it is not difficult to imagine the outcry that would have been caused if the full extent of Norway's intelligence cooperation with the CIA and other US intelligence agencies had become known. It is also worth noting that the few Russian protests that have been registered against intelligence installations on Norwegian soil have tended to be triggered by critical reports in the Norwegian media. Even so, the accumulation of intelligence stations within a short distance from – and in some instances within sight of – Soviet territory did at one stage begin to cause some concern. In 1964, faced with new proposals for expanding the activities, the Chief of Defence Staff found reason to warn against doing things that might irritate the Russians. NIS chief Vilhelm Evang, however, got approval for the plans, remarking that if the Norwegian intelligence effort was not increased, then the western allies would seek to obtain the information in ways that were far more likely to endanger Soviet-Norwegian relations.

From the perspective of Norway's foreign relations in the Cold War it seems reasonable to conclude that the intelligence cooperation with the United States did not, on the whole, damage Norway's policy of reassurance towards the Soviet Union, and may in fact – considering the alternative of a high-profile western intelligence effort in the region – have contributed to the preservation of the high north as a low-tension area in the east-west conflict. Towards the allies, on the other hand, and particularly towards the Americans, Norway's willingness to cooperate doubtless served to counteract allied impressions of Norway as a reluctant ally, considering her many "self-imposed restraints" against becoming fully integrated into allied military activities.

The Northern Flank in the 1970s and 1980s

The effort that has often been called "Norway's struggle for the northern flank" did not have much success during the 1950s, as we have seen. The situation was put in a nutshell by the British Commander-in-Chief of NATO's Northern Command, in a newspaper interview as late as 1962: "In order to secure North Norway one had to be in full control of South Norway. In order to secure South Norway one had to control the Baltic approaches. In order to hold the Baltic approaches one had to control the Danish isles and Jutland. And the key to Jutland is Schleswig-Holstein." The central front on the European continent was, in other words, still the main focus of NATO's European strategy, although it should be noted that the British Intelligence Committee, in a 1956 comment on a NATO threat estimate for the period 1956-1960, said that "as the period advances, and Northern Fleet strength increases, the importance of early seizure of northern Norway will likewise increase."[18] It was not until the late 1960s, however, that the Soviet naval build-up in the north began to cause some concern to Norwegian military planners, and it was to take many more years before the Alliance was willing or able to do anything about counteracting that particular threat.

The 1970s did however see a number of improvements in NATO's willingness to designate forces with the defence of Norway as a high priority, and to pre-position heavy equipment and supplies for forces – mainly American, but also some British and Canadian air and ground forces – that could then be brought in during a crisis. In particular, air defence of the northern flank was significantly improved through the so-called COB (Collocated Operations Bases) programme, which ensured that most of the

Norwegian air bases – themselves built through massive infusions of NATO funds – were organised and equipped for joint operations by Norwegian and earmarked US air force units. Facilities were also arranged for planes from the US Navy's aircraft carriers to transfer their operations to Norwegian airfields. This development continued apace in the 1980s, most noticeably through the arrangement whereby all the heavy equipment needed for a US Marine Amphibious Brigade of about 13 000 men was pre-positioned in central Norway. Although the need for operational flexibility dictated that most of the forces thus designated for Norway might also have to be deployed to crisis situations elsewhere, Norway remained a high priority for a maximum of four brigades and 14–16 air squadrons. In addition, the new US Maritime Strategy developed through the 1980s presaged a decisive turn towards a strong and continued presence of heavy US naval units in the North Atlantic and Norwegian seas, contrasting the previous decade's gradual retreat of the allied maritime defence line to behind the Greenland-Iceland-United Kingdom barrier.

During the 1980s, therefore, while the arms race between the United States and the Soviet Union was intensified, and the war in Afghanistan exacerbated East-West relations, the outlook for Norway's defence was better than at any time before in the Cold War. Most of those developments had been welcomed and indeed encouraged by the Norwegian government, and supported by the public. Norwegian perceptions of the Soviet threat had been sharpened by the Soviet invasion of Afghanistan, another neighbouring country of the USSR. Bilateral relations also took a turn for the worse after the arrest in 1984 of a young and politically ambitious Norwegian diplomat, Arne Treholt, on charges of spying for the Soviets. He was sentenced to 20 years in prison, and it was suggested at the trial that his betrayal had caused almost irreparable damage to Norway's defences. Treholt had also played a role in the 1977 negotiations whereby Norway had agreed to operate a "grey zone" arrangement with the Soviet Union in the Barents Sea, pending a solution of the dispute over the borders of their respective continental shelves and economic zones. The arrangement, which is still in force due to Russian intransigence, was heavily criticised from the start as being one-sided in favour of the Soviets, and also as a dangerous concession to Soviet desires for bilateral deals with its small neighbour. Moreover, 1983 brought another in a long series of incidents of suspected Soviet submarine incursions into Norwegian coastal waters. As usual in those cases the culprit – if indeed there was one – was not identified, but suspicions remained, reinforced by Sweden's "whisky on the rocks" episode in 1981.

Even so, public opinion in Norway, while remarkably consistent in its support of NATO and Norway's membership in the Alliance, was beginning to show a certain Cold War weariness. Was all this defence build-up and military spending really necessary? Would not the arms race, with its

226

thousands of nuclear weapons, increase the danger of war by accident or otherwise? Was not the Cold War becoming an exclusively bilateral contest between the two super-powers, in which their allies were playing the role of pawns? Such questions had periodically been aired earlier in the Cold War, only to be submerged by Soviet actions such as the invasion of Hungary in 1956, Czechoslovakia in 1968, and Afghanistan in 1980. By the mid-1980s, however, the mood of disengagement seemed stronger than ever.

Neutralist Nostalgia?

As noted earlier in this chapter, the government's efforts to increase Norway's own contribution to the country's defence during NATO's rearmament drive from 1951 to 1954 met with much resistance from some cabinet ministers, from strong elements within the Labour Party, and from the "national-conservatives" mentioned earlier. An instinctive dislike of spending money on the military, and a feeling that Norway's armed forces were coming under the control of foreigners, can explain much of that resistance. But it is necessary to ask also if neutralist or even isolationist sentiments were coming back to roost after the menace of war during 1948–51 had receded. Many found it hard to believe that the Soviet Union had expansionist designs beyond the perimeter of its satellites in Europe, and Norway had no serious quarrel of her own with the Russians, having lived in peace with the Eastern neighbour for as long as could be remembered. There was also the deterrent effect of the Atlantic Treaty itself, through the solemn commitment of the western great powers to come to Norway's defence. Besides, if Norwegian territory was strategically important in a Cold War perspective, would not the western powers from sheer self-interest see to it that it did not come under Soviet control? On the other side of the coin was the unease felt by many Norwegians about the Alliance somehow making them co-responsible for the distasteful colonial policies of France and Portugal.

Einar Gerhardsen, who returned to the post of Prime Minister in 1955, had always kept a sensitive finger on the pulse of his party. He may also have been influenced by the more pronounced leftist views of his politically active wife, Werna Gerhardsen. Be that as it may he seemed rather more receptive to such moods than his Foreign Minister Halvard Lange. The first sign of a slight rift between them came as Gerhardsen was the first Prime Minister of a NATO member state to receive an invitation to visit the Soviet Union. Gerhardsen had clearly encouraged the invitation, and the government felt that to reject it would be a provocation. But they were determined to limit the conversations in Moscow to matters of bilateral economic and cultural relations, contrary to Soviet wishes. Lange therefore stayed at home, leaving the Minister for Trade as the only Minister to accompany Gerhardsen. The visit took place in November 1955, and both the Prime Minister and his hosts appeared to regard it as a success. Back home the reactions were decidedly mixed, however. Eyebrows were raised both in government circles and within the party leadership as the Prime Minister brought back proposals for extensive contact and cooperation at the party and trade union level. And in the Foreign Ministry Lange was aghast that Gerhardsen had agreed to include Norway's "bases policy" declaration in the concluding joint statement from the visit, thus making it appear as a bilateral commitment rather than a unilateral declaration.

The differences between Gerhardsen and Lange should not be exaggerated. Lange did not disapprove of contacts that could bring the Soviet Union out of its isolation in regard to the western powers. But he clearly wished to limit such contacts to more mundane matters such as trade and other economic fields, cultural exchange, and sports, avoiding anything which might cast doubt on the firmness of Norway's commitment to the western alliance. The Prime Minister, on the other hand, clearly believed that Soviet-Norwegian dialogue even in the political area might contribute to a general reduction of east-west tensions. The events in Hungary in the autumn of 1956 for a time put a stop to further efforts in that direction. But Gerhardsen's surprise intervention at the NATO summit in Paris in December 1957, proposing a delay of the nuclear buildup in Europe in order to explore the possibility of arms reduction talks with the Soviets, showed that his hopes for dialogue were undiminished. Lange had himself for some time been considering various approaches to arms control, including a ban on nuclear tests and measures to prevent the spread of nuclear weapons. The difference was that he wished to secure alliance backing for such proposals, and deprecated Norwegian solo play as not only useless but also damaging both for the cause itself and for Norway's position in the Alliance. It was Gerhardsen's views that most closely reflected the general public mood in Norway at the time. His views also, at least for the time being, prevented the break-away of the left wing of the Labour Party with their increasingly strident anti-NATO and anti-nuclear stance.

Foreign Minister Lange was a firm believer in quiet diplomacy, and came to see contacts with the East European countries as more fertile ground for exploring the possibilities of reducing east-west tensions. Poland, whose Foreign Minister Adam Rapacki held similar views to Lange on nuclear weapons, was an obvious choice for such contacts, and from 1957 onwards Lange engaged in an active dialogue with him, even drafting a revised version of Rapacki's plan for a gradual build-down of both nuclear and conventional armaments in Central Europe. Both that plan and subsequent modified versions were however turned down by Norway's NATO allies. The ideas also met with strong criticism from more conservative members of the Storting's committee for foreign affairs, and in defence of his views

Lange gave them a glimpse into his philosophy, saying that it ought to be the mission of the smaller powers

> [...] to test every opportunity to seek so to speak a new way of attacking the security and political problems in Europe, in order to escape from the en-trenched positions we have dug ourselves into during a decade and move into a situation where we have a certain freedom of movement and certain possibilities to explore and feel our way towards the other side, to see if there might be areas of common ground, in order that a beginning can be made to loosen to some extent the almost convulsive knot of political problems besetting Europe.[19]

In public Lange, determined not to reveal dissension within the Alliance, of course had to present NATO's objections as his own second thoughts, and this contributed to the misleading impression of him as a somewhat obedi-ent servant of the Alliance.

The impression of Lange as an excessively loyal defender of NATO poli-cy was strengthened by the greater willingness and ability of his successor to present himself as of a more independent mind. John Lyng, who came from the Conservative Party to the post of Foreign Minister when a non-socialist coalition government in 1965 broke the thirty year stretch of La-bour rule, sought to disarm leftist fears that his political affiliation had made him into a cold warrior, by gratuitously challenging or even mocking the hard-liners on the right wing. The change from Lange was more in the make-up than in the substance of policy. But Lyng had the good fortune that his tenure coincided with that of Willy Brandt as Foreign Minister and later Chancellor of the German Federal Republic, whose path-breaking "Ost-Politik" made political approaches to Eastern Europe respectable. Brandt was highly admired in Norway, helped by the fact that he had found refuge in Norway from Nazi Germany in the 1930s, and was a Norwegian citizen from 1941 until he returned to German politics after the war. Nor-way became an ardent supporter of the détente of the later 1960s and 1970s, and Germany's leading role undoubtedly softened the scepticism of NATO which America's war in Vietnam engendered.

Labour's fall from power was partly the result of the left wing having broken away to form the Socialist Peoples' Party in 1961. Norway's with-drawal from NATO was a central element of their platform, and while their electoral support remained modest, their vociferous campaigns for Norway's "self-determination" in regard to both NATO and the European Economic Communities struck neutralist cords in wider circles. Support for Norway's membership of NATO still scored high in the opinion polls, but revulsion against nuclear weapons commanded wide support both in the Labour Par-ty and the parties at the centre of the political spectrum. Thus the Socialist

Peoples' Party in 1975 persuaded the government to formalise an additional "self-imposed restraint", in the shape of an explicit ban on foreign warships calling at Norwegian ports with nuclear weapons on board. Although the ban was a formality – it could not be enforced in view of the immunity from search of such ships, and the allied nuclear powers always refused to confirm or deny the existence of nuclear weapons on board – it was a potential embarrassment to a country which desired a more visible presence of allied naval power in the North and Norwegian Seas.

The nuclear issue came back with a vengeance at the end of the 1970s. After the government in 1961 had confirmed the ban against nuclear weapons on Norwegian soil, it had been a more or less tacit assumption that allied forces coming to assist Norway in a crisis might have nuclear weapons in their arsenals. Certain secret preparations to enable Norwegian forces to operate with such weapons had also been made. But as arms control came to dominate the international security agenda during the 1970s, propelled by huge increases in the nuclear arsenals of the two super-powers, public opinion erupted in a series of anti-nuclear demonstrations everywhere in the west. Elements on the left wing of the Labour Party then decided to reopen discussion about NATO's nuclear strategy. Campaigns were launched against proposals such as the "neutron bomb", which would kill persons without causing material damage, or the installation of a multitude of mid-range nuclear missiles in Europe to counter similar Soviet installations, and in favour of establishing a Nordic zone free from nuclear weapons. This time women's organisations and religious groups were also mobilised, and the movement had the support of many voters at the centre of the political spectrum. In 1979 a well-organised campaign began under the slogan "No to nuclear weapons", which in a short time gained 100 000 members. Their petition in support of a Nordic nuclear-free zone and against nuclear weapons on Norwegian soil even in wartime gathered half a million signatures – about one-eighth of the population.

The Labour government in power at the time was in a quandary, particularly over the proposal to equip NATO forces in Europe with cruise missiles and medium-range ballistic missiles. The purpose was to counter the proliferation in the Warsaw Pact countries of the medium-range SS-20 missile, and NATO's decision in favour of the proposal was accompanied by an offer to the Soviet Union of negotiations with a view to simultaneous and parallel cuts in the number of such missiles. Since there was no question of installing the missiles in Norway the government was in favour of such a combined decision, stressing the negotiation element. But this time the rank and file of the Labour Party revolted, and several of their parliamentarians as well as some government ministers joined in the protest. A hastily composed compromise proposal was worked out, parts of which the Prime Minister managed to persuade the Americans and then the NATO council to agree to. On that basis the government weathered the storm, but the wear and tear caused by the so-called "double decision" and the parallel debate on a Nordic nuclear-free zone contributed to Labour's fall from power in the autumn of 1981. The Conservative government, which then took over, put the question of a nuclear-free zone on ice, and Labour in opposition toned down their advocacy – in part because the Americans had uttered slightly veiled threats to suspend plans for reinforcement forces to Norway if such a zone was established.

The Conservative government, with Kåre Willoch as Prime Minister, soon managed to restore Norway's position as a dependable ally. President Ronald Reagan's "Star Wars" or Strategic Defence Initiative, which came to dominate the agenda during the mid-1980s, was strongly disliked by most of the European NATO members, but Norway muted her public criticism of the programme in order not to disturb the US-Norwegian security relationship. That changed as the Willoch government fell in May 1986, and Labour returned to power. At a meeting of NATO Defence Ministers shortly afterwards Norway's Johan Jørgen Holst refused to sign on to a communiqué expressing general support for US postures as regards defence and space weapons. Norway thereby for the first time joined Denmark and Greece as a so-called "footnote country" – countries that from time to time appended reservations to otherwise agreed NATO declarations and communiqués. The Americans reacted sharply. The work of a joint US-Norwegian study group on security and defence affairs, which for a decade had served as a back-channel to heighten US awareness of the problems of the northern flank, was temporarily suspended. The United States also withdrew an offer to finance the upgrading of Norway's anti-aircraft defence. The crisis blew over, but relations remained cool since the Labour government also decided to sharpen the ban against visiting allied ships carrying nuclear weapons. As New Zealand had just made a decree of that nature, the United States was clearly determined to stop the contagion from spreading, and Norway again had to back down.

The noisiest dispute, however, was over the export to the Soviet shipbuilding industry, by the Norwegian firm Kongsberg Våpenfabrikk and the Japanese Toshiba company, of equipment which had the effect of reducing the propeller noise from submarines. Ever since the beginning of the Cold War the Americans had been pushing for strict export controls of strategic material. Norway and the other European countries generally followed the American lead on the issue, albeit often with some reluctance. In this and other fields the Reagan administration, goaded by Senate conservatives, was determined to enforce a hard line, and the KV/Toshiba affair that erupted in 1987 touched an especially raw nerve, since the expanding submarine fleet was a central feature of the Soviet threat. The Americans demanded satisfaction in a number of ways, and the Norwegian government had to

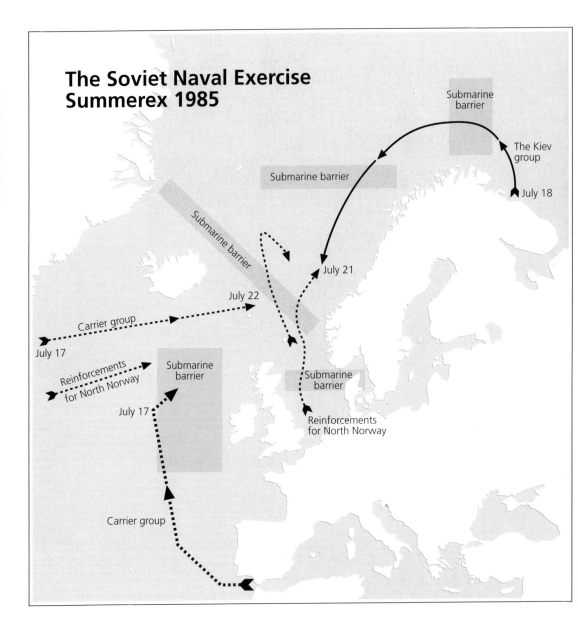

The Soviet Naval Exercise Summerex 1985

Submarine barrier

The Kiev group

July 18

Submarine barrier

Submarine barrier

July 21

July 22

Carrier group

July 17

Reinforcements for North Norway

Submarine barrier

July 17

Submarine barrier

Reinforcements for North Norway

Carrier group

This sketch from Norway's Defence High Command shows the situation during the most extensive Soviet naval exercise, SUMMEREX, in 1985. The rectangles denote barriers established by Soviet submarines against allied reinforcement efforts for Norway (the dotted lines). The curved line extending from the Murmansk coast shows the voyage of a group of Soviet warships led by the aircraft carrier Kiev.

Protest marches against nuclear weapons reached new heights from the late 1970s. The slogan for this rally in 1982 demands "Nordic countries as a nuclear-free zone" – a demand urged by the Soviet Union and also supported by the Finnish government.

employ a varied arsenal of concessions and diplomatic appeals to prevent the dispute from creating a long-term rift. Of particular interest was Norway's warning against giving public opinion an impression that the superpower was resorting to bullying tactics towards a small ally, instead of seeking accommodation based on common interests.

The rifts, discords and sometimes disputes that arose from time to time between Norway and NATO, or between Norway and the United States, varied as we have seen as regards both their nature and their intensity. Apart from the last decade of the Cold War they were not of sufficient importance to dent the general image of Norway as a cooperative and loyal ally, doing her best to contribute to western security in the ways and with the means available to a small nation on NATO's northern frontline. On the whole Norway's governments during the Cold War tended to keep to the security policy line set out by the government in exile during the Second World War: cooperation first, limits to cooperation thereafter. The two main features that set Norway apart from the mainstream of alliance policy were her self-imposed restraints on allied military presence and activities on Norwegian soil, and her anti-nuclear stance in its various permutations. Both those sets of policies could be and were explained as rational and sensible measures to avoid fomenting Soviet feelings of insecurity in a sensitive border region. They were also important as elements in what was sometimes referred to as "the Nordic Balance": a term suggesting a linkage between Norway's self-imposed restraints and restraints on Soviet policy toward Finland. Yet they were in their origins at least partly motivated by what I have called "the isolationist impulse": the desire to seek refuge from the threatening realities of power politics – the wish not to have to share the commitments and responsibilities inherent in an alliance based on "all for one and one for all". Paired with that came the old conviction of "automatic protection", as when one of the leaders of the "No to Nuclear Weapons" in 1983 wrote that NATO "in its own interest will make every effort to hold Norwegian territory."[20] It is this ambivalence between loyalty and separateness which lies behind two contrasting characterisations of Norway that have been current in public debate. One has seen Norway – often somewhat contemptuously – as "the most diligent boy in the NATO school". The other one has called Norway's posture in the Alliance – also somewhat contemptuously – as nothing better than "semi-alignment". Both are clearly wide of the mark. But in a backhanded way they attest to Norway's success in combining a cooperative posture with an astute defence of special interests, concealing a neutralist nostalgia behind a set of perfectly rational arguments.

11. "Our International Material Relations": Cooperation vs. Integration (1945–1994)

Introduction

In 1905 Norway's first Foreign Minister had put "our international material relations" on a par with neutrality as a principal concern for the country's foreign policy.[1] The experience of the Second World War signalled the replacement of neutrality by a commitment to international security cooperation. But there was more to the new internationalism that came to be known as Norway's "Atlantic Policy". The new approach to Norway's relations with the outside world signalled by the government in exile was not limited to security and defence policy. In his radio address of 15 December 1940 Foreign Minister Trygve Lie also spoke of "an economic cooperation which provides social security and prevents crises that can ruin economic life and halt social progress." The framework envisaged embraced primarily the western countries, the British Commonwealth and the United States, Norway's natural economic partners, which also shared the same ideals and traditions of liberty. In his article in The Times of 14 November 1941 he was more specific, and stressed "certain basic facts concerning economic cooperation":

> One is that it is not possible to create political stability without international economic cooperation, another is that there will certainly be no return to the old liberal economic system. The war has made necessary for all countries a national planned economy under the guidance of the state. In the initial post-war period we shall be facing enormous tasks of economic reconstruction, and it is clear that those can only be managed through a common plan. [...] In that way a first step will have been taken towards an international planned economy. The next step will be to achieve regulation of the markets and a coordinated effort to open new markets. This surely is more important than the much talked about issue of free access to raw materials.

Such a plan for making the world safe for social democracy could not be expected to survive subsequent encounters with American free-market liberalism, even in its "New Deal" clothing. But international economic cooperation did take some steps towards a better organised world with the founding, in 1944, of the World Bank and the International Monetary Fund. The first principles of Trygve Lie's programme could therefore be said to be on the way to being fulfilled. But would Norway find the American version of a global economic order acceptable? Norway's reservations against the demands for an accelerated liberalisation of trade, mentioned earlier in relation to the Marshall Plan, and against the vision of Western European economic and political integration, suggested a rocky road ahead.

Of primary importance to Norway was that the country's economic development should be based on the principle of the welfare state, with full employment and equal access to social services. That meant a planned economy on social democratic lines. Moreover, although Norway had suffered comparatively little from the war and the occupation, the government put high priority on a reconstruction that could lay the groundwork for long-term economic progress. This required an emphasis on investment in production equipment and other capital goods at the expense of an accelerated satisfaction of pent-up demands for consumer goods. There was also the problem of protecting Norwegian agriculture and fisheries against competition from countries whose methods of production had the advantages of a higher degree of industrialisation and – in agriculture – a better climate. A high proportion of the Norwegian population, on the coast and in the north, still depended on a combination of small-scale farming and near-shore fishing for their living.[2]

On the other hand Norway could not escape from her exceptionally heavy dependence on foreign trade – about 40 per cent of the Gross National Product. Free trade on a global basis would also benefit the interests of her merchant navy, whose foreign currency earnings were necessary to finance the country's import needs. The problem would be how to square those interests with a determination to maintain tight controls at home. How would Norway react to the inexorable development towards integrated structures in the world economy? Would the isolationist impulse, receding in the face of national security imperatives, reappear as a bar against Norway's integration into trans-national economic structures? The new Foreign Minister, Halvard Lange, appeared to opt for an internationalist approach when he took over in February 1946: Norway would have to adjust her economic plans to "the demands of an organised international cooperation in economic affairs. We must not cling to old concepts of absolute national sovereignty." But the Labour Party drew much of its electoral support from the small-holding and fishing communities, in competition with the parties at the centre of the political spectrum whose isolationist traditions had a strong appeal.

236

European Cooperation without Integration

The Organisation for European Economic Cooperation (OEEC), which from 1948 was the machinery established to administer the Marshall Plan programme in conjunction with the American Economic Cooperation Administration (ECA), was an inter-governmental agency, without the kind of supra-national authority likely to frighten anti-integrationists in Norway or elsewhere. But pressure from the United States for an accelerated liberalisation of trade, starting with the establishment of a customs union, found much support in the member states on the European continent. Great Britain and the Scandinavian countries shared a profound dislike of the idea, and after Norway, Sweden and Denmark had toyed with the idea of a Scandinavian customs union, they joined with Britain in a loose consultative arrangement under the name UNISCAN. Norway's apparent willingness to discuss a Scandinavian customs union was a sham: Swedish industry had during the war further increased its competitive advantage against a much less industrialised Norway, and Norwegian farmers did not stand a chance against the modern and highly efficient Danish agriculture.

A pattern was here revealed which was to be repeated again and again. Faced with pressures for greater integration at the European level, Norway tended to look the other way, feigning renewed interest in Scandinavian cooperation until that, too, began to appear threatening. For a time during the early 1950s Norway also looked towards making NATO the point of departure for an "Atlantic Community", hoping to add a loosely defined political and economic cooperation to the increasingly integrated security community. Speaking at a meeting of the Council of Europe in August, 1950, Finn Moe as chairman of the Storting's committee for foreign affairs said that Norway had

> no intention of creating difficulties in the way of establishing regional agreements, be it a French-Italian union, a French-German union, or an even larger federal union. We only ask that the Norwegian people may themselves decide if they wish to join such a union, considering also that we are all members of a more significant and essential community – the Atlantic Community.[3]

Both the Nordic and the Atlantic framework had stronger appeal in Norway than the European one, although for different reasons. Nordic cooperation had a built-in advantage due to geographic nearness, strong cultural affinities, and very similar languages, and a number of limited cooperative ventures saw the light of day under the aegis of the Nordic Council. But attempts to go beyond practical collaboration to schemes that smacked of integration tended to awaken ghosts from past history, such as Sweden's leadership aspirations, or Norway's fear of being dominated by her erstwhile union partners. The pull of the Atlantic framework had deep roots in Norway's long-standing pro-British orientation, nurtured by trade and shipping interests, reinforced by her reliance on British naval power for security, and intensified through the close ties developed during the war. Although those ties were to some extent personal to the "war generation", and whereas the United States soon took over Britain's place as guarantor of Norway's security, a long time would pass before the US-Norwegian partnership could displace the old Anglo-Norwegian association. What happened from the end of the 1940s was rather that Norway's ties to the two Anglo-Saxon powers seemed to co-exist in a kind of mutually reinforcing relationship. As against all this, "Europe", which in Norwegian as in British parlance meant the continental countries, was still foreign territory – nice places to visit, but one would not want to live there or get too involved with them.[4] French culture was much admired, but at a distance, and it would take a long time before Norwegians could forgive Germany for the invasion and occupation of their country.

The early sector-wise integration efforts in Europe, such as the European Coal and Steel Community, were of no concern to Norway. Those that took an interest in the process regarded such moves as a positive development towards peace in Europe and control of the Germans, but their interest was purely academic since the question of membership did not arise for Norway. The continuing discussion of schemes that pointed towards regional integration in Europe, economic as well as in the defence and security field, did raise the prospect of Norway gradually becoming sidelined. As long as Great Britain shared Norway's scepticism, this was not seen as a serious threat. The extent to which Norway was prepared to rely on close relations with Britain as a counterweight to European integration schemes became apparent in the abortive initiative to link Norway with the foreign exchange and monetary collaboration group known as the sterling area. Norway's primary economic motive was to ensure a continued flow of capital imports as the Marshall Plan was coming to its end. The idea was picked up with some enthusiasm by Britain's ambassador to Norway, who wished to go further, and proposed Norwegian membership in one form or another of the British Commonwealth. It is open to doubt whether such membership, even of an associate nature, would have found sufficiently wide acceptance in Norway. But the British government saw a host of practical difficulties that would have to be overcome – for example having two monarchs in the Commonwealth! – and the Bank of England saw only increased liabilities and few if any advantages in Norway's participation in the sterling bloc.

A Nordic Solution?

The issue of Nordic or Scandinavian cooperation is usually viewed quite differently from abroad than from the inside. Outside observers, seeing the cultural and political similarities, find it difficult to understand why these countries have not long since entered into a cooperation closely resembling a union. Insiders, on the other hand, take the similarities for granted and fix their – perhaps somewhat near-sighted – eyes on what separates them. In the foregoing chapter I have tried to explain the different strategic considerations which lay behind the failure of the Scandinavian Defence Union project in 1948-49. National security being to a large extent a matter for consideration behind closed doors, the failure of that project was not easily understood by the broad public. Regarding economic cooperation, the obstacles were more obvious. The two most obvious ones were, first, the unequal degree of industrialisation, with especially Sweden but also Denmark being far ahead of Norway. The differences here had a long history, but Sweden's advantage had further increased during the Second World War. The second obstacle was in agriculture, where Norway was at a disadvantage due to both topography and climate. Only some areas of south-eastern Norway could to some extent compare with the open and fertile fields of Denmark and central and southern Sweden. The only sphere in which Norway stood to gain in the short term was that of free access to a larger market for fish products. In practically all other respects a long transition period would be needed before Norwegian industry could become competitive with its neighbours.

Discussion about a Scandinavian customs union began as early as 1947, but then as one of three alternative roads to closer cooperation. The other two roads were either an industrial "division of labour" among the three countries within defined areas, or joint industrial projects. A customs union was included at the insistence of Denmark, and Foreign Minister Halvard Lange went along only because he was convinced that a study would reveal the illusory nature of such a scheme. The first report, although it left the door open for further discussion, showed just that. The non-socialist opposition was particularly adamant, and the reactions in Norwegian industrial circles as well as from the farmers were clearly negative. The Fishermen's Union was prepared to study the issue provided Sweden and Denmark removed all import restrictions on Norwegian fish products.

In part to avoid being cast as the wrecker, and also because of a genuine desire to further the modernisation of the Norwegian economy, the Labour government now proposed further investigations on the basis of a partial free trade arrangement. After four more years of study, during which relations became strained by disputes over fishing rights, Norway again found herself in a minority of one in her opposition to both a customs union and a free trade association. The Labour Party, however, was divided on the issue, and in the autumn of 1954 the government proposed new initiatives towards either a customs union or a even a common Scandinavian market. They thought that Norwegian industry was now better prepared to withstand competition from the neighbours, and also saw a need to strengthen the Scandinavian economies against the expansive efforts of an increasingly powerful Western Germany. The non-socialist opposition remained strong, however, based as it was on nationalist fears of being engulfed by its neighbours, as well as on a general scepticism against an accelerated modernisation tinged with socialism which threatened the traditional lifestyles and economic livelihood of their voters in the countryside and coastal districts.

On the level of limited, practical cooperation – with as prime examples the establishment in 1951 of SAS, the Scandinavian Airlines System, followed by a Nordic passport union, and a common Nordic labour market – the Nordic countries made great strides during the 1950s. But Scandinavian integration remained unacceptable to the majority of Norwegians. European economic cooperation, particularly with Great Britain at the centre, although prone to similar objections, seemed more acceptable, for two reasons: Britain shared the same reluctance towards anything that smacked of supranational integration, and western cooperative schemes, provided Britain was in the lead and the United States was a benign onlooker, had the advantage of strengthening Norway's westward political and security links.

Norway at the Cross-Roads of Europe (I)

In the larger framework, and in the absence of better alternatives, the relatively loose cooperation within the OEEC framework, strengthened by the European Payments Union which facilitated multilateral trade through bypassing to some extent the problem of dollar shortages, seemed satisfactory for Norway. But the resurgence of European integration, which in 1957 gave birth to the European Economic Community (EEC) treaty, raised the prospect of sidelining in more acute form. A British initiative, for supplementing the EEC with a free trade area to embrace all the OEEC countries, fell due to French objections, whereupon Britain and the Scandinavian countries, together with Portugal and the two neutral countries Switzerland and Austria, in 1960 formed the European Free Trade Association EFTA. For Norway this was a satisfactory outcome. Membership of EFTA side-stepped the thorny issue of supranational integration, and EFTA embraced at least some of Norway's main trading partners. Norway also managed by hard bargaining to gain important concessions for her fish exports, while retaining a strong protective fence round her agriculture. But a cloud of uncertainty hung over the new organisation, since it was widely suspected that for Great Britain and Denmark, EFTA was only a staging post on the way to the EEC.

240

In 1961 Great Britain and Denmark submitted their first application to join the EEC. One year later Norway followed suit. This dramatic turn-around in Norway's policy towards Europe came after a process which deserves the somewhat trite epithet of "an agonising re-appraisal". The supranational character of the EEC was such a major stumbling-block that the government in public utterances tried to obfuscate it. The escape route of associate membership – termed by critics as "joining without really joining" – was also considered, and some die-hard isolationists would have preferred a simple trade agreement with the EEC. When the application was for full membership, this indicated that elite perceptions of the continental countries had changed somewhat as a result of cooperation in the OEEC and NATO. That shipping,

" LOOK WHAT I MADE OUT OF THE SPARE WHEEL"

A British cartoonist's scathing comment on the difference in size and importance of the Common Market, with de Gaulle at the wheel, and the European Free Trade Area EFTA with British Foreign Secretary Reginald Maudling at the handlebar.

banking, and export industrial circles now favoured full membership may also be taken as a sign of greater self-confidence in their ability to face open competition from abroad. Public opinion was divided on the issue. Among those who were sufficiently well informed to be able to name the six EEC countries, opinion polls found 50 per cent in favour of joining in 1961, the rest being equally split between the "don't knows" and those opposed. One year later the opponents had strengthened their share, and that trend continued even after the Storting with a strong majority had voted in favour of applying for membership, when an opinion poll showed a total of about one-third in favour, one-third against, and one-third "don't knows".[6] A recurring theme among those who were asked to explain their "noes" was that Norway would be unable to compete with the bigger countries.

Norway's formal application contained a great number of reservations and requests for special arrangements, to the obvious dislike of the "hard-core" EEC countries France and Western Germany. It remains an open question whether the negotiations would have produced a mutually acceptable compromise, since the whole process was stopped short by de Gaulle's veto against British membership. Even if a compromise solution had been

This picture from the first campaign against Norway joining the European Common Market, in 1962, was but a foretaste of what was to come at later junctures. The slogans tell the story: "No to the sale of Norway"; "Referendum First"; "Stand Guard around the Constitution and Government by the People".

found, which by general consensus would have had to be put to a consultative referendum, the outcome might still have been a rejection of membership. Historians who have made special studies of the issue tend to think that the outcome would have been negative on both counts.[7] The opposition to membership reflected on the one hand the long-standing small-state scepticism and even fear of being overwhelmed by Germany and the other continental powers, widely felt although seldom explicitly articulated by the general public. On the other hand there was the more rationally based uncertainty as to the chances for survival of Norwegian agriculture, with its small farms and unfavourable climate, of Norwegian fisheries in view of its low degree of industrialisation, and of the country's small-scale industry producing for the domestic market. In a party-political perspective the opposition gathered much of its strength on the left, where the left wing of the Labour Party had just walked out to form the Socialist People's Party with a platform that included opposition to NATO. But the so-called "national-conservatives" could be found in all parties from left to right, with a certain preponderance in the Agrarian – now renamed the Centre – Party.

An opportunity for a rematch seemed to present itself in the beginning of 1967, as Great Britain again knocked on the doors of the EEC. Indications were that de Gaulle would again block Britain's entry, but the mere possibility that the British might succeed made it necessary for Norway to reconsider the membership issue. Since the long period of Labour governments had come to an end in 1965, it was now up to a non-socialist coalition government, with Per Borten of the Centre Party as Prime Minister, to review Norway's position. And to the surprise of many the government managed to agree, and get a clear majority of the Storting to approve, another application – except this time it was an application "to explore the basis for Norway's adherence to the European Communities". All the reservations were still there, with the need to protect agriculture and fisheries in the forefront. A crucial condition was the preservation of Norway's control of the rich fishing grounds within the new limit of 12 nautical miles.

By the time this new application for negotiations was sent, however, it was already clear that the French position had not changed: already at a press conference on 16 May 1967 de Gaulle had expressed his reservations in a way which observers called "a velvet veto". His final veto came half a year later. At this juncture Denmark saw fit to launch a new initiative for Nordic cooperation, with a higher profile than before. It became known as the NORDEK project, and aimed at nothing less than a customs union combined with intimate cooperation in industrial and economic affairs, plus common agriculture and fishery policies. In spite of Norwegian apprehensions that this looked like a new "Kalmar Union"[8], the negotiations produced a draft treaty after only two years. The success attested to the considerable advances made by Nordic cooperation in a variety of limited, practical fields in the years since 1959 under the superstructure of the inter-parliamentary Nordic Council. As a result, Nordic cooperation enjoyed unprecedented popularity among the public. Still the old Norwegian reservations lurked just under the surface, again with the feeling that Norway was bound to be the loser in the economic sense. When those reservations were this time not brought to the fore, the principal reason was that the whole project had an aura of unreality about it: Denmark clearly saw it as a step on the way to Europe, whereas in Norwegian circles a recent study[9] has identified three different views: on one side a "Europe first" group, containing the Conservative Party and parts of Labour and the Liberals, on the opposite side the "Nordic first" camp of the Centre Party plus some others at the centre and on the left, and in the middle a "Nordic in Europe" group, containing those in the Labour Party and others who feared the consequences of a deep split in the country as well as in their own political parties.

The beginning of the end for NORDEK came already at the end of 1969, as the EEC opened the door to new members. This had the effect of making it plainly obvious that NORDEK for two or three of the four countries was a reserve position in case they should fail to gain entry to the EEC on acceptable terms. Finland, out of concern for her special relationship with the Soviet Union, could not go down that road, and pulled out. Denmark and Norway, and Sweden in spite of serious concerns about her neutrality, then again turned their eyes towards Brussels. Norway re-submitted her 1967 application, and introductory negotiations began in June

1970. Attitudes to Europe had undergone considerable change since 1961. A modernised and expanded industrial sector, and the experience of competing in the EFTA markets, had inspired greater self-confidence among the industrialists as well as in the political elite, not only in the Conservative Party and the Labour Party. Even at the centre of the political spectrum attitudes were changing, especially within the Liberal "Venstre" party which had certain traditions of pro-European idealism.

The question, for Norway, was then whether the government coalition would hold through another process of negotiations, and also whether public opinion had now warmed to Europe, in spite of strong counter-currents of late 1960s radicalism and a growing concern about environmental issues. Preliminary discussions within the government and with the EEC suggested that Norway's old concerns about protection for her agriculture and fishery interests had little chance of being acceptable to Brussels – in fact positions seemed to harden on both sides as the rifts within the coalition government worsened, and the EEC on their side moved towards a policy on fisheries which collided head-on with Norwegian demands. In public opinion, opposition to Norwegian membership began to get organised from the summer of 1970, through a well-organised "Popular movement against membership in the Common Market".

In March 1971 the coalition government collapsed under the strain of trying to bridge the widening gulf between the Conservative pro-Europeans and the increasingly sceptical Prime Minister and his centrist colleagues. It then fell to the Labour Party and a strongly pro-European Prime Minister Trygve Bratteli to bring the negotiations to a conclusion. In the final stages the EEC demonstrated some flexibility towards Norwegian demands in the agricultural sector, but the distance between demands and concessions as regards fisheries remained so wide as to force the resignation of the Minister for Fisheries. Over and above the concrete differences, in this as in other spheres, it is possible to discern a difference in approach to formal agreements: the EEC's unwillingness to compromise on the principles underlying the whole EEC structure shielded a more pragmatic attitude to their practice, whereas Norway, from a traditional small-state fear of being overrun by the stronger party when treaties were to be translated into practice, insisted on detailed and explicit guarantees. The government in the end accepted the proposed treaty, which was signed on 22 January 1972. But the subsequent battle for public opinion became an unequal contest between the pro-Europeans' appeal for trust in the goodwill of the European governments, and the opposition's emphasis on the lack of precise guarantees combined with fears of the EEC's alleged inexorable drift towards a European super-state. In that perspective the most remarkable thing about the September 1972 referendum is not that the majority rejected membership, but that the majority was so narrow – 53,5 against, 46,5 in favour.

Norway at the Cross-Roads of Europe (II)

As a consequence of the referendum the Bratteli government now gave way to a centrist coalition government, whose only task was to negotiate a trade agreement with what had in the meantime changed its name to "the European Communities" – EC. The trade agreement was signed in 1973, and the Labour Party then returned to power, determined that while membership of the EC would have to remain a dead issue, it was essential for Norway to have an active policy towards Europe to avoid becoming sidelined. However, with the strength of the anti-EC groupings both inside and outside of Labour, and the lack of interest among the EC countries in retaining links with the northern "dissident", that determination fell on stony ground. Norway thus began a period of indifference towards European events. Three reasons can be found to explain why that period became such a long one. One has to do with the lack of dynamism – sometimes called "Euro-sclerosis" – in the development of the European Communities. The sharp rise of energy costs due to the "oil crisis" of 1973 brought serious economic setbacks and mass unemployment in the EC countries. While not exactly gloating, the opposition in Norway could with some satisfaction contrast the EC's economic troubles with Norway's increasingly oil-rich prosperity. Another reason lay in the strengthening of Norway's ties with NATO and the United States, which removed any fear that the rejection of EC membership might isolate Norway in the security-political field. The third, and perhaps in the long run the most important, reason was the discovery and beginning exploitation of the North Sea oil and gas reserves.

"Sea-faring at first, rulers of the entire North Atlantic. And now we are reaping gold from the bottom of the sea." With those lines from the poem "The country that is different" the poet Rolf Jacobsen sought to express the extraordinary career of a small country which now, after seven centuries in the doldrums since the demise of its mediaeval empire, suddenly found itself awash with an unearned and unexpected wealth. Norway's "oil age" began at the end of the 1960s, after Norway and Great Britain had divided the North Sea between them concerning the right to exploit whatever natural resources the Continental Shelf might be hiding. Few had much hope that those resources were of any great significance, but as Norway had a long tradition of offshore expansionism it was only natural that the country should claim its share when new ground came up for grabs. Foreign oil companies were at first the only ones willing to bet on the existence of large oil and gas reserves in the area, and in 1969 the American Phillips Company turned up trumps in the shape of the "Ekofisk" field. Still the government, in its 1972 report to the Storting recommending membership in the EEC, confined itself to the cautious remark that "if more fields should come into production during the 1970s" the total effect could be "a considerable contribution to the country's export earnings."[10] What next set the ball really

Few Norwegians really believed that the North Sea would yield exploitable resources of oil and natural gas. But in 1969 the American oil company Phillips struck oil in the EKOFISK field at the southwestern tip of Norway's Continental Shelf, and started a bonanza that seems likely to last until the middle of the new century. The rigs in this picture show EKOFISK in 1997. Today, four years later, the company has announced that – similar to Sarepta's jar - the remaining reserves in the field equal the total quantity estimated at the outset of the operation.

rolling was the "oil crisis" of 1973 whereby the major oil producing countries forced the price of crude oil up to unprecedented heights. Six years later oil accounted for nine per cent of the GNP, with no upper limit in sight. Norway's traditional harvest economy, having until then been based on fish, mineral resources and hydro-electric power, had acquired an entirely new face.

Exploring and exploiting oil and gas resources in the stormy waters and great depths of the North Sea meant working at the cutting edge of existing technology, and as a newcomer Norway possessed neither the know-how, the experience or the capital resources needed. Foreign oil companies were therefore invited to apply for concessions, but on terms that guaranteed a major share of the profits for the Norwegian state. Norway here built on a long tradition of securing national control of the country's natural resources, of which energy had been a major component ever since the harnessing of the nation's hydro-electric power "took off" at the beginning of the 20th century.[11] In order to ensure long-term benefits from the new wealth to the country as a whole, a state oil company was established which would retain at least 50 per cent ownership in all concessions, and which after a learning process would hopefully be able to compete with and gradually take over a major share of the activity. The success of "Statoil" in that respect also laid the groundwork for a flourishing and technologically advanced engineering industry serving the oil activity in a number of different ways, constructing exploration and production platforms, building supply ships, and developing various service functions.

Norway's foreign relations could not help but become strongly affected by the country's oil and gas riches, particularly since its own modest

246

consumption left potentially enormous quantities available for export to Europe. In the long run this would reduce the continental countries' dependence on the Middle East for oil, and North Africa and the Soviet Union for natural gas. Norway had suddenly become an interesting player in the European economy, not only as a source of energy supply, but also as an area of activity for the big multinational oil and gas companies. Even Sweden began to take an interest in the Norwegian economy. Already in 1974 Swedish Prime Minister Olof Palme came to Oslo to suggest a kind of Nordic fra-mework for exploitation of Norway's oil resources. As there was a slight smell of carpet-baggery about it, the predictable answer was that Sweden would be welcome to purchase Norwegian oil, but on strictly commercial terms. A more serious initiative was the subsequent plan by the Managing Director of the Swedish automobile firm Volvo for a multi-facetted Swedish-Norwegian industrial cooperation, including the oil, petrochemical, forestry, and automobile sectors. The idea had visions that attracted much interest in both countries, but Volvo's shareholders proved unwilling to share ownership of their firm with Norwegians.

In their handling of the international implications of Norway's "oil age" the principal players involved – the Foreign Ministry, the Oil and Energy Ministry, and not least Statoil – were clearly conscious that they were handling an important national asset, and that they had to take care to see to it that it remained under national control to the greatest extent compatible with the need for foreign capital and expertise. An early test of this came when the western countries in 1974 decided to form the International Energy Agency (IEA) as a counterweight to the power demonstrated during the "oil crisis" in the previous year by OPEC – the Organisation of Oil Exporting Countries. Norway's initial reaction was positive, while stressing that the aim should be dialogue, not confrontation. Norway of course shared OPEC's interest in relatively high albeit stable oil prices, particularly in view of the high cost of exploiting the resources of the North Sea. But very soon a wave of protests arose, portraying the IEA partly as a rich man's club to secure cheap oil supplies for their industrial supremacy, and partly as an attempt to subvert Norway's right to self-determination in her handling of the oil resources – yet another instance of small-state fear of being overrun by bigger powers.

After much soul-searching, in which the need to show solidarity with the western countries for national security reasons was strongly present, Norway joined the IEA with a reservation clause against the Organisation's authority to determine distribution and consumption quotas in a crisis. At the same time Norway strove to maintain a dialogue with OPEC, but without establishing any formal links – another sign that the country sought to ride two horses at the same time. This dualism was to a large extent unavoidable, reflecting Norway's situation as a western country in every respect,

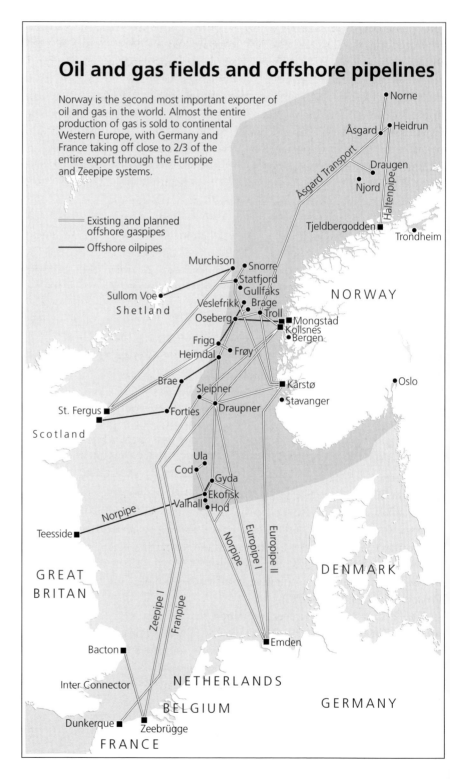

Oil and gas fields and offshore pipelines

Norway is the second most important exporter of oil and gas in the world. Almost the entire production of gas is sold to continental Western Europe, with Germany and France taking off close to 2/3 of the entire export through the Europipe and Zeepipe systems.

Existing and planned offshore gaspipes

Offshore oilpipes

Norne

Åsgard • Heidrun

Åsgard Transport

Draugen

Njord

Haltenpipe

Tjeldbergodden ■ • Trondheim

Murchison • Snorre

• Statfjord

• Gullfaks

Sullom Voe • Veslefrikk • Brage

Shetland Oseberg • ■ Troll

■ Mongstad

Kollsnes

• Bergen

Frigg • Frøy

Heimdal •

Brae • Kårstø ■ • Oslo

Sleipner • Stavanger

St. Fergus ■ • Forties / Draupner

Scotland

Ula

Cod •

• Gyda

• Ekofisk

Valhall • Hod

Norpipe

Teesside ■

NORWAY

Europipe I

Europipe II

Norpipe

GREAT
BRITAN

DENMARK

Zeepipe I

Franpipe

• Emden

Bacton ■

NETHERLANDS

Inter Connector

BELGIUM

GERMANY

Dunkerque ■ Zeebrügge

FRANCE

248

but having common interests with the OPEC countries in the maintenance of relatively high oil prices. The balancing act that this involved was not easy to maintain. The oil price fluctuated wildly, and in periods of very high prices the United States and other western allies put pressure on Norway to push the price down. In periods of very low prices OPEC in their turn urged Norway to join them in cutting production so as to push the price up. On the whole Norway sought to play down the foreign policy implications of her position as an important exporter of oil and natural gas, stressing the intention to let market forces decide which countries to sell to, and at what price. But that was a difficult line to follow in regard to natural gas, since the massive investments in pipelines required long-term contracts.

Norway was right from the start determined not to let her national economy become totally dependent on petroleum, and made conscious efforts to use her new wealth both to strengthen traditional industries, in the face of the drain of manpower towards offshore-related activities, and to develop a wider industrial base. The traditional export commodities, principally fish products, remained very important, even more so after the new international ocean regime by the end of the 1970s had provided Norway with economic zones six to seven times the size of her mainland territory. The European Communities, and especially Western Germany and Great Britain, constituted the most obvious market for Norwegian exports. The revitalisation of European economies in the 1980s, and the surge towards liberalisation, internationalisation, and indeed globalisation of trade and the markets, could not but affect Norway's foreign economic relations. The 1973 trade agreement was no longer sufficient as the EC got on with the process of establishing the "inner market". The return to power of the Labour Party in 1986, with the energetic Gro Harlem Brundtland as the country's first woman Prime Minister, heralded an active Norwegian policy of adjustment to new European cooperative institutions. In the first instance Norway joined the organisations for scientific and technological cooperation, and when the EC began to make strides towards coordination in the field of foreign and security policy Norway made strenuous efforts to obtain some sort of consultative status within the machinery of European Political Cooperation (EPC).

The crucial issue, however, remained that of access to the EC's "inner market". The European Free Trade Area EFTA had lost much of its vitality as Britain and others "defected" to become members of the EC. Still the Nordic EFTA members represented considerable economic strength, and with the active support of the chairman of the European Commission, Jacques Delors, a process of negotiation was begun which in 1992 produced agreement on creating a European Economic Area – EEA. The principal feature of EEA was the establishment of a common industrial market for the EFTA and – since 1991 – the European Union.[12] There was no lack of

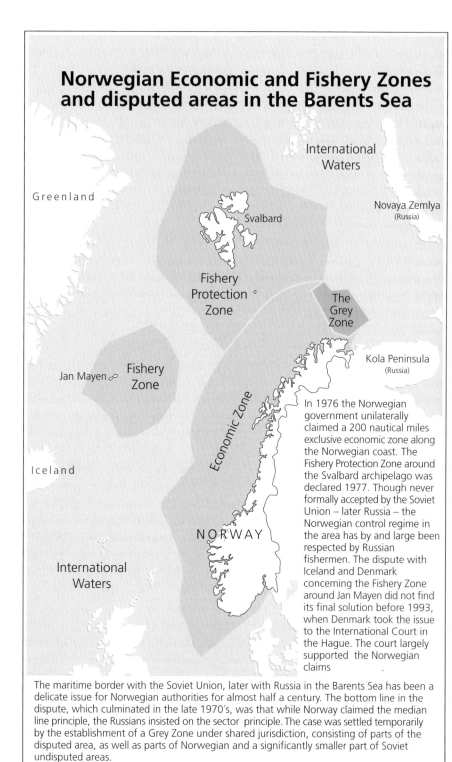

Norwegian Economic and Fishery Zones and disputed areas in the Barents Sea

International Waters

Greenland

Novaya Zemlya (Russia)

Svalbard

Fishery Protection Zone

The Grey Zone

Kola Peninsula (Russia)

Fishery Zone

Jan Mayen

Economic Zone

Iceland

In 1976 the Norwegian government unilaterally claimed a 200 nautical miles exclusive economic zone along the Norwegian coast. The Fishery Protection Zone around the Svalbard archipelago was declared 1977. Though never formally accepted by the Soviet Union – later Russia – the Norwegian control regime in the area has by and large been respected by Russian fishermen. The dispute with Iceland and Denmark concerning the Fishery Zone around Jan Mayen did not find its final solution before 1993, when Denmark took the issue to the International Court in the Hague. The court largely supported the Norwegian claims.

NORWAY

International Waters

The maritime border with the Soviet Union, later with Russia in the Barents Sea has been a delicate issue for Norwegian authorities for almost half a century. The bottom line in the dispute, which culminated in the late 1970's, was that while Norway claimed the median line principle, the Russians insisted on the sector principle. The case was settled temporarily by the establishment of a Grey Zone under shared jurisdiction, consisting of parts of the disputed area, as well as parts of Norwegian and a significantly smaller part of Soviet undisputed areas.

scepticism and even outright opposition against the far-reaching adjustments to EU regulations and directives which the EEA entailed for Norway. Since the EU was the dominant partner in the new organisation, the EFTA countries had to accept the basic provisions of the "acquis communautaire" – the sum total of decisions taken under the EC treaties, in particular as regards the "four freedoms": the free movement of goods, services, capital, and people. A non-socialist coalition government, which took over after Labour suffered a sharp reverse in the 1989 parliamentary election, broke up after only a year due to the Centre Party's fear of losing Norway's "right to self-determination", and the Labour government that returned to power took great pains to conceal that EEA could become a first step towards membership of the EC. That facade became difficult to maintain as first Austria, in 1989, and then Sweden and Finland, in 1991, applied for membership. And in November 1992, six months after signing the EEA treaty, the Brundtland government submitted Norway's new application for membership of the European Union. The EEA treaty was approved by the Storting the year after with a clear majority. But the 35 members who voted against clearly hoped that when push came to shove the majority of the people would find that the EEA made membership of the EU unnecessary.

The negotiations about Norway's application lasted for about a year. The accelerated internationalisation during the foregoing decade meant that integration and supranational structures were not quite the scarecrows they had been on earlier occasions. The EU treaty had also enshrined the so-called "principle of subsidiarity", which aimed to limit the power of the EU to areas where a decision at the Union level was necessary, thus excluding from EU jurisdiction matters which could be decided at the national level. However, fisheries and agriculture were again stumbling-blocks on the way to an agreement. Norway's traditional demands for permanent special status were again put forward, and rejected by the EU, and the compromise solutions agreed were to some extent cheques drawn on the future willingness of the EU to practice those solutions in a spirit of goodwill towards Norway. Just before the opening of the negotiations a new stumbling-block appeared, in the shape of an EU draft directive which seemed to endanger national self-determination in regard to oil and natural gas resources, by challenging Norway's right to take national considerations into account in the granting of concessions for exploration and exploitation. This Norway refused to accept, and after some hard and public bargaining the EU agreed to make significant changes in favour of Norway's position in the final version of the directive.

The omens were hardly favourable as the government in 1994 put its proposal for a membership treaty to the referendum. Already the municipal elections of 1991 had shown considerable progress for the hard-core opposition, the Centre and Socialist Left parties. In the parliamentary elections

As the British cartoonist in a previous illustration, this Norwegian cartoonist has also been struck by the feebleness of any substitute for membership of the European juggernaut – adding for good measure the jubilant "Hurrah" as Norway in the EEA skiff cuts loose from the giant.

of 1993 the opponents had flocked to the Centre Party, which had taken the lead in the well-organised popular "No to EU" campaign. Their tune was much the same as before, with its emphasis on sovereignty, self-determination, grass-roots democracy, and economic support for the livelihood of people in the countryside, on the coast, and in the north. Some of their arguments were difficult to dismiss or refute. Prominent among those was the fear that the pattern of Norwegian governance, with its deliberate policy of a far-reaching distribution of power and economic resources to the scattered communities of such a thinly populated country, would lose out to the inexorable centralisation of power in the EU organs.

Underneath it all one could also detect an attitude not unlike that which Sir Geoffrey Howe, in his resignation speech as British Foreign Secretary, attributed to Margaret Thatcher: an image of "a Continent that is positively teeming with ill-intentioned people scheming to extinguish democracy, to dissolve our national identities, to lead us through the back door into a federal Europe."[13] Against this the "yes" campaign, which got off to a late start since it was determined to await the final treaty proposal, fought a largely defensive battle, trying to convince the people that co-determination through membership was better than a largely illusory self-determination.

A key question in the run-up to the referendum was how Norway's two neighbours to the east, Sweden and Finland, would go. Most observers expected Finland to join the EU, as a decisive step towards that re-alignment with the west which her relationship with the Soviet Union had for so long prevented. There was more doubt about Sweden, whose long-standing tradition of non-alignment seemed to have the force of an unwritten part of the Constitution. Yet Sweden's economy was undergoing a severe crisis, and since the EU at least so far did not conflict with non-alignment in the defence and security field, economic considerations were bound to weigh heavily with the doubters. In Norway no such considerations carried any force. Her western alignment was secured by membership of NATO, and her economic strength meant that arguments about the need to join for economic reasons were lacking in conviction. So on 28 November 1994, after Finland – with a clear majority – and Sweden – with a narrow margin – had voted to join, 52,2 per cent of the Norwegians voted "no" and only 47,8 voted "yes".

12. An Ethical Foreign Policy?

Introduction

In 1906 the young scholar Halvdan Koht, later to become a renowned international historian and Norway's Foreign Minister, published a modest-looking little book with a title that translates as "The Idea of Peace in Norwegian History."[1] The subtitle of the book, more accurately reflecting its contents, was "Norway in the growth of international justice". Koht's central message was that the small democratic countries had a particular mission as spokesmen and pioneers for a peace built on justice and not on power. His attempt to interpret Norwegian history right from the formation of the mediaeval Kingdom as an endless quest for peace is hardly convincing. But he clearly had a point when referring to Norway's promotion of neutrality and arbitration treaties from the end of the 19th century, which I have dealt with in earlier chapters. In the closing passage he expressed the hope that Norway, together with her Scandinavian neighbours and Switzerland, would become the source from which peace among the peoples should spread through the rest of the world. "Peace and justice provide the safest shield for lands and peoples, and the people that make peace their purpose will thereby have gained an honourable place in the history of the world." The emphasis in Koht's book on the arbitration treaties, as well as his account of Norway's successful effort to achieve a peaceful dissolution of the Union with Sweden, show a clear recognition that action and not just words was needed if Norway was to set an example for other states to follow. But Koht was no pacifist – in fact he resigned as chairman of the Norwegian Peace Association when in 1902 it voted to condemn even defensive wars against an external attacker.

After the First World War Norway's record as a pioneer for the peaceful settlement of international disputes continued to rest on a succession of arbitration treaties. Norway's efforts for peace beyond that remained at the verbal level, as noted in an earlier chapter. Her far-reaching unilateral disarmament, although presented as a peace-building effort, had other reasons: the widespread feeling that the World War had been "the war to end all wars", the absence of identifiable external threats to Norwegian security,

and the Labour Party's view of the military as a weapon against the working class. Yet Norwegians tended to view their country as a standard-bearer
for peace, proudly pointing to Fridtjof Nansen's efforts on behalf of the
League of Nations during the famine years in the Soviet Union and in the
resettlement of refugees after the Greco-Turkish imbroglio. The fact that the
awarding of the Nobel Peace Prize was entrusted to Norway – to a committee selected by the Storting – was also regarded as a tribute to Norway
as a peacemaker. Few seemed to notice that Nansen was first and foremost
a pragmatic man of action, with scant regard for the lofty ideals professed
by Norwegian politicians – his efficient resettlement of Moslems from
Greece and Greeks from Turkey looks remarkably similar to what today is
condemned as "ethnic cleansing".[2] As for the Nobel Peace Prize, recent historical research has focused on the awards prior to the Second World War
as a reflection of Norwegian foreign policy.[3] That they reflected the ideals
that Norway hoped would prevail in international affairs is clear. In fact the
list of laureates 1901–1938 suggests a conception of peacemaking as principally the province of mostly since-forgotten idealist thinkers and writers,
with only a sprinkling of practitioners such as Theodore Roosevelt, Austen
Chamberlain, Aristide Briand, Gustav Stresemann – and Fridtjof Nansen.

   On the whole, as I have tried to argue in earlier parts of this book, Norway's quest for peace, international law and disarmament in the period
before the Second World War displayed a curious amalgam of realism,
naiveté, and self-interest. It was based on self-interest in so far as Norway
was a "satisfied" state without "irredenta" that could become the cause of
armed conflict with other states, and therefore had everything to win and
nothing to lose by the elimination of inter-state wars. It was realistic in its
fundamental premise that the survival and well-being of small states
required the replacement of international anarchy, and its antithesis of great
power dominance, by a better organised world based on international justice. It was also naive in its supposition that other states, not enjoying the
advantages of undisputed borders and a reasonably homogenous population, only needed to be persuaded in order to emulate "the Nordic way".

   A policy based on those three elements could not survive unchanged in
the face of the violence of the Second World War and the armed truce of
the Cold War, and Norway's simultaneous transition from having been an
onlooker to becoming an active participant in international power politics.
But the underlying beliefs were to prove remarkably resilient, not only sur-
viving the Cold War but actually becoming strengthened as the world
moved closer to the new millennium. Their make-up may have changed
somewhat as circumstances have altered, but the motive force – the conviction that Norway has a special role to play in leading the world up the
straight and narrow path towards a peace based on international justice and
humanitarian values – has remained surprisingly stable. Some might prefer

to call it Norway's "ethical foreign policy". Here I shall call it "the mission-ary impulse", since I see Norwegians' long and strong traditions of sending missionaries to less fortunate countries as one of the most important roots of Norway's post–World War II efforts for a better and more peaceful world.

1945–1970: Anti-Colonialism, Development Aid, and UN Peacekeeping

Norway's strong and consistent support for the United Nations has been one of the mainstays of her declared foreign policy since the organisation was founded in 1945. Frequent statements of official policy called the UN "the cornerstone of Norwegian foreign policy", and persisted in that char-acterisation – even if modified to "one of the cornerstones" after NATO had taken its place in the country's security equation. The election of wartime Foreign Minister Trygve Lie as the first Secretary General of the UN clearly cemented the world organisation's position in Norwegian pub-lic opinion as the embodiment of ideals which, however elusive, were ne-vertheless just around the corner. If the UN's Security Council proved to be a disappointment, Norway could always turn her attention to the work of the other organs, such as the Economic and Social Council, and the Trusteeship Council. On the eve of resigning as Foreign Minister in order to assume the post of Secretary General, Trygve Lie proudly referred to the work of Norway's great hero Fridtjof Nansen in the humanitarian efforts entrusted to him by the League of Nations in the 1920s, and vowed that Norway would follow his traditions.

We have already seen how Norway was in the forefront of efforts both inside the UN and in other forums to make the fascist Franco regime in Spain an outcast of the civilised world. But it was in the fields of de-coloni-sation and development aid that Norway, often but not always together with her Nordic neighbours, eventually came to see herself as a natural spear-head.[4] Portugal and France, whose policies and conduct towards their Afri-can and East Asian colonies came in for particular criticism, were clearly annoyed. Norway's criticism was however tempered by concern for the two countries' status as Norway's allies in NATO, and was in the early stages more often than not expressed in the closed chambers of the Alliance instead of through public diplomacy in the UN or elsewhere. But as pub-lic opinion in Norway became agitated about France's war in Algeria, the government was forced to take a more open stand. Opinion was more divided towards the war in Indo-China, since that could be seen as part of the containment of a wider communist offensive against western interests and positions. In 1952 Norway in fact supported an unanimous NATO resolution that declared the French struggle in Indo-China as being fully consonant with the aims and ideals of the Atlantic community. But the storm that this created on the domestic front persuaded the government to take a firmer line in the future against anything that could be construed as making Norway "guilty by association" in the colonial wars of her NATO allies. That line was also influenced by the growing importance of the group of non-aligned states in the UN, which expected Norway to "stand up and be counted" in the struggle for independence of the former colonies.

So far Norway's efforts to retain an ethical profile for her foreign policy could be confined to the verbal or rhetorical level. In development aid more was needed, at least money. Norway was in the 1950s not in a financial position to devote any substantial sums to such aid. In fact Norway was herself the recipient of huge amounts of economic and military assistance and infrastructure funds, as noted earlier. The initial sums given by Norway to the various technical assistance programmes of the United Nations and its agencies were extremely modest. From 1954–5 onwards this began to change, partly in order to "compete" with Sweden and Denmark, and Norway and Denmark for a time became the biggest contributors as measured in relation to population and GNP. Generally Norway extolled the virtues of multilateral aid through the UN and its agencies as against the more self-serving country-to-country aid. But in 1952 Norway took the bold step of inaugurating a bilateral programme of aid to the fishing communities of the state of Kerala in southeast India. In addition to generous sums from public funds the programme would benefit from a nation-wide collection of money from private citizens, thus making it not just an impersonal government-funded scheme but one in which the "man in the street" could feel that he had a personal stake.

This poster demonstrates the effort to make the Norwegian aid project for India a real people-to-people effort. The publicity campaign of the "People's action for economically underdeveloped areas" – the latter term had not yet been branded as politically incorrect – also ran a special railway carriage which toured the country with shows by popular radio personalities, performing songs like the one that translates roughly as follows: "We act on our yearnings to build by giving aid to Travancore – our time needs action for the future: This now comes from Norway on eagles' wings."

The person-to-person character of the Indian-Norwegian Fisheries project, and the fact that Norway was the first non-colonial country after the United States to engage in bilateral development aid, was a major public relations coup for the country. Inside Norway, although there was considerable scepticism in more conservative quarters, it served the "missionary impulse" of the parties at the centre of the political spectrum, which drew much of their support from the districts whose voters traditionally supported the various Christian missionary organisations with donations of money. The Labour movement in its turn saw the programme as a brilliant expression of traditional social democratic ideals of international solidarity and humanitarian concern. A more matter-of-fact motive for the programme was to eradicate the poverty that communist expansion fed on. The timing of the initiative also had something to do with giving the public something positive to think about at a time when the political debate was mostly about ever increasing defence budgets. An extra bonus in that respect was, as a note from the Labour Party's central office put it, "to engage in an idealistic venture those many Norwegian 'intellectuals' who find that Norway's apparent dependence on capitalist America gives them breathing problems, and whose only activity so far has been the occasional forays against Norway's foreign policy stance."[5]

India was a natural choice for this pioneering effort. It was the world's largest democracy, they spoke English there, and they had a workable administrative apparatus. The focus on fisheries also seemed an obvious one: here was an activity in which Norwegians were really experts. The reality in India was to prove that assumption somewhat naive, and it took some years before a pattern of larger and motorised boats and a cooperative sales organisation could begin to function. The capital and know-how needed to operate motor boats meant that by and large the middlemen benefited more than the village fishermen that the project was intended to help. Still the project not only persevered but got extended to other areas on the coast, swallowing for a time over half the total Norwegian development aid budget. When it was wound up after twenty years, opinions were – and today still are – divided as to its merits and results. It was criticised from the right as a prime example of "innocents abroad" or a total waste of money, and from the left as having helped the "haves" more than the "have-nots". But at least it seems to have made a major contribution to the creation of a modern Indian fisheries industry, and the prosperity it brought to the towns in the area did gradually filter down to the population in the villages.

Another action-oriented peace effort has been Norway's extensive participation in military or semi-military peacekeeping efforts under the aegis of the United Nations. This effort did not come out of the blue: already in 1920 Norway had responded to an appeal from the League of Nations by preparing a company of soldiers as part of an international force for supervisory and police duties during a referendum on Lithuania's international status. In the event the force was never sent. Norway's peacekeeping effort on behalf of the United Nations began on a small scale in 1949, when five army officers were sent to Kashmir as part of the mission to supervise the armistice there between India and Pakistan. The next contribution was of quite a different kind. In response to an appeal from the UN Command in the war in Korea Norway in 1951 established a mobile field hospital – NORMASH – near Seoul. The principal stage for Norway's participation in UN peacekeeping activities was to be the Middle East, however.

Support in Norway for the new State of Israel was clear and strong from the beginning. The image of the Jewish people, reeling from their heinous persecution by Hitler's Germany, endeavouring to build a small social democratic state in the lands of the Bible, could not fail to appeal to the people of another small social democratic state – people whose religious feelings were aroused by the mere mention of geographic place names from the area. The existence of a missionary society in Norway whose aim was to convert Jews to Protestantism, and the fact that many tended to blame the Jews for the death of Jesus Christ, counted for little against such a wave of sympathy. The rising tensions between Israel and the Arabs in 1956 brought the first Norwegian peacekeepers to the area as officers in the UN Truce Supervision Organisation in Palestine.

Norway's pro-Israeli stance was dented somewhat by the Suez war in the autumn of 1956. Although Israel was here allied with another of Norway's traditional friends, Great Britain, the military action against Egypt was a clear breach of international law, and also threatened to strengthen the position of the Soviet Union in the Middle Eastern powder keg. At the same time Norway as a major shipping nation was concerned to keep the Suez Canal open, and this, as well as the urge to support the United Nations, motivated her co-sponsorship of a General Assembly resolution to establish a "United Nations Emergency Force" (UNEF) to assure and control a cessation of hostilities. Within a few days Norway also had ready a company of infantry soldiers for participation in the force. That contribution was subsequently enlarged as Norway and Denmark joined their forces in the area into one battalion with support elements. During the ten years that UNEF operated in the area, until expelled by Egypt at the outbreak of the Six-Day War with Israel in 1967, more than 11 000 Norwegian soldiers served in the force. In the meantime Norwegian military personnel had contributed over 1000 men to UN operations in the Congo from 1960 to 1964, and participated in short-term observer missions in the Lebanon, Jordan, Yemen and Saudi-Arabia.

1970–2000: "Idealpolitik" on a Wider Front

We have seen earlier how the non-socialist coalition which came to power in Norway in 1965 brought a change of tune in public policy declarations towards the East-West conflict. That change was even more pronounced in relation to events that did not involve Norway directly, but which conflicted with Norwegian values of peace, democracy, and human rights.[6] Television, started on a regular basis by the Norwegian State Broadcasting in 1960, may have had something to do with that. To take one example, John Lyng, as Foreign Minister from 1965 to 1970, did not shrink from sharp public criticism of Nigeria's federal government in its conflict with the break-away state of Biafra. Televised images of Biafra's tearful leader Colonel Ojukwe and the suffering civilians in the area made a deep impression on

259

After 19 years of Labour government Foreign Minister Halvard Lange had to hand over his portfolio to John Lyng (left) from the Conservative Party. The non-socialist coalition which then took over rode into power on a felt "need for change". In retrospect, continuity rather than change prevailed, and the conduct of foreign policy changed more in style than in content.

the Norwegian public, and Church Aid organisations openly sided with the cause of Biafra, thus exerting pressure which at one stage brought the Norwegian government to the brink of direct involvement by way of a recognition of Biafran independence. Nearer to home Norway strongly condemned the so-called Colonels' Coup which overturned the democratically elected government of Greece in 1967, and took the lead in taking the military junta to the bar of the Council of Europe's Commission of Human Rights.

Not unexpectedly, America's war in Vietnam became the focus for protest movements everywhere in the radicalised atmosphere of the later 1960s and early 1970s. Although the protests in Norway were moderate compared to the fever pitch reached in Sweden, where Prime Minister Olof Palme made common cause with the demonstrators, they touched a wide spectrum of the people. Some saw the war in the perspective of a small country fighting for independence against western imperialism, others saw it – with an admixture of anti-Americanism – as foreign intervention in a civil war between forces for progress, however undemocratic, and an unpopular quasi-feudal regime maintained in power through American military strength. Others again were simply shocked by the television pictures of burnt-out villages and dead and wounded civilians, and wanted an end to the killing. As a close ally of the United States the Norwegian government was muted in its public criticism. But in 1967 Foreign Minister Lyng from the rostrum of the UN General Assembly criticised America's war, and called for negotiations. In this he reflected an increasing opposition to US policy also inside the government, particularly from the Ministers of the Liberal "Venstre" party. Mere criticism did not go far enough for the Labour Party, however, and when they returned to power in 1971, Norway became the first NATO member state to recognise North Vietnam, in defiance of strong American protests which only just stopped short of recalling the ambassador "for consultations".

260

The uproar in Norway over the civil war between Nigeria and the break-away state of Biafra owed much to the advent of nation-wide television. Pictures of suffering children brought into people's homes by the new medium stimulated a massive aid project organised by the 'Church Emergency Aid', and compassion for the people of Biafra at one stage brought the government close to recognising the independence of the rebelling state.

Even in the United States' own back yard, Central and South America, Norway during the 1970s began to take an active interest in political developments. There was strong sympathy for Salvador Allende's government which came to power in Chile in 1970, and corresponding fury when General Pinochet carried through his military coup and began a ruthless persecution of the democratic and socialist opposition. After some hesitation the Norwegian embassy in Santiago became a haven for refugees, many of whom were also admitted to political asylum in Norway. The urge to support social democratic solutions to the many problems in that part of the world later led to an intense friendship with Michael Manley, Jamaica's Prime Minister from 1972 until he was deposed in 1980. His socialist leanings, and his friendship with Fidel Castro in nearby Cuba, did not endear him to the United States, but the Norwegian Labour Party, and Odvar Nordli as Prime Minister, saw him as the heroic pioneer for a social democratic solution to the problems of the Americas. Development aid and initiatives for cooperation in shipping and industry followed, but the lustre of Jamaica soon faded.

Norway's attention next became focused on Nicaragua, where the radical Sandinista movement in 1979 succeeded in toppling the repressive Somoza regime. The Labour government took an active part in the efforts of the Socialist International to strengthen the democratic element of the

In Norway as elsewhere protest marches against America's war in Vietnam were on the rise from 1965, and quickly became a rallying point for forces on the left of the political spectrum. Here one of the marches approaches the US Embassy building in Oslo with a banner demanding "Stop the murders in Vietnam".

Sandinistas, and took a clear stand against the Reagan administration's interventionist policy on behalf of the armed resistance against Ortega's government. The non-socialist government which took over in Norway in 1981 was divided in its views, with Prime Minister Kåre Willoch deploring both US policy towards Nicaragua and Ortega's leaning towards Moscow. His Minister for Development Aid, Ms. Reidun Brusletten from the Christian People's Party, still managed to push through the odd idea of sending a "ship of peace" to the Sandinista government as a symbol of Norwegian support. Throughout the 1980s there was however an increasing and widely approved emphasis on much needed relief and development aid towards the people of Nicaragua, which continued during the following decade irrespective of the political colour of either the donor or the recipient government.

The kind of political activism displayed by successive Norwegian governments in favour of left-of-centre and preferably social democratic movements and governments, or liberation movements fighting against their erstwhile colonial overlords, reflected a genuine conviction that the forces they supported were the best hopes for the future of the countries in question. Norway here frequently found herself at odds with many of her allies, not least the United States, whose quest for stability more often than not led Washington to support authoritarian regimes. Occasionally, however, Norway was at odds with herself. Her ideals at times came into conflict with not only her interest in maintaining her links with her allies but also her

262

material or economic interests. Both conflicts were present in Norway's campaign against apartheid in South Africa, and to a lesser extent against the white regime in Rhodesia. There was no doubt about Norway's anti-racist convictions. But Norwegian shipping, and particularly oil tankers, had a major role in maritime transport to those areas, and this brought to the fore an argument used by those who were sceptical towards the idea of Norway as a front-runner in campaigns to boycott or stigmatise repressive regimes: such campaigns had at best no effect, and at worst damaged Norwegian interests, except when part of a wide international effort that included some of the major powers. Solo performances by Norway, the sceptics claimed, were a mere drop in the ocean. Knut Frydenlund, Norway's Foreign Minister from 1973 to 1981 and again from 1986 until his untimely death a year later, clearly had a more realistic view of Norway's role than most political leaders, and saw the danger of policies dictated by domestic opinion rather than by their international effect:

Knut Frydenlund brought to his long service as Foreign Minister (1973–81 and 1986–7) not only a solid basis of experience from the foreign service, but also a profound understanding of the complexities of international relations, and an open, analytical mind which did not immediately appeal to the more doctrinaire factions of the Labour Party. His easy manner still made him a bridge-builder during the turbulence of the late 1970s.

> As Foreign Minister one has to act on those demands from Norwegian opinion and Norwegian political life. But being in an executive role means facing a succession of difficult matters of judgement. One meets other aspects of the issues. An active engagement for human rights may bring burdens in our relations with other countries. It also means that other Norwegian interests suffer when we in one way or another intervene towards other countries. Nor can we avoid noticing that what we ourselves see as a good cause and as an expression of a moral attitude, may be seen by other nations and peoples as moralising and as an expression of conceit.[7]

Less controversial than the verbal political activism of telling other countries what to do were the development aid packages that usually accompanied Norwegian declarations of support. Receiving countries were suitably grateful for what they got, especially money with no strings attached and technical assistance geared towards their own ideas of development. For a long time the "philosophy" behind Norway's aid programmes was that attempts to impose the donor's idea of what the recipient country needed smacked of neo-colonialism, and should be avoided. In practice, of course, Norwegian values and ideas often prevailed. In line with an international trend Norwegian development aid really took off from the end of the 1960s, when a separate Agency with the acronym NORAD was established under the aegis of the Foreign Ministry. One of its tasks was to coordinate the work of private organisations which gradually came to play a major role and to spend a large share of the increasing budgets. This in due course led to what in the 1990s came to be called "the Norwegian model": a close-knit cooperation between state agencies, research institutions, and non-governmental humanitarian organisations. Development aid soon became an immensely popular cause in public opinion, and the political parties competed to propose ever more ambitious targets for the proportion of GNP to be devoted to aid. Norway's oil wealth provided new opportunities for largesse, and in 1982 the country fulfilled its promise as one of the first to allocate one per cent of the GNP to development aid.

In spite of Norway's principal stand in favour of multilateral aid through the United Nations, bilateral aid became increasingly important. Norwegian industry could then benefit, while Norway as a nation enjoyed the higher profile and "soft power" that accrued when aid projects carried the Norwegian flag. The visibility of the Norwegian aid effort would thus be heightened both abroad and at home. Critical voices at home still complained that aid with strings attached smacked of paternalism and selfishness, and for a long time Norway resisted the international trend towards linking aid with recipients' purchases of Norwegian products on a commercial basis. That determination weakened in periods when economic setbacks produced unemployment in branches of the Norwegian export industry. A telling example was the crisis in the shipbuilding industry in the 1970s, which the government decided to solve by offering subsidised and state guaranteed loans to developing countries that wished to purchase ships from Norway. On the face of it the arrangements were extremely successful, as the order books for the shipbuilders filled up. Enormous sums were hence committed as loan guarantees. But by 1980, when the programme was wound up, it was clear that most of the money was lost since the debt-ridden developing countries were unable to repay the loans, and the ships built were anyhow largely unsuited for their needs.

A thorny problem throughout was the selection of worthy recipient countries. Need for aid was an obvious criterion, but since there were needy countries everywhere, choices had to be made in which political considerations had to be taken into account. Thus Botswana was an early choice in order to help that country to free itself from South Africa's dominance. More mundane reasons were also present, as when Tanzania, Kenya and Uganda were among the first African countries to receive aid: like in India they spoke English there, and possessed a relatively well-functioning administration. But Uganda soon dropped out when Idi Amin began to run that country to the ground. In 1972 the Bratteli government set down certain political considerations as explicit criteria. Preference would be given to countries that were clearly development-oriented and emphasised social justice. Even more controversial was the opening for aid to popular movements that fought for national independence. The subsequent addition of such criteria as respect for human rights and democratisation was not controversial, but which of the countries in question could be said to meet such conditions?

Norwegian development aid thus continued to grow and develop as an enormously complex patchwork quilt of countries and projects. At the same time doubts were beginning to emerge about the results and effects of the relatively vast sums spent. The ambitious target of one per cent of GNP meant a lot of money chasing often randomly chosen projects. Evaluations of specific projects gave food for thought, and, in some rightist circles, for wholesale condemnation of the whole concept of development aid. One of the more famous failures was a fisheries project at Lake Turkana in Kenya. Lack of sufficient fish resources and an unstable water supply meant that the modern freezing plant that was built could not be used, which was perhaps just as well since there were no freezer trucks in the country, and the fish would at any rate have been far too expensive for the ordinary Kenyan consumer. But it is another tribute to the strength of the "missionary impulse" that public support for Norwegian development aid has remained remarkably solid to this day. In the 1990s a new philosophy took hold, which emphasised the receiving country's responsibility for doing their part to ensure success for the various projects, in cooperation with the donor country, including the building of an institutional infrastructure as an insurance against waste.

Focus on the Middle East, 1976–1998

Norwegian pro-Israeli feelings showed few signs of abating during the sharpened conflict between Israel, Egypt and Syria from 1967 to 1973. On the contrary, over half of the Storting members joined a "Friends of Israel" caucus when it was formed in 1974. Yet Norway's official policy began to show a more even-handed approach. She had supported UN Resolution 242 and its refusal to condone expansion of Israeli territory as obtained by force, and gave aid to Palestinian refugees. The Palestine Liberation Organisation, PLO, was still regarded as an extremist and terrorist organisation. But after the middle of the 1970s, as the PLO began to show signs of a more moderate stance, unofficial contacts were established. On the official level Foreign Minister Knut Frydenlund in 1974 instructed Norway's ambassador to the UN to vote in favour of letting Yassir Arafat speak to the General Assembly. This produced a wave of criticism from a broad spectrum, not least from his own Labour Party, and again brought relations with the PLO to freezing point.

In 1978, after the Israeli army had entered Southern Lebanon in an effort to stop Palestinian harassment of Israeli settlements, the United Nations

A total of over 50 000
Norwegian military per-
sonnel have participated in
31 UN or UN-mandated
peacekeeping operations
since 1947 – from small
observer missions to regular military units. The
main effort has been in
the Middle East, where
33 000 soldiers have
served in the UNIFIL
force in the Lebanon
(where this picture was
taken) from 1978 to 1998,
and 11 000 in the UNEF
force in Egypt from 1956
to 1967.

established a peacekeeping force in the area – UNIFIL, United Nations
Interim Force in Lebanon. Norway offered a sizeable contribution to the
force in the shape of the NORBATT battalion, at considerable expense
since the UN as usual was short of funds for peacekeeping purposes. As
UNIFIL proved to be anything but an interim force, and Norway became
the greatest single contributor of manpower, about 33 000 Norwegian military personnel came to spend six months or more in southern Lebanon.
Many doubted the usefulness of the force, as the Israelis retained a fair measure of control in the area through native auxiliary militia units, and senior
Norwegian military officers from time to time called for the withdrawal of
the force, pointing to the drain on money and military resources. The force
proved effective in one respect, however: men and women who served, and
who left Norway with a pro-Israeli prejudice, often came back fed up with
Israeli arrogance and sympathetic to the cause of the Palestinians. In the end
it was the need to provide military personnel to Bosnia and Kosovo which
in 1998 brought the final withdrawal of NORBATT.

The other important effect of Norway's presence in the area was a closer contact of Norwegian diplomats and senior politicians with Palestinian
leaders. In that way, and with the Labour Party in the forefront, the foundations were laid for Norway's role as a go-between and later mediator
between the PLO and the Israelis. Sweden was also in the running for such
a role, but her closer ties with the PLO gave Sweden reduced credibility
towards the Israelis and the Americans. Norway's advantage was enhanced

While Norway's close relationship with Israel had long roots, relations with the Palestine Liberation Organisation (PLO) began to be developed from the late 1980s, as Yasser Arafat felt the need for a go-between with good relations with the United States. Norway fitted that bill as a member in good standing of NATO. An important step towards what became the 'Oslo Process' was taken by Foreign Minister Thorvald Stoltenberg when he made an official visit to Arafat in January 1989.

through the personal relations with both Israeli and PLO leaders of a small number of centrally placed members of the Labour Party, one of whom led a research project into living conditions among the Palestinians. The original proposal for Norway to act as a go-between came from the PLO, but Israel held back until Labour returned to power there in 1992 with Yitzhak Rabin as Prime Minister and Shimon Peres – a long-standing friend of Norway's Foreign Minister Thorvald Stoltenberg – as Foreign Minister. Talks began under conditions of extreme secrecy in January 1993 in Oslo, and continued in spite of recurrent crises until a "Declaration of Principles" could be concluded in August that year. Out of deference to the Americans, who would inevitably have a central role in the implementation of the process, the formal signing ceremony took place on the White House lawn in Washington D.C. on 13 September.

The "Oslo Accord" – often just referred to as "Oslo" – has been variously hailed as an historic breakthrough, criticised as a superficial cover over intractable antagonisms, or condemned as deeply flawed in its consecration of Israeli dominance. Today, more than seven years later, the violent and bloody days of the "intifada" seem to have returned: violence is on the increase, and a final peace accord between Palestinians and Israelis still seems some distance away. But the jury is still out, and Norway for one is certainly doing her best both as pacifier and as provider of aid to the Palestinians to keep the process from becoming completely derailed. Whatever the future brings, and assuming that "Oslo" has brought more than just a temporary truce, Norway's "moment in the Middle East" should be credited to a number of factors. On the one side is Norway's long-standing friendship

267

with Israel, coupled with the timely development of close relations also with the Palestinian leaders, while retaining the confidence of the United States that accrued from decades of close cooperation in NATO. On the other side is the importance of a small number of persons who happened to be in positions of influence at the time, and whose "personal chemistry" and sheer perseverance carried them through one near-breakdown after another.

Saving the Globe

Coinciding in time with the Oslo Process, but in marked contrast to the secrecy of that venture, Norway was putting herself at the forefront of a global campaign to save the environment. Occupying centre stage was Norway's energetic and forceful woman Prime Minister, Gro Harlem Brundtland. The country's engagement in such global issues had a precedent which went back to the 1970s. The crisis of the international currency and exchange system following the breakdown of the 1945 Bretton Woods regime of stable exchange rates, and the 1973 "oil crisis", served as background for a 1974 special UN session on the combined problem of the Third World's trade in raw materials and slow economic development. The developing countries claimed that the existing global "terms of trade" favoured the industrialised countries and served to cement the gap between the poorer and the richer countries. They called for a new economic world order, focused in particular on the problem of low and/or wildly fluctuating prices of their raw materials exports.

Norway was traditionally a strong supporter of free trade, on account of her own dependence on external trade as well as her world shipping interests. In 1975, however, the Labour government in a white paper signalled a radical change of policy, proposing structural reforms of the world economy for the benefit of the poorer countries, and advocating preference arrangements for their exports. Such calls for what was termed a "New Economic World Order" clearly appealed to a domestic public opinion which already saw Norway as a frontline campaigner for development aid, decolonisation, peace, and humanitarian principles. But the policy was also borne by a strong conviction that a continuation or deepening of the unequal distribution of wealth in the world could lead to serious conflicts on a global scale – a conviction with roots going back to Trygve Lie's 1940 appeal for a kind of social democratic world order through what he called an "international planned economy".[8]

In the years that followed Norway and the Netherlands in particular worked intensively to persuade other industrialised countries, and especially the major powers, to involve themselves in the process. But a great amount of verbal support could not conceal a general reluctance to meddle with the principle of free markets and trade, and even Norway gradually came to realise that wholesale solutions to global inequalities were too ambitious. The mechanisms of the marketplace, in spite of their shortcomings, were still the best system. Norway also discovered some special interests of her own: the Norwegian merchant navy, with ten per cent of the world's tonnage, feared the trend towards protectionism which might exclude its ships from the bulk of the developing countries' seaborne trade. Norwegian agriculture and textile industry interests were also on their guard against cheap imports from developing countries. Still, although the hope for a "New Economic World Order" on the 1975-80 model receded, the social democratic dream of a world where a fairly free world market might be combined with more social justice, better public health services and more and better schools has lingered in the minds of successive Norwegian governments as well as the minds of other left-of-centre leaders. The label might change: for a while during the late 1990s it began to be called "The Third Way", and in 1999 a Berlin conference of 12 reform-minded leaders plus President Bill Clinton renamed the dream 'Progressive Governance'. It remains to be seen whether that new version will bring the dream any closer to being realised.

The big global crusade in which Gro Harlem Brundtland was to make her mark during the 1980s was to save the environment from the effects of pollution and untrammelled exploitation of the world's limited natural resources. For Norway this was not a new idea. A popular "green" movement had been riding on the crest of the 1960s wave of radicalism, first expressed in "sit-down" protests against new hydro-electric schemes, and in 1972 Norway was the first country to include a special Minister for the Environment in the government. Already during the 1960s the country was becoming concerned about the pollution of the North Sea and the acid rain caused by sulphuric smoke from Europe's heavy industry and coal-fired power plants. Prevailing winds and ocean currents sent much of that pollution straight towards Norway, damaging forests and destroying life in the rivers and lakes. The main culprit as far as Norway was concerned was Great Britain, and the reluctance of successive British governments to take on the massive cost of cleaning up the emissions from British smoke stacks had a markedly detrimental effect on Anglo-Norwegian relations – exemplified by such undiplomatic outbursts as the Norwegian Minister calling his British opposite number a "shitbag". In the meantime environmental concerns had been brought to the fore at a more global level, partly triggered by such major disasters as the Chernobyl explosion, and by the discovery of an "ozone hole" over the Antarctic which suggested that the whole globe was at risk from dangerous ultra-violet rays.

During the 1970s international organisations such as the OECD – the Organisation for Economic Cooperation and Development – and the

Norway's first woman Prime Minister, Gro Harlem Brundtland, made her entry on the national stage as Minister for the Environment in 1974, at the age of 35. Elected chairperson of the Labour Party in 1981, she quickly established herself as an active and forceful leader. The environment remained one of her most cherished causes, and her leadership of the World Commission on Environment and Development made her an important actor on the global stage. But she also had solid insight and understanding of foreign and security policy, and was strongly pro-European. She maintained and strengthened Norway's good relationship with the German Federal Republic, through personal contact with Chancellor Helmuth Kohl. (She had studied medicine in Germany, and spoke better German than English, unlike most Norwegians.)

United Nations began to pay increasing attention to environmental issues. The latter organised special conferences on the issue, and established a United Nations Environment Programme. But as practical results were few and far between, the UN in 1982 appointed a special World Commission on Environment and Development. Gro Harlem Brundtland became its chairperson, and for nearly a decade she and her Commission roamed the globe as an untiring pressure group in favour of the concept of "sustainable development". Her personal energy and determination, coupled with the diplomatic acumen of her close adviser Johan Jørgen Holst, had a major share in making the Commission a more successful venture than many other star-studded international bodies. Another reason for its success was the realisation that economic growth was a precondition for the eradication of poverty and under-development – an important step away from the "zero-growth" message of environmental campaigns such as the "Club of Rome" and others. The Brundtland Commission's 1987 report insisted that it was not only possible but necessary to combine a measure of economic growth with due regard to protection of the environment, if development and social and economic progress were to be sustained in a long-term perspective.

The crowning achievement of the Commission was the United Nations Conference on Economic Development in Rio de Janeiro in 1992, which demonstrated a wide consensus around "declarations of intent". Many were disappointed at the lack of binding commitments from the participating countries. But the entire effort had undoubtedly heightened global consciousness about the problem, and ensured that active concern for the environment would henceforth have a prominent place on the global agenda. On the domestic front the work of the Commission also had a sobering effect, partly by revealing that Norway's own record was not without blemish: Norwegian whaling came in for massive criticism in the debates about marine resources, and the government found it difficult to convince the critics that whales, being a resource like any other, could also be exploited within the boundaries of sustainable development. Norwegian seal-hunting was another target for environmental groups, with pictures on television of beautiful white baby seals being slaughtered by Norwegian "barbarians". At the time of writing environmentalists are also gearing up to protest against plans to hunt down sev-

The conference in Rio de Janeiro in 1992 marked a high point for the global campaign for a better environment, but the many high-minded speeches and resolutions produced few binding commitments.

eral of the small wolf packs that prey on sheep flocks in the border regions toward Sweden – thus further tarnishing Norway's reputation as the guardian of the environment.

The big environment issue of the final decade of the century came to be that of "global warming" or the so-called "greenhouse effect", due to emissions of carbon dioxide and other "climate gases" into the atmosphere which then "trap" the heat radiating from the globe and re-radiates it to the earth and to the oceans – with potentially disastrous effects on the world climate. Here Norway fell into a quandary. The good news was that Norway's reliance on hydro-electric power meant that her emissions of CO_2 per unit of energy were relatively modest. The bad news came later, as an increasing number of countries led by the big industrial powers insisted that reduction targets for emissions should be on a percentage basis that would be the same regardless of the total quantity of CO_2 emitted by each country. The other problem for Norway was the emissions of gases connected with the production and transport of natural gas and petroleum in and from the North Sea. A way out emerged through a proposal from Norway for the establishment of a clearing house where countries could finance much needed reduction processes in other countries and have that reduction "credited to their own account" as it were. The fate of that proposal, however, remains uncertain as this is being written. Here again Norway was caught between the demands from single-issue campaigners that the country should set a good example, and the government's realisation that ideals and interests were not always in harmony.

There remains to be considered a field of activity where Norway's ideals and interests were not in conflict. The accolade earned by the "Oslo Process" towards peace in the Middle East appeared to give currency to the idea that Norway and Norwegians possessed special qualifications as mediators for peace or reconciliation. The country's lack of a colonial or imperial past, its support for the United Nations, and its traditional advocacy of arms control and détente, were the rational arguments most often mentioned as the basis for that idea. Less talked about was Norway's readiness to prop up peace processes with generous amount of money. We have seen above that the at least temporary success of the "Oslo Process" can be explained partly by Norway's patient development of friendship and mutual trust with the parties, and partly by the qualities of individual Norwegians involved in the process. The same explanation holds good for Thorvald Stoltenberg's initial success as the UN's mediator in Yugoslavia: Norway had had close and friendly relations with Tito's Yugoslavia since the end of the Second World War, and Stoltenberg had served in the Norwegian embassy in Belgrade. What Norway lacked on both occasions was the power and influence required to convert a temporary truce into a sustainable peace.

Other mediation efforts during the 1990s had mixed results. Most successful appears to have been the mediation effort in Guatemala, where a six-year process of talks ended in 1996 with a peace agreement that brought to an end 36 years of civil war between the forces of the government and a guerrilla movement. Similar efforts in the Sudan, Sri Lanka and Haiti got nowhere, suggesting that mediation in internal disputes that are deeply rooted in historical or ethnic conflicts require, in addition to special personal qualifications, a profound knowledge of the country and its history which Norwegians do not normally have. (The jury is still out on similar efforts in Colombia, and a renewed effort in Sri Lanka.) Hence there is scant basis for the hubris that could be glimpsed in recent claims by State Secretaries in the Foreign Ministry and others that Norway possesses a kind of "soft power" that gives the country "a formidable reputation" and a position as a "humanitarian great power".

More to the point are the lessons drawn by former State Secretary Jan Egeland, who has been involved in Norwegian peace efforts, and who at the time this is written is Special Representative of the UN Secretary General in Colombia. Speaking from experience, he deprecates even the use of the word "mediator" for what Norwegians have done or can do in conflicts such as the ones mentioned. Norway's role can only be that of an active facilitator or arranger of conditions and circumstances conducive to success. "A mediator needs to have a combination of the muscle of great powers and the expertise of experienced UN negotiators. Norway, which can neither threaten nor cajole reluctant parties to compromise, must continue to be the active facilitator."[9] As for the special advantages that can give Norway such a role he points not to "soft power" but to Norway's smallness, which means that Norwegian representatives can build up close relations with guerrilla leaders without them fearing that they may be betrayed for ulterior motives.

Viewing the wide range of initiatives and actions – in development aid, peacekeeping, humanitarian relief and mediation – that have resulted from the country's emphasis on the ethical or moral dimensions of foreign policy during the last half-century, it seems that Norway has come a long way from her early promotion of international law as the only way to solve conflicts in a peaceful manner. Yet international law is essentially about how states ought to behave. The difference between then and now is therefore principally a question of means. As Norway in the 1940s changed from being basically an onlooker to becoming an active participant in international politics, she also came to realise that the roots of injustice and conflict are far too varied to be explained by or dealt with by reference to international justice. Norwegian development aid, her efforts to promote a New Economic World Order, and the campaigns for the global environment, were clearly based on sensible and forward-looking views about the world's problems.

Norwegian foreign policy has also reflected a realisation that justice is not always served by strict adherence to international law. NATO's war for Kosovo is the latest, and the clearest, example of a situation where humanitarian considerations overrode a strict application of international law's traditionally most hallowed principle – that of respect for state sovereignty. Hence it is still a question of how states ought to behave. What has changed, is that the desire or even need to make states behave the way they ought to, the missionary impulse, has gained strength to the extent of even challenging such a basic rule of the law of nations as non-interference in the internal affairs of another state. Halvdan Koht's 1906 message, that the small democratic countries such as Norway have a special mission as spokesmen and pioneers for a peace built on justice, remains in force. It may have been eclipsed somewhat during the Cold War when, as the realist conception tells us, the imperatives of national security took precedence over moral considerations in the choices made by national leaders. But the decline and end of the Cold War seems to have brought Norway's "missionary impulse" back with a vengeance. It remains to be seen whether Norway manages to steer a middle course between "the two extremes of over-rating the influence of ethics upon international politics or under-estimating it by denying that statesmen and diplomats are moved by anything but considerations of material power."[10]

13. Epilogue: Into the New Millennium

Introduction

Norwegians appear to be entering the new millennium with a considerable amount of confidence in their country's future. It is already one of the richest countries in the world, awash with the billions that keep pouring in from the exploitation of its oil and natural gas resources. Backstage looms another major source of wealth – the resources from the sea, now reaped not only from fishing in open waters but increasingly produced in fish farms along the coast. The demand for its products in the export markets seems insatiable. Critical voices may warn against over-confidence, pointing to the fact that the Norwegian economy remains that of a harvester of finite natural resources. They bemoan the low rate of investment in research and development, which could produce innovation and lay the groundwork for new industry based on "hi-tech" and intelligence. They warn about the fate of Spain, whose gold and silver brought home by the "conquistadores" was wasted on endless wars instead of being invested in the country's economic future, in the end leaving the country poorer than before. Yet their warnings seem to fall on deaf ears, or at least fail to create any sense of urgency.

Along with that confidence, which also means that at least half the population appears to view with equanimity the prospect of Norway remaining outside the European Union for the foreseeable future while one country after the other claims membership of the club, goes a curious lack of confidence in Norway's ability to influence the European Union from within. At the same time Norwegians continue to harbour strong convictions – sometimes verging on hubris – about their country's natural role and special mission as a global influence for peacemaking and human rights.

A recent analysis by a Norwegian political scientist[1] has succinctly described Norway's problem in relation to international integrative processes. As alluded to in the foreword to this book, and drawing on Robert A. Dahl's description[2] of a central dilemma confronting most small democratic countries, its essence is this: The smallness of the country means that there is little distance between the government and the governed, hence the citizen

– individually or, increasingly, through professional organisations – has more influence on national decisions affecting his or her life situation. Yet that smallness also means that the country has relatively little influence over the international conditions that increasingly determine Norway's integrity and welfare. This conundrum is currently reflected in the dilemma Norway faces in relation to the European Union. If Norway remains outside the EU, she may retain more of her internal self-government, but will have little influence on the external parameters for the country's integrity and prosperity. If the country draws closer to the EU, it will increase its influence over the international conditions determining its own welfare and integrity. But it will at the same time reduce the individual Norwegian's influence on his or her situation and conditions of life. It is right and natural for a country to have ambitions to exert as much influence internationally as possible. But ambitions need to be related to a priority of interests, and be carefully calibrated to what is possible.

An unwillingness or inability to assign clear priorities among the aims and means of Norwegian foreign policy remains a problem as the country enters the new millennium. It is possible to see this as a reflection of the history of Norway's foreign relations. I have earlier identified three formative periods in the evolution of Norwegian foreign policy: 1905–1910, when the "classic" Norwegian neutralism took shape; the inter-war period, when Norway wrapped herself in the mantle of a missionary for international law and disarmament; and the 1940s during which the country allied itself with great powers and became an active participant in international power politics. It is possible to see the pervasive influence of all three trends as different ways of overcoming that central dilemma: neutralism, as a wish to build fences around the country's self-determination; the "missionary impulse" as an attempt to influence the international environment from the outside; and active participation in power politics as the result of a determination to exert international influence from within. During the last three decades of the twentieth century it has been possible to preserve an uneasy coexistence among those three trends. Concern about "self-determination" has kept Norway outside the EU, NATO membership has enabled an active participation in power politics, and the "missionary impulse" has exerted itself through the country's "ethical foreign policy".

Two recent developments suggest that this triple juggling act may no longer be possible. Firstly, as decision-making in the European Economic Area becomes more and more of a one-way street, Norway's surrender of some of her sovereignty to the European Union is becoming a cumulative process. Secondly, and more important, recent European moves toward making the EU a major actor in the defence and security field have moved the goalposts as regards Norway's choices. While NATO – with the United States – remains the principal pillar of her security, Norway is now having

275

to determine her relationship with the EU in the defence and security field as well. Gone are the days when Norway could be an associate member of the somewhat toothless Western European Union without this affecting her relationship with the EU.

Norwegian Security after the Cold War

"Europe and America in the 1980s: Must Norway choose?" Such was the provocative title of a high-powered conference held in Oslo in May 1981. Two central concerns served as the background for the contributions of the speakers at the conference. On the European stage there were worries about the foreign policy direction announced by President Ronald Reagan and his new administration. Lambasting the outgoing Carter administration for having weakened America's strength and resolve to stand up against the Soviet "evil empire", the Reagan administration vowed to make the United States and the western world strong again. Many Europeans, although shaken by the Soviet Union's accelerated nuclear arms buildup as well as by the invasion of Afghanistan, saw Reagan's take-over as portending a new Cold War and a renewal of the arms race. In Norway those worries were accentuated by the political turmoil surrounding NATO's decision to install new mid-range nuclear missiles in Europe, as a counter to the proliferation of Soviet SS-20 missiles. The other concern, particular to Norway, was that trans-Atlantic policy splits might force her either to increase her dependence on the United States or move closer to Europe – or be left hanging in the middle, increasingly isolated.

Prime Minister Gro Harlem Brundtland, opening the conference, predictably rejected the choice implied in the conference title. "Norway cannot choose between ties to the Atlantic countries and ties to Europe. Our foreign policy must include both aspects."[3] She acknowledged that the reappraisal then taking place in Washington created uncertainty, but nevertheless emphasised Norway's Atlantic orientation as the bottom line: "Only the United States has sufficient power to stand against the Soviet Union in northern Europe."[4] The Prime Minister thus reflected the primacy of security as the determinant of Norwegian foreign policy throughout the Cold War. Economic interests were important, as the repeated attempts to knock on Europe's door had shown. But the security aspect was present on each occasion, both as a strong argument in favour of membership in the EC or EU, and as perhaps the major area of concern after membership had been rejected: if consultation in NATO increasingly became a dialogue between Brussels and Washington, Norway risked becoming a supplicant without representation on either side. Then her "No" to Europe would have relegated Norway to the margins of international politics also in the security sense.

The 1985 summit meeting between Gorbachov and Reagan signalled the impending end to the Cold War.

During the 1980s there was, in Norway as in most European countries, a growing feeling of Cold War weariness. There was a sense that the arms race was becoming increasingly meaningless, with the thousands of nuclear warheads piling up on both sides of the Iron Curtain – a feeling that the Cold War was turning into a bilateral contest between the two super-powers, with their smaller allies being not much more than pawns in the big game. President Reagan's "Star Wars" programme contributed to that feeling. Mikhail Gorbachov, who took over power in the Kremlin in 1985, came to be seen as representing hopes for a change in the Soviet Union, and opinion polls in Norway suggested that the people regarded Reagan and the United States as the greater obstacle to détente. By 1989, however, the United States could with some justification declare victory for its policy of strength. The Soviet Union, collapsing under the economic burden of the arms race, was about to surrender its East European "empire". Two years later the Soviet Union dissolved itself. The Soviet threat, which since 1949 had been the glue that held NATO together, disappeared, and hopes were high that Eastern Europe, including Russia, was embarking on the road to democracy.

More than the other European NATO member states, however, Norway had good reasons for seeing that the end of the Cold War was not "the end of history". Norwegians had lived for 45 years with the Soviet superpower as their next-door neighbour. During that time they had seen the Soviet

277

Together with the United States, Norway took several initiatives for cooperative ventures with Russia after the Cold War. One of them aimed to contain the contamination of the environment in the north resulting from Soviet military activities in the nuclear field. In 1996 the Defence Ministers of Norway, Russia and the United States at a meeting in Bergen signed a convention to that effect.

North-western Military District develop from a desolate outpost to become the area of the highest concentration of military and especially naval hardware in the world. The Kola Peninsula, with its ice-free inlets and ports, had become the home of the Northern Fleet, which since 1960 contained the major part of the Soviet Union's powerful nuclear missile submarines – the greatest single threat to NATO's Atlantic lines of communication and to North America.

During the 1990s the deterioration of Russia's conventional armed forces, the various arms reduction agreements that had been concluded, and the institution of democratic reform in Russia, meant the disappearance of the short-term and medium-term threat against the West. But Russian democracy is unstable, and Russia remains a power with an enormous arsenal of nuclear weapons. Norway also has an unresolved territorial dispute with Russia concerning jurisdiction in the Barents Sea and the Arctic Ocean. In Norwegian eyes, while the threat might have disappeared, there remained a long-term uncertainty. Initially, therefore, Norway's expenditure on defence was not reduced to the same extent as that of most other European countries. This has now changed, as Norway has embarked on a major downsizing and re-structuring of the defence establishment. How far that downsizing will go, depends presumably on what direction Russian defence and security policy will take under President Putin: already there are indications of a certain reversal to Cold War thinking in Moscow, as evidenced by groundless allegations about Norwegian activities in the north being "threats to their national security".

Already during the 1980s Norway had begun to feel the need for more balance in her security relationships, partly stimulated by the widespread concern about the Reagan administration's more belligerent attitude towards the Soviet Union. While the "alliance within the alliance" that the special relationship with the United States constituted was still important, there was a need to develop closer security and defence ties with the European NATO members. After 1972 all Norway's European NATO allies except Turkey and Iceland were members of the European Communities, including Norway's

278

so to speak "oldest ally", Great Britain. There seemed at least a long-term risk of Norway becoming sidelined into an exclusive reliance on an unequal partnership with the superpower on the other side of the Atlantic. This became a problem as the EU began making efforts towards foreign policy coordination through the EPC – the European Political Cooperation, and then towards vitalising the Western European Union as the defence and security arm of Europe. As a non-member of the EU Norway had to settle for vague consultation arrangements with the EPC, and associate membership of the Western European Union. That was hardly satisfactory for a country that felt it had a lot to gain from, as well as to contribute to, the European security partnership. National security considerations were therefore an important factor as Norway began to assess the state of her foreign relations after the people in 1994 again had rejected membership of the EU.

The Evolution of NATO

A central question, for Norway as for the other European member states, was what would happen to NATO after the Soviet threat had gone. Some thought, and a few hoped, that NATO would simply fold or at least disintegrate. But a NATO summit meeting in London in 1990 showed an organisation with both the will and the ability to reform itself in order to meet new challenges. While the EU had barely begun to talk about a future inclusion of the new democracies of Eastern Europe, NATO moved quickly to establish a consultative relationship with the member states of the former Warsaw Pact as well as with the newly independent states of the former Soviet Union, in the shape of NACC – the North Atlantic Cooperation Council. By 1994 NATO had moved one step further by instituting the Partnership for Peace, where all those countries could begin to cooperate with the Alliance about defence strategy, military planning, and participation in peacekeeping activities. NATO also moved towards closer cooperation with the Western European Union, and with the Organisation for Security and Cooperation in Europe (OSCE).

The greatest uncertainty about NATO's reforming process was its effect on relations with the Russian Federation. Although President Yeltsin and his government had moved towards cooperation with the various organs established under NATO auspices, and Russia subsequently was given special

Johan Jørgen Holst was Norway's foremost security and defence analyst during most of the Cold War, as Research Director and later Director of the Norwegian Institute of Foreign Affairs. His political career began in 1976, and from then until his sudden death in 1994 at the age of 57 he served as State Secretary in the Ministry of Defence, then as State Secretary in the Ministry of Foreign Affairs, until in 1986 he became Defence Minister, and in 1993 Foreign Minister. His strong intellect and profound insight commanded respect, but his efforts to stay within the mainstream of the Labour Party's views on security policy sometimes brought him into conflict with his own convictions.

279

Jørgen Kosmo served as Defence Minister from 1993 to 1997, during the difficult period when US interest in and support for NATO's Northern Flank began to fade behind more urgent concerns in the Middle East and the Balkans. Here the cartoonist shows him declaring that "our security policy remains firm" even while the United States appears to be preparing to reduce its commitment to the region.

consideration through the establishment of a permanent joint council, many quarters within the volatile political environment in Moscow were deeply sceptical. Norway, as the only NATO member with a common border with Russia, had from the beginning of the process stressed the need for an open dialogue with Russia on the broader problem of European security. Norway also took an early initiative for cooperation with Russia in the high north, through programmes to develop the Barents Euro-Arctic Region – an ambitious attempt to transcend borders that during the Cold War used to be impenetrable, and where security considerations are bound to remain a limiting factor for a long time.

The most contentious issue was NATO's decision that the eastern European states, some of which were openly clamouring for admission, might in due course become full members of the organisation. Many thought that decision was at least premature, and pointed to the newly established Partnership for Peace as the best vehicle for security and defence cooperation. Norway had early signalled a cautious attitude: while she understood the desire of those countries to obtain the same security as Norway and the other NATO members enjoyed, any enlargement process had to take time. The applicants would need time to adjust their military institutions and to build defence structures that would enable them to work with the well-established military organs of NATO. It was also necessary to avoid provoking Russia by seeming to establish new frontiers of conflict. On the other hand one risked alienating the new democracies by appearing to give Russia a veto on the manner in which they shaped their national security posture. Still Norway supported the principle of enlargement of NATO once the decision was made.

There was more disagreement about which countries to admit to membership. Poland, Hungary, and the Czech Republic posed no particular problem. The difficulty centred on the Baltic States, which had reclaimed their status as independent nations after the break-up of the Soviet Union. They had from the start cultivated close relations with the Nordic countries, stressing common interests on account of smallness and regional closeness, and many circles in Norway, with the encouragement of the United States, thought Scandinavia ought to take special responsibility for the security and welfare of the Baltic region. At the Madrid NATO Summit in July 1997, Norway's Prime Minister Thorbjørn Jagland was in the forefront of those who urged leaving the door open for the Baltic republics, even if they could not be included in the first enlargement "package". Since then, however, the question of their membership of NATO has receded behind various practical schemes for Baltic cooperation, instituted through a Council of Baltic Sea States where Norway is a member.

In the midst of all those institutional developments NATO had to step in to use its military strength in the former Yugoslavia. As the crisis in Yugoslavia became centred on the break-up of Bosnia, neither NATO – whose forces and command structures were still geared towards a major East–West conflict, nor the WEU – which had ambitions but no forces, were prepared for action. But when the UN Secretary General requested assistance to monitor compliance with UN sanctions against Yugoslavia, both organisations decided to set up naval forces in the Adriatic. From that time onwards NATO's involvement in Bosnia grew from supporting the United Nations Protection Force on the ground to taking control of the entire operation through IFOR – the Implementation Force – whose mission was to supervise the implementation of the Dayton Accords. Bosnia thus became NATO's first venture into operations "out-of-area" – outside the area originally defined in the Washington Treaty as NATO's area of responsibility. Within the limited means at her disposal – in particular her lack of a professional army – Norway has supported and participated in that process from the beginning.

The Kosovo crisis opened a new phase for NATO. After repeated and prolonged attempts to get former Yugoslavia to participate in a peaceful solution, including the failed attempt to put a stop to the violence by introducing a corps of OSCE observers on the ground, NATO began a bombing campaign to force the Serbian army to withdraw from Kosovo. Although the Norwegian government gave full support also to this action, public opinion was somewhat more divided on the issue, especially after the targets for bombing were extended to include infrastructure of more indirect military importance inside Serbia itself. Many also questioned NATO's right to use military force without a direct and explicit mandate from the UN Security Council, and that debate merged with criticism of the so-called "New NATO". Taking their cue from the wording and alleged implications of NATO's new Strategic Concept, formalised at the Washington Summit in April 1999 which marked the Alliance's 50th anniversary, some claimed that this had transformed NATO from a defensive into an aggressive alliance with ambitions to play policeman to the whole world. The majority of the people, and the government, nevertheless supported the principle of outside intervention if necessary to prevent genocide or massive violations of human rights. Norwegian fighter aircraft took part in the air campaign, albeit in a supporting role, and an army battalion joined the land force sent to supervise the pacification of Kosovo – KFOR. At the dawn of the new millennium Norway was also preparing to organise battle-capable forces for future participation in actions of that nature.

Europe on the Move

NATO's actions in the former Yugoslavia on several occasions revealed dissent – mainly, and predictably, between the United States and France – over what should be the proper role of the Alliance. Behind the disagreements lay the clear and somewhat painful realisation that Europe was incapable of mounting any operation of the size required by the Kosovo emergency without massive assistance from the United States, and that the Americans consequently tended to assume command and control of the operation. This gave new impetus to the endeavour to create a more self-sufficient Europe in the military sense, but this time not inside NATO but alongside the Atlantic Alliance. What gave this new attempt more credibility than previous efforts was that Great Britain was prepared to join, and even take the lead. The first move in that direction was the St. Malo Declaration on European defence in December 1998, by which Great Britain joined with France in calling for the development of a separate European capability to act with military force.

The St. Malo initiative was undoubtedly a bit of a surprise to many Norwegians, who tended to believe that they could rely on the British to ensure that NATO, and the trans-Atlantic connection, remained the principal instrument for the handling of major crises in the Euro-Atlantic area. Norway and Great Britain had also shared fears that moves toward a separate European defence organisation, usually promoted by France, would drive a wedge between Europe and the United States. When Norway still gave the initiative a guarded welcome, the explanation can be found in a sense that, with Britain on board, and the other EU countries nodding with varying degrees of enthusiasm, the bandwagon was becoming unstoppable. The choice was then between being sidelined, or joining in order to seek the best possible solution for Norway's own involvement. On the side of NATO, the Washington Summit in April 1999 officially welcomed the ini-

tiatives for a stronger European role, and pledged its cooperation. The St. Malo initiative has since been followed up by the Cologne European Council in June 1999, where NATO's Secretary General Solana was appointed as "Mr. CFSP" to coordinate EU's Common Foreign and Security Policy. Then, at the Helsinki Summit in December that year a decision was made that Europe should by the year 2003 be able to mount a force of 50–60 000 men within sixty days, and to maintain that force in operation for at least one year – requiring a total of at least 200 000 available forces. The purpose was to enable the EU to act in crises "where NATO as a whole is not engaged".

Building on long experiences from participation in UN peacekeeping, but also from a conviction that Norway had a special role in preserving peace in the world, Norway made special efforts to provide forces for the international peacemaking operations in Bosnia and – as here – in Kosovo.

The further development of such a European Security and Defence Identity (ESDI) lies in the future while this is being written. Uncertainties abound about Europe's ability to translate its plans into practice. As the Political Director of the WEU, Alyson Bailes, has recently explained, the policy decisions leave a lot of practical matters to be decided.[5] And as is often said, "the devil is in the details". In the meantime it is important to have a clear understanding of the motivation behind the new European initiatives. They have a history that goes a long way back. The desire for a strong European pillar as a counterweight to American strength is as old as

NATO itself. France wanted it for political reasons, in order to escape from US dominance. But that aim has consistently proved elusive, even after Europe became rich enough to bear comparison with the United States, and therefore presumably rich enough to support a more independent conventional military capability. Kosovo again showed how much Europe lagged behind the United States. For precision bombs, for intelligence capability (especially, but not only, in the field of satellites), for electronic warfare, and for "strategic lift" (the ability to transport forces and equipment on a large scale and at short notice), in all those fields the Americans proved to be miles ahead of the Europeans. Even for troops on the ground an American force was needed.

Possibly even more important as a motivation was the realisation, after Bosnia and Kosovo, that there are many other essential aspects to security than the military factor which is NATO's principal asset. A military occupation can "freeze" an explosive situation, but cannot by itself provide a solution to the deeper causes of misery and violence. Diplomatic and political efforts, humanitarian assistance, democracy building, and economic aid, are prominent among the instruments that are essential to an indivisible security package. The European Union has enormous potentials in all those fields, if it can get its act together. The Stability Pact for South Eastern Europe, established at the Sarajevo Summit in July 1999 at the initiative of the EU, calls for just such a "comprehensive and coherent approach to the region".

On the face of it, there is much to be said for a European capability to act independently of the Americans in crises of European origin. There is no denying the uneasiness felt in most European countries about recent trends in US foreign and security policy. If the new Republican administration succeeds in developing a National Missile Defence into something reminiscent of the Reagan administration's "Star Wars" this may, in addition to creating a crisis in relations with Russia, contribute to a long feared "decoupling" of America from its European allies. Only this time it would have been caused by US policies and not by European resentments of their "big brother". Greater independence for Europe is also desirable for other reasons. There is much force in the argument that it really should not be necessary for the rich countries of Western Europe to call in the United States to help them contain and solve security problems which do not directly threaten American interests. Ideally, therefore, NATO and the European Union should work out arrangements whereby Europe, with the understanding of NATO and with assistance as required from NATO's well-established facilities, could handle crises in its own back yard. But in order to achieve that, two requirements have to be fulfilled. First, those arrangements need to be worked out in a spirit of cooperation with the United States, without the tinge of anti-Americanism that accompanied some earlier attempts by France to assert European independence. Second, the Europeans have to spend more – much more – on their armed forces. In 1999 the European NATO members spent on average 2,3 per cent of their Gross National Product on defence, compared to 3,1 per cent for the United States. (The figure for Norway conforms to the European average.)[6] Will the peoples of Europe accept such a burden? In theory, of course, an integrated European multi-national effort might produce results where present combinations of separate national capabilities have failed. But there is good reason for expressing some doubts about Europe's ability to match American capabilities, even in the narrow area of rapid-reaction peace-keeping, and at least within the time limit that the EU has set for itself.

There is an additional question to be pondered by the EU countries as well as by NATO as a whole: what sort of future crises will the European armed forces be expected to deal with? The debate going on, about the need to get rid of Cold War thinking about East–West problems, and instead concentrate on developing capabilities to deal with future crises of a different kind, is it perhaps another example of the proverbial tendency to prepare for yesterday's war? Is it really likely that other areas in Europe's neighbourhood will explode, like Yugoslavia has done? Also, since the Kosovo operation will need a very large military effort for many years to come in order to maintain peace in that area, will Europe be able to deal with any additional major crisis at the same time? Has not the uncertain success of peace enforcement operations, in the former Yugoslavia as well as in Africa, all but removed western willingness to intervene and get embroiled in similar situations in the future?

The process of devising new structures beside or instead of existing ones is under way. Changes are necessary to meet new post-Cold War challenges, described in NATO's new Strategic Concept as "oppression, ethnic conflict, economic distress, the collapse of political order, and the proliferation of weapons of mass destruction." But it is also necessary to remember what the Strategic Concept says about the longer term: "Notwithstanding positive developments in the strategic environment and the fact that large-scale conventional aggression against the Alliance is highly unlikely, the possibility of such a threat emerging over the longer term exists." Some tend to dismiss this latter concern as a relic of the Cold War. But perhaps we should remind ourselves that it took only six years for Germany to turn its more or less disarmed Weimar democracy into the militarily powerful and aggressive dictatorship which in 1939 started the Second World War. And it took longer than that for the western powers to rearm in order to meet that new threat.

Norway, NATO, and the ESDI

One of the problems mentioned by Alyson Bailes in the article just referred to, and possibly the hardest, will be to give a proper role in the new arrangement for the non–EU Europeans – which is where Norway comes in. But not only Norway – also Turkey and the new Eastern European NATO members Poland, the Czech Republic, and Hungary. As Alyson Bailes notes, those countries "have expertise, regional standing, and concrete military assets which the EU would be well advised to exploit at the stage of building its policies as well as carrying out specific actions." Norway, for one, is clearly prepared to contribute to such an independent European capability for military action. A programme is under way to establish army, air force and naval units which at short notice stand ready to participate in both so-called "Article 5" operations – self-defence of NATO territory – and other international peace operations – so-called "non-Article 5 operations". Even if it is not a question of large forces from such a small population, they will be capable forces. Those forces could also be made available for action under EU auspices. As this is being written, however, the suggested arrangements for bringing non-members of the EU into the ESDI process stop short of allowing them access to the final decision-making. The EU's bottom line still seems to be one of insisting on "full respect for the autonomy of EU decision-making."

In a newspaper article on 8 January 2001 Norway's Defence Minister Bjørn Tore Godal appears to have accepted that Norway will not be able to take part in the EU's military, operational decision-making. "But in spite of those limitations we cannot afford to remain entirely outside the evolving defence and security cooperation in Europe." He also suggested one major reason why Norway cannot afford this:

> Norway is today militarily much less exposed than during the Cold War, but is still important from a strategic point of view. Our enormous ocean areas with their rich natural resources underscore that situation. The situation will still be such that we can be subjected to political or military pressure, and it is not given that NATO's military backing will be relevant in all such eventualities.[7]

In the meantime, however, the defence of Norway continues to depend on NATO. With a population of only 4,5 million she has to defend an area larger than Italy. The distances are enormous: Southern Europeans wishing to visit the North Cape are always surprised to discover that when they get to Oslo they have covered only half the distance. Norway also has responsibility for economic zones at sea that cover an area six to seven times that of her mainland territory. In addition she has to consider how to protect and defend installations at sea which provide an increasing share of Europe's

286

resources of petroleum and natural gas. For all this Norway needs co-operation and assistance from allied countries. Norway looks to NATO as the principal forum for trans-Atlantic consultations in all matters affecting the security of the Euro-Atlantic area. Norway therefore has to hope that the development of a European Security and Defence Identity will proceed in close co-operation with NATO and the United States, avoiding unnecessary duplication of effort.

The dual basis for Norwegian security – Atlantic *and* European – hence remains essentially as Gro Harlem Brundtland expressed it in 1981, and as Johan Jørgen Holst stated it twelve years later:

Thorbjørn Jagland capped a long service to the Labour Party by becoming its chairman in 1992, and took over from Gro Harlem Brundtland as Prime Minister in 1996. He resigned with his Cabinet after disappointing results in the General Elections of 1997, but returned as Foreign Minister in Jens Stoltenberg's Labour government in 2000. His security policy views for a long time placed him left of centre in the party, but his main interest and engagement has been and remains the development of an enlarged European Union – preferably with Norway as a member.

> Norway needs both an Atlantic and a European framework for its security policy. It is not a question of "either-or", but of "both-and". [...] In a period where the states of the European Union will have to take on more of the responsibilities and burdens of the defence of Europe, it is important that Norway preserves that double anchor.[8]

Holst's hope was then of course that Norway would join the EU and thus take part in the process whereby Europe undertook to build a common defence policy. The Foreign Minister in the Labour government which took over in March 2000, Thorbjørn Jagland, has not concealed his preference for Norwegian EU membership. At least for the time being, however, the government appears to have resigned itself to the kind of consultative status in the formation of a European defence identity that is implied in the quoted statement by Defence Minister Godal.

Further Norwegian Dilemmas

For Norway the deeper significance of the European Security and Defence Identity is the fusion of the two central dilemmas: the choice between Europe and America, for national security, and between membership and

Bjørn Tore Godal became a public figure through his leading role in an anti-EEC grouping that called itself "The Labour movement's information committee against Norwegian membership". This did not prevent him from becoming one of Gro Harlem Brundtland's closest collaborators in her government's handling of Norway's relations with the EU during the early 1990s. He served as Minister of Trade through the EEA process, and was Foreign Minister 1994–7, overseeing the completion of the proposed treaty for membership of the EU which was then rejected in the referendum. When Jens Stoltenberg formed his minority Labour government in 2000, Godal became Defence Minister, with the challenge to bring about a major downsizing and re-structuring of the armed forces.

non-membership of the EU, for political and economic reasons. As this is being written there is little sign of the big national debate that such fundamental foreign policy choices at the threshold of the new millennium call for. A kind of answer is provided in the government's report to the Storting on Norway and Europe, submitted on the eve of the first year of the "real" new millennium. Introducing the report Foreign Minister Jagland characterised it as "a response to the fact that there have been important developments in Europe since the beginning of the 1990s", and that it is "intended to lay the groundwork for a broad debate on these developments so that the parties in the Storting can formulate their views on how they can be dealt with." But he also stressed that "it is not a report that is either for or against EU membership".[9] The likelihood is therefore that the deep divisions both within and between the parties as well as in public opinion will remain and that, consequently, any referendum will in the foreseeable future produce a negative answer.

The current and somewhat low-key foreign policy discourse may be illustrated by, on the one hand, the title of a pamphlet posing the worrying question "What now, Little Norway?" On the other hand there is the assertion, from the authoritative source of a recent State Secretary in the Foreign Ministry, that Norway is a "humanitarian great power" and "a heavy player in international efforts for peace and security". It is perhaps easy to dismiss both the "worriers" and the "spin doctors" as being wide of the mark. But the perception gap between them suggests that Norway still has some distance to cover before she is ready to assign clear and explicit priorities among the divergent paths that have led her to where she stands today: the neutralist path, the missionary path, and the path of binding commitments.

This is not a new problem: In 1989 the Ministry of Foreign Affairs submitted a major report to the Storting which is sometimes referred to as "the bible" of Norwegian foreign policy.[10] Its title was "Development trends in the international society and their effects on Norwegian foreign policy". In a chapter on the aims and means of Norwegian foreign policy the government there attempted nothing less than a re-definition of the national interest. The task of the Foreign Ministry, the report said, should be "to promote Norway's interests in its foreign relations, including both our particular interests and the interests we share with other countries."[11] That statement was then followed by a detailed enumeration of a long series of national, regional and global foreign policy interests and aims, without any apparent attempt to assign any kind of priority among them. A slight reservation appeared as regards Norway's ability to exert an influence on global concerns. In order to have "real influence" Norway must here *concentrate her efforts* to areas where our interests are considerable or where we have particular experience, traditions, competence, or resources."[12] But that admonition was then followed by a list of "areas for special effort" which included just about every good cause.

As of today Norwegians' fears of a loss of political "self-determination" prevent Norway from joining the EU, while the country's binding commitments remain with NATO. That seems to leave what I have chosen to call the "missionary impulse" as a kind of common ground. There is of course nothing wrong with wishing to play the mediator and peacemaker: it cannot do much harm, and could conceivably in a few cases do some good. But when a small country like Norway assumes a high profile foreign policy, it is important to make sure that there is a proper balance between shadow and substance. Grand ambitions need an underpinning of actual achievements. Moreover, a high profile needs to be reflected also in regard to essential national interests. Norway, however, celebrated the arrival of the new millennium with two foreign policy initiatives, neither of which had any bearing on her dilemmas or indeed on her national interests. One was the campaign for membership of the UN Security Council, the other was the establishment of a new section for "peace, conciliation, and democracy-building" in the Foreign Ministry. The ultimately successful campaign for a seat on the Security Council has moreover created expectations about Norway's role that seem likely to backfire when the realities of power politics come home to roost.

At a deeper level still, Norway's current dilemma in her relations with the European Union reflects a dichotomy that has been present throughout the twentieth century, formulated but not perceived in Foreign Minister Løvland's 1905 programme of combining political isolationism with economic internationalism. National self-determination was a necessary and self-evident political goal for a nation that had just broken away from a union with another state. However, as the English historian Alfred Cobban wrote a long time ago, "[In] the economic world self-determination is an irrelevant conception." At least for a country like Norway, with an exceptionally heavy dependence on foreign trade in the broadest sense of the term, this has always been true, and has become even more so in the era of liberalisation and even globalisation of the international economy. This has created a long-standing contradiction between what has been termed "the country"'s political exclusiveness and the openness of its economy."[13]

Until now those two strands of foreign policy have been able to maintain an uneasy coexistence, translated into a series of "special arrangements" but stopping short of full membership of international organisations that are likely to impinge on the country's political self-determination. However, a close look at the 1990s suggests that this has been a decade of yet another formative period, in which the economy has gradually replaced national security as the principal determinant of Norwegian foreign relations. Through the instrument of the treaty for the European Economic Area, EEA, Norway achieved the status of an insider in the EU's internal market, albeit remaining a non-member of the Union in the political sense. (It is no mere coincidence that the primacy of economic concerns also has reinforced a long-term trend, noticeable since the 1970s, whereby Germany has replaced Great Britain as Norway's principal partner among the major European powers.)

The EEA was, on the face of it, accepted by a wide majority of parliamentarians – 130 in favour, 35 against – as a satisfactory arrangement of Norway's economic relations with Europe. In fact, those who had rather seen Norway as a full member of the EU, have continued to regret Norway's absences from the closed circles where decisions are made which inevitably affect the country. Those who are against membership, on the other hand, would either have preferred a simple trade agreement, or regard the EEA arrangement as a lesser evil. In either case they remain unconvinced that the status of an outsider in fact means a net loss of national sovereignty, through the obligation to adopt a long series of regulations and obligations decided in forums where Norway has no voice. Integration by way of the EEA has become acceptable because it has taken care of Norway's economic needs. Opting for an economic arrangement of the country's relationship with Europe, while remaining aloof from the political integration that membership of the EU would constitute, has for a time preserved the uneasy balance between an open economy and the aversion against political commitment. Norway's relationship with the European Union will however present new challenges in the years to come, as the EU increasingly looks to add to its largely economic brief that most touchy element of self-determination, namely foreign and security policy.

Notes

1. The Middle Ages

1 Unless otherwise stated this chapter is largely based on Narve Bjørgo's account in Part I of N. Bjørgo, Ø. Rian, and A. Kaartvedt, *Selvstendighet og Union: Fra Middelalderen til 1905* (Vol. 1 *of Norsk utenrikspolitikks historie*) Oslo 1995.

2 I use the term 'empire' here in the OED sense of an 'aggregate of subject territories ruled over by a sovereign state'. The Norwegian term is "Noregsveldet".

3 According to *The Oxford Companion to the English Language*, **norn**, defined as 'the language of ancient Norway and its colonies', may have survived as the spoken language of the common people in the Orkneys and Shetland to the late 18th century, and also left 'striking imprint on dialects, names, culture, and folk memory' in Caithness on the Scottish mainland, and in the West Highlands and Islands'.

4 See the discussion in Per Sveaas Andersen, *Samlingen av Norge og Kristningen av landet 800-1130* (Oslo 1977) pp. 160-168.

5 *Encyclopaedia Britannica* (1998 CD edition.)

6 See e.g. S. Hasund in Vol. III of *Det Norske Folks Liv og Historie* (Oslo 1934) p. 288-293.

2. Union with Denmark 1536–1814

1 I use here the translation of Thomas Kingston Derry in his *A History of Scandinavia* (London 1979) p. 89. His assessment of this "Norway paragraph" is however that it "settled the fate of Norway".

2 Unless otherwise noted this chapter is based on Øystein Rian's account in part 2 of N. Bjørgo, Ø. Rian, A. Kaartvedt, *Selvstendighet og Union: Fra Middelalderen til 1905* (Vol. 1 *of Norsk utenrikspolitikks historie.*) Oslo 1995.

3 Knut Mykland, *Kampen om Norge*, Oslo 1978 (Vol. 8 in the series *Norges Historie*) p. 386. Mykland is also the originator of the thesis that Christian Frederik's hidden agenda was the reunification of Norway and Denmark.

4 Speech to the Constitutional Assembly by the clergyman Nicolai Wergeland, as quoted in Henrik Wergeland, *Norges Konstitutions Historie*, new edition Oslo 1914, p. 278.

3. The Swedish-Norwegian Union 1814–1905

1 Unless otherwise noted this chapter draws heavily on Alf Kaartvedt's account in Part 3 of N. Bjørgo, Ø. Rian, A. Kaartvedt, *Selvstendighet og Union: Fra Middelalderen til 1905* (Vol. 1 *of Norsk utenrikspolitikks historie*) Oslo 1995. The greater emphasis on Norwegian foreign policy interests is however my own.

2 Thomas Kingston Derry, *A History of Modern Norway, 1814-1972* (Clarendon Press, Oxford 1973) p. 68.

3 Jens Arup Seip, *Utsikt over Norges historie* Vol. 2 (Oslo 1981) p. 33, quoting from *Menigmands Blad* 1 June 1875.

4 *Stortingstidende* (Parliamentary Proceedings) 17 April 1871, p. 378.

5 Bjørnstierne Bjørnson, "Russland", in *Verdens Gang* 11 November 1896.

4. The Challenges of Sovereignty

1 Except as otherwise noted this chapter draws heavily on Roald Berg, *Norge på egen hånd, 1905-1920* (Vol. 2 in *Norsk utenrikspolitikks historie*) Oslo 1995. The emphasis on the isolationist urge behind the policy is however my own.

2 See Chapter 3 p. 66.

3 This and the following excerpt are quoted from the documentary collection of J.V. Heiberg (ed.), *Unionens opløsning 1905* (Kristiania 1906) pp. 715-6.

4 R.L. Rothstein, *Alliances and Small Powers* (New York 1968) p. 247.

5 R. Krishna, "India and the Bomb", in *India Quarterly* Vol. XXI (1965) p. 122.

6 G. Liska, *Nations in Alliance* (Baltimore 1962) p. 213. For an extended discussion of my views on non-alignment in its various permutations see e.g. my article "Janus Septentrionalis? The Two Faces of Nordic Non-Alignment" in J. Nevakivi (ed.), *Neutrality in History* (Helsinki 1993) p. 313-324.

7 See Chapter 3, p. 58.

8 The following discussion of the implications of the Integrity Treaty is my own.

5. Norway in the First World War

1 Quotations from O. Riste, *The Neutral Ally* (Oslo and London, 1965) p. 37. This chapter is based on that book as well as on Roald Berg, *Norge på Egen Hånd: 1905-1920* (Vol. 2 in *Norsk utenrikspolitikks historie*) Oslo 1995.

2 *The Neutral Ally*, p. 108.

3 *Ibid.*, p. 109.

4 *Ibid.*, p. 111.

5 Patrick Salmon, *Scandinavia and the Great Powers 1890-1940* (Cambridge University Press, 1997) p. 139.

6 O. Riste, *The Neutral Ally*, p. 175.

7 P. Salmon. *Scandinavia and the Great Powers*, p. 158.

8 O. Riste, *The Neutral Ally*, p. 193.

9 *Ibid.*, p. 209.

6. The Cross-Currents of the Inter-War Period

1 Much of this chapter is based on Odd-Bjørn Fure's work *Mellomkrigstid, 1920-1940* (Vol. 3 in the series *Norsk utenrikspolitikks historie*) Oslo 1996.

2 *Stortingstidende* 1920, Vol. 7a p. 425.

3 As quoted in Odd–Bjørn Fure, *Mellomkrigstid, 1920-1940*, p. 56.

4 See Roald Berg, *Norge på egen hånd, 1905-1920* (Vol. 2 in the series *Norsk uten-rikspolitikks historie*) Oslo 1995, p. 285.

5 See Fure, *Mellomkrigstid* p. 118-9.

6 See Fure, *Mellomkrigstid* p. 131.

7 Fure, *Mellomkrigstid* p. 143, but also Odd Gunnar Skagestad, *Norsk Polarpolitikk*, Oslo 1975, p. 51.

8 Both quotations from Fure, *Mellomkrigstid* p. 87-8.

9 The most detailed – and highly critical – study of Norwegian attitudes to international politics in the period is Nils Ørvik, *Sikkerhetspolitikken 1920-1939: Fra forhistorien til 9. april 1940.* (Vols 1-2, Oslo 1960-61).

10 As quoted in Fure, *Mellomkrigstid* p. 189.

11 James Joll, *Europe since 1870: An International History.* Pelican Books, London 1976, p. 290.

12 Patrick Salmon, *Foreign Policy and National Identity: The Norwegian Integrity Treaty 1907-24* (In the series *Forsvarsstudier* No. 1, 1993). Institutt for forsvarsstudier, Oslo 1993.

13 Fure, *Mellomkrigstid*, p. 197.

14 Quoted in G.M. Gathorne-Hardy, *A Short History of International Affairs 1920-1939* (Oxford University Press 1950) p. 414.

7. War Comes to Norway

1 As quoted in Nils Ørvik, *Sikkerhetspolitikken 1920-1939* (Oslo 1961) Vol. 2 p. 210.)

2 Koht's note of the conversation, with one vital word "ikkje" [not] missing, is printed in his memoirs *For Fred og Fridom i Krigstid 1939-1940* (Oslo 1957) p. 24.

3 As quoted in P. Salmon, *Scandinavia and the Great Powers 1890-1940*, p. 345.

4 From the verbatim report of the Committee's session 9 December 1939, published in Johan Scharffenberg (ed.) *Norske aktstykker til okkupasjonens forhistorie* (Oslo 1950) pp. 138-41.

5 *Ibid.*, p. 307-8.

6 For a more detailed analysis of why the German invasion took both Norway and Britain by surprise see my *Weserübung: Det perfekte strategiske overfall?* (In the series *Forsvarsstudier* No. 4/1990. Institutt for forsvarsstudier, Oslo 1990.) An English version is "A Complete Surprise: The German Invasion of Norway in 1940", in International Commission of Military History, *Acta No. 13* (Helsinki 1991).

7 Translated, with italics added, from Johan Nygaardsvold, *Norge i krig 9. april – 7. juni 1940* (Oslo 1982) p. 166.

8. In the Wartime Alliance

1 For this chapter, apart from my own work *"London-regjeringa": Norge i krigsalliansen 1940-1945* (Oslo 1973-79, 2nd ed. 1995), I draw on Jakob Sverdrup, *Inn i Storpolitikken 1940-1949* (Vol. 4 in *Norsk utenrikspolitikks historie*). Oslo 1996.

294

2 PRO (Public Record Office, London) CAB 85/19, Ministry of Defence to the British Government 10 July 1940.

3 MFA (Ministry of Foreign Affairs) Archives, file 34.1/19, letter from Dr. Arne Ording and others to the government 10 July 1940.

4 Archives of the 1945 Parliamentary Commission of Investigation, box 30.1.17.

5 PRO, FO 371/29421, N 1307/87/30, 8 April 1941.

6 *The Times*, London, 14 November 1941.

7 PRO, FO 371/29422, N 6510/87/30, Sargent Minute 14 November 1941.

8 MFA Archives, file 34.1/19.

9 Erik Opsahl (ed.) *Arne Ordings Dagbøker* (Oslo 2000) p. 100-1.

10 PRO, PREM 4/100/7, "The 'Four Power Plan'" s. 23-4.

11 *Norsk Tidend*, 19 January 1944.

12 On this incident see O. Riste, "An Idea and a Myth: Roosevelt's Free Ports Scheme for Norway", in B. Seyersted (ed.) *Americana Norvegica IV. Norwegian Contributions to American Studies* (Oslo 1973).

13 MFA archives, 34.4/99, Minute by Finance Minister Paul Hartmann 12 April 1943.

14 Trygve Lie, *Hjemover* (Oslo 1958) p. 159.

15 S. Holtsmark (ed.), *Norge og Sovjetunionen 1917-1955: En utenrikspolitisk dokumentasjon* (Oslo 1955) p. 360.

16 PRO, FO 371/36867, N 3010/219/63, 17 June 1943.

17 Excerpts from those diaries are given in Krister Wahlbäck, *Regeringen och Kriget* (Stockholm 1972).

18 See the three-volume documentary collection published by the Norwegian Ministry for Foreign Affairs *Norges forhold til Sverige under krigen 1940-45* (Oslo 1947) Vol. I p. 16-17.

19 PRO, FO 371/48008, doc. N1965/11/42.

9. From War to Cold War

1 Much of this chapter draws on the lucid survey given in Jakob Sverdrup, *Inn i Storpolitikken 1940-1949* (Vol. 4 of *Norsk utenrikspolitikks historie*) Oslo 1996

2 *Documents of the United Nations Conference on International Organisation, San Francisco 1945* (London and New York, 1945) p. 349-50.

3 Editorial in the government's official newspaper *Norsk Tidend* 15 July 1942.

4 John Sanness et al. (eds.), *Festskrift til Arne Ording* (Oslo 1958) p. 140.

5 Wayne S. Cole, *Norway and the United States 1905-1955* (Ames, Iowa 1989) p.121.

6 PRO, FO 371/66021, N 1224/68/30.

7 Magne Skodvin, *Norden eller NATO* (Oslo 1971) p. 131.

8 Magne Skodvin, *Scandinavian or North Atlantic Alliance* (Forsvarsstudier No. 3, 1990) p. 11.

9 See the documentary collection by Sven Holtsmark (ed.), *Norge og Sovjetunionen 1917-1955* (Oslo 1995) p. 405 i. a.

10 Geir Lundestad, *America, Scandinavia and the Cold War 1945-1948* (New York 1980) p. 93.

11 PRO, CAB 131/2, Bevin memorandum to Defence Committee 13 March 1946.

12 The plan was presented as *Stortingsmelding* (White Paper) No. 32 (1945-46).

13 *Stortingsforhandlinger*, 1945-46, 7b, p. 2183.

14 *Foreign Relations of the United States* 1948 Vol. III p. 24-5.

15 See M. Skodvin, *Norden eller NATO*, p. 248.

16 The Scandinavian angle is further explored in my "Scandinavian Union or Western Alliance? Scandinavia at the Crossroads 1948-1949" in Ennio di Nolfo (ed.), *The Atlantic Pact Forty Years Later: A Historical Reappraisal* (Berlin and New York 1991).

17 *Stortingsforhandlinger* 1949, 7a, p. 301.

10. On NATO's Northern Frontline

1 Norwegian security policy, and in particular Norway's relationship with NATO, has been extensively researched and described by historians. For this chapter, in addition to my own work, I have drawn heavily on the relevant volumes of the series *Norsk utenrikspolitikks historie*, viz. Knut E. Eriksen and Helge Ø. Pharo, *Kald Krig og Internasjonalisering, 1949-1965* (Oslo 1997), and Rolf Tamnes, *Oljealder, 1965-1995* (Oslo 1997); on Rolf Tamnes, *The United States and the Cold War in the High North* (Oslo 1991), and a number of publications from the Norwegian Institute for Defence Studies.

2 The headline covered an article by a columnist in *Le Figaro* 25 June 1983 which contained the following sentence: "Soyons francs, qui, en France, en R.F.A., en Italie, en Grande-Bretagne, et même aux Etats-Unis, envisagerait alors sérieusement de mourir pour Nordkyn?" Although occasioned by the increasing numbers of mid-range missiles in Europe, the article, with its obvious reference to western unwillingness to "die for Danzig" when Germany in September 1939 invaded Poland, questioned the very foundation of NATO solidarity.

3 *Aftenposten* 12 September 1949.

4 *Stortingsforhandlinger*, 1950, 7a, p. 1170.

5 Halvdan Koht, *For fred og fridom i krigstid* (Oslo 1957) p. 284.

6 Sigurd Evensmo, *Ut i kulda* (Oslo 1978) p. 71.

7 See e.g. Don Cooke, after describing the signing ceremony in Washington D.C.: "It would be another two years before the superstructure of the North Atlantic Treaty Organisation was finally in place on top of the North Atlantic Treaty." (Don Cooke, *Forging the Alliance: NATO 1945 to 1950*, London 1989, p. 222.)

8 National Archives (US), Record Group 319, P & O 091 Norway TS, encl. "Report by the Joint Strategic Plans Committee on a British JPS report 'Norway – Advice on Defence'."

9 *Stortingsforhandlinger*, 12 December 1951, p. 2543.

10 This point emerges clearly in Mats Berdal's important study *The United States, Norway and the Cold War, 1954-60* (London and New York 1997), e.g. p. 178-9.

11 This section is based on my book *The Norwegian Intelligence Service 1945-1970* (London 1999).

12 Archives of the NIS, copy file H: draft for letter from General Lambrechts to Defence Minister Handal, 12 October 1956.

13 *Ibid.*, p. 104.

14 *Ibid.*, p. 70.

15 For this and other details of the U-2 affair see Rolf Tamnes, *The United States and the Cold War in the High North* (Oslo 1991) p. 178-182.

16 The Finnish authorities apparently agreed to turn a blind eye to those and similar activities unless and until the Soviets got wind of them and demanded that they had to be stopped.

17 As quoted in Rolf Tamnes, *ibid.*, p. 236.

18 Public Record Office, London, CAB 158/24, JIC (56)53 (Final), 13 April 1956.

19 As quoted in Eriksen and Pharo, *Kald Krig og Internasjonalisering*, p. 248.

20 Tove Pihl in her article "Sikkerhet og nedrustning", *Aftenposten*, 18 January 1983.

11. "Our International Material Relations": Cooperation vs. Integration (1945–1994)

1 See Chapter 4 p.75-6.

2 This chapter, like the others on the post-war period, again draws heavily on volumes 5 (K.E. Eriksen and H. Ø. Pharo, *Kald krig og internasjonalisering 1949-1965*) and 6 (R. Tamnes, *Oljealder 1965-1995*) of the series *Norsk utenrikspolitikks historie*. I am also indebted to Helge Pharo's excellent survey article "Ingen vei utenom? Norge i integrasjonsprosessene i Europa 1946-1994" in D.H. Claes and B.S. Tranøy (eds.), *Utenfor, annerledes, og suveren?* (Oslo 1999).

3 *Stortingsmelding* No. 5, 1951, p. 24.

4 It is common usage in the Norwegian language to speak of things happening "nede i Europa" – "down in Europe". As Alan Henrikson's work on "mental maps" suggests, this may have some impact on attitudes. See Alan K. Henrikson, "The Geographical 'Mental Maps' of American Foreign Policy Makers", in *International Political Science Review*, 1:4 (1980) p. 495-530.

5 Although the two terms are often loosely used interchangeably, there is a difference: the term Scandinavia denotes the three culturally, ethnically and geographically closely related countries Sweden, Denmark and Norway, whereas the term Nordic (being in the English language an adjective without a corresponding noun) embraces also Finland and – in most respects – Iceland. In the Scandinavian languages, however, the terms "Norden" and "nordisk" tend to be used indiscriminately, and will be used so here when translated.

6 Opinion polls in B. Alstad (ed.), *Norske meninger I: Norge, nordmenn og verden* (Oslo 1969).

7 Eriksen and Pharo, *Kald Krig og Internasjonalisering* p. 345-52, Pharo in *Utenfor, annerledes, suveren?* p. 26-30, Clive Archer and Ingrid Sogner, *Norway, European Integration and Atlantic Security* (Oslo and London 1998) p. 26-8.

8 See Chapter 1 p. 27.

9 Tamnes, *Oljealder*, p. 169.

10 Ministry of Foreign Affairs, *Stortingsmelding* No. 50, 1971-2, p. 61.

11 See Chapter 4, p. 81-2.

12 Although the European Union – EU – was not formally constituted under that name until 1993, I take the Maastricht Summit of December 1991 as its "datofbirth".

13 *The Guardian Weekly*, 25 November 1990.

12. An Ethical Foreign Policy?

1 Halvdan Koht, *Fredstanken i Noregs-sogo: Noreg i den samfolkelege rettsvoksteren.* (Oslo 1906.)
2 An excellent analysis of Nansen's w
3 See *The Norwegian Nobel Institute Series* Vol. 1 (2000) Nos. 1-3, with essays by Ivar Libæk, Asle Sveen, and Øivind Stenersen.
4 What follows draws mainly on Knut E. Eriksen and Helge Ø. Pharo, *Kald Krig og Internasjonalisering 1949-1965* (Vol., 5 in the series *Norsk Utenrikspolitikks Historie*) Oslo 1997.
5 As quoted in Eriksen/Pharo's volume p. 174.
6 The following draws heavily on the pioneering work on the period by Rolf Tamnes, in his *Oljealder 1965-1995* (Vol. 6 in the series *Norsk utenrikspolitikks historie*) Oslo 1997.)
7 Lecture on 23 May 1984 on "Human rights in Norwegian foreign policy – what we can do and what we ought to do", reproduced in a memorial collection of his speeches edited by his successor Thorvald Stoltenberg and published under the title *En bedre organisert verden* (Oslo 1987). See p. 274, also p. 78.
8 See above Chapter 8 p. 164 and Chapter 11 p. 235-6.
9 Jan Egeland, "Lærdommer fra praktisk fredsarbeid", in *Aftenposten* 14 May 1998.
10 Hans J. Morgenthau, *Politics among Nations* (New York 1973) p. 236. See also Paul Keal (ed.), *Ethics and Foreign Policy* (Canberra 1992).

13. Epilogue: Into the New Millennium

1 Torbjørn L. Knutsen, in Torbjørn L. Knutsen, Gunnar M. Sørbø, Svein Gjerdåker (ed.s), *Norges Utenrikspolitikk* (2nd Edition, Oslo 1997) p. 41.
2 Robert A. Dahl, "A Democratic Dilemma", in *Political Science Quarterly* Vol. XXX (1994) No. 2 pp. 23-34.
3 *NUPI Rapport* No. 54, May 1981, p. 2.
4 *Ibid.*, p. 4.
5 Alyson J.K. Bailes, "NATO's European Pillar: The European Security and Defence Identity." In *Defence Analysis* Vol. 15 No. 3, pp. 305-322.
6 Figures from IISS, *The Military Balance 2000-2001* (Oxford University Press for the International Institute for Strategic Studies, Oxford 2000).
7 Bjørn Tore Godal, "Internasjonal forsvarsinnsats". In *Dagbladet* 8 January 2001.
8 Defence Ministry Press Release No. 2, 1993. Address to "Den polytekniske forening" 2 February 1993, p. 15.
9 Foreign Ministry Press release 1 December 2000.
10 *Stortingsmelding* No. 11 (1989-90): "Om utviklingstrekk i det internasjonale samfunn og virkninger for norsk utenrikspolitikk".
11 *Ibid.*, p. 45.
12 *Ibid.*, p. 50. See also the discussion by Geir Lundestad in his essay "Lange linjer i norsk utenrikspolitikk" in *Internasjonal Politikk* Vol. 57 (1999) No. 2.
13 Torbjørn L. Knutsen, *op.cit.* p. 25.

Suggestions for further reading

Books in English

Books on general Norwegian history

Andenæs, J., Riste, O., Skodvin, M., *Norway and the Second World War* (Oslo 1965 and later editions). A brief popular survey.

Bergh, T., Hanisch, T.J., Pharo, H.Ø., *Growth and Development: The Norwegian Experience 1830–1980* (Oslo 1981).

Danielsen, Rolf, and others, *Norway: A History from the Vikings to Our Own Times* (Oslo 1995). The most up to date version, albeit with little attention to foreign relations.

Derry, Thomas Kingston, *A History of Scandinavia* (London 1979). Somewhat outdated, but still useful as an outside observer's views.

Derry, Thomas Kingston, *A History of Modern Norway 1814–1972* (Oxford 1973).

Hauge, Jens Christian, *The Liberation of Norway* (Oslo 1995). An account by the leader of the Norwegian Military Resistance.

Popperwell, Ronald G., *Norway* (in the series *Nations of the Modern World* (London 1972). Covers mainly, according the introduction, "Norwegian history, life, and culture in the nineteenth and twentieth centuries".

Riste, O., Nøkleby, B., *Norway in World War II: The Resistance Movement* (Oslo 1972 and later editions).

Books on Norwegian Foreign Relations

Archer, C. and Sogner, I., *Norway, European Integration and Atlantic Security* (Oslo and London 1998).

Berdal, Mats R., *The United States, Norway and the Cold War 1954–1960* (London 1997).

Cole, Wayne S., *Norway and the United States 1905–1955* (Ames, Iowa 1989).

Egeland, Jan, *Impotent Superpower – Potent Small State: Potentials and Limitations of Human Rights Objectives in the Foreign Policies of the United States and Norway* (Oslo 1985).

Holst, Johan J. (ed.) *Norwegian Security Policy for the 1980s* (Oslo 1985).

Lindberg, Folke, *Scandinavia in Great Power Politics, 1905–1908* (Stockholm 1958).

Lindgren, Raymond E., *Norway-Sweden: Union, Disunion, and Scandinavian Integration* (Princeton 1959).

Lundestad, Geir, *America, Scandinavia, and the Cold War 1945–1949* (Oslo and New York 1980).

Riste, Olav, *The Neutral Ally: Norway's Relations with Belligerent Powers in the First World War* (Oslo and London 1965).

Riste, Olav *The Norwegian Intelligence Service 1945–1970* (London 1999).

Salmon, Patrick, *Scandinavia and the Great Powers 1890–1940* (Cambridge 1997).

Sawyer, Peter H., *Kings and Vikings. Scandinavia and Europe AD 700–1100* (London 1982 and later editions).

Tamnes, Rolf, *The United States and the Cold War in the High North* (Oslo 1991).

Udgaard, Nils M., *Great Power Politics and Norwegian Foreign Policy: A Study of Norway's Foreign Relations November 1940-February 1948* (Oslo 1973).

Ørvik, Nils, *The Decline of Neutrality 1914–1941* (London 1971).

Books in Norwegian on Norway's Foreign Relations

The central reference work here is the series *Norsk Utenrikspolitikks Historie*, with the following volumes (all with extensive bibliographies):

Vol. 1: Bjørgo, N., Rian, Ø., Kaartvedt, A., *Selvstendighet og Union. Fra Middelalderen til 1905* (Oslo 1995).

Vol. 2: Berg, Roald, *Norge på Egen Hånd. 1905–1920* (Oslo 1995).

Vol. 3: Fure, Odd-Bjørn, *Mellomkrigstid. 1920–1940* (Oslo 1996).

Vol. 4: Sverdrup, Jakob, *Inn i Storpolitikken. 1940–1949* (Oslo 1996).

Vol. 5: Eriksen, K.E., Pharo, H. Ø., *Kald Krig og Internasjonalisering. 1949–1965* (Oslo 1997).

Vol. 6: Tamnes, Rolf, *Oljealder. 1965–1995* (Oslo 1997).

Holtsmark, Sven G. (ed.), *Norge og Sovjetunionen 1917-1955. En utenrikspolitisk dokumentasjon* (Oslo 1995). An extensively annotated collection of documents.

Knutsen, T.L., Sørbø, G., Gjerdåker, S. (ed.s), *Norges Utenrikspolitikk* (Oslo 1997). An uneven collection of thematic studies on specific aspects of Norwegian foreign policy.

Mathisen, Trygve, *Svalbard i internasjonal politikk 1871-1925* (Oslo 1951).

Skodvin, Magne, *Norden eller NATO?* (Oslo 1971).

Skogrand, K. and Tamnes, R. *Fryktens likevekt* (Oslo 2001). An excellent study of Norway's "atomic policy".

Ørvik, Nils, *Sikkerhetspolitikken 1920–1939* (I-II, Oslo 1960–61).

List of abbreviations

AFNORTH	Allied Forces Northern Europe
C-in-C	Commander-in Chief
EC	European Communities
EEA	European Economic Area
EEC	European Economic Community
EFTA	European Free Trade Area
EPC	European Political Cooperation
ESDI	European Security and Defence Initiative
EU	European Union
IEA	International Energy Agency
IFOR	Implementation Force
KFOR	Kosovo Force
KV	Kongsberg Våpenfabrikk
NAT	North Atlantic Treaty
NATO	North Atlantic Treaty Organisation
NIS	Norwegian Intelligence Service
OECD	Organisation for Economic Cooperation and Development
OEEC	Organisation for European Economic Cooperation
OSCE	Organisation for Security and Cooperation In Europe
OPEC	Oil Producing and Exporting Countries
SAS	Scandinavian Airlines System
STANAVFORLANT	Standing Naval Force Atlantic
UK	United Kingdom
UN, UNO	United Nations Organisation
US	United States
USSR	Union of Soviet Socialist Republics
WEU	Western European Union

List of illustrations

Archives, museums and image agencies:
Aschehougs arkiv: p. 48
Bergen Museum: p. 25
Dagsavisen: p. 201
Det Nationalhistoriske Museum på Frederiksborg: p. 35
Forsvarets rekrutterings- og mediasenter: p. 266
Forsvarsmuseet: p. 37, 38, 66, 74, 79, 141, 283
Kunnskapsforlagets arkiv: p. 165
Narvik Kulturkontor, Fotosamlingen: p. 144
Nasjonalbiblioteket avd. Oslo. Billedsamlingen: p. 60, 133, 135
Norges Hjemmefrontmuseum: p. 155
NPS: p. 233, 242, 262
Roar Hagen: p. 252, 280
Scanpix: p. 186, 188, 197, 199, 200, 205, 215, 216, 220, 257, 260, 261, 263, 267, 270, 271, 277, 278, 279, 287, 288
Tom B. Jensens arkiv: 151
Universitetets Oldsaksamling, Oslo: 17

Books:
Chatterton, E. Keble 1938. *Den store blokade.* Oslo: Gyldendal: p. 99
Elgklou, Lars 1978. *Bernadotte. Historien – och historier – om en familj.* Stockholm: Askild & Kärnekull: p. 41
Fasting, Kåre 1955. *Nils Claus Ihlen 1855 – 24. juli – 1955.* Oslo: Gyldendal: p. 91
Griffiths, Richard T. 1992. The Creation of the European Free Trade Association. *EFTA-Bulletin* 1: p. 241
Holmsen, Andreas og Magnus Jensen 1949. *Norges historie,* vol. 2. Oslo: Gyldendal: p. 118
Holmsen, Gunnar 1911. *Spitsbergens natur og historie.* Kristiania: Olaf Norlis Forlag: p. 85
The Illustrated London News. 1940. London: The Illustrated London News & Sketch Ltd.: p. 148
Lie, Trygve 1958. *Hjemover.* Oslo: Tiden: p. 175
Low's War Cartoons. 1941. London: The Cresset Press: p. 152
Løvland, Jørgen 1929. *Menn og minner fra 1905. Av statsminister Løvlands papirer.* Oslo: Gyldendal: p. 70, 76
Norges krig 1940-1945. 1948. Oslo: Gyldendal: p. 160
Norsk våpenhistorisk selskap. Årbok 1981. Oslo: Norsk våpenhistorisk selskap: p. 19
OED Faktaheftet 97 1997. Olje- og energidepartementet: p. 246
Olsen, K. Anker 1955. *Norsk Hydro gjennom 50 år. Et eventyr fra realitetenes verden.* Oslo: Norsk Hydro-Elektrisk Kvælstofaktieselskab: p. 82
Omang, Reidar 1959. *Norsk utenrikstjeneste,* vol. 2, Stormfulle tider 1913-1928. Oslo: Gyldendal: p. 107
Riste, Olav 1987. *Norge i krig,* vol. 7, Utefront. Oslo: Aschehoug: p. 166, 168
Smedal, Gustav 1934. *Nasjonalt forfall: tilbakeblikk og fremtidsmål i Grønlandssaken.* Oslo: Norli: p. 120
Tamnes, Rolf 1991. *The United States and the Cold War in the High North.* Oslo: Ad Notam: p. 208
Vogt, Per 1938. *Jerntid og jobbetid. En skildring av Norge under verdenskrigen.* Oslo: Johan Grundt Tanum: p. 89, 92

Index